Lecture Notes in Computer Science   **15693**

Founding Editors

Gerhard Goos
Juris Hartmanis

Advanced Research in Computing and Software Science
Subline of Lecture Notes in Computer Science

More information about this series at https://link.springer.com/bookseries/558

Artur Boronat · Gordon Fraser

Editors

Fundamental Approaches to Software Engineering

28th International Conference, FASE 2025
Held as Part of the International Joint Conferences on
Theory and Practice of Software, ETAPS 2025
Hamilton, ON, Canada, May 3–8, 2025, Proceedings

 Springer

Editors
Artur Boronat
University of Leicester
Leicester, UK

Gordon Fraser
University of Passau
Passau, Germany

ISSN 0302-9743   ISSN 1611-3349 (electronic)
Lecture Notes in Computer Science
ISBN 978-3-031-90899-6   ISBN 978-3-031-90900-9 (eBook)
https://doi.org/10.1007/978-3-031-90900-9

This Springer imprint is published by the registered company Springer Nature Switzerland AG
The registered company address is: Gewerbestrasse 11, 6330 Cham, Switzerland

If disposing of this product, please recycle the paper.

ETAPS Foreword

Welcome to the 28th ETAPS! ETAPS 2025 took place in Hamilton, Canada. It is the first time ETAPS was held outside of Europe.

ETAPS 2025 was the 28th instance of the International Joint Conferences on Theory and Practice of Software. ETAPS is an annual federated conference established in 1998, and consists of four conferences: ESOP, FASE, FoSSaCS, and TACAS. Each conference has its own Program Committee (PC) and its own Steering Committee (SC). The conferences cover various aspects of software systems, ranging from theoretical computer science to foundations of programming languages, analysis tools, and formal approaches to software engineering. Organizing these conferences in a coherent, highly synchronized conference programme enables researchers to participate in an exciting event, having the possibility to meet many colleagues working in different directions in the field, and to easily attend talks of different conferences. On the weekend before the main conference, numerous satellite workshops took place that attracted many researchers from all over the globe.

ETAPS 2025 received 329 submissions in total, 106 of which were accepted, yielding an overall acceptance rate of 32.2%. I thank all the authors for their interest in ETAPS, all the reviewers for their reviewing efforts, the PC members for their contributions, and in particular the PC (co-)chairs for their hard work in running this entire intensive process. Last but not least, my congratulations to all authors of the accepted papers!

ETAPS 2025 featured the unifying invited speakers Ina Schaefer (Karlsruhe Institute of Technology, Germany) and Matthew B. Dwyer (University of Virginia, USA), and the invited speakers Amal Ahmed (Northeastern University, USA) for ESOP and José Meseguer (University of Illinois Urbana-Champaign, USA) for FASE. Invited tutorials were provided by Suguman Bansal (Georgia Institute of Techology, USA) on reinforcement learning from logical specifications and Arun Ross (Michigan State University, USA) on biometrics.

ETAPS 2025 was organized by McMaster University. The Faculty of Engineering at McMaster University has a reputation for innovative programs, cutting-edge research, leading faculty, and aspiring students. It has earned a strong reputation as a center for academic excellence and innovation. The Faculty has approximately 180 faculty members, along with close to 4,500 undergraduate and 1,000 graduate students. The local organization team consisted of Claudio Menghi and Mark Lawford (general chairs), Melissa Alzaeim (event organizer), Alan Wassyng and Angelo Gargantini (workshop chairs), Sébastien Mosser and Matt Luckcuck (publicity chairs), Patrizio Pelliccione (sponsor chair), Silvia Bonfanti and Andrea Bombarda (web chairs), Jacques Carette and Christos Tsigkanos (local proceedings chair), Lena Liberale and Martin von Mohrenschildt (finance chairs), Damiano Torre and Lina Marsso (registration chairs), and Vera Pantelic and Denise Geiskkovitch (student volunteer chairs).

ETAPS 2025 is further supported by the following associations and societies: ETAPS e.V., EATCS (European Association for Theoretical Computer Science), EAPLS (European Association for Programming Languages and Systems), and EASST (European Association of Software Science and Technology).

The ETAPS Steering Committee consists of an Executive Board, and representatives of the individual ETAPS conferences, as well as representatives of EATCS, EAPLS, and EASST. The Executive Board consists of Marieke Huisman (Twente, chair), Andrzej Wąsowski (Copenhagen), Thomas Noll (Aachen), Jan Kofroň (Prague), Barbara König (Duisburg-Essen), Arnd Hartmanns (Twente), Caterina Urban (Inria), Jan Křetínský (Munich), Elizabeth Polgreen (Edinburgh), and Lenore Zuck (Chicago).

Other members of the steering committee are: Elvira Albert (Madrid), Maurice ter Beek (Pisa), Nathalie Bertrand (Rennes), Dirk Beyer (Munich), Artur Boronat (Leicester), Luís Caires (Lisboa), Ferruccio Damiani (Torino), Gordon Fraser (Passau), Arie Gurfinkel (Waterloo), Reiner Hähnle (Darmstadt), Reiko Heckel (Leicester), Marijn Heule (Pittsburgh), Sebastian Junges (Nijmegen), Joost-Pieter Katoen (Aachen and Twente), Guy Katz (Jerusalem), Delia Kesner (Paris), Fabrice Kordon (Paris), Robbert Krebbers (Nijmegen), Kim Guldstrand Larsen (Aalborg), Mark Lawford (Hamilton), Claudio Menghi (Hamilton and Bergamo), Stefan Milius (Erlangen-Nürnberg), Andrzej Murawski (Oxford), Corina Păsăreanu (Ames), Laure Petrucci (Paris), Peter Y.A. Ryan (Luxembourg), Don Sannella (Edinburgh), Viktor Vafeiadis (Kaiserslautern), and Anton Wijs (Eindhoven).

I would like to take this opportunity to thank all authors, keynote speakers, attendees, organizers of the satellite workshops, and Springer Nature for their support. ETAPS 2025 was also generously supported by Tourism Hamilton and the Tutte Institute for Mathematics and Computing. I hope you all enjoyed ETAPS 2025.

Finally, a big thanks to Claudio, Mark and Melissa and their local organization team for all their enormous efforts to make ETAPS a fantastic event.

May 2025

Marieke Huisman
ETAPS SC Chair
ETAPS e.V. President

Preface

FASE 2025 was the 28th edition of the International Conference on Fundamental Approaches to Software Engineering series. It is a forum for researchers, developers, and users interested in the broad field of software engineering. The topics of interest include requirements, design, architecture, modeling, applications of AI to software engineering and software engineering for AI-based systems, quality, model-driven engineering, processes, and software evolution. FASE 2025 was part of the 28th ETAPS International Joint Conferences on Theory and Practice of Software (ETAPS 2025), held May 3–9 in Hamilton, Canada.

There were four submission categories for FASE:

1. *Research papers* clearly identify and justify a principled advance to the fundamentals of software engineering.
2. *Empirical-evaluation papers* evaluate existing software challenges or critically validate current proposed solutions with scientific means, that is, by empirical studies, controlled experiments, rigorous case studies, and simulations.
3. *New Ideas and Emerging Results (NIER) papers* seek to disrupt the status quo with forward-looking, thought-provoking, innovative research on the foundations of software engineering, as well as lessons learned from the past.
4. *Tool demonstration and data showcase papers* present a new tool, a new tool component, novel extensions to an existing tool, or a new dataset.

This year, 31 papers were submitted to FASE in categories 1–4, consisting of 20 research papers, 6 empirical-evaluation papers, 3 NIER papers, and 4 tool-demonstration and data showcase papers. Each paper underwent a double-blind peer review process, where three program committee members reviewed each submission, with the option to involve subreviewers. The review process spanned 9 weeks, ensuring thorough evaluation and discussion of submissions. It was possible to submit an artifact for evaluation alongside a paper, if made long-term available and declared in the Data-Availability Statement. The program committee extensively discussed the papers and ultimately decided to accept 11 papers included here. This is an acceptance rate of 35%.

Artifacts comprise tools, models, proofs, or other data for validating the results of a paper. The artifact evaluation committee (AEC) reviewed the artifacts based on their documentation, ease of use, and, most importantly, whether the results presented in the corresponding paper could be accurately reproduced. As in 2024 FASE offered a joint voluntary artifact evaluation together with ESOP and FoSSaCS to authors of accepted papers. All of the four artifact submissions that were linked with accepted FASE 2025 submissions met the requirements for the "Artifacts Available" badge. In addition, 2 submissions were awarded the "Artifacts Evaluated – Functional" badge and 1 submission the "Artifacts Evaluated – Reusable" badge.

FASE 2025 was proud to host a keynote by José Meseguer from the University of Illinois at Urbana-Champaign, USA. These proceedings contain the invited paper supporting the keynote. In *Capturing System Designs with Formal Executable Specifications*,

Meseguer argues that capturing system designs in executable formal specifications ab origine is one of the best and most cost-effective ways of developing system designs of high quality and to verify their qualitative and quantitative requirements.

FASE 2025 also hosted Test-Comp 2025, the 7th International Competition on Software Testing. This event evaluated 20 software systems for automatic test-case generation for C programs. From the 14 actively participating teams, the jury selected 5 short papers that describe their test systems. These papers are also published in these proceedings. They were reviewed by a separate program committee (jury). Each of the Test-Comp papers was assessed by at least four jury members. Two sessions in the FASE program were reserved for the presentation of the results: (1) a presentation session with a report by the competition chair and summaries by the developer teams, and (2) an open community meeting.

We would like to thank all the people who helped to make FASE 2025 successful. First, we thank the authors for submitting their papers. The PC members and additional reviewers did a great job: they contributed informed and detailed reports and engaged in the PC discussions. We thank Reiner Hähnle, chair of the FASE steering committee, and Marieke Huisman, chair of the ETAPS steering committee, for their valuable advice. Lastly, we would like to thank the overall organization team of ETAPS 2025. We extend our gratitude to Jacques Carette and Christos Tsigkanos, the local proceedings chairs, for their diligent oversight of the proceedings preparation. We also thank the Artifact Evaluation Committee (AEC) for their assessment of submitted artifacts and the Test-Comp 2025 jury members for their evaluation of competition submissions. Additionally, we appreciate the editorial support of Springer Nature, as well as the local organizers of ETAPS 2025 in Hamilton, Canada, for their efforts in facilitating this event.

Finally, we acknowledge the Gold Open Access publication of these proceedings in the Lecture Notes in Computer Science (LNCS) series, ensuring unrestricted access to the contributions presented at FASE 2025.

March 2025

Artur Boronat
Gordon Fraser
PC Chairs

Laura Bussi
Michalis Kokologiannakis
Ondřej Lengál
Stefan Winter
AEC Chairs

Dirk Beyer
Competition Chair

Organization

Program Committee

Artur Boronat (Chair)	University of Leicester, UK
Gordon Fraser (Chair)	University of Passau, Germany
Tevfik Bultan	University of California at Santa Barbara, USA
Ana Cavalcanti	University of York, UK
Priyanka Darke	Tata Consultancy Services, India
Juan de Lara	Universidad Autonoma de Madrid, Spain
Antinisca Di Marco	University of L'Aquila, Italy
Sigrid Eldh	Ericsson, Sweden
Santiago Escobar	Universitat Politècnica de València, Spain
Carlo A. Furia	USI - Università della Svizzera italiana, Switzerland
José Antonio Hernández López	Linköping University, Sweden
Leen Lambers	Brandenburgische Technische Universität Cottbus-Senftenberg, Germany
Kristóf Marussy	Budapest University of Technology and Economics, Hungary
Mercedes Merayo	Universidad Complutense de Madrid, Spain
Jose Oliveira	University of Minho, Portugal
Fernando Orejas	Universitat Politècnica de Catalunya, Spain
Richard Paige	McMaster University, Canada
Luigia Petre	Åbo Akademi University, Finland
Fiona Polack	University of Hull, UK
Jan Oliver Ringert	Bauhaus University Weimar, Germany
Camilo Rocha	Pontificia Universidad Javeriana Cali, Colombia
José Miguel Rojas	University of Sheffield, UK
Adrian Rutle	Western Norway University of Applied Sciences, Norway
Augusto Sampaio	Federal University of Pernambuco, Brazil
Paola Spoletini	Kennesaw State University, USA
Jun Sun	Singapore Management University, Singapore
Christoph Treude	Singapore Management University, Singapore
Mahsa Varshosaz	IT University of Copenhagen, Denmark
Manuel Wimmer	Johannes Kepler University Linz, Austria
Vadim Zaytsev	Universiteit Twente, The Netherlands

Artifact Evaluation Committee

Laura Bussi (Chair)	University of Pisa, Italy
Stefan Winter (Chair)	LMU Munich, Germany
Michalis Kokologiannakis (Chair)	ETH Zurich, Switzerland
Ondřej Lengál (Chair)	Brno University of Technology, Czech Republic
Alexandre Moine	New York University, USA
András Kovács	University of Gothenburg, Sweden
Andrea Colledan	University of Bologna, Italy
Bernardo Almeida	LASIGE, University of Lisbon, Portugal
David Chocholatý	Brno University of Technology, Czech Republic
Gennaro Zanfardino	University of L'Aquila, Italy
Giordano d'Aloisio	University of L'Aquila, Italy
Gustavo Carvalho	Universidade Federal de Pernambuco, Brazil
Hongjian Jiang	RPTU Kaiserslautern-Landau, Germany
Julia Sapiña	Universitat Politècnica de València, Spain
Loïc Pujet	Stockholm University, Sweden
Loïc Germerie Guizouarn	Université de Rennes, CNRS, Inria, IRISA, France
Lucas Sakizloglou	Brandenburg University of Technology, Germany
Manolis Pitsikalis	National Centre for Scientific Research Demokritos, Greece
Michal Hečko	Brno University of Technology, Czech Republic
Noa Izsak	Ben-Gurion University of the Negev, Israel
Pablo Gómez-Abajo	Universidad Autónoma de Madrid, Spain
Raúl Gutiérrez	Universitat Politècnica de València, Spain
Raúl López-Rueda	Universitat Politècnica de València, Spain
Sougata Bose	University of Liverpool, UK
Soumodev Mal	Chennai Mathematical Institute, India
Srinidhi Nagendra	IRIF, CNRS, Université Paris Cité, Chennai Mathematical Institute, France
Szumi Xie	Eötvös Loránd University, Hungary
Thomas Holger	Universität der Bundeswehr München, Forschungsinstitut CODE, Germany
Vincent Cheval	University of Oxford, UK
Wei-Lun Tsai	Academia Sinica, Taiwan
Zainab Fatmi	University of Oxford, UK
Zsófia Ádám	Budapest University of Technology and Economics, Hungary

Test-Comp 2025 Program Committee and Jury

Dirk Beyer (Chair)	LMU Munich, Germany
Sumesh Divakaran	College of Engineering Trivandrum, India
Marie-Christine Jakobs	LMU Munich, Germany
Zhenbang Chen	National University of Defense Technology, China
Marek Trtík	Masaryk University, Brno, Czechia
Mohannad Aldughaim	University of Manchester/King Saud University, UK/Saudi Arabia
Kaled Alshmrany	University of Manchester/Institute of Public Administration, UK/Saudi Arabia
Yurii Kostyukov	RnD Toolchain Labs, Huawei, China
Léo Andrès	OCamlPro/LMF, France
Thomas Lemberger	LMU Munich, Germany
Adam Štafa	Masaryk University, Brno, Czechia
Martin Jonáš	Masaryk University, Brno, Czechia
Matthias Kettl	LMU Munich, Germany
Joxan Jaffar	National University of Singapore, Singapore
Max Barth	LMU Munich, Germany

FASE 2025 Steering Committee

Reiner Hähnle (Chair)	TU Darmstadt, Germany
Dirk Beyer	Ludwig-Maximilians-Universität München, Germany
Artur Boronat	University of Leicester, UK
Ana Cavalcanti	University of York, UK
Gordon Fraser	University of Passau, Germany
Reiko Heckel	University of Leicester, UK
Marie-Christine Jakobs	Ludwig-Maximilians-Universität München, Germany
Einar Broch Johnsen	University of Oslo, Norway
Leen Lambers	BTU Cottbus-Senftenberg, Germany
Tiziana Margaria	University of Limerick, Ireland
Gabriele Taentzer	Philipps-Universität Marburg, Germany
Sebastian Uchitel	Universidad de Buenos Aires, Argentina and Imperial College London, UK
Andrzej Wąsowski	IT University of Copenhagen, Denmark
Heike Wehrheim	University of Oldenburg, Germany
Manuel Wimmer	Johannes Kepler University Linz, Austria

Additional Reviewers

Supriya Agrawal
Paulo Sérgio Almeida
Levente Bajczi
Martin Eisenberg
Stefan Klikovits

Reinhold Plösch
Sumanth Prabhu
Lucas Sakizloglou
Jorge Sousa Pinto
Kangfeng Ye

Contents

Capturing System Designs with Formal Executable Specifications

José Meseguer$^{(\boxtimes)}$

University of Illinois at Urbana-Champaign, Urbana, IL 61801, USA
meseguer@illinois.edu

Abstract. Basing system designs on informal specifications and apply-ing formal methods after system implementation greatly reduces the ben-efits that formal methods can provide. Systems of high quality and trust-worthiness can be developed in a faster and much more efficient way by capturing system designs with *formal executable specifications* and sub-jecting them to automated formal verification from the earliest stages of system design. Even greater benefits can be gained by making such for-mal designs highly composable and reusable by means of *formal patterns*. The experience on using the rewriting-logic-based language Maude and its tool environment and formal patterns for all these purposes is pre-sented and illustrated with concrete examples. The benefits of combining model-based design approaches with the one based on formal executable specifications is also discussed an illustrated with examples.

Keywords: System Design · Executable Specifications · Formal Pat-terns · Qualitative and Quantitative Properties · Rewriting Logic · Maude

1 Introduction

Many important theoretical and practical advances have taken place in the area of Formal Methods (FMs), and impressive applications have been developed. Furthermore, FMs and their associated tools are now routinely used in many industries. However, their full potential remains partly unexploited. In pg. 57 of a recent FMs survey [47], I gave my own view about their future in a position statement where, among other things, I said (emphasis added):

> Rather than focusing mostly on [code] verification, [formal methods] should support system design, validation, evolution and maintenance from the *earliest stages*. For this, use of *executable formal specifications* for fast system modeling and analysis *before implementation* is crucial.

The problem at present is that many complex systems are still designed in an *informal* manner. This happens not just for the proprietary designs of many companies, but even when international bodies responsible for agreeing on and carefully documenting the standards of a widely used system —e.g., a new com-munication protocol, or a programming language— capture its design mostly informally. Let me give three examples that I know well:

ⓒ The Author(s) 2025
A. Boronat and G. Fraser (Eds.): FASE 2025, LNCS 15693, pp.1–32, 2025.
https://doi.org/10.1007/978-3-031-90900-9_1

1. Until 2007, when S. Chen, J. Meseguer, R. Sasse, H. J. Wang and Y.M. Wang used a formal executable semantics of Internet Explorer (IE) in Maude to uncover 13 new types of visual spoofing attacks on IE [27], hundreds of thousands of dollars were yearly lost due to such kinds of attacks, and no meaningful way existed to predict and prevent new attacks.
2. Until 2012, when C. Ellison and G. Rosu gave the first full formal executable semantics of C (in K, automatically translated to Maude by the K-Maude tool [105,104]) [43], no complete formal specification of C existed. This K semantics uncovered semantic flaws in several C theorem provers.
3. Until 2023, when S. Liu, H. Duan, L. Heimes, M. Bearzi, J. Vieli, D. Basin and A. Perrig gave the first formal executable semantics (in Maude) of the end-to-end name resolution behavior of DNS [61], many attacks were regularly perpetrated on DNS, and several more, which were uncovered in [61], were confirmed on popular DNS implementations.

As the above examples illustrate, the most disastrous consequence of informal specifications is their utter *lack of predictive power*. In fact:

- It is virtually impossible to predict the problematic behaviors of a complex system based on its informal specifications *before it is built*.
- Even after a complex system has been implemented, lack of a formal executable specification makes it very difficult to systematically uncover its often subtle flaws and vulnerabilities.

The second point is illustrated by the systems (1)–(3) described above, which all had heavily tested, mature implementations.[1] But the first point is much more important than the second, for the simple reason that *design errors are typically several orders of magnitude more expensive than coding errors*.

Let me further comment on these two points: formal executable specifications can be used in two different ways: (i) in a **post facto** analysis of an already implemented system, or (ii) one can use formal executable specifications **ab origine**, that is, from the earliest stages of a system's *design*. As the above examples (1)–(3) illustrate, formal executable specifications can be extremely valuable in a *post facto* specification and analysis of a system. However, post facto specification and analysis is neither the most cost effective nor the most fruitful application of FMs for three reasons:

1. Inferring a formal executable specification from a large, already implemented system is very labor-intensive. I have detailed knowledge about this problem in both the case of IE (Example 1) and in the case of the Maude specification of the Cassandra key-value store used in [67].
2. Due to large system size and complexity (easily hundreds of thousands or even millions of lines of code) a formal specification inferred from a system implementation usually provides only *partial knowledge* about the system.

---

[1] In the case of C, the executable specification of Ellison and Rosu was able to pass more tests than those passed by the GNU compiler using the GNU torture suite.

For example, besides the 13 new types of visual spoofing attacks uncovered by the Maude specification of IE, one more attack type was later found because some additional IE functionality had not been modeled in the original Maude specification of IE.

3. While the uncovering of a system's *design flaws* by means of a post facto analysis based on a formal executable specification inferred from its implementation can be extremely valuable, the cost of *fixing* those design flaws *after* the system has been implemented can be quite high: this is an engineering fact of life about late discovery of design errors.

In response to the reasons I have just given, somebody could object as follows:

> *We already knew all that back in the times of stepwise refinement in structured programming. And we have since then learned considerably more about program extraction from propositions in intuitionistic type theory. Isn't all you have said just old hat?*

I would answer that objection by making a crucial distinction between:

- **Formal System Specifications**, in which a *computational mathematical model of a system* is captured by a formal executable specification in a *computational* logic, and
- **Formal Property Specifications**, in which *formal requirements* about the desirable correctness and quantitative properties that a system should satisfy are captured in various, usually *non-executable*, logics.

Both kinds of specifications are essential: they complement each other, and both should be used *ab origine*, since the earliest stages of system design. The problem with the above objection is that it confuses the early uses of *property specifications* —i.e., of formal system requirements expressed, for example, as Hoare logic triples, or as intuitionistic logic propositions— with something completely different, namely, that we should *also* use formal *executable* specifications from the very beginning and that this is crucial. But why? Let me give six reasons:

1. **Formal specifications of large systems may contain bugs**. This applies to both formal requirements and to executable specifications. The big difference is that an executable specification is in fact a *declarative program* that can, not only be tested and debugged like any other program, but can also, as in the case of Maude (see §4), be *model checked* to uncover subtle design flaws in early designs. This kind of debugging is usually not possible for property specifications. Imagine, for example, an *axiomatic semantics* of C in Hoare logic. One cannot use the GNU torture suite —as Ellison and Rosu did for their K semantics of C— to debug a C axiomatic semantics.

2. **KISS**. Since a formal executable specification is a declarative program, the entry barrier for engineers to write such specifications is quite low: just learning another programming language. This is typically not the case for formal property specifications, which may require expert acquaintance with complex logics. Let me give one example from my direct experience about the

use of Maude. In the late 90's and early 2000's I was involved in the early applications of Maude to systems biology [42] that has subsequently been vigorously developed under the leadership of Carolyn Talcott and other researchers. The first Maude executable specification thus developed —a model of a mammalian cell and its molecular biology reactions (over 500 of them)— was not developed by a computer scientist, but by Merryl Knapp, a biologist with no previous acquaintance with Maude. Since Maude axioms are rewrite rules specifying local concurrent transitions in a system, rewrite rules had an obvious one-to-one correspondence with molecular biology reactions.

3. **Small is beautiful.** Formal executable specifications of a system are orders of magnitude *smaller* than system implementations in a conventional language (Examples (1)–(3) underscore this). And they are much more *understandable* than a conventional implementation. For example, the executable formal semantics of C by Ellison and Rosu had about 1,000 rules in K, with each language feature captured by a few rules with an obvious meaning.

4. **Executable specifications are much easier to verify than imperative code.** To begin with, they are simpler and much smaller. A further key advantage is that the verification process *never leaves mathematics*. This is because, as explained in §2, an executable formal specification is a theory T in a computational logic, and its formal requirements are formulas φ in some, usually non-executable, property specification logic. By contrast, an imperative programming language is an *engineering artifact* that needs a precise *mathematical semantics* before any formal program verification worth its name can get off the ground. Even more importantly, verification of formal executable designs can uncover costly *design errors* much more easily and much earlier than verification of system implementations.

5. **Easy, rapid exploration of alternative designs.** In traditional system development it is very costly to explore *alternative designs*, for the obvious reason that informal specifications cannot predict system behavior on which design changes should be based. Since design changes after implementation can be prohibitively expensive, exploration of design alternatives often becomes unfeasible. This is not at all the case when a system design is captured by a formal executable specification: alternative changes are easy to make. In Maude, it may just require changing a few rewrite rules; and quick feedback about the correctness and quantitative properties of alternative designs can easily be gained by automatic verification methods (see §4 and §5.2).

6. **Gold standard for code generation**. If an executable specification language has high performance, a system specification may be directly used as a system implementation. Alternatively, an executable formal design may be either transformed into a correct-by construction implementation as done, for example, in [68], or may be compiled into a lower level language for further efficiency, as done by K's compilation into LLVM.

Having motivated the usefulness of capturing system designs with formal executable specifications, I explain in §2 how a *computational logic* supports such specifications. In §3 I then explain how *formal patterns* can increase the modularity and reusability of formal system designs. Verification of qualitative and quantitative properties of Maude designs is then discussed in §4. I summarize my own experience about formal executable designs in §5. The relationship with model-based design is discussed in §6. Conclusions are presented in §7.

2   Capturing System Designs in a Computational Logic

The ideas I am presenting are *logic-independent*: various logics can be chosen as executable formal specification languages. But not all logics are suitable for this purpose, simply because many, although they are *mechanizable*, i.e., a theorem prover can mechanize their inference rules, are not *executable* in the obvious, intuitive sense that the logic itself, or a suitable subset of its theories, can be efficiently implemented as a *declarative programming language*. I call a logic enjoying these properties a *computational logic*. For example, the λ-calculus, the π-calculus, Horn logic, confluent theories in equational logic, and rewriting logic are all computational logics in this sense. However, not all computational logics can support system specification equally well. For example, the λ-calculus and equational logic can both nicely express *deterministic* systems, but are not a good fit for specifying non-deterministic ones, whereas the opposite is the case for Horn logic. I present below some requirements on a computational logic $\mathcal{L}$ that I have found particularly useful for system specification purposes.

2.1   Requirements on the Computational Logic $\mathcal{L}$

In my own experience, for a computational logic $\mathcal{L}$ to be an expressive *semantic framework* for executable formal system design it is highly desirable that $\mathcal{L}$ supports features such as the following:

1. implementable as a high-performance declarative programming language
2. can naturally specify both deterministic systems and a wide range of concurrent systems, including concurrent object-oriented systems
3. an executable system specification, i.e., a theory T in $\mathcal{L}$, has an associated *initial model*[2] that defines a *mathematical model* of the system thus specified
4. supports logical reflection
5. supports the specification of real-time and probabilistic systems
6. availability of advanced algorithmic and deductive formal verification methods and tools in a variety of *property-specification logics*, including logics expressing quantitative properties.

---

[2] More generally, T can be a *parameterized theory* associating a *free model* to each model of its *parameter theory* P. In this way, T defines a *parametric family of systems*. This desirable property of $\mathcal{L}$ can be captured by the requirement that $\mathcal{L}$ is a *liberal institution* [48].

Let me unpack requirement (6). By requirement (3), a theory T in $\mathcal{L}$ specifying a given system defines a mathematical model of such a system as an initial model $\mathcal{I}_T$, which is precisely the link between the system specification T and its formal requirements R. Formal requirements in R may be expressed in a variety of (typically non-computational) property specification logics. That is, each formal requirement $\varphi \in R$ is a formula in one such logic. The link between T and R is then simple: T meets a formal requirement $\varphi \in R$ iff $\mathcal{I}_T \models_{\mathcal{L}'} \varphi$, where $\mathcal{L}'$ is the property specification logic of formula φ, and $\models_{\mathcal{L}'}$ denotes the *satisfaction relation* between models and formulas in $\mathcal{L}'$. For example, $\mathcal{I}_T$ may provide the mathematical model of a communication protocol, and φ may express a safety or liveness property about such a protocol in some temporal logic. What (6) expects is that advanced algorithmic and deductive formal methods and tools are available to prove formal requirements about $\mathcal{I}_T$ in various property specification logics $\mathcal{L}'$, including logics expressing quantitative properties.

Maude's [28] computational logic, namely, *rewriting logic* [73,24] and its real-time and probabilistic extensions (see [91,63]) provides a semantic framework for system specification meeting requirements (1)–(6). For how requirements (1)–(5) are met by rewriting logic and Maude see [75,74,71,30,91,63]. I discuss in detail how Maude meets requirement (6) in §4.

I explain in §3 below how a computational logic $\mathcal{L}$ meeting requirements (1)–(6) can support *modular* and *reusable* development of system designs by means of *formal patterns*.

3   Formal Patterns for Modular System Design

This section summarizes and borrows ideas from [76,78]. I refer to those two publications for further details. Formal patterns are formally specified *generic solutions to commonly occurring computational problems*. Being generic, a formal pattern applies, not just to a single system, but to a typically infinite class of systems that satisfy specified *semantic requirements*. Application of a formal pattern to a system satisfying the formal pattern's input requirements results in a new system with new functionality that is *correct by construction*. Such correctness takes the form of an *assume-guarantee formal assurance*: assuming that the original system meets the formal pattern's semantic requirements, then the application of the formal pattern to such a system is guaranteed to enjoy specific correctness properties.

Formal patterns are very useful for formal system design because, as it will become clear in what follows, they support a high degree of genericity, reusability and modularity of system designs. In this way, a system design, instead of being a *one of a kind* design that has to be developed and verified from scratch, can reuse many existing generic system components, algorithms and program transformations *for free*, as well as the correctness properties already verified for those components, algorithms and program transformations. This can greatly reduce design and verification efforts and can substantially increase system quality.

3.1   Formal Patterns in Declarative Programming Languages

Mathematically, a formal pattern is a *theory transformation* P that maps a declarative program in a computational logic $\mathcal{L}$, that is, a theory T in the class $\mathcal{C}$ of $\mathcal{L}$-theories satisfying the pattern's input requirements, perhaps with some *additional parameters* $\boldsymbol{p}$, into a new theory $P(T, \boldsymbol{p})$ specifying the new correct-by-construction system generated by P, i.e., we can describe P as a (possibly partial) function,

$$P : \mathcal{C} \times \textit{Params} \ni (T, \boldsymbol{p}) \mapsto P(T, \boldsymbol{p}) \in \textit{Th}_{\mathcal{L}}$$

where $\textit{Th}_{\mathcal{L}}$ denotes the category of finitary theories in the language's computational logic $\mathcal{L}$. I assume throughout that $\mathcal{L}$ enjoys the requirements presented in §2.1. We can therefore view P as a *meta-program*, that is, as a program that transforms a declarative program T into another declarative program $P(T, \boldsymbol{p})$. Thanks to requirement (4) in §2.1 (logical reflection), programs in $\mathcal{L}$ can be meta-represented as data structures,[3] so that the meta-program P is also a program in the same computational logic $\mathcal{L}$.

   Although in some applications (e.g., [2]) the purpose of a formal pattern P may be one of *optimization and/or specialization* of a declarative program $T \in \mathcal{C}$, in $\mathcal{L}$, in many other applications $P(T, \boldsymbol{p})$ may instead be a *substantial extension* of T with completely new features and capabilities; that is, $P(T, \boldsymbol{p})$ is often *a more sophisticated system*, enjoying new features and properties not available in T. Nevertheless, the assume-guarantee properties of P often include the fact that P will in some appropriate sense be *semantics-preserving*. But in general this should not be understood in the sense that T and $P(T, \boldsymbol{p})$ have the same semantics. Instead, the semantics of $P(T, \boldsymbol{p})$ will often *extend* that of T while respecting T itself, which may remain intact as a *subcomponent* of $P(T, \boldsymbol{p})$. This is in fact the case for many formal patterns (see, e.g., [110,112,111,26,4,39,50]). From the point of view of code reusability this means that the *code* of T is *not changed at all* by P. That is, T is kept intact and *encapsulated* as a subcomponent. This gives formal patterns powerful modularity, code understandability and reusability, and verification scalability properties.

   In yet other kinds of examples of formal pattern (e.g., [81,10,68,63,66]), the input theory T may not be kept as a subcomponent of $P(T, \boldsymbol{p})$. Instead, the assume-guarantee properties relating T and $P(T, \boldsymbol{p})$ may include considerably more general semantics-preserving properties such as the existence of a *simulation* or *bisimulation* (including the case of a *stuttering* simulation or bisimulation), between $P(T, \boldsymbol{p})$ and T.

---

[3] In Maude this is supported by its `META-LEVEL` module.

3.2   Application Areas

Formal patterns specified as Maude *meta-programs* have been defined and proved correct in various application areas, including:

1. **Cyber-physical systems**
   - Formal Patterns for Safe Operation of Medical Devices [110,112,111]
   - Physically Asynchronous/Logically Sinchronous (PALS) pattern for real-time distributed systems [83,81], and Multi-Rate PALS [10,8,15]
2. **Security**
   - Cookies [26] (for DDoS protection)
   - Adaptive Selective Verification (ASV) [4] (for DDoS protection)
   - Server Replicator (SR) and ASV+SR [39] (for DDoS protection)
   - Protocol Dialects [46]
3. **Distributed systems' implementation and model checking**
   - The D Transformation [68] for correct-by-construction distributed system implementation.
   - The P, *Sim* and M transformations for statistical model checking (SMC) analysis [63]
   - The M Transformation for automatically verifying consistency properties of Distributed Transaction Systems [66]
4. **Theorem proving and executability transformations**
   - The $\mathcal{E} \mapsto \mathcal{E}^{\equiv}$ [50] and $\boldsymbol{\mathcal{E}} \mapsto \boldsymbol{\mathcal{E}}$: [79] Transformations
   - The $\mathcal{R} \mapsto \overline{\mathcal{R}}_l$ and $\mathcal{R} \mapsto \overline{\mathcal{R}}_{\Sigma_1,l,r}^{\Omega}$ Transformations [77]
   - The $\mathcal{R} \mapsto \mathcal{R}_U$ Transformation [35]
   - Partial Evaluation Transformations [2].

Detailed discussion of the above formal patterns is beyond the scope of this paper. I refer to [76,78] for overviews of many of them, and to the references given for each formal pattern for full details. Nevertheless, the P, *Sim*, M and D transformations, as well as PALS, will make cameo appearances later in the paper.

4   Qualitative and Quantitative Verification of Designs

I explain here how Maude meets requirement (6) from §2.1. Some of the requirements of a Maude system design may be *quantitative*. For example, they may involve time, space, power or performance requirements; and they may involve probabilities. They are typically specified in timed or probabilistic logics. Other requirements, e.g., a system invariant, do not involve quantities and are then called *qualitative*. They are typically specified in standard logics such as first-order logic, temporal logics such as LTL and CTL*, Hoare logic and so on. The difference between these two kinds of properties is not always clear-cut.

Requirement (6) is important for system design because qualitative and quantitative properties are not independent. Quantitative requirements may be as important as non-safety-critical qualitative ones, and a balance between them may be needed. I provide a good illustration of this balancing need in §5.2.

A Maude distributed system design is a rewrite theory $\mathcal{R} = (\Sigma, E, R)$, where (Σ, E) is an equational theory (in fact an equational program) specifying the system's data types and auxiliary functions, and R is a collection of rewrite rules describing the distributed system's *local concurrent transitions*. The initial model $\mathbb{T}_{\mathcal{R}}$ is a mathematical model of the distributed system $\mathcal{R}$, but its states are elements of the initial algebra $\mathbb{T}_{\Sigma/E}$ of its equational theory (Σ, E).

Verification of Qualitative Requirements. Some of the formal requirements of $\mathcal{R}$ may be purely functional and qualitative because they only involve $\mathbb{T}_{\Sigma/E}$. For such requirements, the following Maude tools can verify various functional properties: (i) the Church-Rosser Checker [37]; (ii) the Maude Termination Tool (MTT) [34]; (iii) the Sufficient Completeness Checker (SCC) [51]; and (iv) the New Inductive Theorem Prover (NuITP) [38].

Many other qualitative formal requirements of $\mathcal{R}$ will involve $\mathbb{T}_{\mathcal{R}}$, i.e., the distributed system's behavior. Some of these requirements, expressible in modal logic as reachability requirements (e.g. invariants) or as LTL properties, can be verified in Maude itself, either by (1) *explicit state* model checking features such as: (i) the `search` command, (ii) its LTL model checker; or (iii) the extension of the LTL model checker to verify properties under user-specified strategies reported in [99], which will soon be added to Maude; or by (2) *infinite-state, narrowing-based* model checking of invariants with the `fvu-narrow` command.

Infinite-state model checking of LTL properties is instead supported by the Maude Logical Model Checker tool [7]; and explicit-state model checking in the richer logic LTLR is supported by Maude's LTLR Model Checker tool [9]. Furthermore, the tool described in §6 of [97] makes it possible to model check CLT* and μ-calculus temporal logic properties of Maude designs through an interface to the LTSim model checker [52].

Verification of Quantitative or Mixed Requirements. I view real-time requirements as mixed. The Real-Time Maude tool [91] can model check real-time requirements expressed in either LTL or in timed CTL (TCTL). For quantitative properties of actor-based distributed system designs involving both time and probabilities, properties can be expresses in the QuaTEx quantitative probabilistic temporal logic [1] and can be model checked in the parallel statistical model checker PVesStA [3]. At present, the best tool supporting integrated statistical model checking verification of Maude actor-based distributed system designs is the Actors2PMaude tool [63], because it includes PVesStA as a subcomponent and implements the P, S and M formal patterns mentioned in §3.2, which as explained and demonstrated in [63], makes it much easier for a user to transform a distributed Maude design into a probabilistic rewrite theory in the PMaude language extension [1]. In addition to all these tools, the QMaude tool [98] supports both probabilistic (in PRISM [55] and Storm [32]) and statistical model checking (in MultiVeStA [103]) of probabilisitic rewrite theories.

5   Experience Using Maude in Early System Design

As I have already pointed out, the formal design methodology of using formal executable specifications *ab origine* in system design, implementation and verification is *computational-logic-independent*: any declarative language directly based on a computational logic $\mathcal{L}$ can be used; but I have also pointed out in §2 that not all computational logics are equally expressive, or equally well-suited for designing systems.

All this implies that various computational logics can be and have been used for this purpose. It is outside the scope of this paper to survey all such efforts. What I can do here is to describe efforts which I have fairly detailed knowledge about, namely, those using rewriting logic and Maude for this purpose. Even within Maude, I am sure that there are various such uses I am unfamiliar with. Let me mention several uses of Maude for early system design, implementation and verification that, among others, I know about:

1. Design, implementation and verification of the **IBOS** browser (more on this in §5.1).
2. Design, implementation and verification of the **ROLA** distributed database (more on this in §5.2).
3. The **N-Tube** provably secure inter-domain bandwidth reservation algorithm is a novel network algorithm with strong guarantees against DDoS attacks proposed by T. Weghorn, S. Liu et al. in [115]. N-Tube's design was captured as a rewrite theory in Maude. Furthermore, to subject N-Tube's design to detailed performance analysis by statistical model checking, N-Tube's Maude design was then extended into a *probabilistic rewrite theory* in PMaude and was analyzed by statistical model checking in **PVeStA** [3].
4. Design, implementation and validation of **new Maude language features**. Exploiting rewriting logic's *logical reflection* and its support by Maude's META-LEVEL module, most of the advanced features that have been added to Maude over the years have first been designed, implemented and validated in Maude. This has been greatly helped by the *Full Maude* language extension [36,28], a metalevel Maude program that allows adding new features to Maude by reflection. I like to say that, at any point in time, Full Maude is what Maude *will be*. Only after a long experimentation in Full Maude (or in the Maude-NPA tool [44]) with a new Maude feature has it been later implemented in C++ for greater efficiency. Advanced features that have been so designed and implemented in Maude and have later been added to Maude's C++ implementation include:
   - Parameterized theories, modules, and views.
   - Object-oriented modules.
   - Maude's strategy language.
   - Unification algorithms modulo axioms.
   - Variant narrowing, Variant unification, and Variant-based reachability.
5. Design, implementation and validation of **Formal Tools**. Rewriting logic is a good match for designing and building formal tools. This is so because

it is a flexible *logical framework* [69], which can naturally represent many logics and formal inference systems by representing each inference rule in the given logic or system as a (possibly conditional) rewrite rule. This has been systematically exploited in designing and building formal tools in Maude in two ways:

(1) Formal verifications tools for Maude such as:
   - Maude's Church-Rosser and Coherence Checkers [37].
   - Maude's Termination Tool (MTT) [34].
   - Maude's Sufficient Completeness Checker (SCC) [51].
   - Maude's Logical Model Checker [7].
   - Maude's LTLR Model Checker [9].
   - Maude's Inductive Theorem Prover (ITP) [31].
   - Maude's New Inductive Theorem Prover (NuITP) [38].
   - Real-Time Maude [91]
   - PMaude Tool and statistical model checking environment (Actors2PMaude) [63].

(2) Tools for other logics and specification formalisms such as, e.g.,
   - A *LOTOS* execution and analysis environment [114].
   - *CafeInMaude* translator from CafeOBJ to Maude and its formal verification environment [95].
   - The *L-Framework*, a Maude executable implementation of a meta-logical framework to mechanize and prove properties about a wide variety of sequent-based logics meta-represented as rewrite theories [90].
   - The *HOL/Nuprl* proof translator to transfer large libraries of theorems in the HOL theorem prover to theorems in the classical extension of NuPrl [109]. This translator defined a map of entailment systems (in the sense of the theory of general logics [72]) between the logics of HOL and NuPrl. The hand proof of correctness of this translator was later verified in the Twelf theorem prover [102].
   - The *AADL2Maude* [94] and *SynchAADL2Maude* [13] tools, giving semantics in Real-Time Maude to models of cyber-physical systems in the behavioral subset of the AADL modeling language and supporting model checking verification of such models. These tools are integrated with OSATE. I give more details on both of them in §6.2.

It is impossible to give details within this paper about all the above-mentioned system designs and implementations. I can, however, illustrate the Maude-based design methodology used in all of them by briefly summarizing two such designs, namely, those of **IBOS** and **ROLA**.

5.1 IBOS

After a talk by Shuo Chen at the University of Illinois reporting on how Maude had been used to uncover 13 types of previously unknown visual spoofing attacks on IE, my colleague Sam King came to my office and posed to me the following question, with roughly the following words:

Why don't we design and build a browser that is secure by design?

Sam's question exemplified the enormous advantage of *ab origine* uses of formal executable specifications over *post facto* uses: In a large system like IE with over one million lines of code, it was possible and very useful to use Maude to uncover and correct[4] *some* security vulnerabilities; but it was essentially hopeless to achieve strong security guarantees about the IE implementation itself.

That conversation in my office was the start of a very fruitful 4-person (S. King, J. Meseguer, S. Tang and R. Sasse) collaboration on the design of such a secure-by-design browser: the *Illinois Browser and Operating System* (IBOS). Sam was the Ph.D. advisor of Shuo Tang, and I advised the Ph.D. of Ralf Sasse. Ralf was of course thoroughly familiar with Maude and formal verification. Shuo took my CS 476 course to also become familiar with specification and verification in Maude. The design of IBOS was captured in Maude from the very beginning of the project. Sam and Shuo took the lead on deciding the architecture of IBOS, including that of its small kernel, so as to meet specific security requirements, and also on implementing IBOS in C++, whereas Ralf and I focused on improving the Maude formal design and verifying its security properties. Shuo and Ralf interacted very closely, particularly to ensure that the C++ kernel implementation (about 60,000 lines of C++) developed by Shuo as part of his Ph.D. thesis [113] fully agreed with the Maude design. Ralf undertook the model checking verification of IBOS's security properties as part of his Ph.D. thesis [100]. The four of us reported on the IBOS project and its formal specification and verification in [101]. A deductive verification of the IBOS security properties in reachability logic was later carried out in [106]. I summarize below the description of IBOS given in [101] and [106] and refer to [101,106,113,100,107] for further details.

The IBOS architecture can be graphically described as follows:

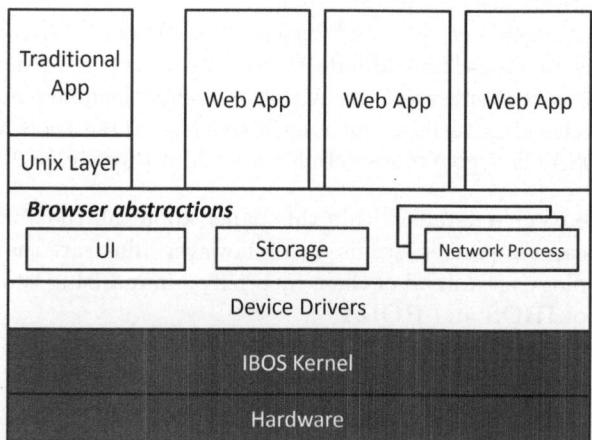

---

[4] The publication of [27] was delayed for about a year to allow the IE team to correct the security vulnerabilities uncovered by the verification of the Maude IE design.

A key security property enforced by IBOS is the *same-origin policy* (SOP): it isolates web apps from different origins, where an origin is represented as a tuple of a protocol, a domain name, and a port number. The main components of IBOS are:

- **Kernel**, built on top of the L4Ka::Pistachio micro-kernel. Its main task is to enforce that inter-process communications meet the IBOS security policies.
- **Network Process**. A network process is responsible for managing network connections to a specific origin. It understands how to encode and decode TCP datagrams and Ethernet frames and can send and receive frames from the network interface card (NIC).
- **Web App** represents a specific instance of a web page loaded in a particular browser tab. Web apps know how to render HTML documents. As per SOP, each web page is labeled by its origin.
- **Browser UI**. The browser user interface (UI) minimally includes the address bar and the mouse pointer and extends to any input mechanism.
- **Display**. The display represents the rendered web app shown to the user; it is blank when no web app has loaded. For security, it cannot modify the UI.

The *security properties* of IBOS can be formally expressed as an *invariant P*, which is itself a conjunction $P = \bigwedge_{1 \leq i \leq 11} P_i$ of eleven simpler invariants [106]. P implies the two main security properties of IBOS, namely, (i) SOP, which is the conjunction $SOP = \bigwedge_{1 \leq i \leq 11} P_i$, and (ii) the *address bar correctness* (ABC) property, which is P_{10}. The invariant $\bigwedge_{1 \leq i \leq 10} P_i$ was verified by Ralf Sasse by model checking [101,100], whereas P itself was deductively verified in reachability logic by Stephen Skeirik as part of his Ph.D. thesis at Illinois [106,107].

IBOS was an academic project. It did not become a commercial product. IBOS demonstrated that a secure browser can be fruitfully designed and implemented by capturing its design *ab origine* in a formal executable specification.

5.2   ROLA

The formal design, verification and implementation in Maude of the Read atOmicity and prevention of Lost updAtes (**ROLA**) distributed database [65] is part of a much bigger joint effort by researchers at the University of Illinois and the University of Oslo to formally specify in Maude and to verify the qualitative (consistency properties) and quantitative (performance properties) of a wide range of industrial and academic distributed databases. To the best of my knowledge, this was the first time that those distributed databases, lacking in virtually all cases any prior formal specifications, were thus formally specified in Maude and analyzed with respect to their consistency and performance properties. I refer to the survey [17] for details about this bigger research effort. What is unique about both ROLA, as compared to all the other industrial and academic distributed data bases described in [17], is that the Maude specifications of all other databases were *post facto* efforts to specify and verify systems already implemented.[5] Instead, ROLA was designed, verified and implemented in Maude *ab origine.*

Another unique aspect of ROLA is that it illustrates how easy, fast and inexpensive it is to *explore the design space* in search of an optimal design (w.r.t. given requirements) by means of executable formal specifications. As already pointed out in §1, it is usually very costly, and seldom done, to explore design alternatives for a system developed from informal specifications. But it is even more difficult and costly to *compare* different distributed systems with respect to some correctness and performance requirements. To begin with, different systems may be implemented in different programming languages, so that experimentally comparing their behavior and performance may not allow answering the counterfactual question: How would they compare if they had been implemented in the *same* programming language? Answering this question might provide partial evidence for the really crucial question: Is the *design* of system *A better* than that of system *B* w.r.t. some given correctness and performance requirements? Let me explain how the design of ROLA provides an answer to this question.

Most modern distributed databases have large numbers of users, sometimes located all over the world, with data stored and replicated across various data centers. For these systems *performance*, and specifically *availability*, is as important as *correctness*, and specifically database *consistency* properties. In distributed database design there is an unavoidable tension between consistency and availability, particularly when the network can be partitioned [23]. The fine art of distributed database system design involves finding the right balance between availability and consistency in the design space. Such a balance actually depends on the kinds of *applications* envisioned for the given database. For example, the database of a social network will typically have considerably weaker consistency requirements than those of a bank or a medical information system; and this can be exploited to increase the performance of a social network.

Exploring the distributed database design space can be guided by the degree of *database consistency* needed for the system in question. Providing a greater degree of consistency than necessary for a given application will often result in loss of performance, including poorer availability. The work of Cerone et al. [25] has provided a formal axiomatization of a hierarchy of increasingly stronger consistency models —with *read atomicity* (**RA**) as the weakest and *serializability* (**SER**) as the stronger—, as pictured in the black-marked models of the consistency hierarchy of Figure 1 from [65]. The significance of ROLA is that it found a previously unexplored sweetspot in the design space by adding one more node to the consistency hierarchy of [25], namely the *update atomic* (UA) consistency, marked in red in Figure 1, and has demonstrated clear performance advantages

---

[5] This should be qualified. New Maude designs of variants or extensions of already-implemented systems were also developed, verified and evaluated, such as alternative designs of Cassandra [62] and RAMP [64], and Megastore-CGC [49], a novel extension of Google's Megastore design. What all this work shows is that formal executable specifications can easily explore design alternatives for already implemented systems.

for this sweetspot, which is well suited for social media applications. The potential usefulness of UA was already conjectured in [25], but was left as a future possibility.

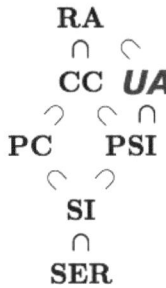

Fig. 1. ROLA's *update atomic* (UA) consistency model added to the hierarchy of consistency models of Cerone et al. [25]

Due to space limitations I refer to [25] for further details on the consistency models in Figure 1, and to [65] for a more detailed discussion of other related consistency models and properties. For my design exploration purposes here, the question I would like to focus on is: What database system designs ensuring either *parallel snapshot isolation* (PSI) (the node right below UA) or something slightly weaker than PSI existed prior to ROLA? The answer is that two such system designs existed, namely, the Walter protocol [108] implementing PSI, and the Jessy protocol [6], implementing the *non-monotonic snapshot isolation* (NMSI) consistency model, which is weaker than PSI but satisfies *causal consistency* (CC). Note that, unlike Walter and Jessy, ROLA does not satisfy CC, but, as explained in [65], CC is not essential for social network applications such as friendship networks. The main question then is: What are the gains in performance obtained by focusing on the UA sweetspot? As I pointed out above, this question would be hard to settle by comparing system implementations of Walter, Jessy and ROLA. Furthermore, it would *require* implementing ROLA before any such comparison became possible, thus defeating the design exploration purpose. However, based on Maude formal executable specifications of Walter, Jessy and ROLA (with the replication features of Walter and Jessy disabled to obtain a fair comparison), and enriching these three specifications with a common probability distribution on the time required for inter-node communication to obtain three associated probabilistic rewrite theories [63], it has been possible to answer this question by statistical model checking analysis using the **PVeStA** tool [3]. The answer is that, as shown in Figure 2 from [65], ROLA clearly outperforms both Walter and Jessy in all performance requirements for all read/write transaction rates.

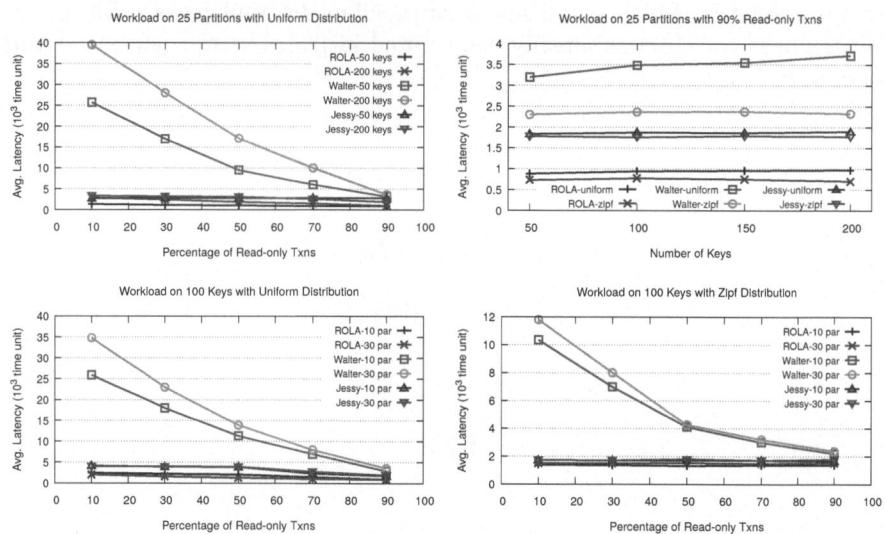

Fig. 2. Average latency comparison across varying workload conditions.

For the model checking verification of ROLA's consistency requirements I refer the reader to §6 of [65]. This still leaves open the matter of ROLA's implementation, and raises the question of how consistent would the ROLA performance predictions be with experimental evaluations of ROLA. These two issues were addressed in the subsequent paper [68]. In fact, [68] answered a much broader question, namely:

> *Is it possible to automatically generate a correct-by-construction implementation of a distributed system design priorly captured in Maude?*

This question was answered by means of a *formal pattern*, namely, the *D-transformation* mentioned in §3.2. The point is that Maude is not only a language to model and verify properties of concurrent systems using the Maude interpreter and its formal tools. Thanks to its support for external objects, including TCP/IP sockets, it is also a language to program and implement open distributed systems [33]. What the *D*-transformation formal pattern does is to transform an object-oriented system design in Maude into a distributed implementation of it, also in Maude, that is *stuttering bisimilar* to the design. Using the *D*-transformation it was then possible to automatically transform the ROLA Maude design into a ROLA implementation and to experimentally evaluate ROLA. As explained in [68], ROLA's distributed implementation was experimentally evaluated in two different scenarios, named ROLA_A and ROLA_B, and the performance predictions for each scenario obtained by statistical model checking of the ROLA design were compared with the corresponding experimental evaluations of its implementation. These results are summarized in Figure 3 from [68] and show a substantial agreement between the ROLA performance predictions and the corresponding experimental evaluations. I refer to [68] for further details.

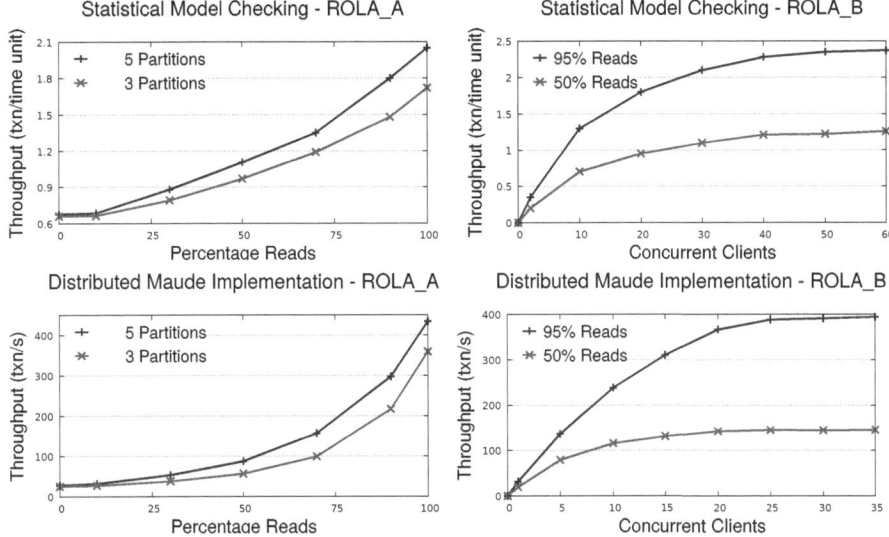

Fig. 3. ROLA: Comparison between statistical model checking (top) and distributed Maude implementation (bottom). Experiments ROLA_A (left) and ROLA_B (right) measure throughput for different number of partitions and different ratios of reads when varying ratios of reads and concurrent clients, respectively.

6   From Modeling Languages to Formal Designs

Software modeling languages are widely used for software design. In this section I discuss the relationships between the model-based approach to design and the approach based on formal executable specification of designs that I have presented here. I would like to begin by asking the question:

> *How can formal executable specifications support and complement model-based system design?*

I, together with other collaborators, as well as many other researchers, have spent substantial efforts over the years trying to provide practical, useful answers to this question. On the one hand, model-based approaches tend to be fairly intuitive and are widely adopted in industry, but it seems fair to say that to the degree to which they lack a formal executable *semantics*, they remain relatively weak in their *predictive power*. On the other hand, the design approach based on formal excutable specifications that I have presented has remarkable capabilities for formally verifying designs and predicting their behaviors. Also, for distributed systems, in the case of Maude, both approaches share a common *object-based* nature. Why not combining both approaches? A practical way to facilitate this combination is to develop *formal plugins* for existing software modeling languages that: (i) provide a *formal semantics* for the models in such a language, and (ii) make simulation and formal analysis of models possible by mapping each model to its formal semantics.

In my view, the simplest and conceptually most satisfactory way of understanding these plugins is as *mappings between modeling languages*. To be concrete for illustration purposes, let me choose Maude. It is perfectly consistent with everything I have said in this paper to call Maude a software *formal modeling language*. Let $\mathcal{M}$ be another software modeling language. Then, a Maude-plugin for $\mathcal{M}$ is simply (the implemention of) a *formal semantics map*:

$$[\![\_]\!] : \mathcal{M} \longrightarrow Maude$$

that assigns to each model $M \in \mathcal{M}$ a corresponding Maude executable specification $[\![M]\!] \in Maude$, that is, a rewrite theory $[\![M]\!]$, which is a formal executable specification of the design formerly captured as M in the modeling language $\mathcal{M}$.

In Maude, mappings of this kind have been defined for a wide range of modeling languages by many researchers including, e.g., [116,88,87,45,53,54,117,5,29,85,84,40,86,20,19,21,22,18,96]. This is just a sample: it is impossible for me to do justice to such a large body of work here. But I can give a flavor for the usefulness of formal plugins by focusing on two important modeling languages for real-time and embedded systems, namely, Ptolemy II [41] and AADL (http://www.aadl.info/). When $\mathcal{M}$ is either Ptolemy II or AADL, the semantic mapping defining the formal plugin is more specific, namely, it has the form:

$$[\![\_]\!] : \mathcal{M} \longrightarrow RealTimeMaude$$

where Real-Time Maude [91] is the language and tool already mentioned in §5. Such a semantic mapping maps each model M in either Ptolemy II or AADL to a formal specification $[\![M]\!]$ in Real-Time Maude, i.e., to a *real-time rewrite theory*, which is a special type of rewrite theory containing a model (which can be either discrete or continuous) of time and modeling time elapse in a system. My discussion of Ptolemy II and AADL below borrows ideas and examples from [14], [13] and [82].

6.1 Ptolemy II

Ptolemy II [41] is a widely used graphical modeling and simulation language tool for real-time and embedded systems. It supports design and simulation of concurrent, real-time, embedded systems expressed in several models of computation (MoCs), such as state machines, data flow, and discrete-event models, that govern the interaction between concurrent components. A user can visually design and simulate hierarchical models, which may combine different MoCs. Furthermore, Ptolemy II has code generation capabilities to translate models into other modeling or programming languages such as C or Java. Discrete-Event (DE) models are among the most central in Ptolemy II. Their semantics is defined by the *tagged signal model* [56]. The work by Bae et al. in [11,14] endows DE models in Ptolemy II with formal analysis capabilities by: (i) defining a semantics for them as real-time rewrite theories; (ii) automating such a formal semantics as a model transformation using Ptolemy II's code generation features; (iii) providing a Real-Time Maude plugin, so that Ptolemy II users can use an extended GUI to define temporal logic properties of their models in an intutitive syntax and can invoke Real-Time Maude from the GUI to model check their models. Let us see an example.

A Ptolemy Example. Figure 4 shows a Ptolemy II model from [14] of a fault-tolerant traffic light system at a pedestrian crossing, consisting of one car

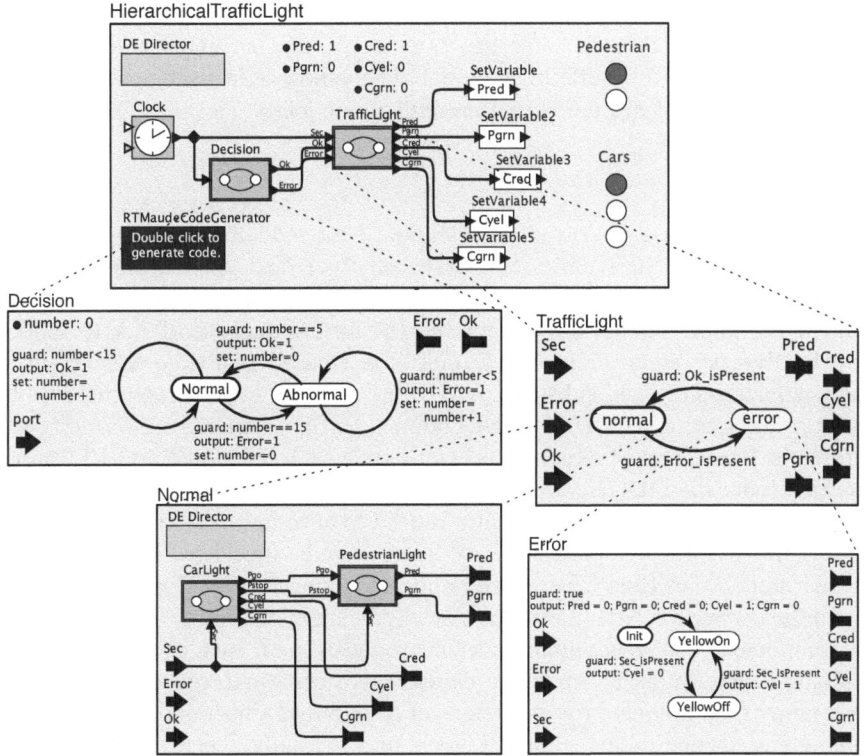

Fig. 4. A hierarchical fault-tolerant traffic light system in Ptolemy II.

light and one pedestrian light. Each light is represented by a set of *set variable* actors (`Pred` and `Pgrn` represent the pedestrian light, and `Cred`, `Cyel`, and

Cgrn represent the car light). A light is *on* iff the corresponding variable has the value 1. The Finite State Machine (FSM) actor Decision "generates" failures and repairs by alternating between staying in location Normal for 15 time units and staying in location for Abnormal for 5 time units, and by sending events to the TrafficLight through its Error and Ok ports accordingly. During normal operations, the lights are controlled by the FSM actors CarLight and PedestrianLight (their FSM's are not shown in the figure) that send values to set the variables; in addition, CarLight sends signals to the PedestrianLight actor through its Pgo and Pstop output ports.

For M this hierarchical Ptolemy II model, the semantic mapping $M \mapsto [\![M]\!]$ realized as a Real-Time Maude plugin associates to M a Real-Time Maude specification that can then be formally analyzed by model checking. I refer to [14] for further details about the real-time rewrite theory $[\![M]\!]$ for this example and the formal verification of its properties.

Real-Time Maude analysis (including automatically generating Real-Time Mude models from Ptolemy II models) of such Ptolemy II DE models has been integrated into Ptolemy II, and has been used, e.g., to uncover a previously undetected flaw in the raffic light model: The yellow light may not be blinking when the taffic light system is in Abnormal mode [60].

6.2   AADL

AADL (http://www.aadl.info/) is a standard for modeling embedded systems that is widely used in avionics and other safety-critical applications. However, AADL lacks a formal semantics, which severely limits both unambiguous communication among model developers and the formal analysis of AADL models. In [94] Ölveczky et al. defined a formal object-based real-time concurrent semantics for a behavioral subset of AADL in rewriting logic, which includes the essential aspects of AADL's behavior annex. Such a semantics is directly executable in Real-Time Maude and provides an AADL simulator and LTL model checking tool called *AADL2Maude. AADL2Maude* is integrated with OSATE, so that OSATE's code generation facility is used to automatically transform AADL models into their corresponding Real-Time Maude specifications. Such transformed models can then be executed and model checked by Real-Time Maude. One difficulty with AADL models is that, by being made up of various hierarchical components that communicate asynchronously with each other, their model checking formal analysis can easily experience a combinatorial explosion. However, many such models express designs of distributed embedded systems which, while being asynchronous, should behave in a virtually synchronous way. This suggests the possibility of using the PALS *formal pattern* [80] already mentioned in §3.2, which reduces distributed real-time systems with virtual synchrony to synchronous ones, to pass from simple synchronous systems, which have much smaller state spaces and are much easier to model check, to semantically equivalent asynchronous systems, which often cannot be directly model checked but can be verified indirectly through their synchronous counterparts. This has led to the design of the Synchronous AADL sublanguage in [13], where the user can specify synchronous AADL models by using a sublanguage of AADL with some special keywords. A synchronous rewriting semantics for such models has also been defined in [13]. Using OSATE's code generation facility, synchronous AADL models can be transformed into their corresponding Real-Time Maude specifications in the *SynchAADL2Maude* tool, which is provided as a plugin to OSATE. Likewise, the user can define temporal logic properties of synchronous AADL models based on their features, without requiring knowledge of the underlying formalism, and can model check such models in Real-Time Maude. More recently, Bae and others have extended Synchronous AADL, including the integration into OSATE, to multirate systems [16], hybrid systems [59,57], and multirate hybrid systems [12,58]. In the hybrid systems cases, the semantics is formalized using rewriting modulo SMT, and the main forms of analysis supported are randomized simulation, (bounded) symbolic reachability analysis, and their combination. Somewhat surprisingly, the performance of such Maude-with-SMT reachability analysis in many cases outperforms dedicated hybrid automata reachability tools such as HyComp, SpaceEx, Flow*, and dReach [59]. The effectiveness of HybridSynchAADL and MR-HybridSynchAADL has been illustrated on systems of collaborating drones.

A Synchronous AADL Example (from [13]). I sketch below a model of an avionics system based on a specification by Steve Miller and Darren Cofer at Rockwell-Collins [83]. A full description of this model is given in [13]; here I just give an impressionistic description of it and refer to [13] for additional details. The details, as such, are not the point of the example: the key point is to illustrate the idea that a synchronous AADL model can be viewed as a synchronous composition of state machines (one such machine per AADL component), which are formalized in the Real-Time Maude semantics as separate objects that change their state synchronously.

In *integrated modular avionics* (IMA), a cabinet is a chassis with a power supply, internal bus, and general purpose computing, I/O, and memory cards. Aircraft applications are implemented using the resources in the cabinets. There are always two or more physically separated cabinets on the aircraft so that physical damage does not take out the computer system. The *active standby* system considers the case of two cabinets and focuses on the logic for deciding which side is *active*. Each side can fail, and a failed side can recover after failure. In case one side fails, the non-failed side should be the active side. In addition, the pilot can toggle the active status of the sides. The full functionality of each side depends on the two sides' perception of the availability of other system components. An AADL-like graphical description of the system is shown in Figure 5, and the following is a fragment of its top-level textual representation, which declares the architecture of the system, with the three subcomponents `sideOne`, `sideTwo`, and `env`, and with immediate data connections (denoted by the arrow '`->`') from the environment to the two sides, and with delayed data connections ('`->>`') between the two sides. Each subcomponent contains a thread specification (not shown) in AADL's behavior annex.

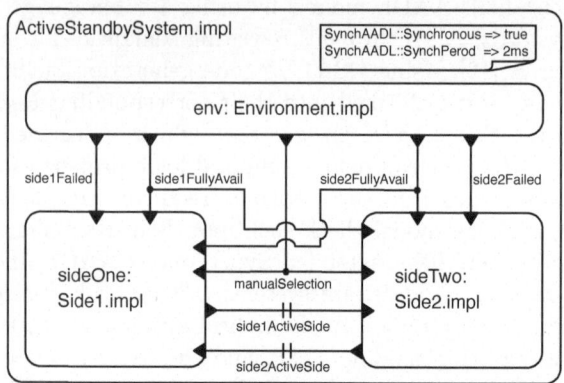

Fig. 5. The architecture of the active standby system.

```
system implementation ActiveStandbySystem.impl
  properties
  SynchAADL::Synchronous => true;    SynchAADL::SynchPeriod  => 2 ms;
  subcomponents
    sideOne: system Side1.impl; sideTwo: system Side2.impl;
    env: system Environment.impl;
  connections
    data port sideOne.side1ActiveSide ->> sideTwo.side1ActiveSide;
    data port sideTwo.side2ActiveSide ->> sideOne.side2ActiveSide;
    data port env.side1FullyAvail -> sideOne.side1FullyAvail;
    data port env.side1FullyAvail -> sideTwo.side1FullyAvail;
    ...
end ActiveStandbySystem.impl;
```

Again, as for Ptolemy II, the key point for AADL is that, for M a synchronous AADL model, the semantic mapping $M \mapsto [\![M]\!]$ realized as an AADL plugin associates to M a Real-Time Maude specification that can then be formally analyzed by model checking. For the details of how this is done for the above active standby example I refer the reader to [13]; and for examples in the further extended plugins of Synchronous AADL to [16,59,57,12,58].

7   Conclusions

I have argued that capturing system designs in executable formal specifications *ab origine* is one of the best and most cost-effective ways of developing system designs of high quality and to verify their qualitative and quantitative requirements. I am not alone in holding this position. My proposed ideas are *logic-independent*, and various researchers have been using different logics for this purpose, not only in academia, but also in industry. For example, researchers at Amazon web services have reported remarkable improvements in their design and verification processes by adopting a formal design approach similar to mine based on Lamport's TLA+ [89].

I have also argued that the choice of the computational logic on which to capture system designs is a non-trivial matter deserving careful decisions; and I have given six requirements that, in my own experience, make a logic enjoying them better suited for the task. I have also addressed the issue of design *modularity and reusability* and have proposed that *formal patterns* can greatly increase modularity and reusability and amortize design and verification efforts.

I have then reported on my own experience in formal system design using rewriting logic and Maude, illustrating that experience with concrete examples. I have also explained the formal verification capabilities for both qualitative and quantitative properties available in Maude and in its formal tool environment.

Finally, I have summarized my own experience and that of many other researchers about the benefits of combining formal-executable-specification-based design and model-based design in a synergistic way by means of *formal plug-ins*, illustrating those benefits by concrete examples in the area of real-time and embedded systems.

The future looks bright, but there are no easy victories. I think that certain high-payoff areas may both greatly benefit from formal-executable-specification-based design and can widely spread those benefits. They include:

- *Standards bodies*, since capturing system standards in formal executable specifications can greatly increase system quality and trustworthiness. The example I mentioned about DNS and its formal specification in [61] dramatically underscores this prediction.
- *Programming languages*, an area I illustrated with the example of the C formal executable semantics in K [43]. Many advances have taken place in the rewiriting logic semantics research project [70,82], and mature technologies based on these advances have been developed in companies such as RV Inc. that make this a ripe area.
- *Formal plugins for software modeling languages.* As I have argued in §6, the synergy between the formal-executable-specification-based and the model-based approaches to system design can yield remarkable benefits. But this requires hard work on well-engineered new plugins and on case studies to facilitate the adoption of this synergistic approach in practice.
- *Generation of efficient correct-by-construction implementations from formal executable designs.* Various research teams are making important advances to eliminate the *formal gap* between verified designs and implementations.

Acknowledgments. I thank the ETAPS organizers for giving me the opportunity of presenting these ideas at ETAPS 2025 in Hamilton, Ontario. I am grateful to Francisco Durán, Santiago Escobar, Si Liu, Narciso Martí-Oliet, Peter Ölveczky and Carolyn Talcott for their very helpful comments that have allowed me to improve the paper.

Disclosure of Interests. The author has no competing interests to declare that are relevant to the content of this article.

References

1. Agha, G., Meseguer, J., Sen, K.: PMaude: Rewrite-based specification language for probabilistic object systems. Electr. Notes Theor. Comput. Sci. **153**(2), 213–239 (2006)
2. Alpuente, M., Cuenca-Ortega, A., Escobar, S., Meseguer, J.: A partial evaluation framework for order-sorted equational programs modulo axioms. J. Log. Algebraic Methods Program. **110** (2020)
3. AlTurki, M., Meseguer, J.: PVeStA: A parallel statistical model-checking and quantitative analysis tool (2011), in Proc. CALCO 2011, Springer LNCS 6859, 386–392
4. AlTurki, M., Meseguer, J., Gunter, C.: Probabilistic modeling and analysis of DoS protection for the ASV protocol. Electr. Notes Theor. Comput. Sci. **234**, 3–18 (2009)
5. Aoumeur, N., Saake, G.: Integrating and rapid-prototyping UML structural and behavioural diagrams using rewriting logic. In: Pidduck, A.B., Mylopoulos, J., Woo, C.C., Özsu, M.T. (eds.) Advanced Information Systems Engineering, 14th International Conference, CAiSE 2002, Toronto, Canada, May 27-31, 2002, Proceedings. Lecture Notes in Computer Science, vol. 2348, pp. 296–310. Springer (2002), http://dx.doi.org/10.1007/3-540-47961-9
6. Ardekani, M.S., Sutra, P., Shapiro, M.: Non-monotonic snapshot isolation: Scalable and strong consistency for geo-replicated transactional systems. In: IEEE 32nd Symposium on Reliable Distributed Systems, SRDS 2013, Braga, Portugal, 1-3 October 2013. pp. 163–172. IEEE Computer Society (2013). https://doi.org/10.1109/SRDS.2013.25, https://doi.org/10.1109/SRDS.2013.25
7. Bae, K., Escobar, S., Meseguer, J.: Abstract Logical Model Checking of Infinite-State Systems Using Narrowing. In: Rewriting Techniques and Applications (RTA'13). LIPIcs, vol. 21, pp. 81–96. Schloss Dagstuhl–Leibniz-Zentrum fuer Informatik (2013)
8. Bae, K., Krisiloff, J., Meseguer, J., Ölveczky, P.C.: Designing and verifying distributed cyber-physical systems using multirate PALS: an airplane turning control system case study. Sci. Comput. Program. **103**, 13–50 (2015)
9. Bae, K., Meseguer, J.: Model checking linear temporal logic of rewriting formulas under localized fairness. Sci. Comput. Program. **99**, 193–234 (2015)
10. Bae, K., Meseguer, J., Ölveczky, P.C.: Formal patterns for multirate distributed real-time systems. Sci. Comput. Program. **91**, 3–44 (2014)
11. Bae, K., Ölveczky, P.C.: Extending the Real-Time Maude semantics of Ptolemy to hierarchical DE models. In: Ölveczky [92], pp. 46–66, http://dx.doi.org/10.4204/EPTCS.36.3
12. Bae, K., Ölveczky, P.C.: Formal model engineering of distributed CPSs using AADL: From behavioral AADL models to Multirate Hybrid Synchronous AADL. In: FACS'23. Lecture Notes in Computer Science, vol. 14485, pp. 127–152. Springer (2023)
13. Bae, K., Ölveczky, P.C., Al-Nayeem, A., Meseguer, J.: Synchronous AADL and its formal analysis in Real-Time Maude. In: Qin, S., Qiu, Z. (eds.) ICFEM. Lecture Notes in Computer Science, vol. 6991, pp. 651–667. Springer (2011)
14. Bae, K., Ölveczky, P.C., Feng, T.H., Lee, E.A., Tripakis, S.: Verifying hierarchical Ptolemy II discrete-event models using Real-Time Maude. Sci. Comput. Program. **77**(12), 1235–1271 (2012)

15. Bae, K., Ölveczky, P.C., Meseguer, J.: Definition, semantics, and analysis of multirate synchronous AADL. In: FM. Lecture Notes in Computer Science, vol. 8442, pp. 94–109. Springer (2014)

16. Bae, K., Ölveczky, P.C., Meseguer, J.: Definition, semantics, and analysis of Multirate Synchronous AADL. In: FM'14. Lecture Notes in Computer Science, vol. 8442, pp. 94–109. Springer (2014)

17. Bobba, R., Grov, J., Gupta, I., Liu, S., Meseguer, J., Ölveczky, P.C., Skeirik, S.: Survivability: Design, formal modeling, and validation of cloud storage systems using Maude. In: Campbell, R.H., Kamhoua, C.A., Kwiat, K.A. (eds.) Assured Cloud Computing, chap. 2, pp. 10–48. Wiley-IEEE Computer Society Press (2018)

18. Boronat, A., Meseguer, J.: An algebraic semantics for MOF. Formal Asp. Comput. **22**(3-4), 269–296 (2010)

19. Boronat, A.: MOMENT: A Formal Framework for MOdel ManageMENT. Ph.D. thesis, Universitat Politècnica de València, Spain (2007)

20. Boronat, A., Carsí, J.A., Ramos, I.: Automatic reengineering in MDA using rewriting logic as transformation engine. In: Gold, N., Systä, T. (eds.) Proceedings of the 9th European Conference on Software Maintenance and Reengineering, CSMR 2005, Manchester, UK, March 21-23, 2005, Proceedings. pp. 228–231. IEEE Computer Society (2005)

21. Boronat, A., Heckel, R., Meseguer, J.: Rewriting logic semantics and verification of model transformations. In: Chechik, M., Wirsing, M. (eds.) Fundamental Approaches to Software Engineering, 12th International Conference, FASE 2009, Held as Part of the Joint European Conferences on Theory and Practice of Software, ETAPS 2009, York, UK, March 22-29, 2009. Proceedings. Lecture Notes in Computer Science, vol. 5503, pp. 18–33. Springer (2009), `http://dx.doi.org/10.1007/978-3-642-00593-0`

22. Boronat, A., Meseguer, J.: MOMENT2: EMF model transformations in Maude. In: Vallecillo, A., Sagardui, G. (eds.) Actas de las XIV Jornadas de Ingeniería del Software y Bases de Datos, JISBD 2009, San Sebastián, España, Septiembre 8-11, 2009. pp. 178–179 (2009)

23. Brewer, E.A.: Towards robust distributed systems (abstract). In: Proceedings of the Nineteenth Annual ACM Symposium on Principles of Distributed Computing. p. 7. ACM (2000)

24. Bruni, R., Meseguer, J.: Semantic foundations for generalized rewrite theories. Theor. Comput. Sci. **360**(1-3), 386–414 (2006)

25. Cerone, A., Bernardi, G., Gotsman, A.: A framework for transactional consistency models with atomic visibility. In: Proc. 26th International Conference on Concurrency Theory, CONCUR 2015. LIPIcs, vol. 42, pp. 58–71. Schloss Dagstuhl - Leibniz-Zentrum fuer Informatik (2015)

26. Chadha, R., Gunter, C.A., Meseguer, J., Shankesi, R., Viswanathan, M.: Modular preservation of safety properties by cookie-based DoS-protection wrappers. In: Proc. FMOODS 2008. LNCS, vol. 5051, pp. 39–58. Springer (2008)

27. Chen, S., Meseguer, J., Sasse, R., Wang, H.J., Wang, Y.M.: A systematic approach to uncover security flaws in GUI logic. In: IEEE Symposium on Security and Privacy. pp. 71–85. IEEE (2007)

28. Clavel, M., Durán, F., Eker, S., Meseguer, J., Lincoln, P., Martí-Oliet, N., Talcott, C.: All About Maude – A High-Performance Logical Framework. Springer LNCS Vol. 4350 (2007)

29. Clavel, M., Egea, M.: ITP/OCL: A rewriting-based validation tool for UML+OCL static class diagrams. In: Johnson, M., Vene, V. (eds.) Algebraic Methodology

and Software Technology, 11th International Conference, AMAST 2006, Kures-saare, Estonia, July 5-8, 2006, Proceedings. Lecture Notes in Computer Science, vol. 4019, pp. 368–373. Springer (2006), http://dx.doi.org/10.1007/11784180

30. Clavel, M., Meseguer, J., Palomino, M.: Reflection in membership equational logic, many-sorted equational logic, Horn logic with equality, and rewriting logic. In: Gadducci, F., Montanari, U. (eds.) Proc. 4th. Intl. Workshop on Rewriting Logic and its Applications. vol. 71. ENTCS, Elsevier (2002)

31. Clavel, M., Palomino, M., Riesco, A.: Introducing the ITP tool: a tutorial. Theoretical Computer Science **12**, 1618–1650 (2006)

32. Dehnert, C., Junges, S., Katoen, J., Volk, M.: A Storm is coming: A modern probabilistic model checker. In: Majumdar, R., Kuncak, V. (eds.) Computer Aided Verification - 29th International Conference, CAV 2017, Heidelberg, Germany, July 24-28, 2017, Proceedings, Part II. Lecture Notes in Computer Science, vol. 10427, pp. 592–600. Springer (2017)

33. Durán, F., Eker, S., Escobar, S., Martí-Oliet, N., Meseguer, J., Rubio, R., Talcott, C.L.: Programming open distributed systems in Maude. In: Bruni, A., Momigliano, A., Pradella, M., Rossi, M., Cheney, J. (eds.) Proceedings of the 26th International Symposium on Principles and Practice of Declarative Programming, PPDP 2024, Milano, Italy, September 9-11, 2024. pp. 7:1–7:12. ACM (2024), https://doi.org/10.1145/3678232.3678237

34. Durán, F., Lucas, S., Meseguer, J.: MTT: The Maude Termination Tool (system description). In: IJCAR 2008. Lecture Notes in Computer Science, vol. 5195, pp. 313–319. Springer (2008)

35. Durán, F., Lucas, S., Meseguer, J.: Termination modulo combinations of equational theories. In: Frontiers of Combining Systems, 7th International Symposium, FroCoS 2009, Trento, Italy, September 16-18, 2009. Proceedings. Lecture Notes in Computer Science, vol. 5749, pp. 246–262. Springer (2009)

36. Durán, F., Meseguer, J.: Maude's module algebra. Sci. Comput. Program. **66**(2), 125–153 (2007)

37. Durán, F., Meseguer, J.: On the Church-Rosser and coherence properties of conditional order-sorted rewrite theories. J. Algebraic and Logic Programming **81**, 816–850 (2012)

38. Durán, F.J., Escobar, S., Meseguer, J., Sapiña, J.: Nuitp: An inductive theorem prover for equational program verification. In: Bruni, A., Momigliano, A., Pradella, M., Rossi, M., Cheney, J. (eds.) Proceedings of the 26th International Symposium on Principles and Practice of Declarative Programming, PPDP 2024, Milano, Italy, September 9-11, 2024. pp. 6:1–6:11. ACM (2024), https://doi.org/10.1145/3678232.3678236

39. Eckhardt, J., Mühlbauer, T., AlTurki, M., Meseguer, J., Wirsing, M.: Stable availability under denial of service attacks through formal patterns. In: de Lara, Zisman (eds.) FASE. LNCS, vol. 7212, pp. 78–93. Springer (2012)

40. Egea, M., Rusu, V.: Formal executable semantics for conformance in the MDE framework. Innovations in Systems and Software Engineering **6**(1-2), 73–81 (2009)

41. Eker, J., Janneck, J.W., Lee, E.A., Liu, J., Liu, X., Ludvig, J., Neuendorffer, S., Sachs, S., Xiong, Y.: Taming heterogeneity—the Ptolemy approach. Proceedings of the IEEE **91**(2), 127–144 (2003)

42. Eker, S., Knapp, M., Laderoute, K., Lincoln, P., Meseguer, J., Sonmez, K.: Pathway logic: Symbolic analysis of biological signaling. In: Proceedings of the Pacific Symposium on Biocomputing. pp. 400–412 (January 2002)

43. Ellison, C., Rosu, G.: An executable formal semantics of C with applications. In: Field, J., Hicks, M. (eds.) POPL. pp. 533–544. ACM (2012)

44. Escobar, S., Meadows, C., Meseguer, J.: Maude-NPA: cryptographic protocol analysis modulo equational properties. In: Foundations of Security Analysis and Design V, FOSAD 2007/2008/2009 Tutorial Lectures, LNCS, vol. 5705, pp. 1–50. Springer (2009)

45. Fernández Alemán, J.L., Toval Álvarez, J.A.: Can intuition become rigorous? Foundations for UML model verification tools. In: Titsworth, F.M. (ed.) Proceedings of the 11th International Symposium on Software Reliability Engineering, ISSRE 2000, San Jose, CA, USA, October 8-11, 2000. pp. 344–355. IEEE Computer Society (2000), http://dx.doi.org/10.1109/ISSRE.2000.885885

46. Galán, D., García, V., Escobar, S., Meadows, C.A., Meseguer, J.: Protocol dialects as formal patterns. In: Tsudik, G., Conti, M., Liang, K., Smaragdakis, G. (eds.) Computer Security - ESORICS 2023 - 28th European Symposium on Research in Computer Security, The Hague, The Netherlands, September 25-29, 2023, Proceedings, Part II. Lecture Notes in Computer Science, vol. 14345, pp. 42–61. Springer (2023)

47. Garavel, H., ter Beek, M.H., van de Pol, J.: The 2020 expert survey on formal methods. In: ter Beek, M.H., Nickovic, D. (eds.) Formal Methods for Industrial Critical Systems - 25th International Conference, FMICS 2020, Vienna, Austria, September 2-3, 2020, Proceedings. Lecture Notes in Computer Science, vol. 12327, pp. 3–69. Springer (2020)

48. Goguen, J., Burstall, R.: Institutions: Abstract model theory for specification and programming. Journal of the ACM **39**(1), 95–146 (1992)

49. Grov, J., Ölveczky, P.C.: Increasing consistency in multi-site data stores: Megastore-CGC and its formal analysis. In: Giannakopoulou, D., Salaün, G. (eds.) Software Engineering and Formal Methods - 12th International Conference, SEFM 2014, Grenoble, France, September 1-5, 2014. Proceedings. Lecture Notes in Computer Science, vol. 8702, pp. 159–174. Springer (2014)

50. Gutiérrez, R., Meseguer, J., Rocha, C.: Order-sorted equality enrichments modulo axioms. Sci. Comput. Program. **99**, 235–261 (2015)

51. Hendrix, J., Meseguer, J., Ohsaki, H.: A sufficient completeness checker for linear order-sorted specifications modulo axioms. In: Automated Reasoning, Third International Joint Conference, IJCAR 2006. pp. 151–155 (2006)

52. Kant, G., Laarman, A., Meijer, J., van de Pol, J., Blom, S., van Dijk, T.: LTSmin: High-performance language-independent model checking. In: Baier, C., Tinelli, C. (eds.) Tools and Algorithms for the Construction and Analysis of Systems - 21st International Conference, TACAS 2015, Held as Part of the European Joint Conferences on Theory and Practice of Software, ETAPS 2015, London, UK, April 11-18, 2015. Proceedings. Lecture Notes in Computer Science, vol. 9035, pp. 692–707. Springer (2015)

53. Knapp, A.: Generating rewrite theories from UML collaborations. In: Futatsugi, K., Nakagawa, A.T., Tamai, T. (eds.) Cafe: An Industrial-Strength Algebraic Formal Method, pp. 97–120. Elsevier (2000)

54. Knapp, A.: A Formal Approach to Object-Oriented Software Engineering. Shaker Verlag, Aachen, Germany (2001), phD thesis, Institut für Informatik, Universität München, 2000.

55. Kwiatkowska, M.Z., Norman, G., Parker, D.: PRISM 4.0: Verification of probabilistic real-time systems. In: Gopalakrishnan, G., Qadeer, S. (eds.) Computer Aided Verification - 23rd International Conference, CAV 2011, Snowbird, UT, USA, July 14-20, 2011. Proceedings. Lecture Notes in Computer Science, vol. 6806, pp. 585–591. Springer (2011)

56. Lee, E.A.: Modeling concurrent real-time processes using discrete events. Ann. Software Eng. **7**, 25–45 (1999)
57. Lee, J., Bae, K., Ölveczky, P.C.: An extension of HybridSynchAADL and its application to collaborating autonomous UAVs. In: ISoLA'22. Lecture Notes in Computer Science, vol. 13703, pp. 47–64. Springer (2022)
58. Lee, J., Bae, K., Ölveczky, P.C.: Rigorous model engineering of hierarchical multirate CPSs in MR-HybridSynchAADL. In: ISoLA'24. Lecture Notes in Computer Science, vol. 15220, pp. 243–262. Springer (2024)
59. Lee, J., Kim, S., Bae, K., Ölveczky, P.C.: HybridSynchAADL: Modeling and formal analysis of virtually synchronous CPSs in AADL. In: CAV'21. Lecture Notes in Computer Science, vol. 12759, pp. 491–504. Springer (2021)
60. Lepri, D., Ábrahám, E., Ölveczky, P.C.: Sound and complete timed CTL model checking of timed Kripke structures and real-time rewrite theories. Science of Computer Programming **99**, 128–192 (2015)
61. Liu, S., Duan, H., Heimes, L., Bearzi, M., Vieli, J., Basin, D.A., Perrig, A.: A formal framework for end-to-end DNS resolution. In: Schulzrinne, H., Misra, V., Kohler, E., Maltz, D.A. (eds.) Proceedings of the ACM SIGCOMM 2023 Conference, ACM SIGCOMM 2023, New York, NY, USA, 10-14 September 2023. pp. 932–949. ACM (2023). https://doi.org/10.1145/3603269.3604870, https://doi.org/10.1145/3603269.3604870
62. Liu, S., Ganhotra, J., Rahman, M.R., Nguyen, S., Gupta, I., Meseguer, J.: Quantitative analysis of consistency in NoSQL key-value stores. Leibniz Trans. Embed. Syst. **4**(1), 03:1–03:26 (2017)
63. Liu, S., Meseguer, J., Ölveczky, P.C., Zhang, M., Basin, D.A.: Bridging the semantic gap between qualitative and quantitative models of distributed systems. Proc. ACM Program. Lang. **6**(OOPSLA2), 315–344 (2022)
64. Liu, S., Ölveczky, P.C., Ganhotra, J., Gupta, I., Meseguer, J.: Exploring design alternatives for RAMP transactions through statistical model checking. In: Proc. Formal Methods and Software Engineering - 19th International Conference on Formal Engineering Methods, ICFEM 2017. Lecture Notes in Computer Science, vol. 10610, pp. 298–314. Springer (2017)
65. Liu, S., Ölveczky, P.C., Wang, Q., Gupta, I., Meseguer, J.: Read atomic transactions with prevention of lost updates: ROLA and its formal analysis. Formal Aspects Comput. **31**(5), 503–540 (2019)
66. Liu, S., Ölveczky, P.C., Zhang, M., Wang, Q., Meseguer, J.: Automatic analysis of consistency properties of distributed transaction systems in Maude. In: Proc. TACAS 2019, Part II. Lecture Notes in Computer Science, vol. 11428, pp. 40–57. Springer (2019)
67. Liu, S., Rahman, M.R., Skeirik, S., Gupta, I., Meseguer, J.: Formal modeling and analysis of Cassandra in Maude. In: Formal Methods and Software Engineering – 16th International Conference on Formal Engineering Methods, ICFEM 2014, Luxembourg, Luxembourg, November 3-5, 2014. Proceedings. Lecture Notes in Computer Science, vol. 8829, pp. 332–347. Springer (2014)
68. Liu, S., Sandur, A., Meseguer, J., Ölveczky, P.C., Wang, Q.: Generating correct-by-construction distributed implementations from formal Maude designs. In: Proc. NASA Formal Methods: 12th International Symposium, NFM 2020,. Lecture Notes in Computer Science, vol. 12229, pp. 22–40. Springer (2020)
69. Martí-Oliet, N., Meseguer, J.: Rewriting logic as a logical and semantic framework. In: Gabbay, D., Guenthner, F. (eds.) Handbook of Philosophical Logic, 2nd. Edition, pp. 1–87. Kluwer Academic Publishers (2002), first published as SRI Tech. Report SRI-CSL-93-05, August 1993

70. Meseguer, J., Roşu, G.: The rewriting logic semantics project. Theoretical Computer Science **373**, 213–237 (2007)
71. Meseguer, J., Talcott, C.: Semantic models for distributed object reflection. In: Proceedings of ECOOP'02, Málaga, Spain, June 2002. pp. 1–36. Springer LNCS 2374 (2002)
72. Meseguer, J.: General logics. In: et al., H.D.E. (ed.) Logic Colloquium'87. pp. 275–329. North-Holland (1989)
73. Meseguer, J.: Conditional rewriting logic as a unified model of concurrency. Theoretical Computer Science **96**(1), 73–155 (1992)
74. Meseguer, J.: A logical theory of concurrent objects and its realization in the Maude language. In: Agha, G., Wegner, P., Yonezawa, A. (eds.) Research Directions in Concurrent Object-Oriented Programming, pp. 314–390. MIT Press (1993)
75. Meseguer, J.: Twenty years of rewriting logic. J. Algebraic and Logic Programming **81**, 721–781 (2012)
76. Meseguer, J.: Taming distributed system complexity through formal patterns. Sci. Comput. Program. **83**, 3–34 (2014)
77. Meseguer, J.: Generalized rewrite theories, coherence completion, and symbolic methods. J. Log. Algebraic Methods Program. **110** (2020)
78. Meseguer, J.: Building correct-by-construction systems with formal patterns. In: Madeira, A., Martins, M.A. (eds.) Recent Trends in Algebraic Development Techniques - 26th IFIP WG 1.3 International Workshop, WADT 2022, Aveiro, Portugal, June 28-30, 2022, Revised Selected Papers. Lecture Notes in Computer Science, vol. 13710, pp. 3–24. Springer (2022)
79. Meseguer, J.: Checking sufficient completeness by inductive theorem proving. In: Bae, K. (ed.) Rewriting Logic and Its Applications - 14th International Workshop, WRLA@ETAPS 2022, Munich, Germany, April 2-3, 2022, Revised Selected Papers. Lecture Notes in Computer Science, vol. 13252, pp. 171–190. Springer (2022)
80. Meseguer, J., Ölveczky, P.C.: Formalization and correctness of the PALS architectural pattern for real-time systems. In: 12th International Conference on Formal Engineering Methods (ICFEM 2010). vol. 6447, pp. 303–320. Springer LNCS (2010)
81. Meseguer, J., Ölveczky, P.C.: Formalization and correctness of the PALS architectural pattern for distributed real-time systems. Theor. Comput. Sci. **451**, 1–37 (2012)
82. Meseguer, J., Rosu, G.: The rewriting logic semantics project: A progress report. Inf. Comput. **231**, 38–69 (2013)
83. Miller, S., Cofer, D., Sha, L., Meseguer, J., Al-Nayeem, A.: Implementing logical synchrony in integrated modular avionics. In: Proc. 28th Digital Avionics Systems Conference. IEEE (2009)
84. Mokhati, F., Badri, M.: Generating Maude specifications from UML use case diagrams. Journal of Object Technology **8**(2), 319–136 (2009)
85. Mokhati, F., Gagnon, P., Badri, M.: Verifying UML diagrams with model checking: A rewriting logic based approach. In: Mathur, A., Wong, W.E. (eds.) Proceedings of the Seventh International Conference on Quality Software, QSIC 2007, Portland, Oregon, USA, October 11-12, 2007. pp. 356–362. IEEE Computer Society (2007)
86. Mokhati, F., Sahraoui, B., Bouzaher, S., Kimour, M.T.: A tool for specifying and validating agents' interaction protocols: From Agent UML to Maude. Journal of Object Technology **9**(3), 59–77 (2010)

87. Nakajima, S.: Using algebraic specification techniques in development of object-oriented frameworks. In: Wing, J.M., Woodcock, J., Davies, J. (eds.) FM'99 - Formal Methods, World Congress on Formal Methods in the Development of Computing Systems, Toulouse, France, September 20-24, 1999, Proceedings, Volume II. Lecture Notes in Computer Science, vol. 1709, pp. 1664–1683. Springer (1999)

88. Nakajima, S., Futatsugi, K.: An object-oriented modeling method for algebraic specifications in CafeOBJ. In: Proceedings of the 19th International Conference on Software Engineering, ICSE'97, Boston, Massachussets, May 17-23, 1997. ACM Press (1997)

89. Newcombe, C., Rath, T., Zhang, F., Munteanu, B., Brooker, M., Deardeuff, M.: How Amazon web services uses formal methods. Commun. ACM **58**(4), 66–73 (2015)

90. Olarte, C., Pimentel, E., Rocha, C.: A rewriting logic approach to specification, proof-search, and meta-proofs in sequent systems. Journal of Logical and Algebraic Methods in Programming **130**, 100827 (2023)

91. Ölveczky, P.C., Meseguer, J.: Semantics and pragmatics of Real-Time Maude. Higher-Order and Symbolic Computation **20**(1–2), 161–196 (2007)

92. Ölveczky, P.C. (ed.): Proceedings of the First International Workshop on Rewriting Techniques for Real-Time Systems, RTRTS 2010, Longyearbyen, Spitsbergen, Norway, April 6-9, 2010. Electronic Proceedings in Theoretical Computer Science, Computing Research Repository (CoRR)

93. Ölveczky, P.C. (ed.): Rewriting Logic and its Applications. 8th International Workshop, WRLA 2010, Held as a Satellite Event of ETAPS 2010, Paphos, Cyprus, March 20-21, 2010, Revised Selected Papers, Lecture Notes in Computer Science, vol. 6381. Springer (2010)

94. Ölveczky, P.C., Boronat, A., Meseguer, J.: Formal semantics and analysis of behavioral AADL models in Real-Time Maude. In: FMOODS/FORTE'10. Lecture Notes in Computer Science, vol. 6117, pp. 47–62. Springer (2010)

95. Riesco, A., Ogata, K.: An integrated tool set for verifying cafeobj specifications. Journal of Systems and Software **189**, 111302 (2022). https://doi.org/https://doi.org/10.1016/j.jss.2022.111302

96. Rivera, J.E., Durán, F., Vallecillo, A.: On the behavioral semantics of real-time domain specific visual languages. In: Ölveczky [93], pp. 174–190

97. Rubio, R., Martí-Oliet, N., Pita, I., Verdejo, A.: Strategies, model checking and branching-time properties in Maude. J. Log. Algebraic Methods Program. **123**, 100700 (2021)

98. Rubio, R., Martí-Oliet, N., Pita, I., Verdejo, A.: QMaude: Quantitative specification and verification in rewriting logic. In: Chechik, M., Katoen, J., Leucker, M. (eds.) Formal Methods - 25th International Symposium, FM 2023, Lübeck, Germany, March 6-10, 2023, Proceedings. Lecture Notes in Computer Science, vol. 14000, pp. 240–259. Springer (2023)

99. Rubio, R., Martí-Oliet, N., Pita, I., Verdejo, A.: Model checking strategy-controlled systems in rewriting logic. CoRR **abs/2401.07616** (2024)

100. Sasse, R.: Security models in rewriting logic for cryptographic protocols and browsers. Ph.D. thesis, University of Illinois at Urbana-Champaign (2012), http://hdl.handle.net/2142/34373

101. Sasse, R., King, S.T., Meseguer, J., Tang, S.: IBOS: A correct-by-construction modular browser. In: FACS 2012. Lecture Notes in Computer Science, vol. 7684, pp. 224–241. Springer (2013)

102. Schürmann, C., Stehr, M.O.: An executable formalization of the hol/nuprl connection in the metalogical framework twelf. pp. 150–166 (11 2006). https://doi.org/10.1007/11916277_11
103. Sebastio, S., Vandin, A.: MultiVeStA: statistical model checking for discrete event simulators. In: Horváth, A., Buchholz, P., Cortellessa, V., Muscariello, L., Squillante, M.S. (eds.) 7th International Conference on Performance Evaluation Methodologies and Tools, ValueTools '13, Torino, Italy, December 10-12, 2013. pp. 310–315. ICST/ACM (2013)
104. Şerbănuţă, T.F.: A Rewriting Approach to Concurrent Programming Language Design and Semantics. Ph.D. thesis, Department of Computer Science, University of Illinois at Urbana-Champaign (2010), http://hdl.handle.net/2142/18252, http://hdl.handle.net/2142/18252
105. Şerbănuţă, T.F., Roşu, G.: K-Maude: A rewriting based tool for semantics of programming languages. In: Ölveczky [93], pp. 104–122
106. Skeirik, S., Meseguer, J., Rocha, C.: Verification of the IBOS browser security properties in reachability logic. In: Proc. WRLA 2020. LNCS, vol. 12328, pp. 176–196. Springer (2020)
107. Skeirik, S.: Rewriting-based symbolic methods for distributed system verification. Ph.D. thesis, University of Illinois at Urbana-Champaign (2019), http://hdl.handle.net/2142/106224
108. Sovran, Y., Power, R., Aguilera, M.K., Li, J.: Transactional storage for geo-replicated systems. In: Wobber, T., Druschel, P. (eds.) Proceedings of the 23rd ACM Symposium on Operating Systems Principles 2011, SOSP 2011, Cascais, Portugal, October 23-26, 2011. pp. 385–400. ACM (2011). https://doi.org/10.1145/2043556.2043592, https://doi.org/10.1145/2043556.2043592
109. Stehr, M.O., Naumov, P., Meseguer, J.: The HOL/NuPRl proof translator— A practical approach to formal interoperability. In: Proc. 14th Intl. Conf. on Theorem Proving In Higher Order Logics (TPHOL'2001) Edinburgh, Scotland, September 2001. pp. 329–345. Springer LNCS 2152 (2001)
110. Sun, M., Meseguer, J.: Distributed real-time emulation of formally-defined patterns for safe medical device control. In: Ölveczky [92], pp. 158–177, http://dx.doi.org/10.4204/EPTCS.36.9
111. Sun, M., Meseguer, J.: Formal specification of button-related fault-tolerance micropatterns. In: Rewriting Logic and Its Applications - 10th International Workshop, WRLA 2014, Held as a Satellite Event of ETAPS, Grenoble, France, April 5-6, 2014, Revised Selected Papers. Lecture Notes in Computer Science, vol. 8663, pp. 263–279. Springer (2014)
112. Sun, M., Meseguer, J., Sha, L.: A formal pattern architecture for safe medical systems. In: Proc. WRLA 2010. vol. 6381, pp. 157–173. Springer LNCS (2010)
113. Tang, S.: Towards Secure Web Browsing. Ph.D. thesis, University of Illinois at Urbana-Champaign (2011), 2011-05-25, http://hdl.handle.net/2142/24307
114. Verdejo, A.: Building tools for LOTOS symbolic semantics in maude. In: Formal Techniques for Networked and Distributed Systems - FORTE 2002, 22nd IFIP WG 6.1 International Conference Houston, Texas, USA, November 11-14, 2002, Proceedings. pp. 292–307 (2002)
115. Weghorn, T., Liu, S., Sprenger, C., Perrig, A., Basin, D.: N-tube: Formally verified secure bandwidth reservation in path-aware internet architectures. In: 2022 IEEE 35th Computer Security Foundations Symposium (CSF). pp. 147–162 (2022)

116. Wirsing, M., Knapp, A.: A formal approach to object-oriented software engineering. In: Meseguer, J. (ed.) Proceedings of the First International Workshop on Rewriting Logic and its Applications, WRLA'96, Asilomar, California, September 3-6, 1996. Electronic Notes in Theoretical Computer Science, vol. 4, pp. 322–360. Elsevier (1996), http://dx.doi.org/10.1016/S1571-0661(04)00046-5

117. Wirsing, M., Knapp, A.: A formal approach to object-oriented software engineering. Theoretical Computer Science **285**(2), 519–560 (2002), http://dx.doi.org/10.1016/S0304-3975(01)00367-X

Towards Large Language Model Guided Kernel Direct Fuzzing

Xie Li[1,2], Zhaoyue Yuan[1,2], Zhenduo Zhang[4],
Youcheng Sun[3,5], and Lijun Zhang[1,2,4(✉)]

[1] Key Laboratory of System Software (Chinese Academy of Sciences) and State Key
Laboratory of Computer Science, Institute of Software, Chinese Academy of Sciences,
Beijing, China
zhanglj@ios.ac.cn
[2] University of Chinese Academy of Sciences, Beijing, China
[3] MBZUAI, Abu Dhabi, United Arab Emirates
[4] Automotive Software Innovation Center, Chongqing, China
[5] The University of Manchester, Manchester, England

Abstract. Direct kernel fuzzing is a targeted approach that focuses on specific areas of the kernel, effectively addressing the challenges of frequent updates and the inherent complexity of operating systems, which are critical infrastructure. This paper introduces SYZAGENT, a framework integrating LLMs with the state-of-the-art kernel fuzzer Syzkaller, where the LLMs are used to guide the mutation and generation of test cases in real-time. We present preliminary results demonstrating that this method is effective on around 67% cases in our benchmark during the experiment.

Keywords: Large Language Model · Fuzzing · Linux Kernel.

1 Introduction

Operating systems (OS) are crucial in modern computing infrastructures, making the correctness and reliability of an OS kernel vital. Fuzzing is a common method for identifying software vulnerabilities and has been notably applied in kernel testing with tools like Syzkaller [3], which has identified many bugs. Despite progress, the complexity of modern OSes can impede fuzzers from reaching deeper code paths. To improve fuzzing efficiency and coverage, researchers have explored ways to better discover and utilize the dependency relations between system calls and tasks [8,9]. Other works have employed reinforcement learning techniques [11] and static analysis methods [6,14] to target previously unreached code during fuzzing.

With the rapid advancement of generative AI [5], the use of large language models (LLMs) in system fuzzing is increasingly recognized [12]. The KernelGPT method [13] has been proposed to utilizing LLMs to generate Syzlang, a domain-specific language for system calls, facilitating improved seed generation and test case creation in Syzkaller [4].

A. Boronat and G. Fraser (Eds.): FASE 2025, LNCS 15693, pp.33–42, 2025.
https://doi.org/10.1007/978-3-031-90900-9_2

Instead of general kernel fuzzing like Syzkaller, this work emphasizes direct kernel fuzzing, which targets specific, often critical areas within the OS kernel to manage the challenges posed by frequent updates and rapid iterations. The Syzdirect approach [10] extends Syzkaller by leveraging the call graph and resource model to provide structured guidance for generating test cases more effectively, enabling the more effective direct kernel fuzzing.

In this work, we integrate LLMs with direct fuzzing of the OS kernel. The source code and fuzzing intermediate results are fed to the LLM dynamically to retrieve guidance for test case generation. Unlike KernelGPT, which focuses on generating Syzlang specifications, and Syzdirect, which utilizes pre-built guidance from the call graph and resource model, our approach employs real-time feedback from the LLM to adapt to changes in the kernel. We implemented our framework, SYZAGENT, to achieve this integration and provide preliminary experimental results demonstrating the effectiveness of the approach. Without loss of generality, GPT-4o [1] is used for the experiments in this paper. In addition, we share insights into the challenges and experiences encountered while integrating LLMs with kernel fuzzers.

2   Motivating Example

Consider a commit changing the function `__anon_inode_getfd` in the Linux kernel, referred to as the *target function*. Our objective is to test the newly introduced code in this commit using guidance from a LLM.

By compiling and analyzing the Linux kernel, we generate a set of *call paths*, which represent the routes from system calls to the target function in the kernel's call graph. Below are two example call paths, where `func1` → `func2` indicates that `func2` is called within the body of `func1`:

`inotify_init` → `do_inotify_init` → `anon_inode_getfd` → `__anon_inode_getfd`

`mock_drm_getfile` → `anon_inode_getfile` → `__anon_inode_getfd`

The first path illustrates a direct call to the target function from a system call (`inotify_init`), while the second involves an indirect call through other functions within two steps. We collect these paths to inform the LLM about potential triggers for the target function. Once identified, the source code from these paths, referred to as *calling code*, will be extracted and used to formulate the initial prompt, as shown in Prompt 1.1 [6].

Prompt 1.1. Initial prompt (before fuzzing)

```
[calling code]
Above is the source code that may call function [target
function], which system calls may trigger the call path
of function [target function]?
```

Upon receiving the initial prompt, the LLM identifies the following system calls that may potentially interact with the target function.

---

[6] Detailed prompts is available at https://github.com/SpencerL-Y/ChatAnalyzer/blob/main/chat_interface.py.

```
[inotify_init, inotify_init1, fsopen, fspick, perf_event_open,
timerfd_create, epoll_create, epoll_create1, eventfd, eventfd2,
signalfd, signalfd4]
```

These system calls represent possible entry points to the target function, and the reason to use the LLM for analysis is to leverage its potential to identify additional system calls, as LLM may provide more diverse outcome since it has been trained on extensive open-source project data.

Subsequently, a kernel fuzzer like Syzkaller is launched with generated test cases using system calls with increased probability to reaching the target. During the fuzzing process, whenever 500 test cases are executed, those that covering functions within 2 steps of the target function are collected, and the covered source code is recorded to create a feedback prompt, as shown in Prompt 1.2.

Prompt 1.2. Feedback prompt (during fuzzing)

```
[calling code]
Above is the source code that may call the target
function [target function], in testing procedure we found
 the following system call programs reach functions that
is close to the target function:
[test cases and covered code]
Generate a list of system calls that if the probability
of generating such system calls in test cases is
increased, the fuzzing process is more possible to reach
our target function: [target function]?
```

After receiving the feedback prompt, the LLM provides an updated list of system calls. With real test cases available, the LLM is more likely to introduce related system calls. In this example, the LLM adds two more system calls, drm_syncobj_handle_to_fd_ioctl and mmap, to the initial list. This improvement in system call generation allows the fuzzing process to cover the target function more frequently in subsequent runs.

3 Approach

The architecture of our proposed approach is depicted in Figure 1, comprising two parts: 1) the original kernel fuzzer Syzkaller, and 2) its LLM extension, SYZAGENT. Below, we introduce each part and explain their interactions.

3.1 Syzkaller

Syzkaller fuzzes the OS kernel by executing finite sequences of system calls with their arguments, where system call comes from a set of system calls S. It creates three task types in the work queue (as shown in Figure 1):

Generation Initial seed programs are generated from manually tuned templates to ensure deeper test cases.

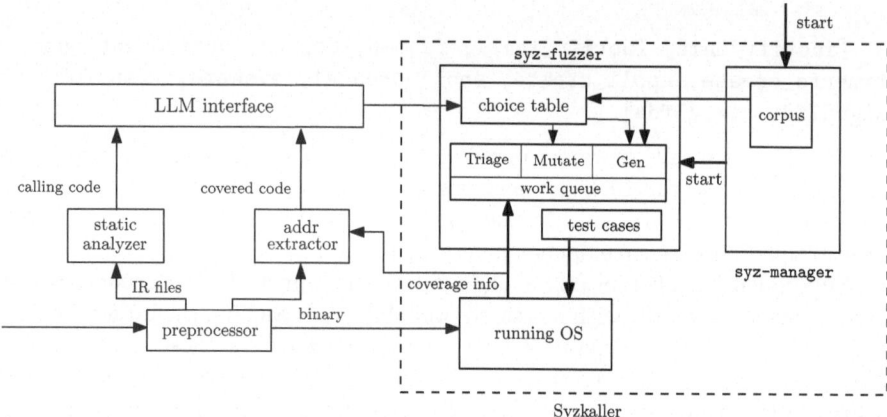

Fig. 1. SYZAGENT extends the existing Syzkaller by applying LLM in fuzzing kernels.

Mutation Mutation is applied to programs selected from a corpus (i.e., previously executed programs with new coverage). During this phase, system calls and their arguments are modified, including adding, removing, or changing system calls. This process is guided by the fuzzing state, which includes a choice table (ct): a two-dimensional array where $ct[c][c']$ represents the probability of generating system call c' after c. System call insertion is either random (5% of the time) or based on probabilities from the choice table. Arguments are generated by considering available resources at the insertion point.

Triage Test cases that triggered new coverage will be verified and minimized by removing redundant system calls, with successful cases added to the corpus as new seeds. Triage tasks take priority in the fuzzing process, followed by generation and mutation if no triage tasks are available.

3.2 SYZAGENT

We propose SYZAGENT to extend Syzkaller, as shown in Figure 1. It integrates an LLM into Syzkaller's generation and modification of the choice table. The LLM influences the fuzzing process in three key procedures: 1. It constructs the initial choice table based on static analysis and LLM analysis results. 2. During fuzzing, it collects some running test cases with coverage information during fuzzing, formulates feedback prompt to obtain guidance on fuzzing from LLM. 3. Finally it updates the choice table using guiding information provided by the LLM. The extension corresponds to the four new components: the *preprocessor*, *static analyzer*, *address extractor*, and *LLM interface*, as shown in Figure 1.

Pre-Processor The pre-processor compiles the OS kernel's source code into a binary image for testing and generates intermediate representations (IR) from LLVM framework [7]. These generated IR files are used for static analysis and are avoided from any optimization to reflect the calling relation as detailed as possible. Additionally, the pre-processor gathers information on all C functions present in the Linux kernel.

Static Analyzer The static analyzer parses and analyzes the IR files generated by the pre-processor, resulting in the call graph of the OS kernel. A *call graph* of the Linux kernel is a graph $G = (C \cup F, E)$, where: C is a finite set of system calls, F is a finite set of other functions, and $E \subseteq (C \cup F) \times (C \cup F)$ represents the set of directed edges in the call graph, showing the calling relationships between functions. Given a target function f_t, the static analyzer performs following tasks:

Job 1: Find all paths from some $s \in C$ to f_t. This corresponds to the first type of call paths in the motivating example.

Job 2: Find all paths from any function f to f_t with length l, where $l < \mathbf{k}$ and $\mathbf{k} \in \mathbb{N}$ is a constant. These are the second type of call paths in the ~~demo~~ motivating example;

Job 3: Identify all *close functions* f_c within a specific *close range* constant $\mathbf{d} \in \mathbb{N}$, where f_c is an n-step predecessor in the call graph and $n \leq \mathbf{d}$. A predecessor refers to a function that directly calls or influences another function in a call path. These functions are denoted by *close area*.

Address Extractor The address extractor matches program counter (PC) points in the compiled Linux kernel binary to their actual locations. Syzkaller uses KCOV [2] for coverage feedback, tracking the PC points reached by test cases. To improve efficiency, PC points in the close area are extracted in advance for quicker coverage checks.

LLM-Interface The LLM interface communicates with the LLM by sending the initial and feedback prompts. It then extracts a set of system calls, S_{inc}, from the LLM feedback to update the choice table.

The choice table is modified as follows: for any system calls c_1 and c_2, let $ct_0[c_1][c_2]$ represent the original choice table value in Syzkaller. The LLM-updated value, $ct_1[c_1][c_2]$, is set to $ct_0[c_1][c_2] + 1$ if either $c_1 \in S_{inc}$ or $c_2 \in S_{inc}$; otherwise, $ct_1[c_1][c_2] = ct_0[c_1][c_2]$. The final choice table is computed by normalizing ct_1 for each row: $ct[c_1][c_2] = \dfrac{ct_1[c_1][c_2]}{\sum_i ct_1[c_1][c_i]}$.

Apart from components above, it is worth mentioning that since LLM analysis runs slower than fuzzing. We sample test cases from all test cases and run LLM analysis in parallel. For every 500 cases sampled, some cases that covered close area will be selected randomly to do the feedback prompting via LLM-interface.

4   Preliminary Experimental Results

We conducted experiments on fuzzing the Linux kernel to demonstrate that our LLM-driven SYZAGENT method: 1) effectively adapts the existing vanilla Syzkaller tool, even breaking its coverage plateau, and 2) offers advantages over the specialized direct kernel fuzzing tool, SyzDirect.

Our experimental setup consisted of a PC equipped with a 13th Gen Intel Core i7-13700 processor and 128GB of memory. The virtual machine under test was configured on QEMU, running a Linux system on an AMD architecture with 4 CPUs and 4GB of memory. Given the 12.8k token limit of the LLM-interface in GPT-4o [1], we selected target functions based on the principle that no function in their call paths should have more than five predecessors to prevent the explosion of number of calling paths of the target function. From this set, we selected a total of 27 target functions which our tool can process currently as our benchmark.

SYZAGENT *vs Syzkaller* In this experiment, each target function was fuzzed using both SYZAGENT and Syzkaller, with each tool tested three times per function, and each run limited to two hours. The fuzzing results from SYZAGENT and Syzkaller are summarized in Table 1. Out of the 27 cases, SYZAGENT achieved a hit rate (the ratio of number of test cases hit close area and the number of all test cases) that surpassed Syzkaller by more than 10% in 8 cases, while it underperformed compared to Syzkaller in only 5 cases. Comparably, we also compute how the increased coverage outperforms the original one, represented as $\omega = \frac{\text{Avg. Diff}}{\text{Avg. Syzkaller Hit Rate}}$ and 18 cases out of 27 have $\omega \geq 10\%$ which is 67%.

These results confirm that the LLM integration in SYZAGENT effectively improves Syzkaller's performance in direct fuzzing, as the majority of cases achieved a higher hit rate when using SYZAGENT.

While this paper primarily focuses on kernel direct fuzzing, during our experiments, we observed that SYZAGENT successfully breaks the Syzkaller coverage plateau. In the 27 direct fuzzing cases, we found that 5 cases achieved higher coverage within a fixed number of test cases, with IDs 4, 19, 25, 26, 27. Figure 2 illustrates the coverage progression for case 27, where deeper target functions were tested, partially validating our hypothesis that the main reason of plateau is the fuzzer lacking a seed that can reach deeper code. However, we also noted that in 6 cases, the cov-

Fig. 2. Coverage-Execution graph for target function `sk_set_bit` within 2h(red line for Syzkaller and blue line for SYZAGENT)

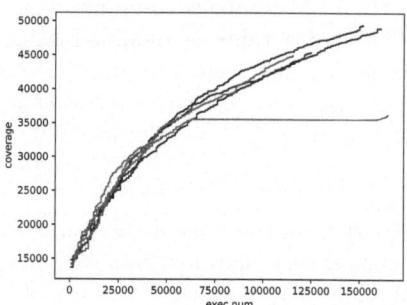

erage performance of SYZAGENT was inferior to that of Syzkaller, while the remaining cases showed similar performance between the two tools. We identify this as another promising new direction emerging from this work, and it will be valuable to investigate this hypothesis further, exploring how to harness the LLM's capabilities to systematically improve kernel fuzzing coverage.

SYZAGENT *vs SyzDirect* An end-to-end comparison with the SyzDirect tool was not feasible due to multiple issues encountered during its installation, configuration, and manual instrumentation requirements.

ID	Target Function	Dist.	SyzAgent Hit %			Syzkaller Hit %			Avg. Diff
			Run 1	Run 2	Run 3	Run 1	Run 2	Run 3	
1	ksys_semctl	1	28.27	28.89	31.8	3.8	5.15	1.11	**26.3**
2	__sys_setfsgid	1	19.1	13.89	9.45	0.0	0.03	0.0	**14.14**
3	do_sched_yield	1	25.15	26.32	41.7	20.57	30.14	26.86	**5.2**
4	vm_acct_memory	2	32.4	28.82	32.84	22.12	17.83	15.27	**12.95**
5	__shmem_file_setup	2	8.82	7.32	7.81	3.79	6.49	4.93	**2.91**
6	io_register_iowq_m...	2	22.05	15.63	18.26	1.02	3.28	2.59	**16.35**
7	__anon_inode_getfile	2	30.47	30.38	30.65	9.97	11.89	11.68	**19.32**
8	copy_fsxattr_from...	3	56.8	56.99	54.75	51.0	49.34	50.1	**6.03**
9	__io_uring_add_...	3	36.02	34.97	28.0	8.9	2.65	11.76	**25.23**
10	keyring_ptr_to_key	3	30.26	21.64	23.95	6.58	2.48	6.47	**20.11**
11	mnt_get_writers	3	77.1	73.33	75.44	67.6	73.84	80.1	1.44
12	futex_requeue_pi_...	3	0.92	0.0	0.0	2.94	0.31	2.0	-1.44
13	wait_for_device_probe	4	0.33	0.31	0.12	0.35	0.14	0.13	**0.05**
14	memcpy_to_page	4	24.07	29.73	34.0	7.1	9.02	0.0	**23.89**
15	kimage_is_dest...	5	1.74	7.69	8.05	0.0	0.06	0.66	**5.59**
16	find_lock_entries	5	40.68	37.72	33.88	38.28	34.67	39.23	0.03
17	fsnotify_data_sb	5	58.2	57.33	61.22	55.73	55.72	60.94	1.45
18	security_inode_set...	5	12.02	10.74	12.86	3.39	4.78	3.61	**7.94**
19	free_partitions	6	13.48	21.94	14.57	28.17	24.73	25.97	-9.63
20	bpf_prog_free	6	0.56	5.12	3.68	1.25	1.5	3.37	**1.08**
21	locks_delete_glob...	6	0.59	0.58	0.0	0.73	0.04	0.56	-0.05
22	pmd_none_or_clear_bad	7	12.92	11.3	16.47	14.72	19.68	18.11	-3.94
23	__submit_bio_noac...	7	31.89	21.5	19.88	20.09	28.69	27.06	-0.86
24	srcu_read_lock_nm...	7	19.89	45.15	26.51	23.62	25.22	20.31	**7.47**
25	trace_wbc_writepage	8	1.82	0.81	3.03	0.79	1.71	0.6	**0.85**
26	sk_set_bit	8	8.21	10.61	6.48	3.09	3.23	6.61	**4.12**
27	sidtab_search_core	8	76.48	77.85	75.68	73.14	76.26	73.34	2.42

Table 1. Experimental Data Comparison between Two Methods ("Dist." denotes the minimum length of call path from some system call to target function. "Hit %" represents the ratio of the test cases that covered close area in the sampled test cases in percentage. "Avg. Diff" denotes the average difference of the hit rate of SyzAgent minus the hit rate of Syzkaller across all runs.)

ID	Target Function	SyzAgent	Syzdirect
1	stable_page_flags	read, pread	ioctl(4 variants), io_uring_enter, read, write, mount
2	fscontext_create_fd	fsopen, fspick	None
3	memfd_fcntl	fcntl, fcntl64, ioctl(UDMABUF_CREATE)	ioctl(UDMABUF_CREATE, UDMABUF_CREATE_LIST), fcntl(getflags)

Table 2. Exemplar system call entry analysis results from SyzAgent and SyzDirect reveal that SyzAgent has advantages over SyzDirect in identifying system call relationships, as highlighted in green. Conversely, SyzDirect excels in detecting argument types, as shown in red, a feature not currently supported by SyzAgent.

Nevertheless, we managed to run SyzDirect's stages for system call entry analysis and conducted a comparison with the LLM-generated results from SYZAGENT. Table 2 presents the results for three target functions in the Linux kernel[7]. In the table, system calls highlighted in green indicate cases where SYZAGENT outperforms SyzDirect, while those in red represent cases where SyzDirect performs better.

In cases with IDs 2 and 3, SYZAGENT identified three additional system call entries compared to SyzDirect. After manually verifying these cases, we found that SyzDirect's call graph analysis was less precise than that of SYZAGENT. For example, in the first case, `io_uring_enter` did not appear to be beneficial for reaching the target function. However, SyzDirect outperformed SYZAGENT in providing specific variants of system calls, likely due to its more detailed call graph model that incorporates resource-producing and consuming relationships, which are currently not included in SYZAGENT analysis. This results in a finer-grained analysis by SyzDirect compared to that of SYZAGENT.

5   Conclusion and Discussion

In this work, we explored the integration of LLM capabilities with OS kernel fuzzers in real-time. Based on our preliminary experimental results, this approach appears effective for direct fuzzing and warrants further investigation. However, our work is still in its early stage, as several advanced techniques, such as the relational graph approach from [9] and more sophisticated static analysis methods like those in [6,14], have not yet been incorporated. Our work also lacks the validation on whether the system calls are correctly generated.

At the implementation level, there are several ways SYZAGENT could be enhanced: 1) Splitting the calling code into smaller segments to facilitate deeper exploration of target functions ; 2) Integrating more closely with Syzkaller to enable LLMs to contribute to argument mutation processes; and 3) Using the distance to the target function of cases that cover nearby areas to select the most promising test cases for generating feedback prompts.

We regard LLMs as a viable solution to the complexities inherent in OS kernel fuzzing, thanks to the vast amount of data on which they are trained and optimized. The combination of LLM capabilities with our real-time feedback framework offers a flexible way to automatically adjust the fuzzing strategy. In the future, we believe it will be important to continue researching how LLMs can boost fuzzing coverage by utilizing information from intermediate results of static analysis and kernel documentation.

Acknowledgments. We gratefully thank Pierre Olivier for providing insights of linux kernel on this study. This work is partly supported by CAS Project for Young Scientists in Basic Research, Grant No.YSBR-040, ISCAS New Cultivation Project ISCAS-PYFX-202201, ISCAS Basic Research ISCAS-JCZD-202302 and the Ministry of Education, Singapore under its Academic Research Fund Tier 3 (Award ID: MOET32020-0004).

---

[7] Commit 304040fb4909f7771caf6f8e8c61dbe51c93505a

References

1. Chatgpt (gpt-4o), `https://www.openai.com/chatgpt`
2. Kcov, `https://github.com/SimonKagstrom/kcov`
3. Syzkaller. `https://github.com/google/syzkaller/`
4. Syzlang. `https://github.com/google/syzkaller/blob/master/docs/syscall_descriptions_syntax.md`
5. Achiam, J., Adler, S., Agarwal, S., Ahmad, L., Akkaya, I., Aleman, F.L., Almeida, D., Altenschmidt, J., Altman, S., Anadkat, S., et al.: Gpt-4 technical report. arXiv preprint arXiv:2303.08774 (2023)
6. Corina, J., Machiry, A., Salls, C., Shoshitaishvili, Y., Hao, S., Kruegel, C., Vigna, G.: DIFUZE: interface aware fuzzing for kernel drivers. In: Proceedings of the 2017 ACM SIGSAC Conference on Computer and Communications Security, CCS 2017, Dallas, TX, USA, October 30 - November 03, 2017. pp. 2123–2138 (2017). `https://doi.org/10.1145/3133956.3134069`
7. Lattner, C., Adve, V.S.: LLVM: A compilation framework for lifelong program analysis & transformation. In: 2nd IEEE / ACM International Symposium on Code Generation and Optimization (CGO 2004), 20-24 March 2004, San Jose, CA, USA. pp. 75–88 (2004). `https://doi.org/10.1109/CGO.2004.1281665`
8. Shen, Y., Sun, H., Jiang, Y., Shi, H., Yang, Y., Chang, W.: Rtkaller: State-aware task generation for RTOS fuzzing. ACM Trans. Embed. Comput. Syst. **20**(5s), 83:1–83:22 (2021). `https://doi.org/10.1145/3477014`
9. Sun, H., Shen, Y., Wang, C., Liu, J., Jiang, Y., Chen, T., Cui, A.: HEALER: relation learning guided kernel fuzzing. In: SOSP '21: ACM SIGOPS 28th Symposium on Operating Systems Principles, Virtual Event / Koblenz, Germany, October 26-29, 2021. pp. 344–358 (2021). `https://doi.org/10.1145/3477132.3483547`
10. Tan, X., Zhang, Y., Lu, J., Xiong, X., Liu, Z., Yang, M.: Syzdirect: Directed grey-box fuzzing for linux kernel. In: Proceedings of the 2023 ACM SIGSAC Conference on Computer and Communications Security, CCS 2023, Copenhagen, Denmark, November 26-30, 2023. pp. 1630–1644 (2023). `https://doi.org/10.1145/3576915.3623146`
11. Wang, D., Zhang, Z., Zhang, H., Qian, Z., Krishnamurthy, S.V., Abu-Ghazaleh, N.B.: Syzvegas: Beating kernel fuzzing odds with reinforcement learning. In: 30th USENIX Security Symposium, USENIX Security 2021, August 11-13, 2021. pp. 2741–2758 (2021)
12. Xia, C.S., Paltenghi, M., Tian, J.L., Pradel, M., Zhang, L.: Fuzz4all: Universal fuzzing with large language models. In: Proceedings of the 46th IEEE/ACM International Conference on Software Engineering, ICSE 2024, Lisbon, Portugal, April 14-20, 2024. pp. 126:1–126:13 (2024). `https://doi.org/10.1145/3597503.3639121`
13. Yang, C., Zhao, Z., Zhang, L.: Kernelgpt: Enhanced kernel fuzzing via large language models. CoRR **abs/2401.00563** (2024). `https://doi.org/10.48550/ARXIV.2401.00563`
14. Zhao, B., Li, Z., Qin, S., Ma, Z., Yuan, M., Zhu, W., Tian, Z., Zhang, C.: State-fuzz: System call-based state-aware linux driver fuzzing. In: 31st USENIX Security Symposium, USENIX Security 2022, Boston, MA, USA, August 10-12, 2022. pp. 3273–3289 (2022)

DeepCRCEval: Revisiting the Evaluation of Code Review Comment Generation

Junyi Lu[1,2], Xiaojia Li[3], Zihan Hua[1,2], Lei Yu[1,2], Shiqi Cheng[1], Li Yang[1(✉)], Fengjun Zhang[1], and Chun Zuo[4]

[1] Institute of Software, Chinese Academy of Sciences, Beijing, China
{yulei2022,chengshiqi,yangli2017,fengjun}@iscas.ac.cn
[2] University of Chinese Academy of Sciences, Beijing, China
{lujunyi21,huazihan22}@mails.ucas.ac.cn
[3] Kuaishou Technology, Beijing, China
lixiaojia03@kuaishou.com
[4] Sinosoft Company Limited, Beijing, China
zuochun@sinosoft.com.cn

Abstract. Code review is a vital but demanding aspect of software development, generating significant interest in automating review comments. Traditional evaluation methods for these comments, primarily based on text similarity, face two major challenges: inconsistent reliability of human-authored comments in open-source projects and the weak correlation of text similarity with objectives like enhancing code quality and detecting defects.

This study empirically analyzes benchmark comments using a novel set of criteria informed by prior research and developer interviews. We then similarly revisit the evaluation of existing methodologies. Our evaluation framework, DeepCRCEval, integrates human evaluators and Large Language Models (LLMs) for a comprehensive reassessment of current techniques based on the criteria set. Besides, we also introduce an innovative and efficient baseline, LLM-Reviewer, leveraging the few-shot learning capabilities of LLMs for a target-oriented comparison.

Our research highlights the limitations of text similarity metrics, finding that less than 10% of benchmark comments are high quality for automation. In contrast, DeepCRCEval effectively distinguishes between high and low-quality comments, proving to be a more reliable evaluation mechanism. Incorporating LLM evaluators into DeepCRCEval significantly boosts efficiency, reducing time and cost by 88.78% and 90.32%, respectively. Furthermore, LLM-Reviewer demonstrates significant potential of focusing task real targets in comment generation.

Keywords: Code review automation · Evaluation framework · Large language models (LLMs) · Text similarity metrics · Defect detection

An extended version of this paper, which includes appendices is available at https://doi.org/10.48550/arXiv.2412.18291

© The Author(s) 2025
A. Boronat and G. Fraser (Eds.): FASE 2025, LNCS 15693, pp. 43–64, 2025.
https://doi.org/10.1007/978-3-031-90900-9_3

1   Introduction

Since Fagan's pioneering work on software inspections in 1976 [7], code review practices have evolved significantly. Early software inspections were formal and resource-intensive, which limited their widespread adoption in the industry. In contrast, Modern Code Review (MCR) has become a vital and streamlined process in both Open-Source Software (OSS) [25–27] and industrial applications [28, 29]. MCR typically involves developers submitting code changes for review, which reviewers then assess to provide feedback on potential issues or improvements. This process may involve mechanisms such as pull requests, changesets, or code patches, depending on the tools and platforms used. A pivotal aspect of MCR is the generation of insightful, constructive comments, essential for guiding developers and pinpointing problems, which is further elaborated upon in the section 'Additional Background' in the appendix of our extended version.

Despite its effectiveness, MCR remains resource-intensive [34]. This challenge has spurred the exploration of automating code review comments to alleviate labor demands [11]. Initial attempts focused on retrieval-based methods using existing comments as references [8, 30]. With the progression of deep learning, the emphasis has shifted to generative approaches. A variety of Code Review Comment Generators (CRCGs) have emerged, notably initiated by Tufano et al. with a T5 transformer architecture [32], later augmented with code-technical language pre-training [31]. Following this trend, models like CodeReviewer [16] and AUGER [14] have further advanced the field, integrating specific pre-training for code review and utilizing review tags to enhance accuracy. Parallel developments include CommentFinder [10], offering an efficient retrieval-based solution, and CCT5 [17], which underscores the importance of considering code changes in comment generation. Later, with the emergence of LLMs, Lu et al. [20] investigate the factors influencing the code review process for both traditional pre-trained language models and LLMs, while Llama-Reviewer [21] marks the first attempt at training code review tasks on LLMs in a parameter-efficient approach. Nevertheless, these models typically employ text similarity metrics such as BLEU [22] and ROUGE [18] for evaluation.

We question the suitability of text similarity as the primary metric for assessing code review comment automation. The dependability of human-written comments in OSS, commonly used as benchmarks, is often subject to scrutiny [1–3, 9, 12, 23, 33]. These comments can be arbitrary and inconsistent, at times offering little more than basic queries or directives like "Why do we need this?" or "Remove this." Unlike traditional text-to-text tasks such as summarization or translation, which seek semantic equivalence, code review comments aim to aid in defect detection and code refinement, requiring deeper insight [1]. Hence, text similarity, as an indirect measurement, falls short of capturing the essence.

Analysis of Benchmark Comments.   The reliability of text similarity metrics for evaluating review comments hinges on the accuracy of the reference text. Yet, the quality and validity of benchmark comments in major datasets, such as the CodeReviewer (CRer) [16] and Tufano datasets [31], often remain ambiguous. To address these ambiguities and provide a more nuanced understanding, we conducted an empirical study analyzing these datasets from four dimensions: 1) Quality: Assessing comments against established quality standards; 2) Category: Evaluating the effectiveness of comments in identifying defects and suggesting improvements, or other potential roles; 3) Tone: Analyzing whether comments clearly state issues or are merely interrogative; 4) Context: Determining if the comments are sufficiently supported by the associated code. For Quality evaluation, we developed criteria based on existing literature about developers' views on code review quality [12], supplemented by our semi-structured interviews and card sorting exercises using affinity diagrams.

DeepCRCEval Stemming from our analysis of benchmark comments, we developed DeepCRCEval, an innovative evaluation framework incorporating both human and LLM evaluators. This framework utilized the criteria of high quality comments identified in the former analysis, and use both scoring and ranking to compare performances. It is geared towards identifying the intrinsic merits of review comments, moving away from the indirect approach of text similarity.

LLM-Reviewer To validate the effectiveness of direct metrics in line with code review objectives, we propose LLM-Reviewer, a lightweight, training-free baseline tool. Traditional methods, reliant on text similarity metrics, may not capture the true essence of code review. In contrast, by harnessing the potential of Large Language Models (LLMs), LLM-Reviewer employs few-shot learning with meticulously crafted prompts. Unlike previous methods, LLM-Reviewer directly addresses the actual aims of code review and controlled the comments' quality with criterion guidance in prompt, more closely mirroring developers' concept of effective review commentary. This baseline also serves as a benchmark to gauge the effectiveness of evaluation frameworks in differentiating high and low-quality review comments.

Revisiting the Evaluation of CRCGs Utilizing DeepCRCEval as our evaluation framework and LLM-Reviewer as our baseline, we reassessed the performance of current state-of-the-art (SOTA) CRCGs. Given the training-free nature of LLM-Reviewer, it was anticipated that other tuned methods would perform at least comparably. However, our findings, derived from both human and LLM evaluators, reveal a considerable shortfall in the performance of existing SOTA CRCGs compared to this benchmark. Our analysis of 1,000 typical code snippets containing defects or code smells demonstrated LLM-Reviewer's proficiency in consistently pinpointing issues, providing well-rounded comments encompassing problem identification, detailed explanation, and possible solutions. In contrast, SOTA CRCGs often produced nonspecific and ambiguous comments, falling short of the review's goals.

Contributions Our significant contributions include:

1. Unveiling the biases in evaluating state-of-the-art (SOTA) CRCGs due to reliance on inappropriate metrics.
2. Developing DeepCRCEval, a versatile evaluation framework employing either human or LLM evaluators, which concentrates on the core essence of comments rather than indirect text similarity measures.

3. Introducing LLM-Reviewer, a pioneering, training-free baseline for code review comment automation.
4. Empirically demonstrating that existing SOTA CRCGs are outperformed by the training-free LLM-Reviewer, indicating potential for improvement.
5. Materials publicly available at https://doi.org/10.5281/zenodo.1051 1726.

The rest of the paper is structured as follows: Section 2 presents the background of our research. Section 3 introduces the overview of the study and our research questions. Section 4 details our analysis of benchmark comments, which aims to prove the limitations of current text similarity measurements. Section 5 illustrates our approach to revisiting the evaluation of code review comment generators, including our dual-granularity human/LLM evaluation framework DeepCRCEval, and a prompt-based LLM baseline LLM-Reviewer. Section 6 shows the results of the reevaluation, as well as key findings and discussions. Section 8 introduces related work on the evaluation of code review comments and the differences between these and our work. Section 9 concludes the paper.

2 Background

2.1 CRCGs and Their Evaluation

For code review automation, researchers predominantly utilize deep learning or information retrieval techniques as code review comment generators (CRCGs) to automatically generate comments for given code snippets. Despite some variations, Figure 1 depicts the typical workflow for training a deep neural network (DNN) model or constructing a retriever for automating code review. Initially, ① a DNN model or a retriever is trained or established using a dataset of code-comment pairs from OSS projects, learning the semantic relationships between code and comments. Then, ② for each test case code snippet, the model or retriever generates or retrieves a comment employing specific decoding or retrieval techniques. Finally, ③ the produced comments are compared against the original ones from the test set, also sourced from OSS projects. Common comparison metrics include BLEU [22] and ROUGE [18], where BLEU assesses the precision of machine translations by measuring the match of N-grams, and ROUGE evaluates the recall of machine-generated summaries based on N-gram co-occurrence. These metrics also guide the training of DNNs.

However, the quality and validity of the original comments extracted from OSS projects are questionable. For example, the comments in Table 1 are not suitable for use as code review comments by **models**, although they might be meaningful for human reviewers. Specifically, "Why do we need this?" is indeed meaningful if it opens a dialogue when by humans. However, CRCGs generate comments only once, without a dialogue-like interaction. If a model outputs this comment, the code author cannot acquire further knowledge as the process has concluded. "Remove this line" provides specific action suggestions. However, without reasons, it could confuse code authors. If by humans, this could be

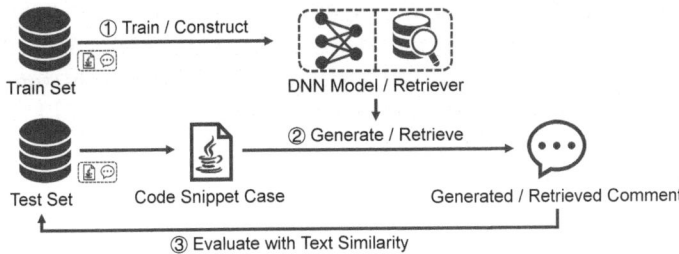

Fig. 1. The overall workflow of learning a deep neural network (DNN) model or retriever to automate code review.

clarified by asking further questions, but for CRCGs the process is already complete. Besides, these two comments are both too general. They lack context and explanation, making it applicable to any code.

Moreover, the text similarity used for comparison are indirect measures of the primary objective, which is to find defects or enhance code. Unlike tasks such as text translation where similar input leads to similar output, review comments can be arbitrary. A same issue can be represented differently, while similar representations might have totally different meanings. Therefore, we posit that there might be an overestimation of the effectiveness of current SOTA CRCGs.

Table 1. Example of unsuitable comments for machine code review.

It's a race to see who merges first, because I bet one of my PRs will cause a conflict with this
why do we need this
remove this line
While I would have liked to resolve all of the N+1 issues related to profiles in this PR this has proved more difficult than anticipated and there's a lot of other good stuff in this PR that I'd really like to get out, so we can keep this around a bit longer.
Can we avoid change names of variable for now? This change is not purely style change and might make those who maintains private patches harder. Such change can be done separately with a more fine grained approach.
I seem to remember we spoke on this earlier in the opposite sense, saying that we want the shortcuts to be added even if they are not displayed.
The same code has been used a few times throughout this file.

2.2   Large Language Models for Evaluations

Large language models have shown capabilities similar to those of human evaluators [13]. Studies have demonstrated that large language models like GPT-4 can achieve higher agreement than human evaluators [6, 15, 24, 35] for ranking preference and scoring. For instance, in the evaluation of general text generation, GPT-4's agreement rate with human evaluations (85%) surpasses the rate of inter-human agreement (81%) [35], a finding echoed in another dataset comparison (69.2% vs. 65.7%) [15]. Considering this, our evaluation framework is based on these works but is more granular and lightweight. We use a chain-of-thought template to inject task-specific knowledge for better scoring and ranking.

Since there is no prior proof of the effectiveness of LLM evaluators in the task of code review comment generation, we adopt both human and LLM evaluators for all evaluation parts of our paper. The LLM evaluators serve as an auxiliary certification, expanding the scope of verification.

3   Overview and Research Questions

Automated code review has garnered significant interest from researchers, yet its evaluation effectiveness has not been sufficiently addressed. This oversight leads to a disconnect between the task objectives and the training processes used. This paper aims to highlight the importance of effective evaluation in code review automation. As depicted in Figure 2, we developed ① DeepCRCEval, a new evaluation framework incorporating both human and LLM evaluators, and ② LLM-Reviewer, a lightweight, training-free, and target-oriented baseline tool. Our study focuses on: **1)** verifying the shortcomings of current evaluation metrics, **2)** manually reassessing the evaluation of existing code review comment generators, **3)** integrating LLM-based alternative evaluators for an extended scope of validation, and **4)** identifying potential improvement directions stemming from the misalignment of task objectives and training processes. The latter two RQs aim to set directions for future research. We next introduce the research questions we aim to investigate and their relationships.

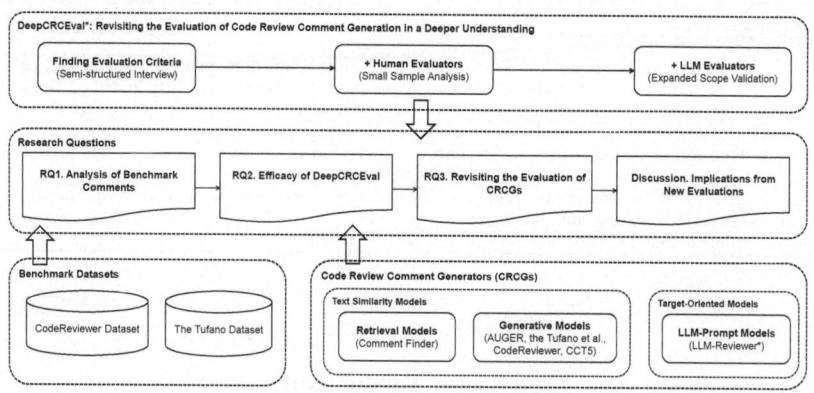

Fig. 2. Overview of our study. * indicates frameworks or models we newly proposed.

RQ1. Analysis of Benchmark Comments: Are the foundations of current evaluation metrics reliable? The reliability of text similarity metrics for evaluating review comments depends on the quality and validation of the reference texts. We first analyze the benchmark reference review comments from four perspectives: quality, category, tone, and context. We present results for each aspect and summarize the relationships between these aspects.

RQ2. Efficacy of DeepCRCEval: Why do we claim that DeepCRCEval provides a deeper evaluation, and why do we integrate LLM evaluators? Before presenting the new results obtained in RQ3, we first examine the differences between our DeepCRCEval and traditional text similarity metrics. Additionally, we evaluate the advantages and disadvantages of using LLM evaluators for expanded scope validation. We report on the efficiency of LLM evaluators and their agreement with human evaluators.

RQ3. Revisiting the Evaluation of CRCGs: What are the actual performances of current CRCGs beyond simple text similarity metrics? By challenging the current text similarity metrics in RQ1, we aim to investigate the actual performances of current CRCGs more deeply. Using our newly proposed evaluation framework, DeepCRCEval, and the new target-oriented model, LLM-Reviewer, as a baseline, we increase the distinction in our analyses. We analyze results from human evaluators as a small sample analysis and from LLM evaluators for expanded scope validation.

Discussion. Implications from New Evaluations: What can we learn to guide further research? The new evaluations aim to guide future research in code review comment generation and propose potential improvement directions. We present the implications derived from our study with case studies.

4 RQ1. Analysis of Benchmark Comments

4.1 Aspects for Analysis

To thoroughly explore previous code review comment datasets, we defining aspects with a qualitative and quantitative process [4], which draws on varied data sources for comprehensive insights, including the review of previous study [12], our semi-structured interviews [19] with seven industry developers, and subsequent card sort and affinity diagram by the authors of this paper. The detailed process are shown in the section 'Finding Quality Evaluation Criteria' in the appendix of our extended version. These gained criteria are utilized for assessing benchmark comment quality, which will also for the subsequent reevaluation.

Quality The multi-step study introduced above culminated in identifying nine key criteria for evaluating the effectiveness of code review comments:

C1. Readability: Clear, easily understandable language.
C2. Relevance: Directly related to the specific code.
C3. Explanation Clarity: Clear elucidation of the issues identified.
C4. Problem Identification: Accurate pinpointing and articulation of bugs.
C5. Actionability: Practical advice for addressing identified issues.
C6. Completeness: Coverage of all issues in the code for comprehensive review.
C7. Specificity: Focus on specific code issues, avoiding generic statements.
C8. Contextual Adequacy: Comments pointing out exact issue locations.
C9. Brevity: Conciseness, conveying essential information without verbosity.

Category We evaluated the comments' ability to detect defects or suggest code improvements using a classification system. This involved adopting the nine categories proposed by Bacchelli et al. [1], such as Code Improvement, Understanding, and Social Communication, and introducing an additional category, "Meaningless Text", for extremely low-quality, uninformative comments.

Tone and Context To examine factors influencing comment validation, we conducted a manual inspection using the Nominal Group Technique (NGT), involving three authors of this paper. Each participant initially prepared individual opinions, later discussed in a structured meeting. The focus was on the aspects with the highest consensus:

- ① **Tone:** Interrogative comments were noted to be less effective, as they often raise questions rather than providing specific, formalized feedback. For example, a comment like "Why this?" is less valuable for identifying defects or suggesting improvements.
- ② **Context:** Comments requiring understanding beyond the provided code snippet (e.g., at the file level) were found challenging, especially in the context of automated code review techniques and their datasets. Comments such as "used a few times throughout this file" lack clarity when only a single method is given as input.

4.2   Analysis Methodology

Analyzing code review comments is a nuanced and labor-intensive task. To manage this, we sampled 100 comments from each of the two primary datasets in this domain: the Tufano dataset [31] and the CodeReviewer dataset [16], abbreviated as Tufano and CRer, respectively. According to the average reliability of 93% for humans in Table 6, the margin of error for 95% confidence level of 100 sample size is within 5%. The Tufano dataset is a monolingual, function-level Java dataset, while the CRer dataset is multilingual and at the diff granularity. Both are constructed from large-scale open-source software repositories and widely utilized in numerous studies. The quality and category is finished with a human scoring system created using QT and and a Delphi Method variant [5] by five master's and doctoral students, respectively. The Tone and context was conducted using the aforementioned NGT sessions by three authors of this study. The detailed process are shown in the section 'Detailed Analysis Methodology for Dateset Comment Quality' in the appendix of our extended version.

4.3   Results of Analysis

We first present the results from each aspect, and then summarize the relationships between each aspect using a Venn diagram in Section 4.3.

Quality Our analysis, illustrated in the upper part of Table 2, indicates that while OSS review comments typically exhibit good readability and brevity, they frequently lack in other critical aspects, reflecting issues of arbitrariness, incompleteness, and irregularity. We designated scores **below 6 (out of 10)** as poor performance indicators for each aspect. The lower part of Table 2 shows the proportion of comments scoring poorly in each aspect. This data highlights deficiencies of comments in aspects other than readability, completeness, and brevity. For example, low scores in explanation clarity or actionability hint at inadequate detail or absence of constructive suggestions, while low relevance, contextual adequacy, or specificity scores suggest a tendency towards vagueness or irrelevance to the code context. LLM evaluations were also conducted, similar to Section 5.1, with detailed results available in Table 'Average quality of comments and percentage of low-quality cases in OSS datasets by LLM evaluators' in the appendix of our extended version.

Table 2. Average quality of comments (❶ upper part, 1-10) and percentage of low-quality cases (❷ lower part, 0%-100%) in OSS datasets. C1-C9 represent aspects mentioned in Section 4.1.

	Dataset	C1	C2	C3	C4	C5	C6	C7	C8	C9
❶	Tufano	8.68	7.07	4.70	5.40	5.81	7.61	6.43	4.89	8.99
	Crer	9.21	6.41	5.23	5.78	5.08	7.40	6.36	6.32	9.03
❷	Tufano	7%	31%	64%	55%	46%	20%	34%	63%	4%
	Crer	1%	48%	57%	52%	64%	31%	35%	43%	0%

Category The classification of comment categories in OSS projects, summarized in Table 3, reveals distinct distributions. In the Tufano dataset, code improvements and defects constitute 64%, while in the CRer dataset, they comprise only 39%. This distribution aligns with previous findings on the proportion of practically useful comments [3]. Comments outside these categories may hold value in specific human code review scenarios but do not align with the core objectives of machine code reviews. For example, comments on deferring tasks to future pull requests, unrelated to the current code, offer limited value.

Tone and Context The analysis shows a significant presence of interrogative comments—38% in the Tufano dataset and 46% in the CRer dataset. Besides, a substantial portion of comments—45% in the Tufano dataset and 54% in the CRer dataset—required out-of-method or out-of-hunk context.

Summary of Analysis The Venn diagrams in Figure 3 for each dataset summarize the interplay of various factors impacting the suitability of reference comments. A notable finding is that only a small fraction of comments in these datasets—3% in the Tufano dataset and 8% in the CRer dataset—qualify as ideal

Table 3. Distribution of comment categories in OSS datasets.

	the Tufano dataset	the CRer dataset
Code Improvement	43%	26%
Understanding	5%	19%
Social Communication	12%	18%
Defects	21%	13%
External Impact	2%	1%
Testing	2%	3%
Review Tool	2%	1%
Knowledge Transfer	1%	8%
Misc	1%	3%
Meaningless Text	11%	8%

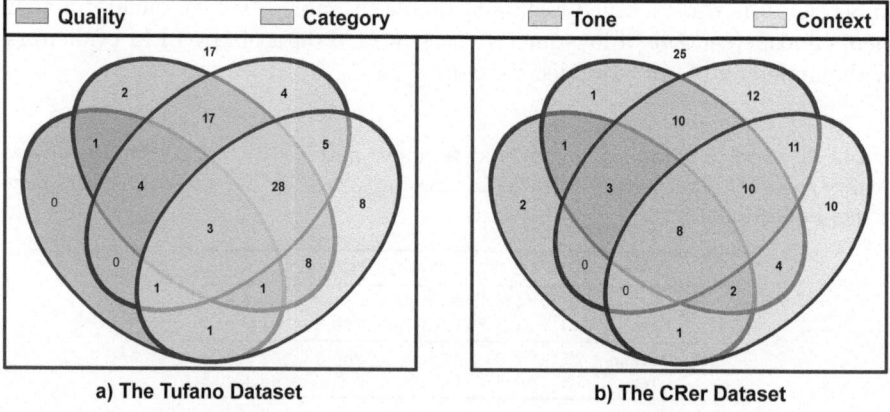

Fig. 3. 4-group Venn diagrams showing the overlap of suitable quality, category, tone, and context in comments.

references. Furthermore, even within this subset, many comments only address minor issues like typos or simple syntax errors.

> **Response to RQ1:** The uncertain quality and validity of benchmark comments undermine their suitability as reference standards, casting doubt on the effectiveness of text similarity as a metric.

5 Revisiting the Evaluation of CRCGs

In light of the inadequacy of text similarity metrics for evaluating Code Review Comment Generators (CRCGs), this section introduces our novel evaluation framework, DeepCRCEval, and a target-oriented baseline, LLM-Reviewer, to reassess the performance of CRCGs.

5.1 DeepCRCEval

Drawing from the criteria established in Section 4.1, we developed DeepCRCE-val, an evaluation framework designed to rigorously analyze the quality of generated comments. DeepCRCEval employs both human and Large Language Model (LLM) evaluators. Initially, we conducted human evaluations on a sampled test set due to cost considerations, then extended the evaluation to the entire test set using LLMs.

Human Evaluators For human evaluations, we developed an executable file using QT, similar to the one in Section 4.3 but enhanced with a comparative ranking task. This tool is also available in our open-source repository.

LLM Evaluators Recognizing the limitations of human scoring, such as cost and time intensity, and challenges in assessing certain aspects like completeness, we incorporated LLM evaluators. Our methodology utilizes a thought-chain-enhanced prompt template, adapted from recent research [35]:

- **Domain-Based Scoring:** In contrast to earlier methods that used a single overall score, we introduced domain-specific scoring across nine different dimensions, allowing for a more detailed and nuanced assessment.
- **Efficient Sorting:** We optimized resource usage by streamlining pairwise comparisons into a consolidated overall sorting, simplifying the process.
- **Chain-of-Thought Integration:** Chain-of-thought (CoT) module was embedded to link scoring and ranking tasks coherently, enhancing the logical flow of evaluations.

The structure of our enhanced prompt template is:

$$P_{Eval} = Des_{Scoring} + G + Obj + Des_{Ranking} + F \tag{1}$$

$$F = F_{Scoring} + CoT + F_{Ranking} \tag{2}$$

where $Des_{Scoring}$ and $Des_{Ranking}$ denote the task descriptions for scoring and ranking, respectively. G comprises guidelines, including notes and criteria descriptions, while Obj represents the objects being evaluated. F outlines the format for the generation, integrating a CoT section for enriched explanations. We delineate each component with "###" for clarity. The detailed prompt template is shown in Table 'Detailed prompt template for LLM evaluators' in the appendix of our extended version. To minimize bias, evaluations were performed twice for each case, once in descending and once in ascending order.

5.2 Selected CRCGs

For our analysis, we first selected all current state-of-the-art (SOTA) CRCGs published in top-tier conferences. This includes models like Tufano et al. [31],

AUGER [14], CodeReviewer [16], and CCT5 [17], primarily based on DNN models, alongside CommentFinder [10], which uses retrieval techniques. Notably, all these CRCGs have been trained or constructed using data from OSS projects and guided by text similarity metrics, which may not align well with the primary goal of identifying defects or enhancing code.

To evaluate CRCG performance effectively, an appropriate baseline is crucial. We sought a baseline that directly targets defect detection and code improvement. Given the absence of such a baseline in existing literature, we introduce LLM-Reviewer, a novel, straightforward, and fair baseline. It resembles DNNs but does not require additional training.

5.3   LLM-Reviewer

Figure 4 illustrates the workflow of LLM-Reviewer. Distinct from traditional CRCGs, LLM-Reviewer operates without the need for a training set. The process for each new code snippet is: ① Integration of the code with a pre-defined prompt. ② Feeding this combined input into the selected LLM to generate a comment. ③ Direct evaluation of the generated comment's quality using DeepCRCEval.

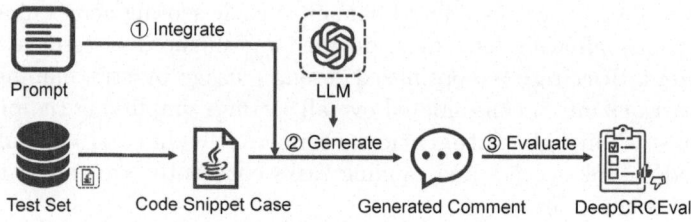

Fig. 4. The overall workflow of LLM-Reviewer.

The pre-defined prompt is bolstered with specific guidance and few-shot instructions. The utilized in-context prompt is:

$$P_{Reviewer} = Des_{Gen} + G_{Gen} + Demo^k \tag{3}$$

where Des_{Gen} offers concise directives for generating code review comments, G_{Gen} encompasses guidelines including notes and criteria descriptions (as discussed in Section 4.1), and $Demo^k$ features k randomly chosen demonstrations, adhering to k-shot learning principles. For this study, we opted for $k = 3$, balancing input length with informative content. Each prompt component is clearly separated by "###" as detailed in Table 'Detailed prompt template for LLM-Reviewer' in the appendix of our extended version.

This prompt is then integrated with the code snippet under review before being fed into the LLM for comment generation. It is worth noting that we use a similar prompt template to the one used for prompt evaluation. This similarity is why we refer to LLM-Reviewer as a target-oriented model. Unlike other text similarity models, the similar prompt template constrains LLM-Reviewer's response to the expected target. Additionally, as a countermeasure against bias, we use human evaluators throughout the entire study.

5.4   Other Experimental Details

Testing Set Since LLM-Reviewer does not require a training dataset, we selected a set of 1,000 code cases with typical issues for testing. These cases are processed by humans to enhance simplicity, and thus to reduce the risk of data leakage. Each case is guaranteed to contain at least one significant issue within one or a few functions, compatible with the input format of earlier CRCGs. We used ROUGE-L to remove duplicates. This test set is also accessible in our open-source repository. For baselines, we utilized their respective training sets.

Implementation of Baselines The implementation of baseline CRCGs involved different approaches. For Tufano et al. [31], AUGER [14], and CCT5 [17], we leveraged their publicly available models. CommentFinder [10] was replicated using the original dataset and code, while CodeReviewer [16] was obtained through fine-tuning their pre-trained model with provided scripts. All GPT-4 usages within the DeepCRCEval framework and our LLM-Reviewer were implemented using the OpenAI Python library, with a temperature setting of 0.1 and a token limit of 8192.

6   RQ2-RQ3: Empirical Findings

This section presents our empirical findings, detailing the performance of various CRCGs as evaluated by our framework DeepCRCEval.

6.1   RQ2. Efficacy of DeepCRCEval

This subsection examines the efficacy of our DeepCRCEval framework, specifically assessing the criteria used for evaluation and the integration of LLMs.

Effectiveness of Criteria Our evaluation framework, DeepCRCEval, surpasses traditional text similarity metrics in two key areas: discrimination and comprehensiveness.

Discrimination Prior studies often reported marginal improvements in text similarity metrics, like a less than 1% increase in BLEU scores. Such negligible enhancements do not reliably indicate an improvement in comment quality, as corroborated by our reevaluations. While newer baselines like CCT5 and AUGER reported improvements in text similarity, they did not surpass their predecessor, Tufano et al., in effectiveness—a conclusion also supported by our qualitative case studies. In contrast, DeepCRCEval, with its well-defined criteria, offers a higher degree of discrimination across various aspects. Moreover, our ranking process provides a direct and comparative analysis of comment quality.

Table 4. Comparison of average time and cost per case per evaluator between human and LLM evaluators.

Evaluator	Single Comment		Performance Comparison	
	Time (s)	Cost ($)	Time (s)	Cost ($)
Humans	224.45	0.62	752.65	2.09
LLMs	25.18	0.06	68.69	0.17

Table 5. Levels of agreement between humans and LLMs.

Evaluators	C1	C2	C3	C4	C5	C6	C7	C8	C9
Humans	0.89	0.94	0.94	0.94	0.95	0.91	0.94	0.95	0.90
LLMs	0.62	0.68	0.83	0.80	0.81	0.72	0.79	0.78	0.62

Comprehensiveness DeepCRCEval's second advantage is its ability to offer a holistic evaluation. Unlike previous studies that could not elucidate why their methods were superior using text similarity metrics, DeepCRCEval, by incorporating domain-specific criteria, sheds light on the strengths and weaknesses of different models, providing a more rounded assessment.

Efficacy of LLM Evaluators Integrating LLMs as evaluators aims to enhance automation and minimize cost.

Efficiency To demonstrate the efficiency of LLM evaluators compared to human evaluators, we analyzed the average time and cost per case. Human evaluators were paid $10 per hour, while LLM evaluations were costed based on API charges ($0.03 per 1000 input tokens, $0.06 per 1000 output tokens). Table 4 contrasts the average time and cost for both single comment evaluations and comparative performance analyses. The results underscore the significant reduction in time and cost achieved with LLM evaluators.

Effectiveness We utilized the Inter-class Correlation Coefficient (ICC) to gauge the concordance between LLM and human evaluators, setting the average human scores as the reference. Table 5 details their agreements across various evaluation aspects. Specifically, for each quality metric, two coefficients are reported: one represents the agreement between human evaluators and the reference scores (Human vs. Reference), and the other captures the agreement between LLM outputs and the reference scores (LLM vs. Reference). Despite a marginally lower agreement in some areas, the LLM evaluators achieved high concordance (above 0.75) in aspects like Explanation Clarity, Problem Identification, Actionability, Specificity, and Contextual Adequacy. In aspects where LLM and human evaluators diverged, we observed distinct scoring tendencies. For example, humans were prone to extreme ratings in Readability and Relevance, while LLMs offered more evenly distributed scores. LLMs also considered grammatical and syntactic factors in Brevity, unlike humans who focused on content length and relevance.

> **Response to RQ2:** DeepCRCEval enhances the discrimination and comprehensiveness of evaluations. Employing LLMs as evaluators significantly reduces costs while maintaining a commendable level of reliability.

6.2   RQ3. Results for Baselines by DeepCRCEval

Utilizing DeepCRCEval, as delineated in Section 5.1, we reassessed the quality of comments generated by different CRCGs. The scoring and ranking outcomes from both evaluator types were averaged to derive final results.

Scoring The scoring results, presented in the first part of Table 6, demonstrate a notable superiority of our newly proposed baseline, LLM-Reviewer, across almost all evaluation aspects. This performance advantage is attributed to LLM-Reviewer's direct alignment with the objectives of the code review task, guided by specific quality criteria. In contrast, previous methods, steered by indirect text similarity metrics, often underperformed in several aspects, failing to achieve holistic excellence in comment quality.

Table 6. Average Scoring results by DeepCRCEval (both human and LLM evaluators).

Method Name	Scoring (1-10, Higher = Better) (H. represents Humans and M. represents LLMs)																	
	C1		C2		C3		C4		C5		C6		C7		C8		C9	
	H.	M.	H.	M.	H.	M.	H.	M.	H.	M.	H.	M.	H.	M.	H.	M.	H.	M.
Tufano	8.33	6.36	4.97	3.65	1.40	3.44	1.87	3.35	2.03	3.54	1.87	3.27	2.13	3.57	2.13	4.26	8.87	8.16
CommentFinder	8.27	6.52	2.23	2.77	1.43	2.76	1.27	2.54	1.20	2.71	1.23	2.53	1.30	2.76	1.30	3.43	8.83	8.29
CodeReviewer	7.83	7.13	5.93	3.68	1.00	3.38	2.27	3.29	1.77	3.53	1.90	3.17	2.50	3.54	3.20	4.35	9.50	8.37
AUGER	8.33	4.98	1.93	2.27	1.00	2.16	1.00	2.04	1.13	2.09	1.17	2.04	1.00	2.19	1.07	2.84	9.17	8.43
CCT5	9.63	7.53	3.30	2.90	1.00	2.66	1.23	2.55	1.03	2.60	1.00	2.51	1.23	2.77	1.70	3.79	9.83	9.27
LLM-Reviewer	**9.97**	**9.24**	**10.00**	**9.55**	**9.67**	**9.17**	**9.80**	**9.40**	**9.83**	**9.12**	**9.37**	**8.89**	**9.87**	**9.32**	**9.90**	**9.59**	**9.97**	8.23

Table 7. Average ranking results by DeepCRCEval (both human and LLM evaluators).

	Tufano et al.	CommentFinder	CodeReviewer	AUGER	CCT5	LLM-Reviewer
Humans	2.77	4.77	2.67	5.77	4.03	**1**
LLMs	3.3	4.17	3.33	5.19	4.00	**1**

Ranking The ranking results, depicted in the second part of Table 7, unequivocally place LLM-Reviewer at the top, as acknowledged by both human and LLM evaluators. Following LLM-Reviewer, Tufano and CodeReviewer were closely matched in quality, occupying the second and third positions, respectively. CCT5 was ranked fourth, CommentFinder fifth, and AUGER lagged at the sixth position.

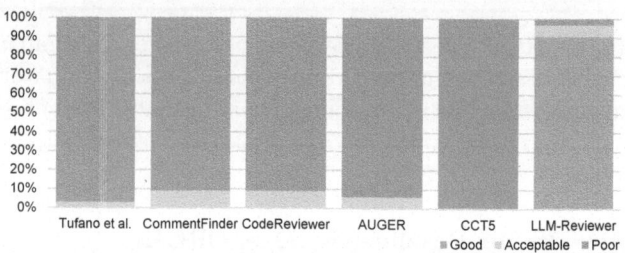

Fig. 5. User feedback ratings distribution for "Good", "Acceptable", and "Poor".

> **Response to RQ3:** LLM-Reviewer, guided by direct task objectives and explicit criteria, excels in generating high-quality review comments, surpassing previous models.

7 Discussion

7.1 Implications

Our findings highlight the limitations of existing text similarity metrics in evaluating code review comment generation. Our proposed framework, DeepCRCE-val, demonstrates superior ability in discriminating between high and low-quality reviews, offering a more comprehensive assessment. Additionally, our new baseline, LLM-Reviewer, guided by direct targets and specific criteria, outperforms previous models.

To assess its practical utility, we tested a web application developed using the Gradio library with 5 industry developers. Users were instructed to input code snippets, and the application provided generated comments from each model. User feedback on total 66 cases, categorized as "Good" (I), "Acceptable" (II), or "Poor" (III), is summarized in Figure 5. The feedback corroborates our findings: comments generated by LLM-Reviewer, noted for their quality and effectiveness, received more "Good" ratings. This user input highlights the potential direction for future research, emphasizing the need to delve into deeper, domain-specific features rather than treating code review as a standard text-to-text task.

> **Implications:** For code review comment generation, researchers should prioritize the fundamental objectives of code reviews instead of focusing merely on textual similarity. Incorporating the specific goals of code reviews directly into the training methodologies seems promising.

7.2 Case Study

For a qualitative comparison, we present two case studies in Table 8—one highlighting a defect and another focusing on code improvement. These cases contrast high-quality comments from LLM-Reviewer with those of lower quality from other baselines. Comments from baseline models often suffer from a lack of relevance or generality, potentially confusing developers. This deficiency may stem from their reliance on indirect text similarity metrics, leading to suboptimal outcomes. Conversely, LLM-Reviewer's comments are notably superior, providing precise, clear explanations of problems, their causes, and suggested solutions, corroborating our previous findings.

Table 8. Case studies comparing baseline comments.

Case 1: DeadLock Issue

```
public class SyncExample {
    private final Object lock1 = new Object();
    private final Object lock2 = new Object();
    public void method1() {
        synchronized(lock1) {
            synchronized(lock2) {
                System.out.println("Lock1 then Lock2");
            }
        }
    }
    public void method2() {
        synchronized(lock2) {
            synchronized(lock1) {
                System.out.println("Lock2 then Lock1");
            }
        }
    }
}
```

Source	Comment
Tufano et al.	This is exactly the same class, you can't have two methods, one with the same name, and another with the same name.
CommentFinder	May want to get rid of this System.out running loose here in this test case.
CodeReviewer	Why is this needed?
AUGER	yes i think we should have this in the hoosier state lock block
CCT5	Remove this line.
LLM-Reviewer	In "SyncExample" class, "method1" and "method2" obtain locks in a different order. If they are called concurrently, it can lead to a deadlock where each method is waiting for the other to release a lock. Always acquire locks in the same order to prevent deadlocks.

Case 2: Map Performance Issue

```
public void processMap(Map<String, Integer> map, String key) {
    if (map.containsKey(key)) {
        Integer value = map.get(key);
        System.out.println(value);
    }
}
```

Source	Comment
Tufano et al.	Can we make this a logger?
CommentFinder	> I would rather use the first version and avoid the cast to M. Is that OK? Please cast (M) map.put(key, value). We save an additional Tuple instance which scales for many calls. I see our collections as low-level, they should be as performant as possible. A cast is fast.
CodeReviewer	Remove this file, its irrelevant to this PR.
AUGER	why do we need this
CCT5	Please remove this.
LLM-Reviewer	The "processMap" method performs two lookups: one for "containsKey" and another for "get". This is inefficient. Instead, use "get" directly and check if the result is null. It performs the operation in a single lookup, improving efficiency.

Case Study: LLM-Reviewer's high-quality comments deliver concise, clear explanations of issues, their roots, and potential fixes, contrasting with the irrelevant or generic comments from other models.

7.3 Threats to Validity

Several factors are crucial for assessing the validity of our findings. Firstly, our selection of large language models (LLMs), specifically GPT-4, was a deliberate decision. For DeepCRCEval, GPT-4 was chosen to emulate human evaluators because of its advanced capabilities. Likewise, GPT-4 served as the foundation for LLM-Reviewer due to its status as a leading and representative LLM. Another consideration is the focus on the Java programming language for our code review task. While Java has specific characteristics that differ from other languages, it is the most commonly used language in prior research, making it suitable for comparison. Finally, the scope of our reevaluation needs acknowledgment. We used graduate computer science students as proxies for actual developers in human evaluations. These students have significant programming experience, making them a reasonable approximation. Additionally, due to the high costs of manual analysis, our study covered a relatively small sample size. To mitigate this, we used LLM evaluators for broader analysis and compared the concordance between human and LLM evaluations, ensuring a thorough and robust assessment.

However, using LLMs to evaluate LLMs still potentially introduces bias, which is why we also used human evaluators. The introduction of LLM-Reviewer aims to highlight the significant room for improvement in existing CRCGs. The results show that they score particularly low compared to LLM-Reviewer, a discrepancy even more pronounced when by humans, which cannot be wholly attributed to bias.

8 Related Work

The automation and evaluation of machine code review comments are recent developments, aligning with longstanding research interests in assessing the quality of human-written comments. Traditional evaluations predominantly focused on the "usefulness" of comments. Early methods, exemplified by Bosu et al. [3], employed decision trees and hand-crafted rules to categorize comments as "useful" or "not useful", often based on subsequent code modifications or "wontfix" labels. Rahman et al. [23] refined this approach by emphasizing comments' "change-triggering" characteristics, incorporating textual content and reviewer experience into their predictive models. Hasan et al. [9] expanded this further by integrating additional features from review contexts and reviewer backgrounds. A notable advancement came with Yang et al. [33], who introduced a BERT-based scoring system across four dimensions (emotion, question, evaluation, and suggestion), marking a shift towards a more detailed and explanatory evaluation, beyond extensive feature engineering.

However, Yang et al.'s methodology diverges from ours in two key respects. First, their model assesses human-generated comments, whereas our focus is on **machine**-generated comments aimed at enhancing code review quality. This necessitates a more granular evaluation, emphasizing clarity and effectiveness in addressing actual defects or improvements, as detailed in Section 2.1. Second, our approach demands a deeper evaluation, analyzing the interaction between **code**

and comment pairs, while previous research primarily targeted comments alone. Without including code as a target, it is impossible to judge perspectives related to actual issues in the code. Finally, we utilize the emergent abilities of **LLMs** like in-context learning. Earlier models like BERT lacked the depth required for such analysis, but recent LLM advancements, especially GPT-4, have shown near-human comprehension in understanding both code and language. Hence, DeepCRCEval incorporates LLM evaluators to complement human evaluation, balancing reliability with reduced time and cost.

9   Conclusion

This study challenges the prevailing evaluation methodology for CRCGs, arguing that text similarity metrics like BLEU and ROUGE-L are inadequate due to the questionable quality and validity of benchmark comments. As a solution, we introduced DeepCRCEval, a framework directly addressing developers' concerns, and LLM-Reviewer, a lightweight, training-free baseline for CRCG evaluation. LLM-Reviewer, guided by clear and direct task goals and criteria, contrasts with methods relying on text similarity for training.

Our empirical findings suggest that CRCGs might overstate their improvements when focused on text similarity metrics, often producing comments that are irrelevant or overly generic. In contrast, LLM-Reviewer demonstrates the ability to provide clear, concise explanations of issues, their causes, and potential solutions, even without specific training. DeepCRCEval offers superior discrimination and comprehensiveness compared to previous metrics, and significantly reduces costs while maintaining reliable evaluation standards when employing LLMs as alternative evaluators. Our work lays a foundation for task-specific evaluations for code review comment generation, and highlights that future researchers should not neglect the original objectives of the code review.

Acknowledgments. This work was supported by the National Key Research and Development Program of China (No. 2023YFB3307202) and the Alliance of International Science Organizations Collaborative Research Program (No. ANSO-CR-KP-2022-03).

References

1. Bacchelli, A., Bird, C.: Expectations, outcomes, and challenges of modern code review. In: 2013 35th International Conference on Software Engineering (ICSE). pp. 712–721 (2013). https://doi.org/10.1109/ICSE.2013.6606617
2. Bosu, A., Carver, J.C., Bird, C., Orbeck, J., Chockley, C.: Process aspects and social dynamics of contemporary code review: Insights from open source development and industrial practice at microsoft. IEEE Transactions on Software Engineering **43**(1), 56–75 (2017). https://doi.org/10.1109/TSE.2016.2576451
3. Bosu, A., Greiler, M., Bird, C.: Characteristics of useful code reviews: An empirical study at microsoft. In: 2015 IEEE/ACM 12th Working Conference on Mining Software Repositories. pp. 146–156 (2015). https://doi.org/10.1109/MSR.2015.21

4. Creswell, J.W., Creswell, J.D.: Research design: Qualitative, quantitative, and mixed methods approaches. Sage publications (2017)
5. Dalkey, N., Helmer, O.: An experimental application of the delphi method to the use of experts. Management science **9**(3), 458–467 (1963)
6. Dubois, Y., Li, X., Taori, R., Zhang, T., Gulrajani, I., Ba, J., Guestrin, C., Liang, P., Hashimoto, T.B.: Alpacafarm: A simulation framework for methods that learn from human feedback. arXiv preprint arXiv:2305.14387 (2023)
7. Fagan, M.: Design and code inspections to reduce errors in program development. In: Software pioneers, pp. 575–607. Springer (2002)
8. Gupta, A., Sundaresan, N.: Intelligent code reviews using deep learning. In: Proceedings of the 24th ACM SIGKDD International Conference on Knowledge Discovery and Data Mining (KDD'18) Deep Learning Day (2018)
9. Hasan, M., Iqbal, A., Islam, M.R.U., Rahman, A.I., Bosu, A.: Using a balanced scorecard to identify opportunities to improve code review effectiveness: An industrial experience report. Empirical Softw. Engg. **26**(6) (nov 2021). https://doi.org/10.1007/s10664-021-10038-w, https://doi.org/10.1007/s10664-021-10038-w
10. Hong, Y., Tantithamthavorn, C., Thongtanunam, P., Aleti, A.: Commentfinder: a simpler, faster, more accurate code review comments recommendation. In: Proceedings of the 30th ACM Joint European Software Engineering Conference and Symposium on the Foundations of Software Engineering. pp. 507–519 (2022)
11. Hua, Z.H., Yang, L., Lu, J.Y., Zuo, C.: Survey on code review automation research. Ruan Jian Xue Bao/Journal of Software **35**(7), 3265–3290 (2024) (in Chinese). http://www.jos.org.cn/1000-9825/7112.htm
12. Kononenko, O., Baysal, O., Godfrey, M.W.: Code review quality: How developers see it. In: 2016 IEEE/ACM 38th International Conference on Software Engineering (ICSE). pp. 1028–1038 (2016). https://doi.org/10.1145/2884781.2884840
13. Li, D., Jiang, B., Huang, L., Beigi, A., Zhao, C., Tan, Z., Bhattacharjee, A., Jiang, Y., Chen, C., Wu, T., et al.: From generation to judgment: Opportunities and challenges of llm-as-a-judge. arXiv preprint arXiv:2411.16594 (2024)
14. Li, L., Yang, L., Jiang, H., Yan, J., Luo, T., Hua, Z., Liang, G., Zuo, C.: Auger: automatically generating review comments with pre-training models. In: Proceedings of the 30th ACM Joint European Software Engineering Conference and Symposium on the Foundations of Software Engineering. pp. 1009–1021 (2022)
15. Li, X., Zhang, T., Dubois, Y., Taori, R., Gulrajani, I., Guestrin, C., Liang, P., Hashimoto, T.B.: Alpacaeval: An automatic evaluator of instruction-following models. https://github.com/tatsu-lab/alpaca_eval (2023)
16. Li, Z., Lu, S., Guo, D., Duan, N., Jannu, S., Jenks, G., Majumder, D., Green, J., Svyatkovskiy, A., Fu, S., et al.: Automating code review activities by large-scale pre-training. In: Proceedings of the 30th ACM Joint European Software Engineering Conference and Symposium on the Foundations of Software Engineering. pp. 1035–1047 (2022)
17. Lin, B., Wang, S., Liu, Z., Liu, Y., Xia, X., Mao, X.: Cct5: A code-change-oriented pre-trained model. In: Proceedings of the 38th IEEE/ACM International Conference on Automated Software Engineering (2023)
18. Lin, C.Y.: Rouge: A package for automatic evaluation of summaries. In: Text summarization branches out. pp. 74–81 (2004)
19. Lindlof, T.R., Taylor, B.C.: Qualitative communication research methods. Sage publications (2017)
20. Lu, J., Li, Z., Shen, C., Yang, L., Zuo, C.: Exploring the impact of code review factors on the code review comment generation. Automated Software Engineering **31**(2), 71 (2024)

21. Lu, J., Yu, L., Li, X., Yang, L., Zuo, C.: Llama-reviewer: Advancing code review automation with large language models through parameter-efficient fine-tuning. In: 2023 IEEE 34th International Symposium on Software Reliability Engineering (ISSRE). pp. 647–658. IEEE (2023)

22. Papineni, K., Roukos, S., Ward, T., Zhu, W.J.: Bleu: a method for automatic evaluation of machine translation. In: Proceedings of the 40th annual meeting of the Association for Computational Linguistics. pp. 311–318 (2002)

23. Rahman, M.M., Roy, C.K., Kula, R.G.: Predicting usefulness of code review comments using textual features and developer experience. In: 2017 IEEE/ACM 14th International Conference on Mining Software Repositories (MSR). pp. 215–226 (2017). https://doi.org/10.1109/MSR.2017.17

24. Ray: Aviary: Study stochastic parrots in the wild. https://github.com/ray-project/aviary (2023)

25. Rigby, P.C., Bird, C.: Convergent contemporary software peer review practices. In: Proceedings of the 2013 9th joint meeting on foundations of software engineering. pp. 202–212 (2013)

26. Rigby, P.C., German, D.M., Cowen, L., Storey, M.A.: Peer review on open-source software projects: Parameters, statistical models, and theory. ACM Transactions on Software Engineering and Methodology (TOSEM) **23**(4), 1–33 (2014)

27. Rigby, P.C., German, D.M., Storey, M.A.: Open source software peer review practices: a case study of the apache server. In: Proceedings of the 30th international conference on Software engineering. pp. 541–550 (2008)

28. Sadowski, C., Söderberg, E., Church, L., Sipko, M., Bacchelli, A.: Modern code review: a case study at google. In: Proceedings of the 40th International Conference on Software Engineering: Software Engineering in Practice. pp. 181–190 (2018)

29. Shan, Q., Sukhdeo, D., Huang, Q., Rogers, S., Chen, L., Paradis, E., Rigby, P.C., Nagappan, N.: Using nudges to accelerate code reviews at scale. In: Proceedings of the 30th ACM Joint European Software Engineering Conference and Symposium on the Foundations of Software Engineering. pp. 472–482 (2022)

30. Siow, J.K., Gao, C., Fan, L., Chen, S., Liu, Y.: Core: Automating review recommendation for code changes. In: 2020 IEEE 27th International Conference on Software Analysis, Evolution and Reengineering (SANER). pp. 284–295. IEEE (2020)

31. Tufano, R., Masiero, S., Mastropaolo, A., Pascarella, L., Poshyvanyk, D., Bavota, G.: Using pre-trained models to boost code review automation. In: Proceedings of the 44th International Conference on Software Engineering. pp. 2291–2302 (2022)

32. Tufano, R., Pascarella, L., Tufano, M., Poshyvanyk, D., Bavota, G.: Towards automating code review activities. In: 2021 IEEE/ACM 43rd International Conference on Software Engineering (ICSE). pp. 163–174. IEEE (2021)

33. Yang, L., Xu, J., Zhang, Y., Zhang, H., Bacchelli, A.: Evacrc: Evaluating code review comments. In: Proceedings of the 31st ACM Joint European Software Engineering Conference and Symposium on the Foundations of Software Engineering. p. 275–287. ESEC/FSE 2023, Association for Computing Machinery, New York, NY, USA (2023). https://doi.org/10.1145/3611643.3616245, https://doi.org/10.1145/3611643.3616245

34. Yang, X., Kula, R.G., Yoshida, N., Iida, H.: Mining the modern code review repositories: A dataset of people, process and product. In: Proceedings of the 13th International Conference on Mining Software Repositories. pp. 460–463 (2016)

35. Zheng, L., Chiang, W.L., Sheng, Y., Zhuang, S., Wu, Z., Zhuang, Y., Lin, Z., Li, Z., Li, D., Xing, E., et al.: Judging llm-as-a-judge with mt-bench and chatbot arena. Advances in Neural Information Processing Systems (2023)

VOCE: A Virtual On-Call Engineer for Automated Alert Incident Analysis Using a Large Language Model

Jia Chen[1] , Xiaolei Chen[1] , Jie Shi[1] , Peng Wang[1(✉)] ,
and Wei Wang[1]

Fudan University, Shanghai, China
pengwang5@fudan.edu.cn

Abstract. In a service system, operations engineers generally deploy numerous monitoring mechanisms in system components to detect anomalies caused by system faults and generate alerts, also known as alarms, that record the phenomenon of anomalies. Due to the topological relationships between system components, a system fault in a system component may affect other components and result in various local anomalies and generate multiple alerts across different components. Therefore, to facilitate troubleshooting, alerts of the same system fault are usually correlated into one group, called alert incident. However, although there are existing approaches that can automatically correlate alerts for operations engineers, analyzing alert incidents still rely on manual work. In this paper, we propose an approach, VOCE (Virtual On-Call Engineer). Using the emerging capabilities of a large language model, VOCE can automatically comprehend the anomaly information described by alerts and emulate the process of operations engineers analyzing an alert incident. Extensive experiments conducted on real alert incidents and two popular large language models demonstrate the effectiveness and efficiency of VOCE in automatically analyzing alert incidents.

Keywords: Alert Incident Analysis· Anomalies · Industrial Cases · Large Language Model · AI Supported Operations.

1 Introduction

In an online service system, faults are usually inevitable due to the large scale and complexity of the system [30]. There are many factors that cause system faults, such as insufficient memory, hardware problem, configuration error, and software bugs [58]. System faults can damage system availability and reduce customer satisfaction, resulting in a huge economic loss for organizations [6]. Therefore, in order to detect or even predict system faults, operations engineers usually monitor various aspects of the service system, such as logs [19,14,32,49], KPIs [21,57,37,8], and traces [58,31,33]. When the monitoring data are abnormal, the corresponding alerts, also referred to as alarms, recording local

© The Author(s) 2025
A. Boronat and G. Fraser (Eds.): FASE 2025, LNCS 15693, pp.65–88, 2025.
https://doi.org/10.1007/978-3-031-90900-9_4

anomalies of the system, will be generated. Therefore, according to alerts, operations engineers can diagnose system faults straightforwardly.

The components of a service system are interconnected through topological relationships; therefore, a fault in one component can impact the functionality of others, resulting in various local anomalies and generating multiple alerts across different components [9]. To reduce the workload of operations engineers, numerous research efforts [52,5,9,10] have been dedicated to link alerts of the same fault into a group, which is also called an alert incident.

However, these methods can only help operations engineers link alerts and obtain alert incidents and cannot replace their role in conducting a thorough incident analysis. Due to the need for strong contextual understanding and logical reasoning abilities, the analysis of alert incidents still relies extensively on manual work. Operations engineers leverage anomaly information recorded in alerts in conjunction with experiential knowledge to analyze alert incidents. The process of analyzing an alert incident typically involves three main steps.

1. Comprehending anomalies recorded by alerts.
2. Inferring the propagation process of the anomalies.
3. Identifying the originating alert, which records the originating anomaly that triggers other anomalies.

Table 1 illustrates an alert incident where the first alert indicates that the call to microservice A on host "21.99.218.233" failed. The second alert shows a drop in the success rate of microservice B accessing microservice A's interface. The third alert reports the unexpected shutdown of host "21.99.218.233". In this example, the originating anomaly of the system fault is the unexpected shutdown of host "21.99.218.233", which triggered the anomaly of microservice A when invoked by "11.99.218.200". Additionally, microservice B, deployed on "11.99.218.235", encountered an anomaly while attempting to call microservice A. Therefore, the third alert is the originating alert.

Table 1. An example of alert incident

Timestamp	Source	Content
2023-05-06 12:00	11.99.218.200	Microservice (A) call failed, IP: 21.99.218.233.
2023-05-06 12:01	11.99.218.235	The success rate of microservice (B) accessing the interface of microservice (A) $\leq 75\%$.
2023-05-06 12:09	21.99.218.233	Error: 21.99.218.233 shut down 637 seconds ago.

Nowadays, with the ever-increasing scale of parameters and data in pre-trained models, large language models (LLMs for short) with tens or even hundreds of billions of parameters have emerged with capabilities beyond conventional models[47,36]. These capabilities include in-context learning, instruction learning, and chain of thought (step-by-step reasoning)[55].

In-context learning capability allows large language models to generate expected output without requiring additional training or gradient update with natural language instruction and/or several task demonstrations[4]. The instruction learning capability empowers large language models to follow task instructions in input text without using explicit examples[39,35,46]. The chain of thought or step-by-step reasoning capability empowers large language models to solve complex tasks using the prompt mechanism that involves intermediate reasoning steps to obtain the final answer[55,48].

The emergent capabilities enable large language models to automatically analyze and infer the expected result based on the input text provided. Therefore, in this paper, we take the lead in employing large language models to emulate the process of operations engineers analyzing alert incidents.

We first use real alert incidents to investigate the key alert information that operations experts take into account when analyzing alert incidents. Then, according to the investigation result, we propose a large language model-based method, VOCE (Virtual On-Call Engineer), to emulate the process of operations experts analyzing alert incidents. More specifically, for an alert incident, VOCE can comprehend the local anomalies recorded by each alert within the incident, infer the propagation of the anomalies, and suggest the alert recording the most likely originating anomaly that triggers other anomalies.

The contributions of this paper are as follows.

1. We use real incident data to investigate the analysis process carried out by operations experts regarding alert incidents. Based on the result of the investigation, we summarize the key alert information that operations experts take into account when analyzing an alert incident.
2. We introduce an automated method, VOCE (Virtual On-Call Engineer), which adopts a large language model to automatically analyze an alert incident. VOCE emulates the process of operations experts analyzing alert incidents, enabling a large language model to comprehend alerts and automatically suggest the alert recording most likely originating anomaly that triggers other anomalies.
3. We conducted an experimental study to evaluate the performance of VOCE based on real-world alert incidents. Experimental results demonstrate the effectiveness of VOCE in automatically analyzing alert incidents.

2 Related Work

For alert analysis, there are many studies with different purposes. Some focus on predicting system faults [11,53], and some focus on linking alerts of the same system fault [29,52,5,10,9].

Studies for system fault prediction focus on predicting system faults according to signal alerts. Chen et al. propose AirAlert [11] to predict outage faults before they actually occur to minimize service downtime and ensure high system availability. Specifically, AirAlert analyzes the relationships between outage faults and alerting signals by a Bayesian network and predicts outage faults using a robust gradient-boosting tree-based classification approach. Zhao et al. [53] propose eWarn to online predict whether a system fault will occur in the near future based on alerts. Specifically, eWarn first extracts some textual and statistical features from alerts to represent omen alert patterns for a system fault and then builds a classification model to predict the occurrence of a system fault. While proactive fault prediction can help operations engineers anticipate potential system issues, the responsibility for alert analysis still resides with the engineers themselves. Thus, in this paper, we present an approach that aims to reduce the workload of operations engineers in alert analysis.

The studies for alert linking focus on linking alerts triggered by the same system fault into the same incident. Lin et al. [29] try to link alerts by alert contents to gain some insight into a system fault. Zhao et al. [52] propose AlertStorm to detect alert storm faults, which lead to overwhelming numbers of alerts in a short time, and link alerts of alert storm faults according to alert contents and system topology. Both the two approaches adopt Jaccard to measure textual similarity between alert contents. LiDAR [10] and OAS [5] employ neural networks to mine common semantic information between alerts, thereby linking alerts of the same system fault. Nevertheless, LiDAR additionally incorporates the topological relationships between system components associated with alerts, while OAS further takes into account the behavioral information of alerts. In addition, Chen et al. presents DyAlert [9], a dynamic graph neural network-based approach to linking alerts. These existing approaches primarily rely on statistical features or train neural networks using labeled data to learn potential relationships between alerts. However, their criteria may differ from those used by operations engineers during manual analysis, which can lead to inaccurate results. In this paper, the proposed approach leverages a large language model to simulate the alert analysis process of operations engineers. As a result, it achieves more accurate and expert-consistent outcomes.

For large language models, they have been shown to be effective for various tasks. Their success can be highly attributed to their ability to understand the intentions of users and complete tasks in a zero-shot or a few-shot fashion [4,39,35]. Due to these emergent abilities, several frameworks have been proposed to motivate large language models to reason before reaching the final conclusions. Kojima et al. [26] and Wei et al. [48] prompt large language models to automatically write step-by-step solutions to solve math problems and other reasoning tasks. Gao et al. [18] apply this technique in writing Python programs. Chen et al. [7] and Shinn et al. [40] instruct large language models to self-debug their generated code. In the field of system operations, there are studies [3] indicating the potentials of large language models, but none of them fully exploits the inherent reasoning abilities of large language models or leverages prior knowledge for alert incident analysis.

3   Background

In this section, we define alerts and alert incidents, then explore key information factors considered in alert analysis, and finally discuss the current applications and potential of large language models in system operations and maintenance.

3.1   Alert

An alert usually has three basic attributes: timestamp, source, and content, which are described below.

1. **Timestamp**: The time at which the alert is generated.
2. **Source**: The system component where the alert is generated, which is usually the IP of the system component.
3. **Content**: The text that records an anomaly of the system component.

An alert incident is a group of alerts that are caused by the same system fault. There are some existing studies [5,52,10,9,29] to automatically link alerts into incidents. Some companies also have their own specific alert linking approaches. These approaches usually link alerts by measuring the semantic similarity of alert contents or the topological distance between alert sources. Since the research goal of this paper is to analyze incidents instead of linking alerts, we will not go into the details of linking alerts.

In this paper, for an alert incident, we formally define it as $I = [a_1, a_2, \cdots, a_n]$, where a_i $(1 \leq i \leq n)$ is an alert in the incident. Moreover, $a_i = (t_i, s_i, w_i, e_i)$, where t_i is the timestamp, s_i is the alert source, w_i is the alert content, and e_i is the template id of a_i parsed by Section 4.1, which represents the type of anomaly recorded by the alert.

3.2   Key Alert Information

In addition to the above three basic attributes, some other inherent or deduced information factors are also considered in the process of alert incident analysis. To figure out how operations engineers analyze alerts, drawing from previous studies [53,54,41] and insights from operations engineers at Company A, we summarize the following four types of information factors that are typically taken into account during alert analysis.

1. **Order**: The chronological order of an alert in an incident according to timestamps. It may reflect the propagation sequence of anomalies corresponding to the same system fault.
2. **System Layer**: The infrastructure layer to which the anomaly of an alert belongs within a system. The structure of a service system is often divided into different layers [12], such as database layer, network layer, application layer, etc. System components in higher layers usually rely on the functionality of system components in lower layers during task execution. Typically, anomalies in lower-layer components can impact the proper functioning of higher-layer components. For example, a network connection anomaly at the network layer may lead to a service execution failure at the application layer.
3. **Impact Scope**: The impact scope of the anomaly indicated by an alert. For example, a single microservice or the entire service system.
4. **Severity**: The extent of damage to system services caused by the anomaly of an alert. Generally, more severe alerts result in greater damage.

In this paper, we investigate alert incidents from a real service system of Company A over a one-month period (2022/09/01 00:00 to 2022/09/30 23:59), which includes 10,680 alerts and 827 incidents. We enlist two operations engineers to retrospectively analyze an alert incident and label the originating alert, which indicates the most likely originating anomaly that triggers other anomalies in the incident. If a consensus cannot be reached, a third expert will be engaged to review the annotations, with the minority deferring to the majority opinion. Then, for each incident, we assess whether the labeled originating alert has the first order, the lowest system layer, the broadest impact scope, and the highest severity. Table 2 demonstrates experimental results, which statistics the proportion of incidents with the highest priority of originating alerts for each type of information factor.

Table 2. Statistical results for key information factors

Information Factor	Proportion (%)
Order	45.34
System Layer	**94.56**
Impact Scope	**95.16**
Severity	**93.35**

Based on Table 2, we can find that, for the alert incidents of Company A over a one-month period, the originating alerts for more than 93% of incidents have the lowest system layers, the broadest impact scope, and the highest severity. Additionally, only about 45% of the originating alerts are the first generated. Therefore, the experimental findings reveal that system layer, impact scope, and severity are significant information factors in assessing whether an alert indicates the originating anomaly of a system fault. Nonetheless, the order of an originating alert does not necessarily precede other alerts. This is because, in a real production environment, due to varying sensitivities in monitoring mechanisms for different anomalies, originating anomalies may not activate monitoring mechanisms and generate alerts first.

3.3   Large Language Models

The Large Language Model (LLM) possesses the ability to comprehend provided textual information from users and systematically analyze this information based on user instructions, thereby progressively deriving reasonable outputs [55]. Such large language models have demonstrated notable achievements across various domains, such as chat bots [23], search engines [22], software testing [25], and system maintenance [3].

The study of Microsoft [3] shows that, when provided with a phenomenon description of a system fault, large language models can effectively infer a plausible fault reason. However, the fundamental research objective of this study differs from our work. In this study, the model is fed a pre-summarized description of a system fault rather than raw alert data. Its output is a speculative explanation of a potential fault reason, rather than a detailed suggestion of the originating alert and its source. Nonetheless, existing study demonstrates the potential application of large models in the field of system operations.

According to Section 3.2, operations engineers, when analyzing an alert incident, tend to extract several specific information factors from alerts. Therefore, in this paper, with the emergent abilities of LLMs, we use LLMs to extract these factors and to emulate real operations engineers in: comprehending anomalies recorded by alerts; inferring the propagation process of the anomalies; suggesting the originating alert.

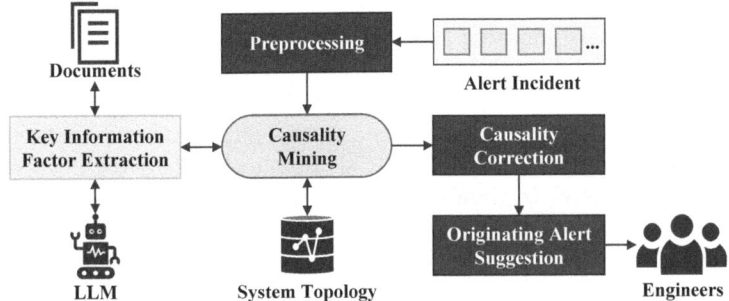

Fig. 1. The overview of VOCE (Virtual On-Call Engineer).

4   Approach

The objective of VOCE (Virtual On-Call Engineer) is to utilize the emergent capabilities of large language models [55] to emulate how operations engineers analyze alert incidents, thereby enhancing operational efficiency. Fig. 1 shows the overview of VOCE. It first preprocesses each alert in an incident as introduced in Section 4.1. Then, according to the investigation in Section 3.2, in key information factor extraction, VOCE utilizes a large language model to extract key information factors from alerts.

In causality mining, VOCE analyzes the propagation process of system faults underlying an alert incident by examining the topological relationships between different system components. It is important to note that while these relationships may be directional in some systems, the direction of fault propagation does not necessarily align with the direction of the topological relationships among the components

Fig. 2 shows a toy example. The topological relationship between "source 1" and "source 2" is directional. "Source 1", a virtual machine, is deployed on "source 2", a physical machine. Both "fault 1" and "fault 2" impact "source 1" and "source 2". However, these two faults propagate in opposite directions between

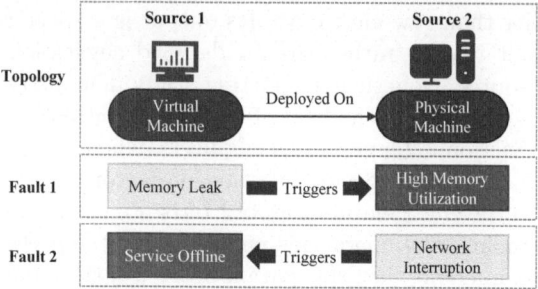

Fig. 2. A toy example of system fault propagation.

the two sources. The originating anomaly of "fault 1" is the memory leak anomaly of "source 1", which triggers the high memory utilization anomaly of "source 2". Conversely, the originating anomaly of "fault 2" is the network interruption anomaly of "source 2", which triggers the service offline anomaly of "source 1".

Therefore, in causality mining, VOCE combines system topology data and key information factors to mine the causalities between anomalies of different system components. In causality correction, VOCE further employs statistical information to validate the extracted causalities and correct the inaccurate ones. Finally, in originating alert suggestion, for an alert incident, based on previous analysis results, VOCE suggests the alert which records the originating anomaly that triggers other anomalies in an incident, called originating alert.

4.1   Preprocessing

Alert content, which records the anomaly of the system component, commonly consists of two parts, variable parameters and invariant keywords [20]. Invariant keywords describe the phenomenon of the anomaly detected by a detection mechanism, and variable parameters record some system metrics, such as CPU usage and memory usage. The text composed of invariant keywords is also called the alert template [20]. For example, in Table 1, the template of the second alert is "The success rate of microservice ($<*>$) accessing the interface of microservice ($<*>$) $\leq <*>$%", where "$<*>$" is the placeholder for a variable parameter.

Thus, alerts belonging to the same template record the same type of system anomaly. To assist an LLM distinguish between different types of anomalies, we first tokenize alert contents, filter out variable parameters, and then derive templates from the processed alert contents [20,2,27,13,45]. Since Drain [20] is a widely-used online parser [5,51,19,49], we adopt it to parse templates. After the parsing task, each alert will be assigned a template, which is identified by a unique number, e_i ($1 \leq i \leq n$).

4.2   Key Information Factor Extraction

According to the investigation in Section 3.2, in addition to the basic alert attributes, timestamp, source, and content, there are three key information factors that are typically taken into account during engineers analyzing alert incidents: system layer, impact scope, and severity. In an alert incident, the originating anomaly usually has a lower system layer, broader impact scope, and higher severity than other anomalies recorded by the alerts in the incident.

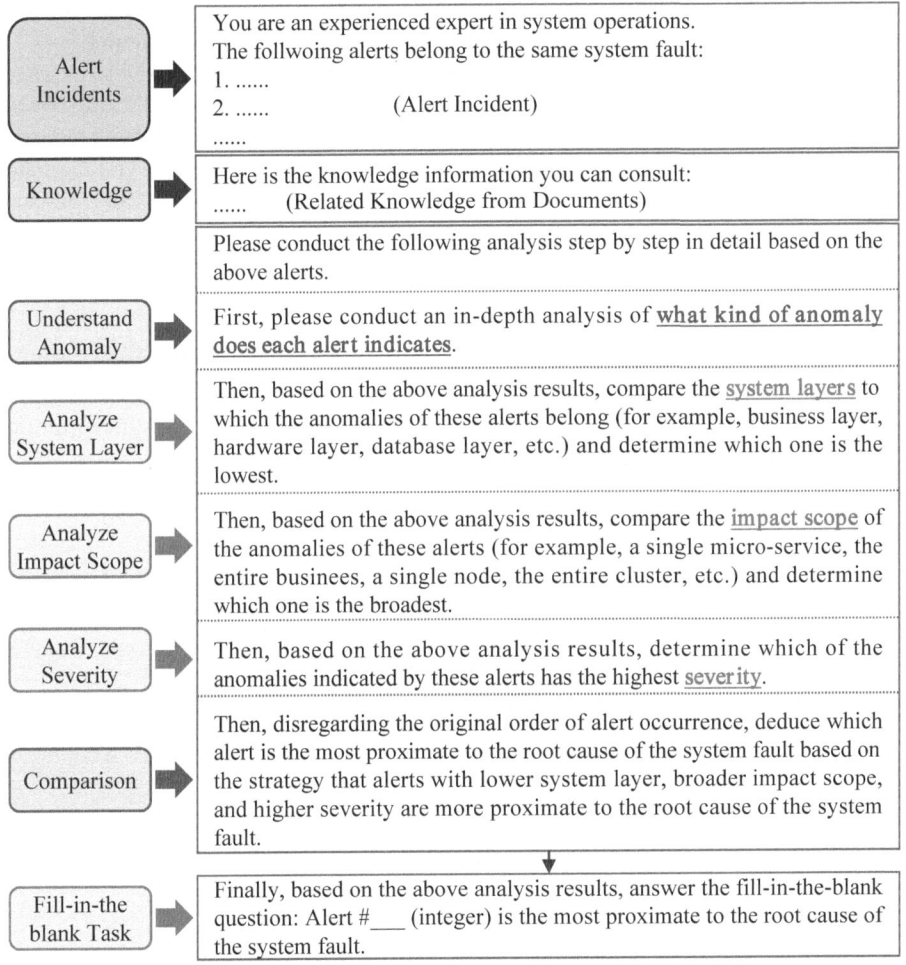

Fig. 3. The process of key information factor extraction.

Therefore, we adopt a large language model to emulate the process of operations engineers when analyzing alert incidents. Fig. 3 shows the chain-of-thought (CoT) prompts for querying the model. Specifically, we first provide an alert incident needed to be analyzed and related knowledge retrieved from documents by semantic similarly [28]. Then, we require the model to understand the anomaly indicated by each alert. Moreover, based on the investigation in Section 3.2, we prompt the model to step-by-step carry out the following analyses [26].

We instruct the model to extract and analyze three key factors for each alert: system layer, impact scope, and severity. Then, we instruct the model to compare and suggest the originating alert based on the finding that the originating anomaly typically has a lower system layer, broader impact scope, and higher severity. Finally, we design a fill-in-the-blank task with a standardized answering structure to facilitate the automated parsing of the output of the model.

Although the prompts in Fig. 3 can instruct a large language model to extract key information factors (system layer, impact scope, and severity) from alerts and suggest the originating alert, we refrain from directly employing the prompts to analyze an alert incident. Because it may be challenging for a large language model to accurately figure out the anomalies recorded by alerts and infer precise causal relationships between the anomalies in a single task.

4.3 Causality Mining

An alert incident can encompass multiple alerts from various sources, complicating the ability of a large language model to identify the originating alert in a single task. To address this challenge, we propose a hierarchical causality mining approach that breaks down alert incident analysis into several sub-tasks, each focusing on fewer alerts and sources.

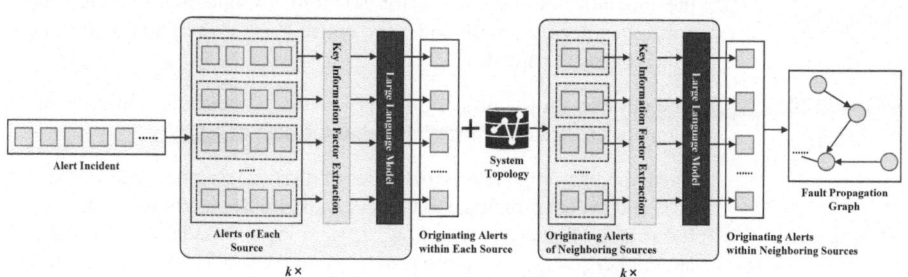

Fig. 4. The process of causality mining.

Usually, within an individual source (system component), various anomaly detection mechanisms are deployed. As a result, in an alert incident, an individual source may contain multiple alerts. Therefore, as shown in Fig. 4, we first focus the perspective of the large language model on an individual source. Based on the prompts in Section 4.2, we can instruct the model to only analyze .the relationship between anomalies within an individual source and suggest the originating alert within the source.

Then, according to the system topology, we mine the causality between the anomalies of each two neighboring sources. We instruct the large language model using the prompts in Section 4.2 to determine which of the originating alerts from the two neighboring sources is more likely to record the true originating anomaly of the underlying system fault. Such a result indicates the propagation direction of the system fault between the two neighboring sources.

To stabilize the inference performance of the large language model, each analysis task is repeated k times [50], and the alert that is selected the most times is the final result. With mined causalities, we can construct a propagation graph, $G = \{E, V\}$, of the system fault underlying a given alert incident. V is the node set that consists of the sources involved in the incident. E is the edge set, in which each edge is a directed edge. For two neighboring sources in G, the propagation direction of the system fault between them is the "opposite" direction of the edge between them.

4.4   Causality Correction

To improve the robustness of VOCE, we validate and refine the propagation directions between sources in the propagation graph, G. Since alerts with the same template record the same type of anomaly, sources containing the same set of alert templates should have similar causal relationships in G.

Therefore, we first classify sources based on the alert templates they contain, grouping sources that share the same set of alert templates into the same type. The classifying result is denoted as $T = [S_1, S_2, S_3, ...S_o]$, where o is the number of types, and S_i $(1 \leq i \leq o)$ is the set of sources that belong to the i-th type. Then, we can calculate the number of edges directed from sources of the i-th type to sources of the j-th type, denoted as $cnt_{i,j} = |(u, v)|u \in S_i, v \in S_j, (u, v) \in E|$. E is the edge set of G. Therefore, if $cnt(i, j) > cnt(j, i)$, the underlying system fault is more likely to propagate from the i-th source type to the j-th source type, and vice versa. Based on such statistical results, we can further correct the directed edges in G that violates the statistical results.

4.5   Originating Alert Suggestion

The fault propagation graph, G, reveals the propagation process of the system fault indicated by a given alert incident. Thus, the source with a higher centrality in G is more likely to be where the originating anomaly occurs. There are many approaches to calculate the centrality of nodes in a graph, such as degree centrality taking the degree of a node as the node centrality [17], betweenness centrality taking the number of shortest paths through a node as the node centrality [16], and closeness centrality taking the sum of the shortest distances from a node to other nodes as the node centrality [15].

In G, for an alert source, its centrality should be determined by the fault propagation relationships in the graph. The direction of the edge between two neighboring sources in G is opposite to the propagation direction of the system fault between the sources. Thus, the more other sources can reach a source through the directed edges in G, the more likely the source is where the originating anamoly occurs.

Eigenvector centrality [34] transmits the centrality score of each node to its neighboring nodes through the edges in a graph, thus a node that can be reached by more other nodes is likely to have a higher centrality score. Therefore, we choose eigenvector centrality [34] to measure the centrality of the sources in G. As a result, we suggest that the originating alert of the source is the alert that records the true originating anomaly.

5   EVALUATION

To evaluate the performance of VOCE, we exploit real-world datasets from a large commercial company A to address the following research questions.

- RQ1: How does VOCE perform in analyzing alert incidents?
- RQ2: How does VOCE perform in terms of efficiency?
- RQ3: How does the parameter k in causality mining affect the performance?

5.1   Experiment Setup

Dataset We exploit real-world alerts from Company A within one month, 2022/09/01 00:00 to 2022/09/30 23:59. A is a large commercial company, providing service for more than a billion users from hundreds of countries. The dataset contains 10680 alerts and 827 incidents. On average, each incident involves 12.91 alerts. For each alert incident, we engaged two operations engineers to conduct a retrospective analysis and label the originating alert. If consensus is not achieved, a third expert will be called in to review the annotations, with the minority deferring to the majority view.

Compared Approaches We utilize two popular large language models, GPT [1,24] and LLaMA [43,44], to evaluate the performance of VOCE.

1. **VOCE-GPT**: We adopt GPT-4o from OpenAI [1,24] as the based model of VOCE. we integrate VOCE with GPT-4o by the OpenAI API service.
2. **VOCE-LLaMA**: Since LLaMA [43,44] is a widely used open-source model for many language task[42,56,38], we also implement VOCE with LLaMA. We choose LLaMA-2 with 13 billion parameters from Meta [44].
3. **CoT-GPT**: We adopt GPT-4o and the chain of thoughts in Section 4.2 to analyze an alert incident step by step.
4. **CoT-LLaMA**: Similar to the above, we adopt LLaMA and the chain of thoughts in Section 4.2 to analyze an alert incident.
5. **Prompt-GPT**: We instruct the model to straightforwardly suggest the originating alert for an alert incident using the prompts in Fig. 5.
6. **Prompt-LLaMA**: Similar to the above, we adopt LLaMA as the base model to straightforwardly suggest the originating alert for an alert incident.

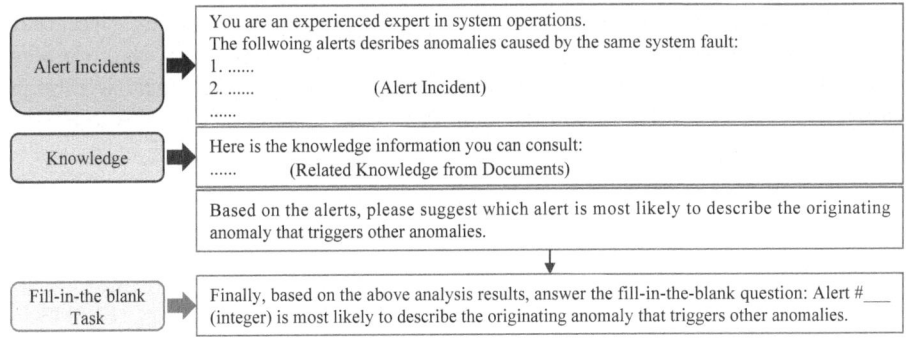

Fig. 5. The prompts of naive approaches.

Implementation All experiments are conducted on a server with 2 * Intel(R) Xeon(R) Platinum 8358 CPU @ 2.60GHz, 1007.0 GB physical memory and 8 Nvidia A40 GPU. Each GPU has 46 GB memory. The OS of the server is Ubuntu 22.04.2 LTS. All experimental approaches are implemented with Python 3.10, and the GPT-4o API service is provided by OpenAI [1,24]. Meta has released three sizes of LLaMA-2 models, 7 billion, 13 billion, and 70 billion parameters [44]. Due to the limitations of computing resources, we choose the largest LLaMA-2 model that our server can support, the model with 13 billion parameters. We deploy a LLaMA-2 model on each GPU in our server. The parameter k in causality mining is set to 5. During experiments, we distribute requests for the LLaMA-2 model evenly across these 8 instances in parallel.

Metrics To evaluate the effectiveness of an experimental approach, we calculate the analyzing accuracy of the approach. Specifically, the accuracy is defined as $\frac{N'}{N}$, where N is the total number of incidents and N' is the number of incidents whose originating alerts are correctly suggested by an experimental approach. In addition, to measure the efficiency of an experimental approach, we calculate the average time cost for the experimental approach to process an alert incident.

5.2   Evaluation Results

To answer the proposed research questions, we evaluate VOCE from three aspects, the effectiveness of VOCE, the efficiency of VOCE, and the impact of the parameter k in causality mining.

RQ1: the effectiveness of VOCE To address RQ1, Table 3 presents the performance of experimental approaches, while Fig. 6 provides a comparison. We can find that, for different base models, VOCE consistently achieves the highest accuracy (>80%), which proves the effectiveness of VOCE. More specifically, for each base model, the accuracy of VOCE is higher than that of the CoT-based approach, while the accuracy of the CoT-based approach is higher than that of the prompt-based approach. Such experimental findings prove that the key alert information we found in Section 4.2 and the hierarchical causality mining strategy we propose in Section 4.3 can effectively instruct the large language model in analyzing an alert incident and suggesting the originating alert.

Table 3. The performance of experimental approaches.

Approach	VOCE		CoT		Prompt	
Model	**GPT**	**LLaMA**	**GPT**	**LLaMA**	**GPT**	**LLaMA**
Accuracy (%)	88.90	81.26	84.19	77.51	81.30	71.58
Time Cost (s)	56.79	279.91	16.96	133.57	2.29	52.89

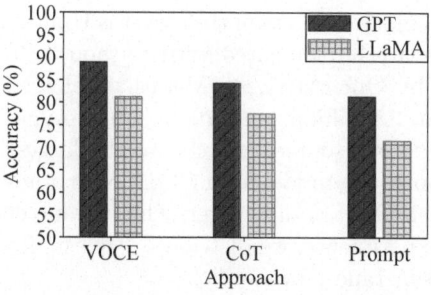

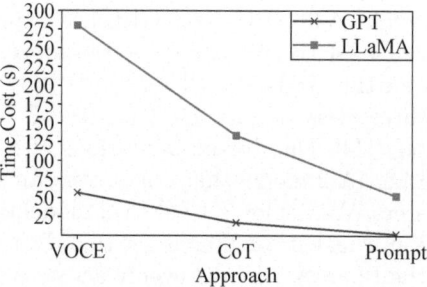

(a) The comparison of effectiveness.   (b) The comparison of efficiency.

Fig. 6. The comparison of the performance of different approaches.

In addition, from Fig. 6(a), we can find that the accuracy of each type of GPT-based approach is higher than that of the same type of LLaMA-based approach. This demonstrates that the commercial GPT-4o model exhibits greater emergent capabilities than LLaMA-2 with 13 billion parameters.

RQ2: the efficiency of VOCE To address RQ2, as shown in Table 3 and Fig. 6(b), we calculate the average time cost for each approach in analyzing an alert incident. We can find that, for different base models, VOCE takes more time to analyze an alert incident than other approaches. This is because the key information extraction and hierarchical causality mining strategy in VOCE require more computation. Nevertheless, the average time cost of VOCE-GPT is less than 1 minute, and the average time cost for VOCE-LLaMA is less than 5 minutes. Moreover, in Company A, operations engineers typically take about 15 minutes to analyze an alert incident. Therefore, the efficiency of VOCE can meet the needs of practical operational tasks.

Moreover, we can also find that the time cost of each type of LLaMA-based approach is more than that of the same type of GPT-based approach. This is because the API service of LLaMA is deployed on 8 GPUs in our experimental environment, and each GPU has an instance of LLaMA model. In our experiments, we distribute the requests for the LLaMA model to these 8 instances as evenly as possible. However, GPT-4o is a commercial model, whose API service is provided by OpenAI, and OpenAI is supposed to have far more computing resources than our experimental environment. Therefore, due to the limitation of computing resources, the time cost of LLaMA-based approaches is greater than that of GPT-based approaches. However, the LLaMA-based approach can still analyze an alert incident in less than five minutes on average, demonstrating the efficiency of our approaches.

RQ3: the impact of k To address RQ3, we evaluate the performance of VOCE under different values of k. We adopt GPT as the base model and vary k from 1 to 10. The result is shown in Fig. 7, where Fig. 7(a) shows the accuracy result and Fig. 7(b) shows the time cost result. For a confidence interval of 5 at a 95% confidence level, we sample 263 incidents to evaluate the impact of k.

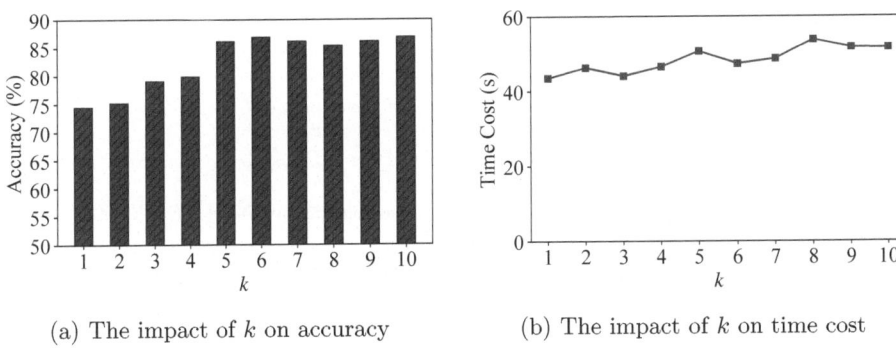

(a) The impact of k on accuracy   (b) The impact of k on time cost

Fig. 7. The impact of k on the performance of VOCE.

From Fig. 7(a), we can find that, as the value of k increases, the accuracy of VOCE also increases at first, and then it gradually stabilizes. This is because a larger k allows VOCE to rely on more analytical results from a large language model for each originating alert suggestion, enhancing the robustness of suggestion results. In addition, as shown in Fig. 7(b), despite some slight fluctuations, the time cost of VOCE does not significantly increase with k. This is because the requests to the service of a large language model in VOCE are parallel. Thus, the time cost of VOCE is not strongly related to k when there are sufficient computing resources to support the service of the model.

Overall, a larger k enables the model to analyze a greater number of outcomes, thereby enhancing the robustness of the final results. However, a larger

k also incurs higher computational costs. In scenarios where the deployment resources are limited, this can lead to increased time costs. Consequently, we recommend that the selection of k should be carefully evaluated based on the available deployment resources and the desired model performance.

5.3   Case Study

Table 4 presents an incident involving an offline fault in a microservice. The alerts from "10.16.141.247" record that microservice A is offline and the call success rate for microservice D is below the threshold. The alerts from "10.16.127.162" record that the call success rate for microservice B is below the threshold, which has affected the service requests from consumer X. The alert from "10.16.150.106" also records a decreased call success rate for microservice C. These three sources belong to the same service system and have interdependent topological relationships. According to expert analysis, the fault of this alert incident stems from the offline of microservice A in "10.16.141.247", which in turn triggers the microservices, B, C and D, to be unable to provide services normally.

Table 4. The alert incident of a microservice offline fault

Timestamp	Source	Content
2023-03-09 22:01	10.16.141.247	Microservice (A) is offline.
2023-03-09 22:02	10.16.127.162	The success rate of the interface to the microservice (B) is below 75%.
2023-03-09 22:03	10.16.150.106	The success rate of the interface to the microservice (C) is below 75%.
2023-03-09 22:04	10.16.141.247	The success rate of the interface to the microservice (D) is below 75%.
2023-03-09 22:04	10.16.127.162	Consumer (X) accessing the microservice (B) interface failed.
2023-03-09 22:05	10.16.127.162	The success rate of the interface in the microservice (B) accessed by the Consumer (X) is below 75%.

Fig. 8 shows the originating alert within each source and the fault propagation graph of the incident, both of which are inferred by VOCE-GPT. The direction of fault propagation is the opposite direction of the edge. We can find that VOCE successfully mined the causality that the offline of microservice A triggers microservices B, C, and D to malfunction. In the fault propagation graph, since "10.16.127.162" and "10.16.150.106" both can ultimately reach "10.16.141.247", "10.16.141.247" has a stronger centrality than the other two sources. As a result, VOCE suggests that "10.16.141.247" is the source where the originating anomaly occurs, and thus the first alert in Table 4, which indicates the offline anomaly of microservice A, is the originating alert.

However, VOCE mistakenly identified a causal link between the anomalies of microservice B and microservice C, as shown by the dotted line in Fig. 8. Due to the robustness of the eigenvector centrality [34] adopted by VOCE, such a redundant edge does not interfere with the final originating alert suggestion.

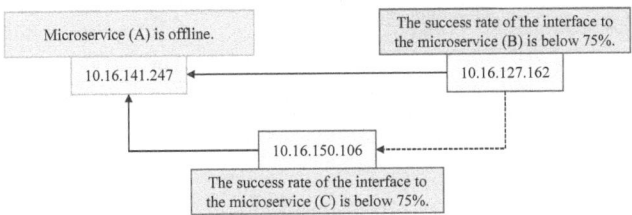

Fig. 8. The fault propagation graph mined by VOCE.

Step 1: In-Depth Analysis of Each Alert

......

Step 2: Compare System Layers of Anomalies
Alert 1: The anomaly pertains to the Microservice Layer since it involves a specific microservice that is offline.
Alert 2: The anomaly pertains to the Application Layer because it deals with the performance of the interface interacting with a microservice.
Lowest System Layer: **The Microservice Layer (Alert 1) is lower than the Application Layer (Alert 2) since it represents a more fundamental failure of a service itself.**

Step 3: Compare Impact Scope of Anomalies
Alert 1: This anomaly impacts a single microservice (CLOUDCALL-SYSTEM) and potentially all dependent services, but its scope is limited to the functionality provided by that microservice.
Alert 2: This anomaly affects the interface to the AIIC-CCBANKQUERY-SERVICE, which may be used by multiple clients or services, thus its impact can extend to any service or application relying on that interface.
Broadest Impact Scope: **Alert 2 has a broader impact because, while it affects a specific microservice, it indicates performance degradation in a service that could be more widely used across multiple clients or applications.**

Step 4: Identify Highest Severity Anomaly
Alert 1: The severity is high due to the complete unavailability of the CLOUDCALL-SYSTEM microservice, which could halt operations relying on it.
Alert 2: The severity is moderate. Although there is an issue with the success rate, the service itself is still operational, meaning it can continue to serve requests, albeit with reduced effectiveness.
Highest Severity: **Alert 1 has the highest severity due to the complete offline status of a critical microservice.**

Step 5: Identify Most Likely Originating Anomaly
Using the strategy that anomalies with a lower system layer, broader impact scope, and higher severity are more likely to describe the originating anomaly:
Alert 1 (CLOUDCALL-SYSTEM is offline) has the lowest layer and highest severity.
Alert 2 (success rate below 75%) has a broader impact but does not indicate a complete failure of the service.

Based on the analysis, **Alert 1 is most likely to describe the originating anomaly that triggers other anomalies**. **The offline status of a crucial microservice would likely lead to performance issues in other interconnected services**, thereby aligning with the characteristics that signal it as the originating anomaly of subsequent issues.

Fig. 9. The analysis process of VOCE.

Although eigenvector centrality is robust to redundant edges, practical deployment can incorporate strategies to filter them out, improving the accuracy of results. For example, predefined rules can be established to eliminate edges that are definitely not traversed by faults. Additionally, since fault propagation graphs are easily interpretable by engineers, redundant edges can be identified and removed through expert review.

To further illustrate the process of VOCE in mining causalities between different sources, Fig. 9 shows the analysis process undertaken by VOCE-GPT to deduce the causal relationship between "10.16.141.247" and "10.16.127.162". According to the underlined content in Fig. 9, we can find that a large language model does indeed exhibit the ability to emulate the processes of operations engineers analyzing alert incidents.

6 Discussion

6.1 Threats to Validity

For the internal threat to validity, the parameter k in causality mining determines the stability of the performance of the large language model. In RQ3, we investigate the impact of k on VOCE and thus choose the optimal value of k for other experiments. Moreover, the originating alert of each incident in the experimental data is manually labeled, introducing potential labeling noise. To reduce the threat, we invite two operations engineers to conduct a retrospective labeling. If they cannot reach a consensus, a third expert will review the annotations, with the minority deferring to the majority. Although mislabeling is hard to avoid during the manual process, we believe that the amount of noises in labeling is small.

For the external threat to validity, since VOCE is based on a large language model, the performance of VOCE relys on the emergent capabilities of the large language model. To mitigate this threat, we evaluate the performance of VOCE using two widely-used large language models, GPT-4o [1,24] and LLaMA [43,44]. GPT-4o is a popular commercial large language model and LLaMA is a prominent open-source large language model. Therefore, the effectiveness and efficiency of VOCE based on these two mainstream models can prove the ability of VOCE to analyze alert incidents.

Additionally, our dataset consists of one month of alerts from Company A, which may limit its diversity and the generalizability of our approaches. However, as a large commercial entity providing financial services to over a billion users across numerous countries, Company A serves as a representative online service system that generates sufficient complex data. The results of VOCE on the real dataset of Company A indicate that our approach is sufficiently generalizable to benefit other companies. In the future, we will deploy VOCE on more service systems. We see no intrinsic limitations that would prevent VOCE from working reliably on different online service systems.

6.2 Limitations

To enhance the robustness of VOCE and facilitate its practical deployment in real-word operational environments, it is essential to address the following issues.

System Topology Incompleteness: VOCE leverages system topology to reveal the propagation process of system faults. However, in practice, system topology information may be incomplete or unavailable. To address this limitation, it is crucial to ensure proper maintenance of comprehensive system topology data to ensure the applicability of VOCE.

Missing Originating Anomalies in Alerts: VOCE assumes that the originating anomaly of a fault is captured by monitoring systems and recorded by alerts. In cases where monitoring coverage is insufficient, identifying the originating anomaly solely based on alerts may be challenging. Therefore, robust monitoring and alerting mechanisms are essential.

Lack of Proactive Fault Resolution: While VOCE automates alert analysis, it cannot proactively resolve faults. Automated fault resolution requires standardized troubleshooting procedures. In practice, troubleshooting involves a diverse range of procedures such as SQL queries, Bash scripts, custom scripts, and specialized software tools, which often lack uniformity. This diversity poses challenges for LLMs in learning and executing such procedures. Addressing this limitation requires not only enabling LLMs to understand expert troubleshooting workflows but also establishing standardized troubleshooting procedures.

Hybrid Human-Machine Workflows: To ensure consistency between the analysis provided by VOCE and expert assessments, a hybrid human-machine workflow can be introduced. Since VOCE emulates the analysis processes of operations engineers, engineers can seamlessly intervene at various stages. For example, during Causality Mining, engineers can review and validate the causal relationships inferred by VOCE between system components, which is often more efficient than analyzing raw alerts. During Causality Correction, the directed edges in the fault propagation graph intuitively represent fault propagation, allowing engineers to refine any incorrect dependencies identified by VOCE.

7   Conclusion

In this paper, we propose an approach VOCE (Virtual On-call Engineer) to automatically analyze alert incidents through a large language model. We first use real alert incidents to investigate the analysis process undertaken by operations experts regarding alert incidents. Then, according to the investigation result, VOCE uses a large language model to emulate the process of operations experts analyzing alert incidents. More Specifically, VOCE first comprehends the local anomalies recorded by the alerts from different system components (sources), then deduces the propagation graph of the system fault indicated by an alert incident, and finally suggests the originating alert.

We conduct extensive experiments on real alert incidents and the results demonstrate that VOCE can effectively and efficiently analyze alert incidents. Currently, VOCE can only analyze an alert incident. It lacks the ability to proactively address the fault underlying an alert incident. In the future, we will endow VOCE with advanced reasoning and autonomous operational execution abilities, enabling it to independently resolve an alert incident after analysis.

References

1. Achiam, J., Adler, S., Agarwal, S., Ahmad, L., Akkaya, I., Aleman, F.L., Almeida, D., Altenschmidt, J., Altman, S., Anadkat, S., et al.: Gpt-4 technical report. arXiv preprint arXiv:2303.08774 (2023)

2. Agrawal, A., Karlupia, R., Gupta, R.: Logan: A distributed online log parser. In: IEEE 35th International Conference on Data Engineering (ICDE). pp. 1946–1951. IEEE (2019)
3. Ahmed, T., Ghosh, S., Bansal, C., Zimmermann, T., Zhang, X., Rajmohan, S.: Recommending root-cause and mitigation steps for cloud incidents using large language models. In: Proceedings of the 45th International Conference on Software Engineering. p. 1737–1749. ICSE '23, IEEE Press (2023)
4. Brown, T.B., Mann, B., Ryder, N., Subbiah, M., Kaplan, J., Dhariwal, P., Neelakantan, A., Shyam, P., Sastry, G., Askell, A., Agarwal, S., Herbert-Voss, A., Krueger, G., Henighan, T., Child, R., Ramesh, A., Ziegler, D.M., Wu, J., Winter, C., Hesse, C., Chen, M., Sigler, E., Litwin, M., Gray, S., Chess, B., Clark, J., Berner, C., McCandlish, S., Radford, A., Sutskever, I., Amodei, D.: Language models are few-shot learners. In: Proceedings of the 34th International Conference on Neural Information Processing Systems. NIPS'20, Curran Associates Inc., Red Hook, NY, USA (2020)
5. Chen, J., Wang, P., Wang, W.: Online summarizing alerts through semantic and behavior information. In: 2022 IEEE/ACM 44th International Conference on Software Engineering (ICSE). pp. 1646–1657 (2022)
6. Chen, J., He, X., Lin, Q., Xu, Y., Zhang, H., Hao, D., Gao, F., Xu, Z., Dang, Y., Zhang, D.: An empirical investigation of incident triage for online service systems. In: IEEE/ACM 41st International Conference on Software Engineering: Software Engineering in Practice. pp. 111–120. IEEE (2019)
7. Chen, X., Lin, M., Schärli, N., Zhou, D.: Teaching large language models to self-debug (2023)
8. Chen, X., Deng, L., Huang, F., Zhang, C., Zhang, Z., Zhao, Y., Zheng, K.: Daemon: Unsupervised anomaly detection and interpretation for multivariate time series. In: 2021 IEEE 37th International Conference on Data Engineering (ICDE). pp. 2225–2230 (2021)
9. Chen, Y., Zhang, C., Dong, Z., Yang, D., Peng, X., Ou, J., Yang, H., Wu, Z., Qu, X., Li, W.: Dynamic graph neural networks-based alert link prediction for online service systems. In: 2023 38th IEEE/ACM International Conference on Automated Software Engineering (ASE). pp. 79–90 (2023)
10. Chen, Y., Yang, X., Dong, H., He, X., Zhang, H., Lin, Q., Chen, J., Zhao, P., Kang, Y., Gao, F., Xu, Z., Zhang, D.: Identifying linked incidents in large-scale online service systems. In: Proceedings of the 28th ACM Joint Meeting on European Software Engineering Conference and Symposium on the Foundations of Software Engineering. p. 304–314. ESEC/FSE 2020, Association for Computing Machinery, New York, NY, USA (2020)
11. Chen, Y., Yang, X., Lin, Q., Zhang, H., Gao, F., Xu, Z., Dang, Y., Zhang, D., Dong, H., Xu, Y., Li, H., Kang, Y.: Outage prediction and diagnosis for cloud service systems. In: The World Wide Web Conference. p. 2659–2665. ACM, New York, NY, USA (2019)
12. Chen, Z., Liu, J., Su, Y., Zhang, H., Wen, X., Ling, X., Yang, Y., Lyu, M.R.: Graph-based incident aggregation for large-scale online service systems. In: 2021 36th IEEE/ACM International Conference on Automated Software Engineering (ASE). pp. 430–442 (2021)
13. Du, M., Li, F.: Spell: Streaming parsing of system event logs. In: 2016 IEEE 16th International Conference on Data Mining (ICDM). pp. 859–864 (2016)
14. Du, M., Li, F., Zheng, G., Srikumar, V.: Deeplog: Anomaly detection and diagnosis from system logs through deep learning. In: Proceedings of the 2017 ACM

SIGSAC Conference on Computer and Communications Security. pp. 1285–1298. ACM (2017)

15. Evans, T.S., Chen, B.: Linking the network centrality measures closeness and degree. Communications Physics **5**(1), 172 (2022)

16. Freeman, L.C.: A set of measures of centrality based on betweenness. Sociometry pp. 35–41 (1977)

17. Freeman, L.C.: Centrality in social networks conceptual clarification. Social Networks **1**(3), 215–239 (1978)

18. Gao, L., Madaan, A., Zhou, S., Alon, U., Liu, P., Yang, Y., Callan, J., Neubig, G.: PAL: Program-aided language models. In: Krause, A., Brunskill, E., Cho, K., Engelhardt, B., Sabato, S., Scarlett, J. (eds.) Proceedings of the 40th International Conference on Machine Learning. Proceedings of Machine Learning Research, vol. 202, pp. 10764–10799. PMLR (23–29 Jul 2023)

19. Han, S., Wu, Q., Zhang, H., Qin, B., Hu, J., Shi, X., Liu, L., Yin, X.: Log-based anomaly detection with robust feature extraction and online learning. IEEE Transactions on Information Forensics and Security **16**, 2300–2311 (2021)

20. He, P., Zhu, J., Zheng, Z., Lyu, M.R.: Drain: An online log parsing approach with fixed depth tree. In: 2017 IEEE International Conference on Web Services (ICWS). pp. 33–40. IEEE (2017)

21. Hundman, K., Constantinou, V., Laporte, C., Colwell, I., Soderstrom, T.: Detecting spacecraft anomalies using lstms and nonparametric dynamic thresholding. In: Proceedings of the 24th ACM SIGKDD International Conference on Knowledge Discovery & Data Mining. p. 387–395. Association for Computing Machinery, New York, NY, USA (2018)

22. Inc., M.: Bing (2024), `https://www.bing.com`

23. Inc., O.: Chatgpt (2024), `https://openai.com/chatgpt`

24. Inc., O.: Gpt-4o (2024), `https://openai.com/index/hello-gpt-4o`

25. Kang, S., Yoon, J., Yoo, S.: Large language models are few-shot testers: Exploring llm-based general bug reproduction. In: Proceedings of the 45th International Conference on Software Engineering. p. 2312–2323. ICSE '23, IEEE Press (2023)

26. Kojima, T., Gu, S.S., Reid, M., Matsuo, Y., Iwasawa, Y.: Large language models are zero-shot reasoners. In: Koyejo, S., Mohamed, S., Agarwal, A., Belgrave, D., Cho, K., Oh, A. (eds.) Advances in Neural Information Processing Systems. vol. 35, pp. 22199–22213. Curran Associates, Inc. (2022)

27. Le, V.H., Zhang, H.: Log parsing with prompt-based few-shot learning. In: 2023 IEEE/ACM 45th International Conference on Software Engineering (ICSE). pp. 2438–2449 (2023)

28. Lewis, P., Perez, E., Piktus, A., Petroni, F., Karpukhin, V., Goyal, N., Küttler, H., Lewis, M., Yih, W.t., Rocktäschel, T., Riedel, S., Kiela, D.: Retrieval-augmented generation for knowledge-intensive nlp tasks. In: Proceedings of the 34th International Conference on Neural Information Processing Systems. NIPS '20, Curran Associates Inc., Red Hook, NY, USA (2020)

29. Lin, D., Raghu, R., Ramamurthy, V., Yu, J., Radhakrishnan, R., Fernandez, J.: Unveiling clusters of events for alert and incident management in large-scale enterprise it. In: Proceedings of the 20th ACM SIGKDD International Conference on Knowledge Discovery and Data Mining. p. 1630–1639. ACM, New York, NY, USA (2014)

30. Lin, Q., Zhang, H., Lou, J.G., Zhang, Y., Chen, X.: Log clustering based problem identification for online service systems. In: Proceedings of the 38th International Conference on Software Engineering Companion. p. 102–111. ACM, New York, NY, USA (2016)

31. Liu, P., Xu, H., Ouyang, Q., Jiao, R., Chen, Z., Zhang, S., Yang, J., Mo, L., Zeng, J., Xue, W., Pei, D.: Unsupervised detection of microservice trace anomalies through service-level deep bayesian networks. In: IEEE 31st International Symposium on Software Reliability Engineering (ISSRE). pp. 48–58. IEEE (2020)

32. Meng, W., Liu, Y., Zhu, Y., Zhang, S., Pei, D., Liu, Y., Chen, Y., Zhang, R., Tao, S., Sun, P., Zhou, R.: Loganomaly: Unsupervised detection of sequential and quantitative anomalies in unstructured logs. In: Proceedings of the 28th International Joint Conference on Artificial Intelligence. pp. 4739–4745. IJCAI Organization (7 2019)

33. Nedelkoski, S., Cardoso, J., Kao, O.: Anomaly detection and classification using distributed tracing and deep learning. In: 19th IEEE/ACM International Symposium on Cluster, Cloud and Grid Computing (CCGRID). pp. 241–250. IEEE (2019)

34. Negre, C.F., Morzan, U.N., Hendrickson, H.P., Pal, R., Lisi, G.P., Loria, J.P., Rivalta, I., Ho, J., Batista, V.S.: Eigenvector centrality for characterization of protein allosteric pathways. Proceedings of the National Academy of Sciences **115**(52), E12201–E12208 (2018)

35. Ouyang, L., Wu, J., Jiang, X., Almeida, D., Wainwright, C.L., Mishkin, P., Zhang, C., Agarwal, S., Slama, K., Ray, A., Schulman, J., Hilton, J., Kelton, F., Miller, L., Simens, M., Askell, A., Welinder, P., Christiano, P., Leike, J., Lowe, R.: Training language models to follow instructions with human feedback (2022)

36. Rae, J.W., Borgeaud, S., Cai, T., Millican, K., Hoffmann, J., Song, F., Aslanides, J., Henderson, S., Ring, R., Young, S., Rutherford, E., Hennigan, T., Menick, J., Cassirer, A., Powell, R., van den Driessche, G., Hendricks, L.A., Rauh, M., Huang, P.S., Glaese, A., Welbl, J., Dathathri, S., Huang, S., Uesato, J., Mellor, J., Higgins, I., Creswell, A., McAleese, N., Wu, A., Elsen, E., Jayakumar, S., Buchatskaya, E., Budden, D., Sutherland, E., Simonyan, K., Paganini, M., Sifre, L., Martens, L., Li, X.L., Kuncoro, A., Nematzadeh, A., Gribovskaya, E., Donato, D., Lazaridou, A., Mensch, A., Lespiau, J.B., Tsimpoukelli, M., Grigorev, N., Fritz, D., Sottiaux, T., Pajarskas, M., Pohlen, T., Gong, Z., Toyama, D., de Masson d'Autume, C., Li, Y., Terzi, T., Mikulik, V., Babuschkin, I., Clark, A., de Las Casas, D., Guy, A., Jones, C., Bradbury, J., Johnson, M., Hechtman, B., Weidinger, L., Gabriel, I., Isaac, W., Lockhart, E., Osindero, S., Rimell, L., Dyer, C., Vinyals, O., Ayoub, K., Stanway, J., Bennett, L., Hassabis, D., Kavukcuoglu, K., Irving, G.: Scaling language models: Methods, analysis & insights from training gopher (2021)

37. Ren, H., Xu, B., Wang, Y., Yi, C., Huang, C., Kou, X., Xing, T., Yang, M., Tong, J., Zhang, Q.: Time-series anomaly detection service at microsoft. In: Proceedings of the 25th ACM SIGKDD International Conference on Knowledge Discovery & Data Mining. p. 3009–3017. Association for Computing Machinery, New York, NY, USA (2019)

38. Rozière, B., Gehring, J., Gloeckle, F., Sootla, S., Gat, I., Tan, X.E., Adi, Y., Liu, J., Remez, T., Rapin, J., Kozhevnikov, A., Evtimov, I., Bitton, J., Bhatt, M., Ferrer, C.C., Grattafiori, A., Xiong, W., Défossez, A., Copet, J., Azhar, F., Touvron, H., Martin, L., Usunier, N., Scialom, T., Synnaeve, G.: Code llama: Open foundation models for code (2023)

39. Sanh, V., Webson, A., Raffel, C., Bach, S.H., Sutawika, L., Alyafeai, Z., Chaffin, A., Stiegler, A., Scao, T.L., Raja, A., Dey, M., Bari, M.S., Xu, C., Thakker, U., Sharma, S.S., Szczechla, E., Kim, T., Chhablani, G., Nayak, N., Datta, D., Chang, J., Jiang, M.T.J., Wang, H., Manica, M., Shen, S., Yong, Z.X., Pandey, H., Bawden, R., Wang, T., Neeraj, T., Rozen, J., Sharma, A., Santilli, A., Fevry, T., Fries, J.A.,

Teehan, R., Bers, T., Biderman, S., Gao, L., Wolf, T., Rush, A.M.: Multitask prompted training enables zero-shot task generalization (2021)

40. Shinn, N., Cassano, F., Labash, B., Gopinath, A., Narasimhan, K., Yao, S.: Reflexion: Language agents with verbal reinforcement learning (2023)

41. Tang, L., Li, T., Pinel, F., Shwartz, L., Grabarnik, G.: Optimizing system monitoring configurations for non-actionable alerts. In: 2012 IEEE Network Operations and Management Symposium. pp. 34–42 (2012)

42. Taori, R., Gulrajani, I., Zhang, T., Dubois, Y., Li, X., Guestrin, C., Liang, P., Hashimoto, T.B.: Stanford alpaca: An instruction-following llama model. https://github.com/tatsu-lab/stanford_alpaca (2023)

43. Touvron, H., Lavril, T., Izacard, G., Martinet, X., Lachaux, M.A., Lacroix, T., Rozière, B., Goyal, N., Hambro, E., Azhar, F., Rodriguez, A., Joulin, A., Grave, E., Lample, G.: Llama: Open and efficient foundation language models (2023)

44. Touvron, H., Martin, L., Stone, K., Albert, P., Almahairi, A., Babaei, Y., Bashlykov, N., Batra, S., Bhargava, P., Bhosale, S., Bikel, D., Blecher, L., Ferrer, C.C., Chen, M., Cucurull, G., Esiobu, D., Fernandes, J., Fu, J., Fu, W., Fuller, B., Gao, C., Goswami, V., Goyal, N., Hartshorn, A., Hosseini, S., Hou, R., Inan, H., Kardas, M., Kerkez, V., Khabsa, M., Kloumann, I., Korenev, A., Koura, P.S., Lachaux, M.A., Lavril, T., Lee, J., Liskovich, D., Lu, Y., Mao, Y., Martinet, X., Mihaylov, T., Mishra, P., Molybog, I., Nie, Y., Poulton, A., Reizenstein, J., Rungta, R., Saladi, K., Schelten, A., Silva, R., Smith, E.M., Subramanian, R., Tan, X.E., Tang, B., Taylor, R., Williams, A., Kuan, J.X., Xu, P., Yan, Z., Zarov, I., Zhang, Y., Fan, A., Kambadur, M., Narang, S., Rodriguez, A., Stojnic, R., Edunov, S., Scialom, T.: Llama 2: Open foundation and fine-tuned chat models (2023)

45. Wang, X., Zhang, X., Li, L., He, S., Zhang, H., Liu, Y., Zheng, L., Kang, Y., Lin, Q., Dang, Y., Rajmohan, S., Zhang, D.: Spine: A scalable log parser with feedback guidance. In: Proceedings of the 30th ACM Joint European Software Engineering Conference and Symposium on the Foundations of Software Engineering. p. 1198–1208. ESEC/FSE 2022, Association for Computing Machinery, New York, NY, USA (2022)

46. Wei, J., Bosma, M., Zhao, V.Y., Guu, K., Yu, A.W., Lester, B., Du, N., Dai, A.M., Le, Q.V.: Finetuned language models are zero-shot learners (2021)

47. Wei, J., Tay, Y., Bommasani, R., Raffel, C., Zoph, B., Borgeaud, S., Yogatama, D., Bosma, M., Zhou, D., Metzler, D., Chi, E.H., Hashimoto, T., Vinyals, O., Liang, P., Dean, J., Fedus, W.: Emergent abilities of large language models (2022)

48. Wei, J., Wang, X., Schuurmans, D., Bosma, M., ichter, b., Xia, F., Chi, E., Le, Q.V., Zhou, D.: Chain-of-thought prompting elicits reasoning in large language models. In: Koyejo, S., Mohamed, S., Agarwal, A., Belgrave, D., Cho, K., Oh, A. (eds.) Advances in Neural Information Processing Systems. vol. 35, pp. 24824–24837. Curran Associates, Inc. (2022)

49. Yang, L., Chen, J., Wang, Z., Wang, W., Jiang, J., Dong, X., Zhang, W.: Plelog: Semi-supervised log-based anomaly detection via probabilistic label estimation. In: 2021 IEEE/ACM 43rd International Conference on Software Engineering: Companion Proceedings (ICSE-Companion). pp. 230–231 (2021)

50. Yao, S., Yu, D., Zhao, J., Shafran, I., Griffiths, T.L., Cao, Y., Narasimhan, K.: Tree of thoughts: Deliberate problem solving with large language models (2023)

51. Zhang, X., Xu, Y., Lin, Q., Qiao, B., Zhang, H., Dang, Y., Xie, C., Yang, X., Cheng, Q., Li, Z., Chen, J., He, X., Yao, R., Lou, J.G., Chintalapati, M., Shen, F., Zhang, D.: Robust log-based anomaly detection on unstable log data. In: Proceedings of the 2019 27th ACM Joint Meeting on European Software Engineering Conference

and Symposium on the Foundations of Software Engineering. p. 807–817. ACM, New York, NY, USA (2019)

52. Zhao, N., Chen, J., Peng, X., Wang, H., Wu, X., Zhang, Y., Chen, Z., Zheng, X., Nie, X., Wang, G., Wu, Y., Zhou, F., Zhang, W., Sui, K., Pei, D.: Understanding and handling alert storm for online service systems. In: Proceedings of the ACM/IEEE 42nd International Conference on Software Engineering: Software Engineering in Practice. p. 162–171. ACM, New York, NY, USA (2020)

53. Zhao, N., Chen, J., Wang, Z., Peng, X., Wang, G., Wu, Y., Zhou, F., Feng, Z., Nie, X., Zhang, W., Sui, K., Pei, D.: Real-time incident prediction for online service systems. In: Proceedings of the 28th ACM Joint Meeting on European Software Engineering Conference and Symposium on the Foundations of Software Engineering. p. 315–326. ACM, New York, NY, USA (2020)

54. Zhao, N., Jin, P., Wang, L., Yang, X., Liu, R., Zhang, W., Sui, K., Pei, D.: Automatically and adaptively identifying severe alerts for online service systems. In: IEEE Conference on Computer Communications. pp. 2420–2429. IEEE (2020)

55. Zhao, W.X., Zhou, K., Li, J., Tang, T., Wang, X., Hou, Y., Min, Y., Zhang, B., Zhang, J., Dong, Z., Du, Y., Yang, C., Chen, Y., Chen, Z., Jiang, J., Ren, R., Li, Y., Tang, X., Liu, Z., Liu, P., Nie, J.Y., Wen, J.R.: A survey of large language models (2023)

56. Zheng, L., Chiang, W.L., Sheng, Y., Zhuang, S., Wu, Z., Zhuang, Y., Lin, Z., Li, Z., Li, D., Xing, E.P., Zhang, H., Gonzalez, J.E., Stoica, I.: Judging llm-as-a-judge with mt-bench and chatbot arena (2023)

57. Zhou, B., Liu, S., Hooi, B., Cheng, X., Ye, J.: Beatgan: Anomalous rhythm detection using adversarially generated time series. In: Proceedings of the Twenty-Eighth International Joint Conference on Artificial Intelligence, IJCAI-19. pp. 4433–4439. International Joint Conferences on Artificial Intelligence Organization (7 2019)

58. Zhou, X., Peng, X., Xie, T., Sun, J., Ji, C., Liu, D., Xiang, Q., He, C.: Latent error prediction and fault localization for microservice applications by learning from system trace logs. In: Proceedings of the 27th ACM Joint Meeting on European Software Engineering Conference and Symposium on the Foundations of Software Engineering. p. 683–694. ACM, New York, NY, USA (2019)

HYBRIDIZE FUNCTIONS: A Tool for Automatically Refactoring Imperative Deep Learning Programs to Graph Execution

Raffi Khatchadourian[1,2] ![ORCID], Tatiana Castro Vélez[2], Mehdi Bagherzadeh[3] ![ORCID],
Nan Jia[2], and Anita Raja[1,2] ![ORCID]

[1] CUNY Hunter College, New York, NY USA
{khatchad,anita.raja}@hunter.cuny.edu
[2] CUNY Graduate Center, New York, NY USA
{tcastrovelez,njia}@gradcenter.cuny.edu
[3] Oakland University, Rochester, MI USA
mbagherzadeh@oakland.edu

Abstract. Efficiency is essential to support responsiveness w.r.t. ever-growing datasets, especially for Deep Learning (DL) systems. DL frameworks have traditionally embraced *deferred* execution-style DL code—supporting symbolic, graph-based Deep Neural Network (DNN) computation. While scalable, such development is error-prone, non-intuitive, and difficult to debug. Consequently, more natural, imperative DL frameworks encouraging *eager* execution have emerged but at the expense of run-time performance. Though hybrid approaches aim for the "best of both worlds," using them effectively requires subtle considerations to make code amenable to safe, accurate, and efficient graph execution—avoiding performance bottlenecks and semantically inequivalent results. We discuss the engineering aspects of a refactoring tool that automatically determines when it is safe and potentially advantageous to migrate imperative DL code to graph execution and vice-versa.

Keywords: deep learning · refactoring · imperative programs · graphs

1 Introduction

Machine Learning (ML), including Deep Learning (DL), systems are pervasive, and—as datasets grow—efficiency becomes essential to support responsiveness [53]. Efficient DL frameworks have traditionally embraced a *deferred* execution-style that supports symbolic, graph-based Deep Neural Network (DNN) computation [10, 21]. While scalable, development is error-prone, cumbersome, and difficult to debug [25, 26, 51, 52]. Contrarily, more natural, less error-prone, and easier-to-debug *imperative* DL frameworks [3, 12, 40] encouraging *eager* execution have emerged. They are, however, less efficient and scalable as their deferred-execution counterparts [10, 18, 20, 29, 37, 40]. Thus, hybrid approaches [4, 18, 37] execute imperative DL programs as static graphs at run-time. For example, in "TensorFlow" [1], *AutoGraph* [37] can enhance run-time performance by decorating (annotating) appropriate Python function(s) with @tf.function (Fig. 1).

A. Boronat and G. Fraser (Eds.): FASE 2025, LNCS 15693, pp.89–100, 2025.
https://doi.org/10.1007/978-3-031-90900-9_5

Though promising, hybrid approaches require non-trivial metadata [29] and exhibit limitations and known issues [19] with native program constructs. Subtle considerations are required to make code amenable to safe, accurate, and efficient graph execution [5, 7, 8, 9]. Alternative approaches [29, 34, 44] may impose custom Python interpreters or

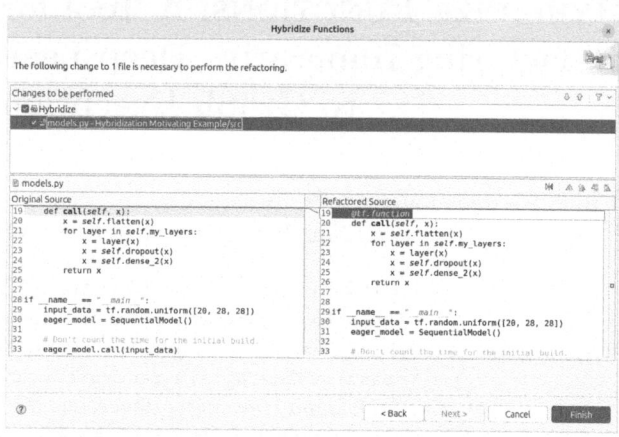

Fig. 1. Screenshot of the HYBRIDIZE FUNCTIONS.

require additional or concurrently running components, which may be impractical for industry, support only specific Python constructs, or still require function decoration. Thus, developers are burdened with *manually* specifying the functions to be converted. Advances in DL are likely to be futile if they cannot be effectively used. Manual analysis and refactoring (semantics-preserving, source-to-source transformation) to achieve optimal results can be overwhelming, error- and omission-prone [13] and is further complicated by the increasing amount of Object-Orientation (OO) in DL code [12] and dynamically-typed languages (e.g., Python), where concrete runtime information is sparse at development time.

In this paper, we report on the design and implementation of a fully automated, publicly available, and open-source refactoring tool named HYBRIDIZE FUNCTIONS [24] that transforms otherwise eagerly-executed imperative (Python) DL code for enhanced performance. The tool—implemented as a *PyDev* [50] *Eclipse* [16] Integrated Development Environment (IDE) plug-in that integrates static analyses from *WALA* [45] and "Ariadne" [15]—assists developers in specifying whether such code could be reliably and efficiently executed as graphs at run-time. Although it works on Python code, the tool nevertheless utilizes the Java Development Tools (JDT) [17] refactoring infrastructure [6] with a UI, preview pane, and refactoring unit tests. The approach at the tool's foundation is based on a novel tensor (matrix-like data structures) analysis specifically for imperative DL code—infers when it is safe and potentially advantageous to migrate imperative DL code to graph execution or eagerly executing code already running as graphs.

Our tool interprocedurally identifies—at the project-level—Python functions that can execute more efficiently as hybrid functions and which may be *hindered* by hybrid execution. It also discovers potential side-effects in Python functions to transform functions to either execute eagerly or in hybrid mode safely. Though the refactorings operate on imperative DL code that is easier-to-debug than its deferred-execution counterparts, they themselves do not improve debuggability but instead enable *performant* yet easily-debuggable (imperative) DL code.

```
1                                          1  import tensorflow as tf
2  class SequentialModel(tf.keras.Model):  2  class SequentialModel(tf.keras.Model):
3    def __init__(self, **kwargs):         3    def __init__(self, **kwargs):
4      super(SequentialModel, self)         4      super(SequentialModel, self)
5        .__init__(...)                     5        .__init__(...)
6      self.flatten = layers.Flatten(       6      self.flatten = layers.Flatten(
7      input_shape=(28, 28))                7      input_shape=(28, 28))
8      num_layers = 100 # Add layers.       8      num_layers = 100 # Add layers.
9      self.layers = [layers                9      self.layers = [layers
10       .Dense(64,activation="relu")       10       .Dense(64,activation="relu")
11       for n in range(num_layers)]        11       for n in range(num_layers)]
12     self.dropout = layers.Dropout(0.2)   12     self.dropout = layers.Dropout(0.2)
13     self.dense_2 = layers.Dense(10)      13     self.dense_2 = layers.Dense(10)
14                                          14
15                                          15  @tf.function
16   def __call__(self, x):                 16   def __call__(self, x):
17     x = self.flatten(x)                  17     x = self.flatten(x)
18     for layer in self.layers:            18     for layer in self.layers:
19       x = layer(x)                       19       x = layer(x)
20     x = self.dropout(x)                  20     x = self.dropout(x)
21     x = self.dense_2(x)                  21     x = self.dense_2(x)
22     return x                             22     return x
```

(a) Code snippet before refactoring.   (b) Improved code via refactoring.

Listing 1.1. "TensorFlow" imperative (OO) DL model code [20].

The tool was evaluated on 19 Python imperative DL programs of varying size and domain with a total of 132.05 K lines of code, where we found that 42.56% of candidate functions were refactorable, with an observed average speedup of 2.16 during performance testing. Due to its popularity and extensive analysis by previous work [11, 23, 25, 27, 35, 38, 51, 52], we focus on hybridization in "Tensor-Flow". In this paper, we discuss engineering challenges we faced in implementing the tool used in the study. We make the following specific contributions:

Implementation and motivation. Our tool's novel engineering aspects are detailed with a focus on its integration of tensor type inference at the instruction-based IR level with a Python development IDE plug-in. Also, architecture, API usage, data representations, algorithms, implementation issues, and a more comprehensive motivation are outlined.

Modernization engineering. We detail engineering aspects of our modernization effort of "Ariadne" in adding new enhancements, including new Python language features and additional library modeling.

2   Motivation

We present examples that highlight some of the challenges associated with analyzing and refactoring imperative DL code to be executed as graphs at run-time with improved efficiency. Listing 1.1a portrays "TensorFlow" imperative (OO) DL code representing a modestly-sized model for classifying images. By default, this code runs eagerly; however, it may be possible to enhance performance by executing it as a graph at run-time. Listing 1.1b, lines 1 and 15 display the refactoring with the imperative DL code executed as a graph at run-time (added code is underlined). *AutoGraph* [37] is now used to potentially improve performance by decorating call() with @tf.function. At run-time, call()'s execution will be "traced" and an equivalent graph will be generated [19]. In this case, a speedup $\left({runtime_{old}}/{runtime_{new}} \right)$ of ∼9.22 ensues [31]. Though promising, using hybridization reliably *and* efficiently is challenging [7, 8, 9, 19, 29]. If used incorrectly, hybridization may yield programs that result in unexpected run-time behavior. For instance, side-effect producing, native Python statements are problematic for `tf.function`-decorated functions [19]. Because their executions are traced, a function's behavior is "etched" (frozen) into its corresponding graph and thus can have unexpected results.

3   Implementation

3.1   Architecture and Dependencies

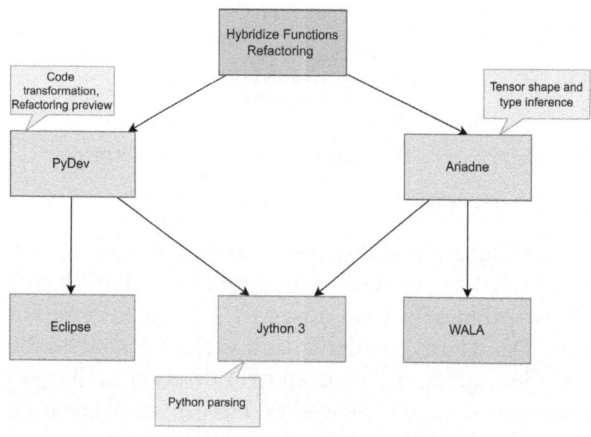

Fig. 2. Overall architecture.

Figure 2 shows the overall architecture of our tool and the dependencies it builds upon. HYBRIDIZE FUNCTIONS [24] is implemented as a publicly available, open-source *PyDev* [50] *Eclipse* [16] IDE plug-in and built upon the *WALA* [45] "Ariadne" [15] analysis framework. *Eclipse* is leveraged for its existing, well documented and integrated refactoring framework and test engine [6], including transformation APIs (e.g., `ASTRewrite`), refactoring preview pane (Fig. 1), precondition checking (e.g., `Refactoring.checkInitialConditions()`, `Refactoring.checkFinalPreconditions()`), and refactoring testing (e.g., `RefactoringTest`).

A challenge in building the tool was to rework much of the existing Java (JDT) refactoring tooling to work with Python. For example, we re-engineered a common framework for building Java refactoring tools [32] to factor out refactoring components that are language agnostic and ones that were specific for Java. In HYBRIDIZE FUNCTIONS, we then extend the parts that are language agnostic to work with Python. This approach allowed us to reuse much of the existing Java refactoring tooling, which is well-tested and robust, and only focus on the parts that are specific to Python. Although *PyDev* is—itself—an *Eclipse* plug-in that provides Python development support within *Eclipse*—including refactoring—it also uses *Eclipse* native refactoring APIs. Instead, we use *PyDev* for other features, as subsequently described.

PyDev is used for efficient program entity indexing, extensive refactoring support [6], and that it is completely open-source for all Python development. We built atop of *PyDev* a fully-qualified name (FQN) lookup that uses the indexing—ideal for large projects—and use it to resolve decorator names. *PyDev* uses Jython for Python parsing (Fig. 2).

WALA is used for static analyses, such as ModRef, for which we built our side-effect analysis upon. "Ariadne", which depends on *WALA*, is used for its Python and tensor analysis, including type inference and ("TensorFlow") library modeling. The tensor type inference is used to determine which functions should be hybridized, as those with tensor parameters are ideal for tracing as demonstrated in §2. The library modeling allows us to simulate the static analysis of large libraries like "TensorFlow" without actually running the tool. The modeling also allows us to track tensor values accepted and returned by library API. Though "TensorFlow" includes type hints that could also be used to track tensor values flowing into functions, they do not assist with the graph construction. For transformation, *PyDev* ASTs with source symbol bindings are used as an intermediate representation (IR), while the static analysis consumes a Static Single Assignment (SSA) [43] IR.

Both *PyDev* and "Ariadne" use Jython 3 for generating Python ASTs (Fig. 2). Thus, there is some redundancy in the AST generation, however, the ASTs are consumed for different purposes. Future work may involve decoupling the Python ASTs from both tools to have a single intermediate representation for both. There are some representation differences with the ASTs produced by "Ariadne" and that produces by *PyDev* that complicate the AST matching. For example, "Ariadne" considers type hints part of a parameter expression while *PyDev* does not.

3.2   Static Analysis Integration

Though both *PyDev* and "Ariadne" initially represent the Python source code as ASTs, as *PyDev* is an IDE plug-in with refactoring support, such a representation is necessary to perform transformations on the *source* code. "Ariadne", on the other hand, transforms the Python ASTs to "CAsts" (Common Abstract Syntax Trees), which are part of *WALA*, i.e., its underlying framework. CAst is meant to represent multiple languages using a single ASTs and is commonly used by the JavaScript tooling supported by *WALA*. The CAst is then transformed to SSA IR, which is the typical input form for advanced static analyses. Thus, in our plug-in, because our input is a *PyDev* project (in AST) and because we eventually transform the source code (i.e., the AST), a mapping mechanism is necessary to correlate the original ASTs with the *WALA* produced SSA IR. In other words, we need to correlate the results obtained by the static analysis with the input source code so that we know which elements to transform and which not to transform. To do this, we adopt a similar mechanism as Khatchadourian *et al.* [33]. Specifically, we approximate the original source location of the resulting IR using various attributes. The matching is non-trivial as the SSA (3-operand address format; similar to assembly or bytecode) is very different than the Python source code. We match the file names, functions, and line numbers, as well as discover if the SSA element is a parameter or not (for function candidate selection). By finding the parameter number in the IR, we then match that with the parameter expression in the original AST. A key difference here between Khatchadourian *et al.* [33] is that, in their approach, the Java bytecode is analyzed, making it more difficult to correlate the results with the original source code. In our case, we have the original source code in CAst form, which makes the correlation easier, as CAst can store the original source positions. It is possible to do this in bytecode analysis, but the line numbers are approximated.

Although "Ariadne" has Python parsing capabilities, we integrated it with *PyDev* due to its excellent and long-lived refactoring support for Python, including refactoring preview pane, element GUI selection, and refactoring undo history. In other words, "Ariadne", like *WALA*, is an program *analysis* framework and thus does not have AST manipulation capabilities that have been traditionally found in IDEs. *PyDev*—an IDE plug-in—can *transform* Python ASTs. An alternative is to use the analysis results from "Ariadne" to guide refactoring recommendations that are then sent to the IDE via the Language Server Protocol (LSP) [36]. Then, an IDE receiving the LSP messages would be responsible for executing the refactoring. However, refactoring support in LSP is currently pending [28, 46].

3.3   Modernizing Ariadne

Prior to our integration, "Ariadne" only worked on "TensorFlow" 1 code, i.e., deferred-execution style DL code. Specifically, it did not analysis summaries for API that is typical used by "TensorFlow" 2 clients, i.e., imperative DL code, and did not support Python constructs that were commonly used in this paradigm. We augmented "Ariadne" to analyze imperative Deep Learning (Python) code by vastly expanding the XML summaries to support a wide variety of popular "TensorFlow" 2 APIs. We also added support for Python module packages [41], wild card imports, intra-package references (relative imports; `from .. import X`) [42], package initialization scripts, automatic discovery of unit test entry points, iteration of non-scalar tensor datasets [22], modeling of additional and popular libraries [2, 39], and analyzing static and class methods, custom decorators, and callable objects (functors) (heavily used by *Keras* models). We have contributed these enhancements back to the open-source "Ariadne" project [47].

To implement wild card imports, we use a queue that inserts only at the beginning. Then, when we detect a wild card, the last wild card import to be seen in the Python file is considered first. This resolves a potential situation where multiple libraries can export the same name.

We further enable "Ariadne" to process code in Python module packages [41], i.e., having the input code being spread out among multiple files and directories. Although the original analysis is interprocedural, it did not originally support module packages, i.e., spanning local Python modules in complex directory structures. We implement this enhancement using a `PYTHONPATH` variable that is optionally used as input to our analysis. This variable is a sequence of systems paths where the analysis should look for modules and resembles the variable used by the Python interpreter (a similar variable is used in *PyDev* [50]). We modified "Ariadne" such that when it finds a Python module that resides in a path contained in `PYTHONPATH`, it adjusts the call graph node identifier so that other modules may find it through `import` statements.

Related to packages, we also enhanced "Ariadne" to support package initialization scripts. To denote a (sub)package, typically, an (empty) `__init__.py` file would be placed in the (sub)package directory. The Python interpreter then treats any scripts in the directory as part of the package. However, this file may

```
1  <Code body of function Lscript nlpgnn/models/__init__.py>
2  global:global script nlpgnn/models/__init__.py = v1
3  ...
4  v260 = global:global script nlpgnn/models/bert.py
5  v262 = fieldref v260.v259:#BERT
6  putfield v1.< PythonLoader, LRoot, BERT, <PythonLoader,LRoot> > = v262
```

Listing 1.2. SSA IR snippet produced from Fig. 3. Text beginning with # is a comment.

also have package initialization code contained within it. A common idiom is to include `import` statements here so that the scripts within the package can be more easily referenced by clients by only using the package name. For example, the `models` package initialization code in Fig. 3 enables clients to more simply import the BERT model using `from nlpgnn.models import bert`. Without the initialization code, `bert` would refer to the `bert` *module* (`bert.py`) instead of the *class* representing the BERT model in `bert.py`.

To achieve this, we breakdown two cases; one for explicit imports and one for wildcards (the latter is shown in Fig. 3). For the first case, we add to the SSA IR a field to the globally exported value representing the `__init__.py` module (`v1` in Lst. 1.2). The client SSA IR then references the name from the module as if the module *contains* the code declaring the name as opposed to import-

```
from .albert import *
from .bert import *
from .GAT import *
```

Fig. 3. Snippet of a `models` package initialization code (`models/__init__.py`) [30].

ing it itself, as shown on line 6 in Lst. 1.2. The wild card (second) is more challenging and requires manipulating the pointer analysis as we have done with general wild card imports as described above but adding more flexibility in discovering the location of the instance, i.e., we add a two-step jump to the instance from the client code. Essentially, we substitute the package's initialization script for the current script when we detect that the package is being imported.

As mentioned earlier, we also add support for intra-package references (relative imports; `from .. import X`) [42], which were popular in our subject set. They also may take the form of `from ...Y import X`, where `Y` is a module in the specified relative package and `Y` a name defined in `X`, e.g., a function, class, or variable.

We add the ability to analyze static and class methods to "Ariadne". We do so by adding a class metadata variable to the constructor call and the trampoline in the SSA. The trampoline for class methods passes the class instance rather than an object instance. Complicating the matter somewhat is the ability to use an instance on the LHS, for which the class must be extracted.

3.4 Transformation

To transform a function to hybrid, we add the `@tf.function` decorator to the definition of the function. However, we first compute the correct prefix to use by analyzing the import statements in the file. In Python, import statements can reside anywhere in the file and may be scoped to certain blocks. Moreover, import statements can be repeated, with the closest import taking precedence over preceding ones. Lastly, imports can be arbitrarily aliased, e.g., `import tensorflow`, `import tensorflow as tf`, and `import tensorflow as ta` are all valid ways to import the "TensorFlow" library. The inserted decorator would then depend on this import. The aforementioned examples would result in the decorators `@tensorflow.function`, `@tf.function`, and `@ta.function`, respectively.

To transform a function to eager, we remove the `@tf.function` decorator by first finding it in a potential list of decorators for the function in question. Like the previous case, finding the decorator is dependent on the import statements. Thanks to *PyDev*'s indexing, however, this turns out to be an easier case; we simply look up the decorator expression in *PyDev*'s database to see if it resolves to `@tf.function`. Note that a simple text search may result in incorrect removals; we encountered instances in our subject set where `@tf.function` did not refer to anything in "TensorFlow" but rather a custom entity, perhaps for mocking.

4   Evaluation Summary

We applied our approach to 19 open-source Python imperative DL programs of varying size and domain, with thousands of source lines of code ranging from 0.12 to 36.72. Our tool considered 766 Python functions, automatically refactoring 42.56% despite being highly conservative. During a run-time performance evaluation, we measured an average relative model training speedup of 2.16 (a memory consumption measurement is pending). Python is a complex language with many dynamic features; thus, our tool may not sound in all cases. To gauge the extent our tool produces correct results, we also measured model accuracy and loss before and after refactoring and found negligible differences. Our results suggest that our tool can nevertheless improve model training speed without introducing significant semantic differences. This is most likely due to our tool's conservativeness, practitioners not favoring highly complex features [49], and "Ariadne" supporting some dynamic features like callbacks. While it possible for our tool to hybridize an incompatible function, the negligible differences in model accuracy and loss further suggest that these situations were avoided on our subjects. And the improved speedup suggests that it does not introduce retracing, although additional testing is currently ongoing. Code readability could also be impacted; however, our tool only adds or removes a single function decorator.

5   Conclusion & Future Work

Our automated refactoring tool, HYBRIDIZE FUNCTIONS, assists developers with writing optimal imperative DL Python code. It is open-source and available as a *PyDev Eclipse* plug-in. The tool integrates an Eclipse-based refactoring with the Python static analyses offered by *WALA* "Ariadne", for which we expanded for modern versions of "TensorFlow" and modern Python constructs that are commonly used in imperative DL programs. Nineteen Python DL projects totaling 132.05 K lines of code were used in the tools assessment, and a speedup of 2.16 on the refactored code was observed. In the future, we will explore incorporating advanced container-based analyses [14, 48] and automatically splitting DL code into more functions to increase hybridization opportunities.

Acknowledgments This material is based upon work supported by the National Science Foundation under Award Nos. CCF 2200343, CNS 2213763, and CCF 2343750.

References

1. Abadi, M., Barham, P., Chen, J., Chen, Z., Davis, A., Dean, J., Devin, M., Ghemawat, S., Irving, G., Isard, M., Kudlur, M., Levenberg, J., Monga, R., Moore, S., Murray, D.G., Steiner, B., Tucker, P., Vasudevan, V., Warden, P., Wicke, M., Yu, Y., Zheng, X.: TensorFlow: A System for Large-Scale Machine Learning. In: Symposium on Operating Systems Design and Implementation (2016)
2. Abseil, *abseil/abseil-py*, (2024). https://github.com/abseil/abseil-py (visited on 06/26/2024).
3. Agrawal, A., Modi, A.N., Passos, A., Lavoie, A., Agarwal, A., Shankar, A., Ganichev, I., Levenberg, J., Hong, M., Monga, R., Cai, S.: TensorFlow Eager: A Multi-Stage, Python-Embedded DSL for Machine Learning, (2019). arXiv: 1903.01855 [cs.PL].
4. Apache, Hybridize. Apache MXNet documentation, (2021). https://mxnet.apache.org/versions/1.8.0/api/python/docs/tutorials/packages/gluon/blocks/hybridize.html (visited on 04/08/2021)
5. Baker, W., O'Connor, M., Shahamiri, S.R., Terragni, V.: Detect, Fix, and Verify TensorFlow API Misuses. In: International Conference on Software Analysis, Evolution and Reengineering, pp. 1–5 (2022)
6. Bäumer, D., Gamma, E., Kiezun, A.: "Integrating refactoring support into a Java development tool".
7. Cao, J., Chen, B., Sun, C., Hu, L., Peng, X.: Characterizing Performance Bugs in Deep Learning Systems, (2021). arXiv: 2112.01771 [cs.SE].
8. Cao, J., Chen, B., Sun, C., Hu, L., Wu, S., Peng, X.: Understanding Performance Problems in Deep Learning Systems. In: FSE. FSE '22, pp. 357–369. ACM (2022). https://doi.org/10.1145/3540250.3549123
9. Castro Vélez, T., Khatchadourian, R., Bagherzadeh, M., Raja, A.: Challenges in Migrating Imperative Deep Learning Programs to Graph Execution: An Empirical Study. In: MSR. MSR '22. ACM (2022). https://doi.org/10.1145/3524842.3528455
10. Chen, T., Li, M., Li, Y., Lin, M., Wang, N., Wang, M., Xiao, T., Xu, B., Zhang, C., Zhang, Z.: MXNet: A Flexible and Efficient Machine Learning Library for Heterogeneous Distributed Systems. In: Workshop on Machine Learning Systems at NIPS (2015). arXiv: 1512.01274 [cs.DC]
11. Chen, Z., Yao, H., Lou, Y., Cao, Y., Liu, Y., Wang, H., Liu, X.: An Empirical Study on Deployment Faults of Deep Learning Based Mobile Applications. In: ICSE. IEEE (2021). https://doi.org/10.1109/icse43902.2021.00068
12. Chollet, F.: Deep Learning with Python. Manning (2020)
13. Dig, D., Marrero, J., Ernst, M.D.: Refactoring sequential Java code for concurrency via concurrent libraries. In: ICSE, pp. 397–407 (2009). https://doi.org/10.1109/ICSE.2009.5070539
14. Dillig, I., Dillig, T., Aiken, A.: Precise reasoning for programs using containers. SIGPLAN Not. **46**(1), 187–200 (2011). https://doi.org/10.1145/1925844.1926407. https://dl.acm.org/doi/10.1145/1925844.1926407 (visited on 10/11/2023)
15. Dolby, J., Shinnar, A., Allain, A., Reinen, J.: Ariadne. Analysis for Machine Learning Programs. In: MAPL, pp. 1–10. ACM (2018). https://doi.org/10.1145/3211346.3211349
16. Eclipse Foundation, Eclipse IDE, (2024). https://eclipseide.org/ (visited on 09/10/2024)
17. Eclipse Foundation, Eclipse JDT, (2025). https://github.com/eclipse-jdt (visited on 01/30/2025)

18. Facebook Inc., PyTorch. TorchScript, en. (2019). https://pytorch.org/docs/stable/jit.html (visited on 02/19/2021)
19. Google LLC, Better performance with tf.function, (2021). https://tensorflow.org/guide/function (visited on 02/19/2021)
20. Google LLC, Introduction to graphs and tf.function, (2022). https://tensorflow.org/guide/intro_to_graphs (visited on 01/20/2022)
21. Google LLC, Migrate your TensorFlow 1 code to TensorFlow 2, (2021). https://tensorflow.org/guide/migrate (visited on 05/27/2021)
22. Google LLC, tf.data.Dataset. TensorFlow, version 2.9.3. (2023). https://www.tensorflow.org/versions/r2.9/api_docs/python/tf/data/Dataset (visited on 12/15/2023)
23. Humbatova, N., Jahangirova, G., Bavota, G., Riccio, V., Stocco, A., Tonella, P.: Taxonomy of real faults in Deep Learning systems. In: ICSE (2020). https://doi.org/10.1145/3377811.3380395
24. *Hybridize-Functions-Refactoring*, (2024). https://github.com/ponder-lab/Hybridize-Functions-Refactoring (visited on 09/30/2024).
25. Islam, M.J., Nguyen, G., Pan, R., Rajan, H.: A comprehensive study on Deep Learning bug characteristics. In: FSE (2019). https://doi.org/10.1145/3338906.3338955
26. Islam, M.J., Nguyen, H.A., Pan, R., Rajan, H.: What Do Developers Ask About ML Libraries? A Large-scale Study Using Stack Overflow, (2019). arXiv: 1906.11940 [cs.SE].
27. Islam, M.J., Pan, R., Nguyen, G., Rajan, H.: Repairing Deep Neural Networks: Fix Patterns and Challenges. In: ICSE (2020). https://doi.org/10.1145/3377811.3380378
28. Istria, M.: An operation for refactorings. Issue #61. microsoft/language-server-protocol, Microsoft. (2021). https://github.com/microsoft/language-server-protocol/issues/61 (visited on 05/10/2023)
29. Jeong, E., Cho, S., Yu, G.-I., Jeong, J.S., Shin, D.-J., Kim, T., Chun, B.-G.: Speculative Symbolic Graph Execution of Imperative Deep Learning Programs. SIGOPS Oper. Syst. Rev. **53**(1), 26–33 (2019). https://doi.org/10.1145/3352020.3352025
30. Kaiyinzhou, NLPGNN/nlpgnn/models/__init__.py, (2020). https://github.com/kyzhouhzau/NLPGNN/blob/b9ecec2c6df/nlpgnn/models/__init__.py (visited on 07/21/2024)
31. Khatchadourian, R.: graph_execution_time_comparison.ipynb, (2021). https://bit.ly/3bwrhVt (visited on 11/03/2021)
32. Khatchadourian, R., Arefin, M., Friedman, O.: *ponder-lab/Common-Eclipse-Refactoring-Framework*, version v3.6.0 (2024). https://doi.org/10.5281/zenodo.13873498. https://github.com/ponder-lab/Common-Eclipse-Refactoring-Framework.
33. Khatchadourian, R., Tang, Y., Bagherzadeh, M., Ahmed, S.: Safe Automated Refactoring for Intelligent Parallelization of Java 8 Streams. In: ICSE. ICSE '19, pp. 619–630. IEEE Press (2019). https://doi.org/10.1109/ICSE.2019.00072
34. Kim, T., Jeong, E., Kim, G.-W., Koo, Y., Kim, S., Yu, G.-I., Chun, B.-G.: Terra: Imperative-Symbolic Co-Execution of Imperative Deep Learning Programs. In: International Conference on Neural Information Processing Systems. NIPS '21, pp. 1468–1480 (2021)
35. Liu, J., Huang, Q., Xia, X., Shihab, E., Lo, D., Li, S.: Is Using Deep Learning Frameworks Free? Characterizing Technical Debt in Deep Learning Frameworks. In: ICSE. ICSE-SEIS '20 (2020). https://doi.org/10.1145/3377815.3381377

36. Microsoft Corporation, Language Server Protocol, (2022). https://microsoft.github.io/language-server-protocol (visited on 05/10/2023)

37. Moldovan, D., Decker, J.M., Wang, F., Johnson, A.A., Lee, B.K., Nado, Z., Sculley, D., Rompf, T., Wiltschko, A.B.: AutoGraph: Imperative-style Coding with Graph-based Performance, (2019). arXiv: 1810.08061 [cs.PL].

38. Nikanjam, A., Khomh, F.: Design Smells in Deep Learning Programs: An Empirical Study. In: International Conference on Software Maintenance and Evolution, pp. 332–342. IEEE (2021). https://doi.org/10.1109/ICSME52107.2021.00036

39. Pallets, Click, (2014). http://click.palletsprojects.com (visited on 06/25/2024)

40. Paszke, A., Gross, S., Massa, F., Lerer, A., Bradbury, J., Chanan, G., Killeen, T., Lin, Z., Gimelshein, N., Antiga, L., Desmaison, A., Köpf, A., Yang, E., DeVito, Z., Raison, M., Tejani, A., Chilamkurthy, S., Steiner, B., Fang, L., Bai, J., Chintala, S.: PyTorch: An Imperative Style, High-Performance Deep Learning Library, (2019). arXiv: 1912.01703 [cs.LG].

41. Python Software Foundation, Modules. Packages, (2024). https://docs.python.org/3/tutorial/modules.html#packages (visited on 04/10/2024)

42. Python Software Foundation, Modules. Intra-package References. Packages, (2024). https://docs.python.org/3/tutorial/modules.html#intra-package-references (visited on 04/12/2024)

43. Rosen, B.K., Wegman, M.N., Zadeck, F.K.: Global Value Numbers and Redundant Computations. In: Symposium on Principles of Programming Languages, pp. 12–27 (1988). https://doi.org/10.1145/73560.73562

44. Suhan, A., Libenzi, D., Zhang, A., Schuh, P., Saeta, B., Sohn, J.Y., Shabalin, D.: LazyTensor: combining eager execution with domain-specific compilers. (2021). https://doi.org/10.48550/ARXIV.2102.13267. arXiv: 2102.13267 [cs.PL]

45. *T.J. Watson Libraries for Analysis*, (2024). https://github.com/wala/WALA (visited on 09/10/2024). original-date: 2012-04-05T18:57:03Z.

46. Tuppeny, D.: Support refactors that require user input/options. Issue #1164. microsoft/language-server-protocol, Microsoft. (2023). https://github.com/microsoft/language-server-protocol/issues/1164 (visited on 05/10/2023)

47. WALA, *wala/ML*, (2024). http://github.com/wala/ML (visited on 09/12/2024).

48. Xu, G., Rountev, A.: Precise memory leak detection for java software using container profiling. ACM Trans. Softw. Eng. Methodol. **22**(3), 1–28 (2013). https://doi.org/10.1145/2491509.2491511

49. Yang, Y., Milanova, A., Hirzel, M.: Complex Python Features in the Wild. In: MSR, pp. 282–293. ACM (2022). https://doi.org/10.1145/3524842.3528467

50. Zadrozny, F.: PyDev, (2023). https://www.pydev.org (visited on 05/31/2023)

51. Zhang, T., Gao, C., Ma, L., Lyu, M., Kim, M.: An Empirical Study of Common Challenges in Developing Deep Learning Applications. In: International Symposium on Software Reliability Engineering (2019). https://doi.org/10.1109/ISSRE.2019.00020

52. Zhang, Y., Chen, Y., Cheung, S.-C., Xiong, Y., Zhang, L.: An Empirical Study on TensorFlow Program Bugs. In: International Symposium on Software Testing and Analysis (2018). https://doi.org/10.1145/3213846.3213866

53. Zhou, W., Zhao, Y., Zhang, G., Shen, X.: HARP: Holistic Analysis for Refactoring Python-Based Analytics Programs. In: ICSE (2020). https://doi.org/10.1145/3377811.3380434

Compositional Learning for Synchronous Parallel Automata

Mahboubeh Samadi[1(✉)], Aryan Bastany[2], and Hossein Hojjat[1]

[1] Tehran Institute for Advanced Studies, Khatam University, Tehran, Iran
{m.samadi,h.hojjat}@teias.institute
[2] University of Tehran, Tehran, Iran
a_bastanyaryan_b@ut.ac.ir

Abstract. Automata learning is an approach for extracting a model in the shape of an automaton from a black-box system. This approach has recently gained much attention in both industry and academia. In this paper, we introduce a compositional automata learning algorithm for systems comprising synchronous parallel components. Our algorithm assumes no prior knowledge about the number of components, their individual alphabets, and the synchronizing alphabets. The learning process is automatic and figures out the alphabet symbols on-the-fly during learning the components. We prove that the proposed algorithm terminates and correctly learns the individual components. We use a number of case studies from the industrial automotive domain and synthetic benchmarks to evaluate the performance of the proposed algorithm. The experimental results show that the algorithm requires significantly fewer input symbols and resets to learn the system compositionally.

1 Introduction

Active automata learning [1] is a promising approach for extracting a model in the shape of an automaton from a black-box system. This technique can be quite handy when engineers need to understand how a legacy or sophisticated system operates. The extracted model is concise, abstract, and quite helpful in practice. Active automata learning has recently gained much attention: it has been used for learning sophisticated industrial systems such as communication and security protocols [2], biometric passports [3], smart cards [4], and network protocols [5].

In automata learning, a learner interacts with a teacher who knows the System Under Learning (SUL), and poses queries to learn the system model. The original algorithm L* [1] is proposed to learn a model of a system as a deterministic finite automaton, and other extensions of L* are introduced in [6,7,8,9,10] to learn richer models. Using L* to learn industrial large models may lead to a huge number of queries which grows quadratically with the number of model states [11]. Instead, compositional learning where a system is learned through learning its components is a promising approach to resolve this problem [12]. In [11,12,13,14], compositional learning algorithms are introduced where [12] and [14] are the closest works to our work. In [12], a *synchronous* parallel composition algorithm is introduced where the alphabets of components are known to the learner beforehand and the components interact synchronously. In [14],

© The Author(s) 2025
A. Boronat and G. Fraser (Eds.): FASE 2025, LNCS 15693, pp. 101–121, 2025.
https://doi.org/10.1007/978-3-031-90900-9_6

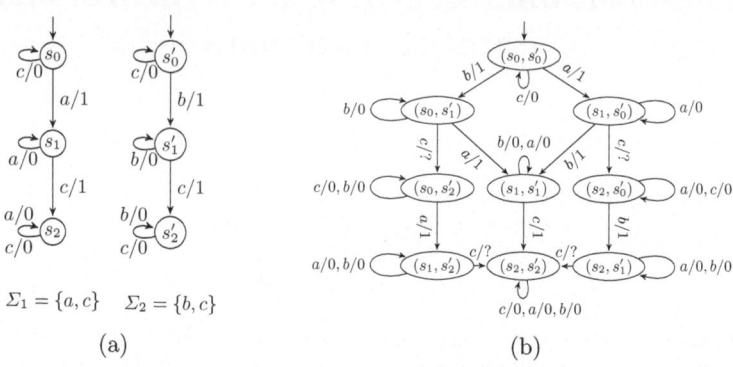

Fig. 1: (a) Two Mealy machines with alphabets $\{a, c\}$ and $\{b, c\}$ (b) Synchronous parallel composition of two Mealy machines synchronizing on c

a compositional algorithm is introduced as an extension of L^* where the individual components are learned without any knowledge about the number of components and their individual alphabets. However, in [14], components are not synchronized and there is no communication among them.

In this paper, we introduce a *synchronous compositional* learning algorithm as an extension of the algorithm proposed in [14] in which systems comprising *synchronous* components are learned compositionally. In our approach, individual components are learned without any knowledge about the number of components, their individual alphabets, and the synchronizing alphabets. We learn such information automatically and on-the-fly, and learn the composite model by applying L^* to the individual components. We learn a system model in the form of a Mealy machine [15]. A Mealy machine is a finite-state machine in which the transitions produce an output value based on the current state and the current input symbol. Following the model learning literature [1,14], we assume that the system model under learning is *deterministic* [16] where there is exactly *one* output and target state for a source state and a given input. In other words, the next state is uniquely determined by the given state, input, *and* output. We show by an example that the synchronous parallel composition of two deterministic Mealy machines may lead to a *pseudo-nondeterministic* Mealy machine [17] where there is more than one output for the given state and the given input.

Example. Consider two deterministic Mealy machines M_1 and M_2 (Fig. 1(a)) with input alphabets $\{a, c\}$, and $\{b, c\}$. These machines synchronize on the shared action c where c has different outputs 0 and 1. Fig. 1(b) shows the synchronous parallel composition of M_1 and M_2 where composing $s_0 \xrightarrow{c/0} s_0$ and $s_1' \xrightarrow{c/1} s_2'$ results in $(s_0, s_1') \xrightarrow{c/?} (s_0, s_2')$ and ? denotes the non-deterministic output which can be either 0 or 1.

In this paper, we assume that each synchronizing action must have a *unique* output wherever it is used across the whole system. This assumption avoids output non-determinism: the synchronous parallel composition of two deterministic Mealy machines remains deterministic. Output determinism is also assumed in [18,19,20] and compatible with many benchmarks in railway [21,22] and automotive [23,24] domains. We also investigated the outputs of actions in some benchmarks (details in Section 5) and found that on average around ∼46 percent of the actions have unique outputs. However, the assumption that synchronizing actions have unique outputs everywhere may be overkill in some cases (the output value should be the same only at the point of communication, not throughout the whole system). Without this assumption, the proposed algorithm cannot detect the synchronizing actions and the individual components, but it learns the parallel composition of automata correctly. We leave investigating the general case as future work.

In the proposed approach, we learn the SUL in separate components. If the alphabets of the components are not disjoint, then their intersection denotes the synchronizing actions. Initially, we start with a partition comprising only singleton sets and assume that all actions can be synchronizing actions. If we find an action with two different outputs, then we remove it from the set of synchronizing actions. The total behavior of the system is obtained by constructing the synchronous parallel composition of the components. We process the counter-example CE returned from the teacher and iteratively update the set of synchronizing actions. For each of the two actions involved in CE, we *merge* their corresponding input sets if they do not belong to the set of synchronizing actions. Otherwise, we *add* the synchronizing action to the sets including the non-synchronizing actions of CE.

Running Example Consider the SUL of Fig. 2(a) with two synchronous components and the alphabets $\{a, c\}$ and $\{b, c\}$. Fig. 2(b) shows the synchronous parallel composition of two components. Initially, we assume that the set of synchronizing actions is $sync = \{a, b, c\}$. We start by partitioning the alphabet into singleton sets of elements, i.e., $\{a\}, \{b\}, \{c\}$, where each set corresponds to one component. The parallel composition of the three learned Mealy machines of Fig. 2(c) does not comply with the original system of Fig. 2(b). Hence, the teacher returns a counter-example. For example, $CE = ca$ is a counter-example as this string generates the output 01 in Fig. 2(b) but the output sequence in Fig. 2(c) is 00. As the action a has two outputs 0 and 1, we remove it from the set of synchronizing actions, i.e., $sync = \{b, c\}$. Two actions c and a are both involved in the minimum counter-example. A counter-example is minimal if any of its prefixes is not a counter-example. In this way, a minimal counter example does not have extra actions and only consists of a sequence of actions that leads to generating different outputs. Hence, we conclude that c and a must belong to one component and hence we add the synchronizing action c to the set including a, i.e., $\{a, c\}, \{b\}$ (details about the methods of *partition* and *merge* can be found in Section 3). Then, we restart the learning process which leads to the Mealy machines in Fig. 2(d). As the learning process continues, the teacher returns a

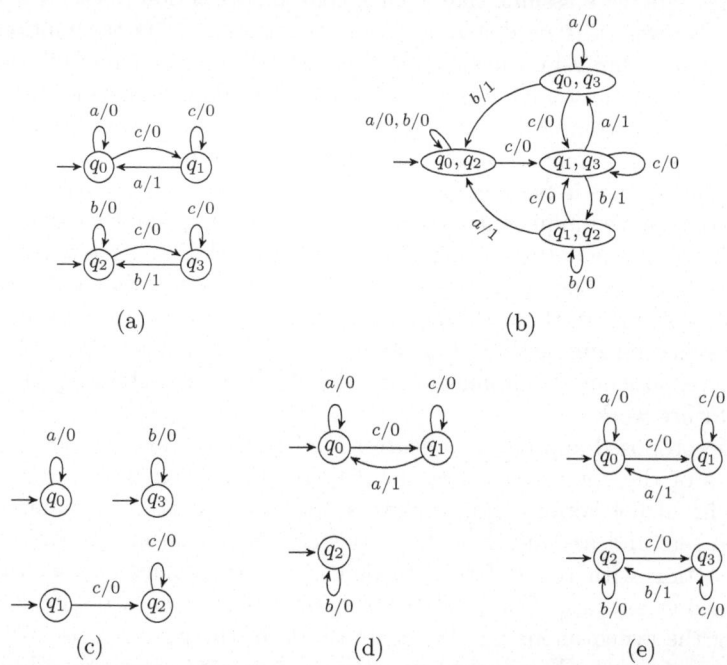

Fig. 2: (a) Initial model: two parallel Mealy machines, (b) Synchronous parallel composition of (a), (c) Partition input alphabet to $\{\{a\}, \{b\}, \{c\}\}$ and learn each component individually, (d) Use a counter-example ca to update components, (e) Use a counter-example cb to update components

counter-example $CE = cb$ which generates the output 01 in Fig. 2(b) but the output sequence is 00 in Fig. 2(d). As the action b has two outputs 0 and 1, we remove it from the set of synchronizing actions which results in $sync = \{c\}$. We conclude that b and c must belong to one component as the counter-example includes both actions b and c. However, we do not merge the input sets $\{a, c\}$ and $\{b\}$ as a and b may belong to two distinct components synchronized on c. Instead, we add c to the set $\{b\}$ which results in $\{a, c\}$ and $\{b, c\}$ (Fig. 2(e)). The synchronous parallel composition of components in Fig. 2(e) is equal to Fig. 2(b). Hence, the teacher does not return a counter-example and the original system's components are learned.

In the following, we summarize our main contributions:

- We introduce a compositional algorithm for parallel synchronous automata. The learner does not know the number of automata, their individual alphabets, and the synchronizing alphabets (Section 3).
- We provide a theoretical proof of the proposed algorithm and prove that the algorithm terminates and the components are learned correctly (Section 4).

- We evaluate the performance of the proposed algorithm on the two sets of benchmarking systems called *synthetic* and *realistic*. For the synthetic systems, we generate random components that can synchronize based on the patterns that reflect the real-world network topologies. For the realistic system, we use a benchmark based on an industrial automotive system (Section 5).

2 Preliminaries and Background

In this section, we first give some preliminaries about the notion of a Mealy machine as the underlying system model, the parallel composition and decomposition of Mealy machines, and the concept of (in)dependent actions. Then, we recall the basic concepts of active automata learning and the L* algorithm.

2.1 Mealy Machines

Mealy machines are the generalizations of finite automata in which the transitions produce outputs:

Definition 1 (Mealy Machine). *A Mealy machine is a six-tuple $(S, s_0, I, O, \delta, \lambda)$:*

- *S is a finite set of internal states, $s_0 \in S$ is the initial state,*
- *I is a non-empty set of actions, representing the input alphabet,*
- *O is a non-empty set of outputs,*
- *$\delta : S \times I \to S$ is a state transition function,*
- *$\lambda : S \times I \to O$ is an output function.*

A Mealy machine starts in the initial state s_0 and accepts a sequence of actions to produce an equally-sized sequence of outputs. For each $s, s' \in S$, $i \in I$, and $o \in O$, we use $\delta(s, i) = s'$ to denote that the next state of s is s', $\lambda(s, i) = o$ to denote that the output upon receiving an input i is o.

2.2 (De)Composing Mealy Machines

In this section, we first define the synchronizing actions and the synchronous parallel composition of Mealy machines, and then explain how a Mealy machine can be decomposed into smaller Mealy machines. In a parallel composition of Mealy machines, we assume that whenever two machines share a common action symbol, this symbol is a synchronizing action and the Mealy machines must synchronize on that symbol. This is essentially similar to CSP-style multi-way communications [25], where multiple machines need to synchronize at the common action name. To prevent non-deterministic behavior, as explained in Section 1, we strictly require that each synchronizing action has a unique output.

Definition 2 (Synchronizing Action). *For n Mealy machines $M_i = (S_i, s_{0_i}, I_i, O_i, \delta_i, \lambda_i)$, s.t $i \in \{1, \ldots, n\}$, an action u is a synchronizing action iff:*

- *There exists M_j and M_k such that $u \in I_j \cap I_k$ and for every $s \in S_j$ and $s' \in S_k$, $\lambda_j(s, u) = \lambda_k(s', u)$.*

- *In any M_j, there are no states $s, s' \in S_j$ such that $\lambda_j(s, u) \neq \lambda_j(s', u)$.*

We assume any action shared among some Mealy machines is a synchronizing action. An action that is not shared between any Mealy machines is a *local* action.

Definition 3 (Synchronous Parallel Composition). *Given n Mealy machines $M_i = (S_i, s_{0_i}, I_i, O_i, \delta_i, \lambda_i)$, s.t $i \in \{1, \ldots, n\}$, their synchronous parallel composition, denoted by $\|_{i=1}^{n} M_i$, defined as $(S, s_0, I, O, \delta, \lambda)$ where $S = S_1 \times \ldots \times S_n$, $s_0 = (s_{0_1}, \ldots, s_{0_n})$, $I = \bigcup_{i \in \{1,\ldots,n\}} I_i$, $O = \bigcup_{i \in \{1,\ldots,n\}} O_i$, $\lambda((s_1, \ldots, s_j, \ldots, s_n), u) = \lambda_j(s_j, u)$ and δ is defined as the following:*

- *For each $j \in \{1, \ldots, n\}$, the local action u can be performed independently if $u \in I_j$ and there does not exist $k \in \{1, \ldots, n\}$, such that $j \neq k$ and $u \in I_k$. In this case, δ is defined as*

$$\delta((s_1, \ldots, s_j, \ldots, s_n), u) = (s_1, \ldots, \delta_j(s_j, u), \ldots, s_n)$$

- *The synchronizing action u can be performed by the Mealy machines that include u. For each $j \in \{1, \ldots, n\}$, we define $\delta'_j(s_j, u)$ to denote the next state of s_j after performing the synchronizing action u. If $u \in I_j$ then $\delta'_j(s_j, u) = \delta_j(s_j, u)$, and if $u \notin I_j$ then $\delta'_j(s_j, u) = s_j$. In this case, δ is defined as*

$$\delta((s_1, \ldots, s_j, \ldots, s_n), u) = (\delta'_1(s_1, u), \ldots, \delta'_j(s_j, u), \ldots, \delta'_n(s_n, u))$$

As the output of a synchronizing action is the same in all Mealy machines, the last condition implies that the output of an action in the composed Mealy machine is the same as its output in the individual Mealy machine.

Next, we first define how a Mealy machine can be decomposed into some Mealy machines, then define (in)dependent actions, and simple Mealy machines.

Definition 4 (Projection of a Mealy Machine [14]). *The projection of a Mealy machine $M = (S, s_0, I, O, \delta, \lambda)$ on a set of inputs $I' \subseteq I$, denoted by $P(M, I')$, is a Mealy machine $(S, s_0, I', O', \delta', \lambda')$, where*

- $\delta'(s, a) = \delta(s, a)$ *for $a \in I', s \in S$,*
- $\lambda'(s, a) = \lambda(s, a)$ *for $a \in I', s \in S$, and*
- $O' = \{o \in O \mid \exists a \in I', \exists s \in S \cdot \lambda(s, a) = o\}$.

Example. Consider two Mealy machines in Fig. 2(a) where alphabets are $\Sigma_1 = \{a, c\}$ and $\Sigma_2 = \{b, c\}$. The shared action c is a synchronizing action, and a and b are the local actions. The synchronizing action c has a unique output 0 in both Mealy machines. The synchronous parallel composition of these two Mealy machines is denoted in Fig. 2(b). The projection of a Mealy machine in Fig. 2(b) on the input alphabets $\{a\}$, $\{b\}$, and $\{c\}$ are represented in Fig. 2(c).

Definition 5 (Independent Cover [14]). *Consider a Mealy machine M with a set of inputs I. The subsets $I_1, \ldots, I_n \subseteq I$ form an independent cover of I when for any sequence of inputs as u', $\lambda_{P(M,I_1)\|\ldots\|P(M,I_n)}(u') = \lambda_M(u')$.*

Intuitively, an independent cover represents individual components where some components are synchronized on shared actions.

Definition 6 (Independent Actions). *Consider a set of inputs I, and $\{I_1, \ldots, I_i, \ldots, I_j, \ldots, I_n\}$ an independent cover of I ($i \neq j$). Two actions u and v where at least one of them is non-synchronizing are independent if $u \in I_i$ and $v \in I_j$.*

Definition 7 (Dependent Actions). *Consider a set of inputs I, and $\{I_1, \ldots, I_i, \ldots, I_n\}$ an independent cover of I. Two actions u and v where at least one of them is a non-synchronizing action, are dependent if $u \in I_i$ and $v \in I_i$.*

Definition 8 (Simple Mealy Machine). *A Mealy machine M is simple if it consists of dependent actions, and no Mealy machines exist like M_1 and M_2 such that $M = M_1 \| M_2$.*

Example. The cover $\{\{a\}, \{b\}, \{c\}\}$ in Fig. 2(c) is not an independent cover as $\lambda_M(aca) = 001$ but $\lambda_{P(M,\{a\})\|P(M,\{b\})\|P(M,\{c\})}(aca) = 000$. Two actions a and b in Fig. 2(a) are independent as they belong to two subsets of $\{\{a,c\}, \{b,c\}\}$, and a and c are dependent as they belong to one set of $\{\{a,c\}, \{a,b\}\}$. Each of the two Mealy machines in Fig. 2(a) are the simple Mealy machines as they are not the synchronous parallel composition of other machines and their actions are dependent on each other.

2.3   Model Learning

Active model learning [1] is a technique for learning the behavior of a black box system by formulating a hypothesis $\mathscr{H}$ about the behavior of an SUL as a finite state machine. The *learner* can pose two types of queries to a *teacher* about the SUL that only the teacher knows: (1) *Membership Queries*, where the learner asks whether a target SUL includes a sequence of actions, (2) *Equivalence Queries* (EQ), where the learner proposes a hypothesis $\mathscr{H}$ about the "language" of the SUL and asks whether $\mathscr{H}$ and the SUL are equivalent. The learner organizes the received information from the teacher in an *observation table*:

Definition 9 (Observation Table [1]). *An observation table is a triple (S, E, T), where $S \subseteq I^*$ is a prefix-closed set of input strings, $E \subseteq I^+$ is a suffix-closed set of input strings, and T can be seen as a table. The rows of T are labeled by elements from $S \cup (S, I)$ where (S, I) represents the set of all possible extensions of prefixes by adding a single symbol from I to each element in S, columns are labeled by elements from E, and $T(s, e)$ is the SUL's output suffix for the input sequence s.e where s.e represents the string formed by concatenating a prefix string s with a suffix string e.*

The L^* algorithm initially starts with S only containing the empty word ϵ, and E equals the set of inputs alphabet I. To construct a hypothesis $\mathcal{H}$, the observation table must have two properties namely *closeness* and *consistency*. An observation table is *closed* iff for all $w \in S.I$ there is a $w' \in S$ that for all $e \in E$, $T(w, e) = T(w', e)$ holds. An observation table is *consistent* iff for all $s_1, s_2 \in S$, such that for all $e \in E$, $T(s_1, e) = T(s_2, e)$, it holds that $T(s_1.\alpha, e) = T(s_2.\alpha, e)$ for all $\alpha \in I, e \in E$.

The learner queries are posed until these two properties hold, and a hypothesis $\mathcal{H}$ is formulated. Then, the teacher returns either a counterexample (CE) denoting the non-conformance, or 'yes', if $\mathcal{H}$ is equivalent to the SUL. If a counter-example is found, it is incorporated into the observation table by adding its prefixes/suffixes to the observation table, and the updated table is again checked for closedness and consistency. The L* algorithm is guaranteed to eventually produce a hypothesis $\mathcal{H}$ which is the same as the SUL.

As we aim to learn the system in terms of synchronous components separately, we need to define the projection operator that removes all the transitions that are not in the projected alphabet. The proposed algorithm learns a blackbox system with respect to its projection on the actions of each component.

Definition 10 (L* with Projected Actions [14]). *Given a Mealy machine* $M = (S, s_0, I, O, \delta, \lambda)$ *and* $I' \subseteq I$, $L^*(M, I')$ *returns* $P(M, I')$ *by running algorithm* L^* *with the projected action* I' *on* M.

3   Synchronous Compositional Learning Algorithm

In this section, we introduce an extension of the CL* algorithm [14] named *Synchronous Compositional Learning* Algorithm (SCL*). In [14], components have no communication and they are not synchronized with each other. In this paper, we compositionally learn an unknown system $M = \|_{i=1}^{n} M_i$ consisting of n parallel synchronous components where each component's input and the synchronizing actions are not known and we learn such information on-the-fly.

We initially assume that each component has an input alphabet and the set of synchronizing actions *sync* is equal to the union of the input alphabets of all components. The main idea behind learning the synchronizing actions in SCL* is to observe the outputs of actions. Based on Definition 2 and the uniformity of the outputs of synchronizing actions, which implies that outputs of synchronizing actions are unique, if the algorithm discovers different outputs for an action u, it concludes that u cannot be a synchronizing action and so it removes u from *sync*. The set of the input alphabets of components $I^F = \{I_1, \ldots, I_n\}$ is a cover of the total system's input alphabet. The goal is to find a cover I^F where each $I_i \in I^F$ corresponds to a component i. When I_i and I_j have a non-empty intersection, it means that they synchronize on the shared actions. To reach such a cover, we start with an initial cover with singleton sets including only one action. Assume that the teacher returns a counter-example $u_1 \ldots u_m$ in response to an equivalence query. For each pair of actions $u_\ell \in I_i$ and $u_r \in I_j$ such that u_ℓ does

---

Algorithm 1 Synchronous Compositional Learning Algorithm (SCL^*)

Result: $\mathcal{H}$
Input: $I^F = \{I_1, \ldots, I_n\}, M$

1: $sync := \bigcup_{i:1\ldots n} I_i$ where $I_i \in I^F$
2: $OutSync := \emptyset$
3: $\mathcal{H} \leftarrow LearnSyncInParts(M, I^F)$
4: **for each** $u \in sync$ **do**
5:     **if** $\exists s_i, s_j \in S \cdot \mathcal{H} = (S, s_0, I, O, \delta, \lambda) \wedge \lambda(s_i, u) \neq \lambda(s_j, u)$ **then**
6:         $sync := sync \setminus \{u\}$
7:     **else** $OutSync := OutSync \cup \{u \mapsto \lambda(s_i, u)\}$
8: $CE \leftarrow \textsc{Equivalence-Query}(\mathcal{H}, M)$
9: **while** $CE \neq yes$ **do**
10:     $ProcessCE(CE)$
11:     $\mathcal{H} \leftarrow LearnSyncInParts(M, I^F)$
12:     $CE \leftarrow \textsc{Equivalence-Query}(\mathcal{H}, M)$
13: $sync := sync \setminus \{u \mid \nexists I_i, I_j \in I^F \cdot u \in I_i \wedge u \in I_j\}$
14: *return* $\mathcal{H}$

---

not belong to *sync*, if $I_1, \ldots, I_n$ does not form an independent cover according to Definition 5, i.e., $\lambda_{P(M,I_1) \| \ldots \| P(M,I_n)}(u_\ell u_r) \neq \lambda_M(u_\ell u_r)$, we conclude that u_ℓ and u_r are dependent and they must belong to one input set. We merge I_i and I_j if u_r also does not belong to *sync*. If u_r belongs to *sync*, we add u_r to I_i which includes u_ℓ. The reason is that if u_r is actually a synchronizing action, then the components i and j must synchronize on u_r. Hence, u_r must belong to both input sets I_i and I_j. As the algorithm continues, if we find that u_r is not actually a synchronizing action, then we merge I_i and I_j. We will prove (Proposition 2) that the counter-example $u_1 \ldots u_m$ consists of at least one non-synchronizing action as the Mealy machine is deterministic and the outputs of synchronizing actions are also unique. Therefore, a sequence of synchronizing actions in the SUL and the learned model will always generate the same sequence of outputs.

After updating I^F, we learn the system with the projected alphabet for each $I_k \in I^F$, and compute the product of the obtained components with synchronous parallel composition. This scenario is iterated until the result is equivalent to the original system, and the teacher returns no counter-example.

In the following, we introduce the SCL* algorithm in detail to learn a system consisting of synchronous components where each component can be modeled by a simple Mealy machine. To this end, we first introduce some definitions used in the algorithm.

Definition 11 (LearnSyncInParts). *The LearnSyncInParts function gets* $M = (S, s_0, I, O, \delta, \lambda)$ *and the cover* $I^F = \{I_1, \ldots, I_n\}$ *of* I *and returns the synchronous parallel composition of the learned components.*

$$LearnSyncInParts(M, I^F) = L^*(M, I_1) \| \cdots \| L^*(M, I_n)$$

Definition 12 (DependentSets). *The function DependentSets gets a counter-example CE, an input cover* I^F, *and a synchronizing set sync, and returns the* *input sets from I^F that contain at least one non-synchronizing action of CE:*

$$DependentSets(CE, I^F, sync) = \{I_j \mid I_j \in I^F, \exists i \cdot CE[i] \notin sync \wedge CE[i] \in I_j\}$$

, where $CE[i]$ refers to the ith symbol of CE.

Example. If $I^F = \{\{a, b\}, \{c, d\}, \{e, f\}\}$, $sync = \{b, d\}$, and $CE = bce$, then $DependentSets(CE, I^F, sync) = \{\{c, d\}, \{e, f\}\}$.

Definition 13 (Merge). *The function Merge gets two covers I_1^F and I_2^F, and updates I_1^F according to the sets in I_2^F. To this end, it removes the sets of I_2^F from I_1^F and adds their union to I_1^F: $Merge(I_1^F, I_2^F) = (I_1^F \setminus I_2^F) \cup \{\bigcup_{I_j \in I_2^F} I_j\}$*

Example. If $I_1^F = \{\{a\}, \{b\}, \{c, d\}\}$, $I_2^F = \{\{b\}, \{c, d\}\}$ then $Merge(I_1^F, I_2^F) = \{\{a\}, \{b, c, d\}\}$

Algorithm 1 shows the pseudo-code of learning a system compositionally including components that synchronized on some actions. The algorithm is called with the singleton covering I^F of the alphabet I and the original system M, i.e., if the input alphabet is $I = \{u_1, u_2, \ldots, u_n\}$, then the initial cover of the alphabet will be $I^F = \{\{u_1\}, \{u_2\}, \ldots, \{u_n\}\}$. Initially, on line 1, we set the synchronizing actions, i.e., $sync$, as the union of all input alphabets in I^F. Then, the *LearnSyncInParts* method, on line 3, learns each of the components given the corresponding alphabet set using the algorithm L^* and returns the synchronous composition of the learned components. Regarding the learned components, we update the hypothetical synchronizing actions, $sync$. Based on our assumption, if there is a synchronizing action like u with different outputs in $\mathcal{H}$, we find that u cannot be a synchronizing action, and hence, remove u from $sync$, on lines 4-6. Otherwise, we store the corresponding output of each synchronizing action in the mapping *OutSync*, on line 7. This mapping maintains the set of tuples including the actions and their corresponding unique outputs. On line 8, we ask the teacher whether the hypothesis $\mathcal{H}$ is equivalent to M. If the teacher returns "yes" for this equivalence query, the algorithm terminates and returns $\mathcal{H}$. Otherwise, the counter-example is processed by the procedure *ProcessCE* in Algorithm 2, and then an(other) iteration of the loop is performed until the correct hypothesis $\mathcal{H}$ is learned, on lines 10-12. The $sync$ set may also contain non-synchronizing actions with unique outputs. On line 13, such actions are removed from $sync$ if they are not shared among some sets of I^F.

Algorithm 2 is a procedure that updates the global variables I^F and $sync$ based on the counter-example CE. The function $Output(CE,M)$ returns the corresponding output of the counter-example, on line 2. If the counter-example contains an action like u that its output is different from the corresponding output in the mapping *OutSync*, then we find that u is not a synchronizing action. Hence, we remove u from $sync$ and *OutSync*, on lines 4-6. Then, we must update the input sets of I^F as u may be in different input sets as a synchronizing action. To this end, we find such sets and merge them on lines 7-8 (by Proposition 1, we explain the necessity of merging such input sets and prove its correctness). After

---

Algorithm 2 Process Counter-Example

Input: CE
Effect: Updating the global variables I^F, $sync$, and $OutSync$

1: **procedure** $ProcessCE$
2:     $OutCE \leftarrow Output(CE, M)$
3:     **for each** $u \in sync$ **do**
4:         **if** $\exists i \cdot CE[i] = u \wedge \exists \{u \mapsto x\} \in OutSync \cdot OutCE[i] \neq x$ **then**
5:             $sync := sync \setminus \{u\}$
6:             $OutSync := OutSync \setminus \{u \mapsto x\}$
7:             $I^s := \{I_j \mid I_j \in I^F \wedge u \in I_j\}$
8:             $I^F \leftarrow Merge(I^F, I^s)$
9:     $I^D \leftarrow DependentSets(CE, I^F, sync)$
10:     **for each** $u_r \in sync$ **s.t** $\exists i \cdot CE[i] = u_r$ **do** $I^D \leftarrow I^D \cup \{\{u_r\}\}$
11:     $I^F \leftarrow Merge(I^F, I^D)$
12: **end procedure**

---

updating the synchronizing actions, we must update I^F based on the counter-example CE. The *DependentSets* method, on line 9, extracts the sets of I^F that are dependent on each other based on the non-synchronizing actions of CE. These sets are merged with the synchronizing actions participating in CE, on lines 10-11.

Proposition 1. *Let I^F be an input cover, and sync be the synchronizing actions. If two input sets $I_i, I_j \in I^F$ have a shared action u, and u is detected as a non-synchronizing action, then I_i and I_j must be merged.*

Proof. According to Algorithm 1, initially all actions belong to *sync*, and the actions with different outputs are removed from *sync*. Assume that in Algorithm 2, lines 4-6, I^F includes two input sets $I_i = \{a_1, \ldots, a_n, u\}$ and $I_j = \{b_1, \ldots, b_m, u\}$ while u is detected as a non-synchronizing action. By Definition 7, each set consists of dependent actions, and hence, the actions $a_1, \ldots, a_n$ are dependent on the non-synchronizing action u, and $b_1, \ldots, b_m$ are also dependent on u. As u is a non-synchronizing action, by the transitive relationship, we can conclude that $a_1, \ldots, a_n$ are also dependent on $b_1, \ldots, b_m$. As a result, we remove I_i and I_j from I^F and instead add their union $\{a_1, \ldots, a_n, b_1, \ldots, b_m, u\}$ to I^F.   □

3.1   Minimum Counter-Examples

We aim to find a counter-example with minimal length where any of its prefixes are not a counter-example. If the teacher returns a non-minimal counter-example, some input sets may be merged incorrectly [14]. We extend the algorithm proposed in [14] to minimize the returned counter-example according to the synchronizing actions. We iteratively take a counter-example CE and return the smallest prefix of CE which is also a counter-example. To this end, we select the input sets I^M including synchronizing and non-synchronizing actions participating in CE. Then, we iteratively get a subset of I^M, merge its members, and produce a set A. The projection of CE on A is returned as a minimum counter-example if the SUL and the hypothesis model produce different outputs.

In the next section, we prove that the SCL* algorithm terminates and the synchronous components are learned correctly.

4   Properties of the SCL* Algorithm

To prove the correctness and termination of the SCL* algorithm, we first prove that if the algorithm terminates, then the shared actions among input sets in I^F belong to *sync*. Then, we prove that a counter-example has at least one non-synchronizing action.

Lemma 1. *Let I^F be an input cover and sync be the synchronizing actions. If the algorithm SCL* terminates in a round where I^F includes I_i, I_j as two input sets with a common action u, i.e., $u \in I_i \cap I_j$, then u belongs to the set of synchronizing actions, i.e., $u \in sync$.*

Proof. We prove this by a contradiction. Assume that u exists in two input sets I_i and I_j while it does not belong to *sync*. By Proposition 1, I_i and I_j must be merged as u is found as a non-synchronizing action. However, this contradicts that the algorithm terminates in a round that I^F includes two distinct input sets I_i and I_j.   □

Proposition 2. *Given an input cover I^F and the synchronizing actions sync, if the teacher returns a counter-example CE, then CE has at least one action like u such that $u \notin sync$.*

Proof. We prove this by a contradiction. Assume that $I^F = \{\{u\}, \{v\}\}$ and all actions of CE like u and v belong to *sync*. By Definition 5, the teacher returns a counter-example if $\lambda_{P(M,u)\|P(M,v)}(uv) = \lambda_M(uv)$ does not hold. In this way, two cases can be assumed: (1) $\lambda_M(uv) \neq \lambda_{P(M,\{u\})\|P(M,\{v\})}(uv)$ holds, and (2) $\lambda_{P(M,\{u\})\|P(M,\{v\})}(uv)$ is not defined. The first case contradicts the assumption that u, v are the synchronizing actions as the outputs of the synchronizing actions must be unique in the system. In the second case, there is a sequence of action uv such that $\lambda_M(uv)$ is defined in M, but $\lambda_{P(M,\{u\})\|P(M,\{v\})}(uv)$ is not defined. As the Mealy machine is deterministic, this case happens if there is an action with different outputs in CE which is a contradiction.   □

The next proposition from [14] indicates that the actions participating in CE belong to different input sets.

Proposition 3. *Let I^F be an input cover and CE be a counter-example. If CE has at least two actions u and v, then u and v do not belong to the same input set of I^F.*

As the actions of CE belong to different input sets, we prove that different input sets of I^F must be merged if and only if they include non-synchronizing actions participating in CE.

Proposition 4. *Let I^F be an input cover, sync be the set of synchronizing actions, and CE be a counter-example. Two input sets $I_i, I_j \in I^F$, where $|I_i| > 1$, $|I_j| > 1$, must be merged iff CE has at least two actions $u, v \notin$ sync such that $u \in I_i$, $v \in I_j$.*

Proof. Proof by contradiction and using Proposition 2.

$\square$

Corollary 1. *If the counter-example includes a synchronizing action u and a non-synchronizing action v, the synchronizing action $u \in$ sync must be added to an input set of I^F including v.*

Now, we prove that the size of an input cover I^F is decreased, and the algorithm SCL^* will eventually terminate.

Lemma 2. *At each round of the algorithm SCL^*, if the counter-example CE has at least two non-synchronizing actions, then the size of I^F is decreased by at least one.*

Proof. Proof by using Propositions 1, 3, and 4.

$\square$

Theorem 1. *The Synchronous Compositional Learning Algorithm terminates.*

Proof. There are three cases according to the synchronizing actions: (1) If there is no synchronizing action among components, the proposed algorithm reduces to the algorithm CL^* [14]. As CL^* eventually terminates, we conclude that our algorithm also terminates. (2) If all actions are synchronizing, then by Proposition 2, the teacher does not return a counter-example. As a result, the SUL is equivalent to the learned model and hence the algorithm terminates. (3) If there are some synchronizing actions among components, then some sets in an input cover $I^F = \{I_1, \ldots, I_n\}$ intersect on synchronizing actions. By Lemma 2, if the returned counter-example has at least two non-synchronizing actions, then the size of I^F is decreased. Furthermore, by Proposition 1, if a shared action u is found as a non-synchronizing action, then those sets that include u are removed from I^F and their union is added to I^F and hence the size of I^F is decreased. If after k rounds, the size of input cover I^F does not decrease anymore, then it is concluded that the counter-example does not include at least two non-synchronizing actions. In this way, only synchronizing actions are added to other input sets as the algorithm continues. The number of alphabet and synchronizing actions are finite; hence, the algorithm terminates after finite rounds. $\square$

In the following, we prove that if the algorithm terminates, then *sync* only includes synchronizing actions.

Lemma 3. *Let I^F be an input cover and sync be the synchronizing actions. If the algorithm SCL^* terminates, then sync includes only the synchronizing actions.*

Proof. Proof by using Lemma 1 and Proposition 4.

$\square$

Now, we prove that the algorithm eventually learns the compositional model including the synchronous components correctly.

Theorem 2. *Given an input cover I^F, the SCL* Algorithm learns the compositional model including the synchronous components correctly.*

Proof. Proof by contradiction using Theorem 1, Lemma 2 and Lemma 3.

$\square$

5   Evaluation and Experimental Results

In this section, we first check how much our assumption is practical in some real benchmarks. To this aim, we performed statistical work on a number of benchmarks [3] and checked what percentage of actions have the same output in the model. Table 3 shows that on average 46 percent of actions have unique outputs in these benchmarks and hence our assumption is practical.

ASML	TLS	TCP	Biometric Passport	ESM Controller	QUIC Protocol	Xray-system
61%	40%	36%	73%	33%	40%	41%

Fig. 3: Percentage of actions with unique outputs in some benchmarks

We also evaluate the performance of our algorithm on some real and synthetic benchmarks. To this aim, we implemented the SCL* algorithm[4] on top of the *LearnLib* framework [26] which is a library for automata learning. We compare the SCL* algorithm with L* by evaluating the number of resets and input symbols. The number of resets denotes how many times a finite state machine must be reset and back to the known state during the execution of queries[14]. This parameter is an important factor in learning practical systems as they are time-consuming [27]. The number of input symbols is the total number of input alphabets among components. This parameter declares the total cost of a learning model as the queries used in the model learning have many different lengths. The total number of input symbols is a more accurate metric for comparison of learning algorithms than the number of queries [28].

We need a set of benchmarks to evaluate the performance of the SCL* algorithm regarding the two metrics. We use *realistic* and *synthetic* benchmarks. For the realistic benchmarks, we choose the Body Comfort System (BCS) [23], which is an automotive software product line (SPL) of a Volkswagen Golf model. For the synthetic benchmarks, we generate some components randomly with different numbers of states and various alphabets. We compose three to nine components for both benchmarks using the synchronous parallel composition (Definition 3).

---

[3] Available on https://automata.cs.ru.nl
[4] https://github.com/AryanBastani/SCL-Star

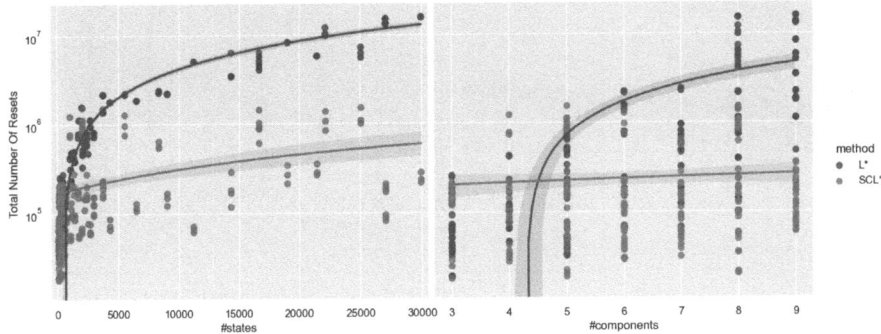

Fig. 4: Total number of resets in SCL* and L* (realistic benchmarks)

The compositional model has a minimum of 100 and a maximum of 30000 states. We do not evaluate the metrics for fewer than 100 states since the advantage of compositional learning is not significant for small systems. In addition, most models of the realistic benchmark do not have more than 30000 states. We repeat each experiment three times and evaluate the experiments on a single-machine quad-core (Intel i5-1135G7 2.42GHz) with 16 GB RAM.

5.1   Realistic Benchmarks

We evaluate the performance of the SCL* algorithm on a realistic system called Body Comfort System (BCS). This system is an automotive software product line of a Volkswagen Golf model. This model has 27 components which have three types of connectors called *input*, *output*, and *internal*. The internal connectors denote interactions among components and input/output connectors constitute the communication with the environment [29]. As Mealy machines are the underlying model of SCL*, we use the finite state machines of these components which are constructed in [30] and consider the internal connectors as the synchronizing actions.

Fig. 4 and Fig. 5 show how the number of states and components affects the number of resets and input symbols. The plots denote the executed tests where red plots correspond to the execution of L* and green plots correspond to the execution of SCL*. The right-hand side of both figures shows the effect of compositional learning when the number of parallel components increases while the number of states remains fixed. The performance of the two algorithms is almost the same in cases where the number of states is small. By increasing the number of states, the compositional learning algorithm SCL* is more scalable.

5.2   Synthetic Benchmarks

We develop a test case generator, which is inspired by [12], to generate a synthetic benchmark. This tool generates some components in the form of Mealy machines

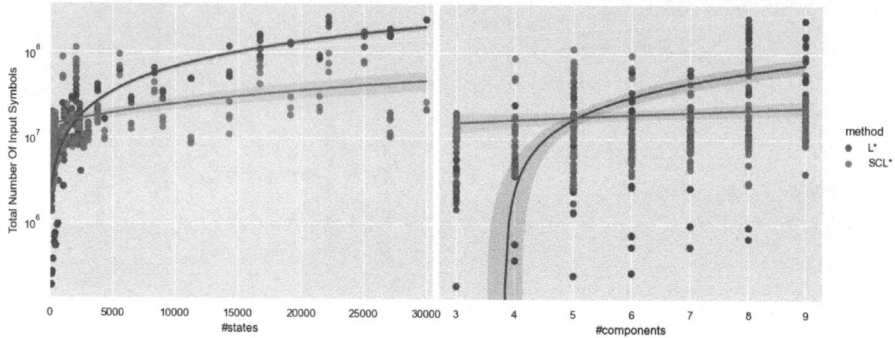

Fig. 5: Total number of input symbols in SCL* and L* (realistic benchmarks)

where each Mealy machine has a random number of states between two and five. The components communicate synchronously regarding the four topologies (Fig. 6) that reflect the real-world network topologies [31]. We randomly assign alphabets to each component in which each component has at least one non-synchronizing action in addition to synchronizing actions.

point to point   star   mesh   ring

Fig. 6: Synchronization topologies in a synthetic benchmark

In Fig. 6, each topology denotes how components can synchronize where the vertices represent the components and edges represent the shared synchronizing actions. In the *point to point* topology, each synchronizing action can be shared only between two components, and all components are not necessarily synchronized. All components must synchronize by *mesh*, while all components synchronize only with one component in *star*. In the *ring* topology, components synchronize in a circular form and synchronize with two components of the circle.

Fig. 7 and Fig. 8 indicate how the number of states and components affects the number of resets and input symbols. Similar to the realistic benchmarks, the colored plots denote the executed test. We use different colors to show the results for various topologies: green for point-to-point, blue for ring, orange for star, and red for mesh. In addition, dashed lines correspond to the execution of L*, and solid lines correspond to the execution of SCL*.

The result shows that SCL* is more scalable than L* when the number of states is increased. For the mesh topology, we cannot evaluate the algorithms

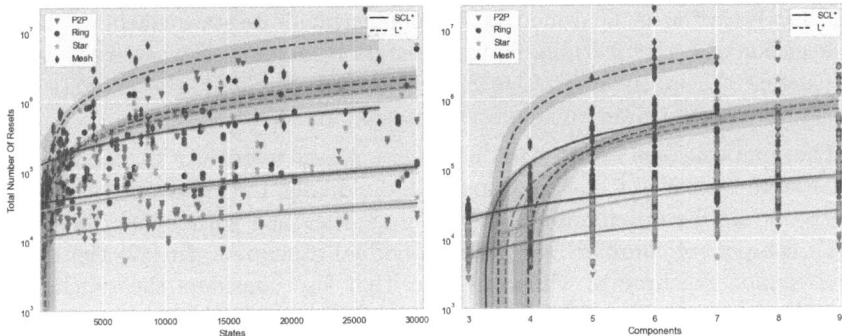

Fig. 7: Total number of resets in SCL* and L* (synthetic benchmarks)

on a system that includes more than seven components (27000 states) due to the memory overflow. Similar to the realistic benchmarks, the right-hand side of both figures shows the effect of compositional learning when the number of parallel components increases while the number of states remains fixed.

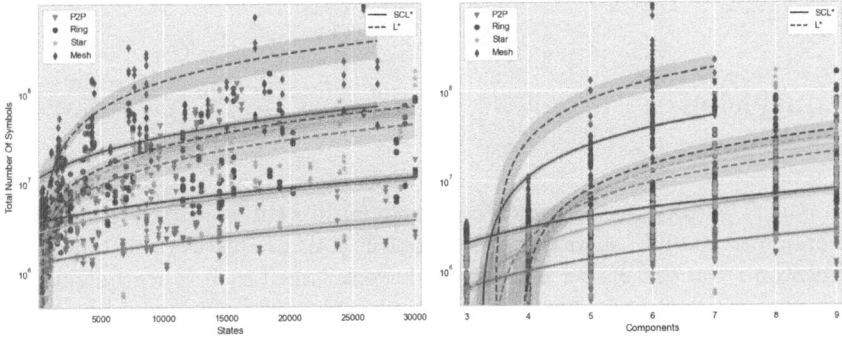

Fig. 8: Total number of input symbols in SCL* and L* (synthetic benchmarks)

6 Related Work

This work builds on the rich literature of active automata learning that aim to find the model of a black-box system by posing queries and iteratively building a hypothesis. These approaches are the extension of the L* algorithm to find the richer models of a system, and learn the system either monolithically or compositionally. For instance, in [10,32,33] the underlying system is learned monolithically. In [10], an extension of L* to pomset automata is introduced which learns the concurrent computations. A monolithic approach is introduced in [32] to learn the asynchronously communicating finite state machines. In [33], an extension of L* for learning finite automata is introduced where they assume the existence of an incomplete teacher who does not know the answers to all queries, and they answer such queries by using an SMT solver.

The compositional approaches, which are closest to our works, learn the parallel system by learning each component individually. In [14], an extension of L* is introduced where individual components are learned without any knowledge of the component number and their individual alphabets. In [14] the components cannot synchronize while our algorithm also considers the synchronization among components. The algorithm of [13] learns the parallel interleaving of Moore machines with decomposable outputs. Each component can be learned by the L* algorithm, and the output of components are explicitly specified. In our work, there are dependencies between components in which some components must be synchronized, and we identify the components and assign outputs to them on-the-fly. In [11], an algorithm to learn the synchronous parallel labeled transitions systems is introduced. However, they assume a priori knowledge of dependencies among actions. In our work, we do not know the synchronizing actions and learn them on-the-fly. In [12], a synchronous compositional learning algorithm is introduced by knowing the alphabet of components. However, we have no knowledge about the alphabet of components and synchronizing actions.

7   Conclusion

In this paper, we introduce a synchronous compositional learning algorithm as an extension of the CL* algorithm presented in [14]. In this work, components can synchronize on the shared actions. We have assumed each synchronizing action has a unique output in a system to maintain the output determinism of the compositional model. The proposed algorithm learns the model of the individual components. We have proved that our algorithm will eventually terminate and learn the model of the individual components correctly. We use two sets of benchmarks to evaluate the performance of our algorithm. One set corresponds to the synthetic benchmark where random components are generated and synchronized based on a special pattern of network topologies. Another set corresponds to the realistic benchmark of an automotive product line model. We have shown that by increasing the number of states and components in a system, the proposed algorithm is more scalable than L*. In future, we aim to relax the restriction on the synchronizing actions's outputs in which each synchronizing action has different outputs in the system.

Data Availability Statement. Our tool is available at https://doi.org/10. 6084/m9.figshare.28236761.

References

1. D. Angluin, Learning regular sets from queries and counterexamples, Journal of Information and Computation, Elsevier, 75 (2) (1987) 87–106. `doi:10.1016/0890-5401(87)90052-6`.

2. P. Fiterau-Brostean, T. Lenaertsand, E. Poll, et.al, Model learning and model checking of SSH implementations, in: 24th International SPIN Symposium on Model Checking of Software, ACM, (2017). `doi:10.1145/3092282.3092289`.

3. F. Aarts, J. Schmaltz, F. Vaandrager, Inference and abstraction of the biometric passport, in: 4th International Symposium on Leveraging Applications, ISoLA, Springer, (2010). `doi:10.1007/978-3-642-16558-0_54`.

4. F. Aarts, J. de Ruiter, Formal models of bank cards for free, in: Sixth International Conference on Software Testing, Verification and Validation, IEEE, (2013). `doi:10.1109/ICSTW.2013.60`.

5. P. Fiterau-Brostean, R. Vaandrager, Combining model learning and model checking to analyze TCP implementations, in: International Conference on Computer Aided Verification, Springer, (2016). `doi:10.1007/978-3-319-41540-6_25`.

6. G. Argyros, L. D'Antoni, The learnability of symbolic automata, in: In International Conference on Computer Aided Verification, Springer, (2018). `doi:10.1007/978-3-319-96145-323`.

7. S. Cassel, F. Howar, B. Jonsson, B. Steffen, Active learning for extended finite state machines, Journal of Formal Aspects of Computing, ACM, 28 (2) (2016) 233–263. `doi:10.1007/s00165-016-0355-5`.

8. J. Moerman, M. Sammartino, A. Silva, B. Klin, Learning nominal automata, in: ACM SIGPLAN Notices, (2017). `doi:10.1145/3009837.3009879`.

9. D. Angluin, D. Fisman, Learning regular omega languages, Journal of Theory Computer Science, Elsevier, 75 (2) (1987) 57–72. `doi:10.1016/j.tcs.2016.07.031`.

10. G. Heerdt, T. Kapp´e, J. Rot, A. Silva, Learning pomset automata, in: 21th International Conference on FoSSaCS, Springer, (2021). `doi:10.1007/978-3-030-71995-1_26`.

11. O. Duhaiby, J. Groote, Active learning of decomposable systems, in: 8th International Conference on Formal Methods in Software Engineering, ACM, (2020). `doi:10.1145/3372020.3391560`.

12. T. Neele, M. Sammartino, Compositional automata learning of synchronous systems, in: Conferance of Fundamental Approaches to Software Engineering , Springer, (2023). `doi:10.1007/978-3-031-30826-0_3`.

13. J. Moerman, Learning product automata, in: Proceedings of The 14th International Conference on Grammatical Inference, (2018). `doi:10.48550/arXiv.1705.02850`.

14. F. Labbaf, J. Groote, H. Hojjat, M. Mousavi, Compositional learning for interleaving parallel automata, in: Conference on Foundations of Software Science and Computation Structures, Springer, (2023). `doi:10.1007/978-3-031-30829-1_20`.

15. G. Mealy, A method for synthesizing sequential circuits, The Bell System Technical Journal, IEEE, 34 (5) (1955) 1045– 1079. `doi:10.1002/j.1538-7305.1955.tb03788.x`.

16. F. Aarts, F. Vaandrager, Learning I/O automata, in: In 21th International Conference on Concurrency, Springer, Lecture Notes in Computer Science, (2010). `doi:10.1007/978-3-642-15375-4_6`.

17. S. P. Khatri, A. Narayan, S. C. Krishnan, K. McMillan, et.al, Engineering change in a non-deterministic FSM setting, in: Proceedings of the 33st Conference on Design Automation, IEEE, (1996). `doi:10.1109/DAC.1996.545618`.

18. S. Paiva, A. Simao, Generation of complete test suites from mealy input/output transition systems, in: Conference of Formal Aspects of Computing , ACM, (2015). doi:10.1007/s00165-015-0350-2.

19. S. Paiva, A. Simao, M. Varshosaz, et al, Complete IOCO test cases: a case study, in: Proceedings of the 7th International Workshop on Automating Test Case Design, Selection, and Evaluation , ACM, (2016). doi:10.1145/2994291.2994297.

20. R. Hierons, The complexity of asynchronous model based testing, Journal of Theoretical Computer Science, Elsevier, 45 (1) (2012) 70– 82. doi:10.1016/j.tcs.2012.05.038.

21. C. Braunstein, A. E. Haxthausen, W. Huang, et al, Complete model-based equivalence class testing for the ETCS ceiling speed monitor, in: Proceeding of SEFM, Springer, (2014). doi:10.1007/978-3-319-11737-9_25.

22. U. S. C. Braunstein, J. Peleska, et al, A sysml test model and test suite for the ETCS ceiling speed monitor, in: Work Package 4 OETCS/WP4/CSM 01/00, University of Bremen, (2014).

23. S. Lity, R. Lachmann, M. Lochau, I. Schaefer, Delta-oriented software product line test models-the body comfort system case study., in: Technical Report 2012-07, (2012).

24. J. Peleska, A. Honisch, F. Lapschies, et al, A real-world benchmark model for testing concurrent real-time systems in the automotive domain, in: Proceedings of ICTSS, Springer, (2011). doi:10.1007/978-3-642-24580-0_11.

25. C. Hoare, Communicating sequential processes, in: Prentice-Hall International 37 series in computer science, (1985). doi:10.1145/359576.359585.

26. H. Raffelt, B. Steffen, Learnlib: A library for automata learning and experimentation, in: Fundamental Approaches to Software Engineering, (2006). doi:10.1145/1081180.1081189.

27. R. Rivest, R. Schapire, Inference of finite automata using homing sequences, in: Information and Computation, Elsevier, (1993). doi:10.1006/inco.1993.1021.

28. F. Vaandrager, Model learning, in: Communications of the ACM, (2017). doi:10.1145/2967606.

29. S. Lity, R. Lachmann, M. Lochau, I. Schaefer, Delta-oriented test case prioritization for integration testing of software product lines., in: Proceedings of the 19th International Conference on Software Product Line, ACM, (2015). doi:10.1145/2791060.2791073.

30. S. Tavassoli, C. Damasceno, R. Khosravi, M. Mousavi, Adaptive behavioral model learning for software product lines, in: 26th International Systems and Software Product Line Conference, ACM, (2022). doi:10.1145/3546932.3546991.

31. W. Tomasi, Introduction to Data Communications and Networking, Pearson Prentice Hall, (2005). doi:10.1201/9781315368658-1.

32. B. Bollig, J. Katoen, C. Kern, Learning communicating automata from MSCs 36 (3) (2010) 390–408. doi:10.1109/TSE.2009.89.

33. M. Moeller, W. Thomas, S. Alaia, K. Caleb, F. Nate, S. Alexandra, Automata learning with an incomplete teacher, in: 37th European Conference on Object-Oriented Programming, LIPICs, (2023). doi:10.4230/LIPIcs.ECOOP.2023.21.

Symbolic State Partitioning
for Reinforcement Learning

Mohsen Ghaffari[1]([⊠]) [iD], Mahsa Varshosaz[1] [iD],
Einar Broch Johnsen[2] [iD], and Andrzej Wąsowski[1] [iD]

[1] ITU, Copenhagen, Denmark
{mohg, mahv, wasowski}@itu.dk
[2] University of Oslo, Oslo, Norway
einarj@ifi.uio.no

Abstract. Tabular reinforcement learning methods cannot operate directly on continuous state spaces. One solution to this problem is to partition the state space. A good partitioning enables generalization during learning and more efficient exploitation of prior experiences. Consequently, the learning process becomes faster and produces more reliable policies. However, partitioning introduces approximation, which is particularly harmful in the presence of nonlinear relations between state components. An ideal partition should be as coarse as possible, while capturing the key structure of the state space for the given problem. This work extracts partitions from the environment dynamics by symbolic execution. We show that symbolic partitioning improves state space coverage with respect to environmental behavior and allows reinforcement learning to perform better for sparse rewards. We evaluate symbolic state space partitioning with respect to precision, scalability, learning agent performance and state space coverage for the learned policies.

Keywords: Reinforcement Learning · Symbolic Execution · State Space Partitioning

1 Introduction

Reinforcement learning is a form of active learning, where an agent learns to make decisions to maximize a reward signal. The agent interacts with an environment and takes actions based on its current state. The environment rewards the agent, which uses the reward value to update its decision-making policy (see Fig. 2). Reinforcement learning has applications in many domains: robotics [22], gaming [44], electronics [15], and healthcare [54]. This method can automatically synthesize controllers for many challenging control problems [43]; however, dedicated approximation techniques, hereunder deep learning, are needed for continuous state spaces. Unfortunately, despite many successes with continuous problems, Deep Reinforcement Learning suffers from low explainability and lack

Supplementary Information The online version contains supplementary material available at https://doi.org/10.1007/978-3-031-90900-9_7

of convergence guarantees. At the same time, discrete (tabular) learning methods have been shown to be more explainable [27,37,51,55] and to yield policies for which it is easier to assure safety [13,18,48], for instance using formal verification [1,20,45]. Thus, finding a good state space representation for discrete learning remains an active research area [3,9,17,26,28,35,52].

To adapt a continuous state space for discrete learning, one exploits partial observability to merge regions of the state space into discrete partitions. Each part in a partition represents a subset of the states of the agent. Ideally, all states in a part capture meaningful aspects of the environment—best if they share the same optimal action in the optimal policy. Consequently, a good partitioning is highly problem specific. For instance, in safety critical environments, it is essential to identify small "singularities"—regions that require special handling—even if they are very small. Otherwise, if such regions are included in a larger part, the control policy will not be able to distinguish them from the surrounding parts, leading to high variance in operation time and slow convergence of learning.

The trade-off between the size of the partitions and the optimality and convergence of reinforcement learning remains a challenge [3,9,26,28,35,52]. Policies obtained for coarse partitions are unreliable. Large fine partitions make reinforcement learning slow. The dominant methods are *tiling* and *vector quantization* [26,28,35,52]; neither is adaptive to the structure of the state space. They ignore nonlinear dependencies between state components even though quadratic behaviors are common in control systems. So far, the shape of the state space partitions has hardly been studied in the literature.

In this work, we investigate the use of *symbolic execution* to extract approximate adaptive partitions that reflect the problem dynamics. *Symbolic execution* [8,21] is a classic foundational technique for dynamic program analysis, originating in software engineering and deductive verification research and commonly used for test input generation [49] and in interactive theorem provers (e.g. [2]). A symbolic executor generates a set of *path conditions* (PC), constraints that must hold for each execution path that the program can take. These conditions partition the state space of the executed program into groups that share the same execution path. Our hypothesis is that *the path conditions obtained by symbolic execution of an environment model (the step and reward functions) provide a useful state space partition for reinforcement learning*. The branches in the environment program likely reflect important aspects of the problem dynamics that should be respected by an optimal policy. We test this hypothesis by:

- Defining a symbolic partitioning method and establishing its basic theoretical properties. This method, SymPar, is adaptive to the problem semantics, general (i.e., not developed for a specific problem), and automatic (given a symbolically executable environment program).
- Implementing the method on top of the Symbolic PathFinder, an established symbolic executor for Java programs (JVM programs) [36]
- Evaluating SymPar empirically against other offline and online partitioning approaches, and against deep reinforcement learning methods. The experiments show that symbolic partitioning can allow the agent to learn better policies than with the baselines.

To the best of our knowledge, this is the first time that symbolic execution has been used to breath semantic knowledge into an otherwise statistical reinforcement learning process. We see it as an interesting case of a transfer of concepts from software engineering and formal methods to machine learning. It does break with the tradition of reinforcement learning to treat environments as black boxes. It is however consistent with common practice of using reinforcement learning for software defined problems and with pre-training robotic agents in simulators, as software problems and simulators are amenable to symbolic execution.

The paper proceeds as follows. Section 2 reviews the relevant state of the art. Section 3 recalls the required preliminaries and definitions. Our state space abstraction method is detailed in Sect. 4. In Sect. 5 we present the evaluation design, and then discuss the experiment results (Sect. 6). We discuss the limitations of our method in Sect. 7. Finally, Sect. 8 concludes the paper and presents future work.

2   Related Work

We study partitioning, or a discrete abstraction, of the state space in reinforcement learning by mapping from a continuous state space to a discrete one or by aggregating discrete states. To the best of our knowledge, the earliest use of partitioning, was the BOXES system [29]. The Parti-game algorithm [33] automatically partitions state spaces but applies only to tasks with known goal regions and requires a greedy local controller. While tile coding is a classic method for partitioning [4], it often demands extensive engineering effort to avoid misleading the agent with suboptimal partitions. Lanzi et al. [25] extended learning classifier systems to use tile coding. Techniques such as vector quantization [26,28,35,52] and decision trees [41,46,53] lack adaptability to the properties of the state space and may overlook non-linear dependencies among state components. Techniques that gradually refine a coarse partition during the learning process [3,9,17,28,52] are time-intensive, and require generating numerous parts to achieve better approximations near the boundaries of nonlinear functions. Unlike other methods, SymPar incurs no direct learning cost (it is offline), requires no engineering effort (it is automated), and is not problem specific in contrast to some of the existing techniques (it is general). It produces a partition that effectively captures non-linear dependencies as well as narrow parts, without incurring additional costs or increasing the number of parts at the boundaries.

The concept of bisimulation metrics [11,12] defines two states as being behaviorally similar if they (1) yield comparable immediate rewards and (2) transition to states that are behaviorally aligned. Bisimulation metrics have been employed to reduce the dimensionality of state spaces through the aggregation of states. However, they have not been extensively explored due to their high computational costs. Moreover, note that bisimulation-minimization-based state-space-abstraction is too fine-grained for the problem at hand. It requires that any states lumped together exhibit the same behavior. This is an unnecessary constraint from the reinforcement learning perspective, which takes no preference over behaviors provided that they lead to the same long-term reward. As long as

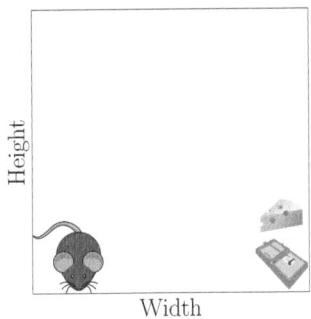

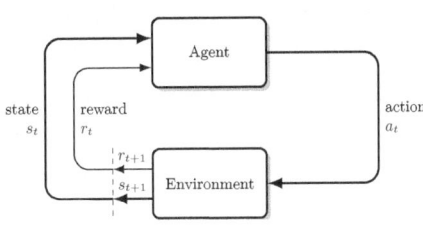

Fig. 1. Navigation environment. A mouse agent in a continuous rectangular board needs to find the cheese, while not stepping on the trap.

Fig. 2. Reinforcement learning schematic.

the same long-term reward estimate is expected for the same (best) local action in two states, it is theoretically sufficient for the two states to be lumped together. For this reason it is worth exploring weaker principles than bisimulation metrics for reducing dimensionality.

3 Background

Reinforcement Learning (see Fig. 2). A Partially Observable Markov Decision Process is a tuple $\mathcal{M} = (\overline{\mathcal{S}}, \overline{\mathcal{S}}_0, \mathcal{A}, \mathcal{S}, \mathcal{O}, \mathcal{T}, \mathcal{R}, \mathcal{F})$, where $\overline{\mathcal{S}}$ is a set of states, $\overline{\mathcal{S}}_0 \in$ pdf $\overline{\mathcal{S}}$ is a probability density function for initial states, $\mathcal{A}$ is a finite set of actions, $\mathcal{S}$ is a finite set of observable states, $\mathcal{O} \in \overline{\mathcal{S}} \to \mathcal{S}$ is a total observation function, $\mathcal{T} \in \overline{\mathcal{S}} \times \mathcal{A} \to$ pdf $\overline{\mathcal{S}}$ is the transition probability function, $\mathcal{R} \in \overline{\mathcal{S}} \times \mathcal{A} \to \mathbb{R}$ is the reward function, and $\mathcal{F} \in \mathcal{S} \to \{0, 1\}$ is a predicate defining final states. The task is to find a policy $\pi : \mathcal{S} \to \text{Dist}(\mathcal{A})$ that maximizes the expected accumulated reward [43], where Dist is the probability mass function over $\mathcal{A}$.

Example 1 *A mouse sits in the bottom-left corner of a room with dimensions $W \times H$. A mousetrap is placed in the bottom-right corner, and a piece of cheese next to it (Fig. 1). The mouse moves with a fixed velocity in four directions: up, down, left, right. Its goal is to find the cheese but avoid the trap. The states $\overline{\mathcal{S}}$ are ordered pairs representing the mouse's position in the room. The set of initial states $\overline{\mathcal{S}}_0$ is fixed to $(1, 1)$, a Dirac distribution. We define the actions as the set of all possible movements for the mouse: $\mathcal{A} = \{(d, v) : d \in \mathcal{D}, v \in \mathcal{V}\}$, where $\mathcal{D} = \{U, D, R, L\}$ and $\mathcal{V} = \{r_1, r_2, \ldots, r_n \mid r_i \in \mathbb{R}^+\}$. $\mathcal{S}$ can be any partitioning of the room space and $\mathcal{O}$ is the map from the real position of the mouse to the part containing it. Our goal is to find the partition, i.e., $\mathcal{S}$ and $\mathcal{O}$. The reward function $\mathcal{R}$ is zero when mouse finds the cheese, -1000 when the mouse moves into the trap, and -1 otherwise. For simplicity, we let the environment be deterministic, so $\mathcal{T}$ is a deterministic movement of the mouse from a position by a given action to a new position. The final state predicate $\mathcal{F}$ holds for the cheese and trap positions and not otherwise.*

S-ASSIGN	$(x = e, \sigma, k, \phi)$	$\rightarrow$	$(\text{skip}, \sigma[x \mapsto \sigma e], k, \phi)$
S-IF-T	$(\text{if } b : s_1 \text{ else} : s_2, \sigma, k, \phi)$	$\rightarrow$	$(s_1, \sigma, k, \phi \wedge \sigma b)$
S-IF-F	$(\text{if } b : s_1 \text{ else} : s_2, \sigma, k, \phi)$	$\rightarrow$	$(s_2, \sigma, k, \phi \wedge \sigma \neg b)$
S-WHILE-T	$(\text{while } b : s, \sigma, k, \phi)$	$\rightarrow$	$(s ; \text{ while } b : s, \sigma, k, \phi \wedge \sigma b)$
S-WHILE-F	$(\text{while } b : s, \sigma, k, \phi)$	$\rightarrow$	$(\text{skip} ; \sigma, k, \phi \wedge \sigma \neg b)$
S-SMLP	$(x \sim \text{rnd}, \sigma, k, \phi)$	$\rightarrow$	$(\text{skip}, \sigma[x \mapsto y_k], k + 1, \phi)$

Fig. 3. Symbolic execution rules for an idealized probabilistic language. Each judgement is a quadruple: the program, the symbolic store (σ), the sample index (k), the current path condition (ϕ).

Partitioning. Partitioning is "the process of mapping a representation of a problem onto a new representation" [16]. A *partition* over a set $\overline{S}$ of states is a family of sets $p_1, \ldots, p_n \subseteq \overline{S}$ such that $p_1 \cup \ldots \cup p_n = \overline{S}$ and $p_i \cap p_j = \emptyset$ for $1 \leq i < j \leq n$. The sets in a partition are called parts. The set of all partitionings is partially ordered: we talk about coarseness (granularity) of partitions. A partition $\mathcal{P}'$ is *coarser* than $\mathcal{P}$ (and $\mathcal{P}$ is *finer* than $\mathcal{P}'$) if $\forall p \in \mathcal{P}. \exists p' \in \mathcal{P}'. p \subseteq p'$. Recall that the space of partitions is isomorphic to the space of equivalence relations over a set.

Symbolic Execution is a program analysis technique that systematically explores program behaviors by solving symbolic constraints obtained from conjoining the program's branch conditions [21]. Symbolic execution extends normal execution by running the basic operators of a language using symbolic inputs (variables) and producing symbolic formulas as output. A symbolic execution of a program produces a set of *path conditions*—logical expressions that encode conditions on the input symbols to follow a particular path in the program.

For a program over input arguments $I = \{v_1, v_2, \ldots, v_k\}$, a path condition $\phi \in PC(I')$ is a quantifier-free logical formula defined on $I' = \{\vartheta_1, \vartheta_2, \ldots, \vartheta_k\}$, where each symbolic variable ϑ_i represents an initial value for v_i.

We briefly outline a definition of symbolic execution for a minimal language (for more details, see, e.g., [5]). Let V be a set of program variables, Ops a set of arithmetic operations, $x \in V$, $n \in \mathbb{R}$, and $op \in \text{Ops}$. We consider programs generated by the following grammar:

$e ::= x \mid n \mid op(e_1, \ldots, e_n)$

$b ::= \text{True} \mid \text{False} \mid b_1 \text{ AND } b_2 \mid b_1 \text{ OR } b_2 \mid \neg b \mid b_1 \leq b_2 \mid e_1 < e_2 \mid e_1 == e_2$

$s ::= x = e \mid x \sim \text{rnd} \mid s_1; s_2 \mid \text{if } b : s_1 \text{ else} : s_2 \mid \text{while } b : s \mid \text{skip}$

A symbolic store, denoted by σ maps input program variables $I \subseteq V$ to expressions, generated by productions e above. An update to a symbolic store is denoted $\sigma[x = e]$. It replaces the entry for variable x with the expression e. An expression can be interpreted in a symbolic store by applying (substituting) its mapping to the expression syntax (written $e\sigma$).

Figure 3 gives the symbolic execution rules for the above language, in terms of traces (it computes a path condition ϕ for a terminating trace). In the reduction rules, ϕ represents the path condition and k denotes the sampling index. The first rule defines the symbolic assignment. An assignment does not change the path conditions, but updates the symbolic store σ. When encountering conditional statements, the symbolic executor splits into two branches. For the true case (rule S-IF-T) the path condition is extended with the head condition of the branch, for the false case (S-IF-F), the path condition is extended with the negation of the branch condition. Similarly, for a *while* loop two branches are generated, with an analogous effect on path conditions. The last rule executes the randomized sampling statement. It simply allocates a new symbolic variable y_k for the unknown result of sampling, and advances the sampling index [50]. Figure 5 shows the path conditions obtained by applying similar rules to above for the code to the left (Fig. 4). The first path condition $PC^{(U,1)}$ corresponds to the branch where condition d==1 is true in the program.

The above rules can be used to prove basic properties of symbolic execution. For example, since branch conditions are always introduced in dual rules, the path conditions of a program are mutually exclusive [5].

Practical symbolic executors have been realized for full scale programming languages. Although we defined symbolic execution at the level of syntax, the two most popular symbolic executors operate on compiled bytecode [6,36]. In presence of loops and recursion, symbolic execution does not terminate. To halt symbolic execution, we can set a predefined timeout in terms of an iteration limit or a program statement limit. This produces an approximation of the set of path conditions.

4   Partitioning Using Symbolic Execution

We present the idea of symbolic partitioning using a single agent with the environment modeled as a computer program. The program (*Env*) is implementing a single step-transition ($\mathcal{T}$) in the environment with the corresponding reward ($\mathcal{R}$). We use symbolic execution to analyze the environment program *Env*, then partition the state space using the obtained path conditions. The partition serves as the observation function $\mathcal{O}$. The entire process is automatic and generic—we can follow the same procedure for all problems.

Example 2 *Figure 4 shows the environment program for the 10×10 navigation problem (Example 1). For simplicity, we assume the agent can move one unit in each direction, so $\mathcal{V} = \{1\}$ and $\mathcal{A} = \{U, D, R, L\} \times \mathcal{V}$. The path conditions in Fig. 5 are obtained by symbolically executing the step and reward functions using symbolic inputs x and y and a concrete input from $\mathcal{A}$. Using path conditions in partitioning requires a translation from the symbolic executor syntax into the programming language used to implement the partitioning process, as the executor will generate abstract value names.*

A good partition maintains the Markov property, so that the same action is optimal for all unobservable states abstracted by the same part. Unfortunately,

```
1  W = 10 # Width
2  H = 10 # Height
3  def step(x, y, d, v):
4    if d == 1: # UP
5      if y < H:
6        return x, y+v
7    if d == 2: # DOWN
8      if y > 1:
9        return x, y-v
10   if d == 3: # LEFT
11     if x > 1:
12       return x-v, y
13   if d == 4: # RIGHT
14     if x < W:
15       return x+v, y
16   return x, y
17
18 def reward(x, y, d, v):
19   if x == W:
20     if y == 2:
21       return 0.0 # Cheese
22     if y == 1:
23       return -1000.0 # Trap
24   return -1.0
25
```

$PC^{(U,1)}$

$5, 19, 20 \quad y < 10 \wedge x = 10 \wedge y + 1 = 2$

$5, 19, !20 \quad y < 10 \wedge x = 10 \wedge y + 1 \neq 2$

$5, !19 \quad y < 10 \wedge x \neq 10$

$!5, 19 \quad y \geq 10 \wedge x = 10$

$!5, !19 \quad y \geq 10 \wedge x \neq 10$

$PC^{(D,1)}$

$8, 19, 20 \quad y > 1 \wedge x = 10 \wedge y - 1 = 2$

$8, 19, !20, 22 \quad y > 1 \wedge x = 10 \wedge y - 1 \neq 2 \wedge y - 1 = 1$

$8, 19, !20, !22 \quad y > 1 \wedge x = 10 \wedge y - 1 \neq 2 \wedge y - 1 \neq 1$

$8, !19 \quad y > 1 \wedge x \neq 10$

$!8, 19, !20, 22 \quad y \leq 1 \wedge x = 10 \wedge y = 1$

$!8, !19 \quad y \leq 1 \wedge x \neq 10$

$PC^{(L,1)}$

$11, !19 \quad x > 1 \wedge x - 1 \neq 10$

$!11, !19 \quad x \leq 1 \wedge x \neq 10$

$PC^{(R,1)}$

$14, 19, 20 \quad x < 10 \wedge x + 1 = 10 \wedge y = 2$

$14, 19, !20, 22 \quad x < 10 \wedge x + 1 = 10 \wedge y \neq 2 \wedge y = 1$

$14, 19, !20, !22 \quad x < 10 \wedge x + 1 = 10 \wedge y \neq 2 \wedge y \neq 1$

$14, !19 \quad x < 10 \wedge x + 1 \neq 10$

$!14, 19, 20 \quad x \geq 10 \wedge x = 10 \wedge y = 2$

$!14, 19, !20, 22 \quad x \geq 10 \wedge x = 10 \wedge y \neq 2 \wedge y = 1$

$!14, 19, !20, !22 \quad x \geq 10 \wedge x = 10 \wedge y \neq 1 \wedge y \neq 1$

Fig. 4. The environment program $(\mathcal{T}, \mathcal{R})$ for the navigation problem (Fig. 1).

Fig. 5. Path conditions collected by symbolic execution. The numbers (to the left) refer to line numbers in the program of Fig. 4.

this means that a good partition can be selected only once we know a good policy—after learning. To overcome this, SymPar heuristically bundles states into the same part if they induce the same execution path in the environment program. We use an off-the-shelf symbolic executor to extract all possible path conditions from Env, by using $\overline{\mathcal{S}}$ as symbolic input and actions from $\mathcal{A}$ as concrete input. The result is a set PC of path conditions for each concrete action: $PC = \{PC^{a_0}, PC^{a_1}, \ldots, PC^{a_m}\}$, where $PC^a = \{PC_0^a, PC_1^a, \ldots, PC_{k_a}^a\}$. The set PC^a contains the path conditions computed for action a, and k_a is the number of all path conditions obtained by running Env symbolically, for a concrete action a.

Running the environment program for any concrete state satisfying a condition PC_i^a with action a will execute the same program path. However, the partitioning for reinforcement learning needs to be action independent (the same for all actions). So the obtained path conditions cannot be used directly for the partitioning. Consider $PC_i^{a_1} \in PC^{a_1}$ and $PC_j^{a_2} \in PC^{a_2}$, arbitrary path conditions for some actions a_1, a_2. To make sure that the same program path will be taken from a concrete state for both actions, we need to create a part that corresponds to the intersection of both path conditions: $PC_i^{a_1} \wedge PC_j^{a_2}$. In general, each set in PC

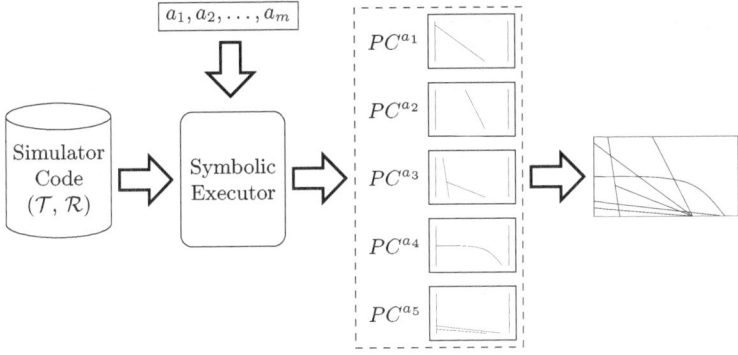

Fig. 6. Overview of SymPar.

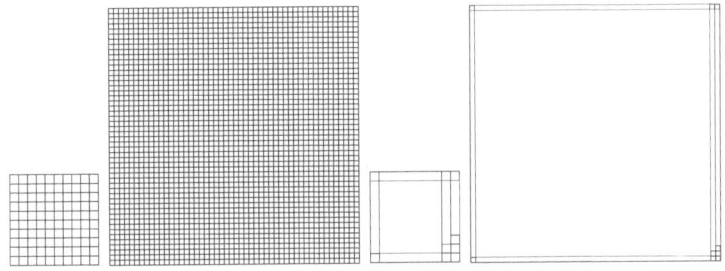

Fig. 7. Using tile coding (left) and SymPar (right) for 10×10 and 50×50 navigation

defines partitions of the state space for different actions. To make them compatible, we need to compute the unique coarsest partition finer than those induced by the path conditions for any action, which is a standard operation in order theory [10]. In this case, this amounts to computing all intersections of partitions for all actions, and removing the empty intersections using an SMT check.

The process of symbolic state space partitioning is summarized in Fig. 6 and Alg. 1. SymPar executes the environment program symbolically. For each action, a set of path conditions is collected. In the figure, $|\mathcal{A}| = 5$ and, accordingly, five sets of path conditions are collected (shown as rectangles). Each rectangle is divided into a group of regions, each of which maps to a path condition. Thus, the rectangles illustrate the state space that is discretized by the path conditions. Note that the border of each region can be a unique path condition (an expression with equality relation) or a part of neighbour regions (an expression with inequality relation). The final partition is shown as another rectangle that contains the overlap between the regions from the previous step.

Example 3 *Figure 7 (left) shows the partitioning of the Navigation problem using tile coding [4] for two room sizes. Numerous cells share the same policy, prompting the question of why they should be divided. SymPar achieves a much*

Algorithm 1 Partitioning with Symbolic Execution (SymPar)

Input: Env, $\mathcal{A}$
Output: $\mathcal{P}$ (a partitioning of $\overline{\mathcal{S}}$)

1: $PC \leftarrow \emptyset$
2: **for** $a \in \mathcal{A}$ **do**
3:     $PC^a, \Psi \leftarrow$ SymExec (Env, symbolic $\overline{\mathcal{S}}$, concrete a)   // Ψ is the set of sampling variables
4:     Add distribution support constraints for all variables $\overline{\mathcal{S}} \in \Psi$ to PC^a
5:     Existentially quantify all sampling variables in PC^a // may introduce overlaps of conditions
6:     $PC'^a \leftarrow \emptyset$
7:     **for** $p, q \in PC^a$ **do if SAT** $(p \wedge q)$ $PC'^a \leftarrow PC'^a \cup \{p \wedge q\}$
8:     $PC^a \leftarrow PC'^a$
9: $\mathcal{P} \leftarrow PC^{\mathcal{A}[0]}$
10: **for** $a \in \mathcal{A} - \{\mathcal{A}[0]\}$ **do**
11:     $\mathcal{P}' \leftarrow \emptyset$
12:     **for** $p \in \mathcal{P}, q \in PC^a$ **do if SAT** $(p \wedge q)$ **then** $\mathcal{P}' \leftarrow \mathcal{P}' \cup \{p \wedge q\}$
13:     $\mathcal{P} \leftarrow \mathcal{P}'$
14: $\mathcal{P} \leftarrow \mathcal{P} \cup \{\sim \bigvee_{p \in \mathcal{P}} p\}$
15: **return** $\mathcal{P}$

---

coarser partition than the initial tiling, by discovering that for many tiles the dynamics is the same (right).

We handle stochasticity of the environment by allowing environment programs to be probabilistic and then following rule S-SMLP in symbolic execution (Fig. 3). We introduce a new symbolic variable whenever a random variable is sampled in the program [23,50]. Consequently, our path conditions also contain these sampling variables. To make the process more reliable, one can generate constraints, limiting them to the support of the distribution. For example, for sampling from a uniform distribution $U[\alpha, \beta]$, the sampling variable n_v is subject to two constraints: $n_v \geq \alpha$ and $n_v \leq \beta$. In order to be able to compute the partition over state variables only, as above, we existentially quantify the sampling variables out. This may introduce overlaps between the conditions, so we compute their intersection at this stage before proceeding (see lines 6-9 in Alg. 1).

Since the entire setup uses logical representations and an SMT solver, we exploit it further to generate witnesses for all parts, even the smallest ones. We use them to seed reinforcement learning episodes, ensuring that each part has been visited at least once. Consequently the agent is guaranteed to learn from all the paths in the environment program. This can be further improved by constraining with a reachability predicate (not used in our examples).

Properties of SymPar. SymPar on the specifics of the environment implementation. Distinct implementations of the simulated environment may result in different partitioning outcomes for a given problem. On the other hand, the outcome is independent of the size of state space. Recall that in Fig. 7 (right) the number of parts is the same for the small and the large room.

A partition is by definition total: every state in the input space is included in a part, ensuring the entire state space is fully covered. As symbolic execution does not terminate for many interesting programs (programs with loops have infinitely many symbolic paths), one typically stops symbolic execution after a designated timeout. This can leave a part of the state space unexplored. Hence, a partitioning obtained from path conditions generated by symbolic execution may not cover all the state space. SymPar makes the obtained partition total by adding the complement of the union of the computed partitions, to cover for the unexplored paths (l. 14 in Alg. 1). Thus, the following property holds:

Theorem 1. *The set $\mathcal{P}$ obtained in Alg. 1 is a partition (i.e., it is total):* $\forall \bar{s} \in \overline{S} \; \exists! \, \mathcal{P}_0 \in \mathcal{P} \cdot \bar{s} \in \mathcal{P}_0.$

The cost of SymPar amounts to exploring all paths in the program symbolically and then computing the coarsest partition. The symbolic execution involves generating a number of paths exponential in the number of branch points in the program (and at each branch one needs to solve an SMT problem—which is in principle undecidable, but works well for many practical problems). A practical approach is to bound the depth of exploration of paths by symbolic executor for more complex programs. Computing the coarsest partition requires solving $|\mathcal{P}|^{|\mathcal{A}|}$ number of SMT problems where $|\mathcal{P}|$ is the upper bound on the number of parts (symbolic paths) and $|\mathcal{A}|$ is the number of actions. The other operations involved in this process such as computing and storing the path conditions in the required syntax are polynomial and efficient in practice.

Theorem 2. *Let PC^a be the set of path conditions produced by SymPar for each of the actions $a \in \mathcal{A}$. The size of the final partition $\mathcal{P}$ returned by SymPar is bounded from below by each $|PC^a|$ and from above by $\prod_{a \in \mathcal{A}} |PC^a|$.*

The theorem follows from the fact that $\mathcal{P}$ is finer than any of the PC^as and the algorithm for computing the coarsest partition finer than a set of partitions can in the worst case intersect each part in each set PC^a with all the parts in the partitions of the other actions.

Note that SymPar is a heuristic and approximate method. To appreciate this, define the optimal partition to be the unique partition in which each part contains all states with the same action in the optimal policy (the optimal partition is an inverse image of the optimal policy for all actions). The partitions produced by SymPar are neither always coarser or always finer than the optimal one. This can be shown with simple counterexamples. For an environment with only one action, the optimal partition has only one part as the optimal policy maps the same action for all states. But Sympar will generate more than one part (a finer partition) if the simulation program contains branching. For problems without branching in the simulator such as cart pole problem, Sympar produces only one part. However, the optimal partition contains more than one part as optimal actions for all states in the state space are not the same. To understand the significance of this approximation in practice, we evaluate SymPar empirically against the existing methods.

5   Evaluation Setup

The partitioning of the state space faces a trade-off: on one hand, the granularity of the partition should be fine enough to distinguish crucial differences between states in the state space. On the other hand, this granularity should be chosen to avoid a combinatorial explosion, where the number of possible parts becomes unmanageably large. Achieving this balance is essential for efficient and effective learning. In this section, we explore this trade-off and evaluate the performance of our implementation in SymPar empirically by addressing the following research questions:

RQ1 *How much smaller are the SymPar partitions compared to other methods, and how do these smaller partitions impact learning performance?*

RQ2 *How does the granularity of the partition affect the learning performance?*

RQ3 *How does SymPar scale with increasing state space sizes?*

RQ4 *How well does SymPar group together behaviorally similar states?*

We compare SymPar to CAT-RL [9] (online partitioning) and with tile coding techniques (offline partitioning) for different examples [43]. Tile coding is a classic technique for partitioning. It splits each feature of the state into rectangular tiles of the same size. Although there are new problem specific versions, we opt for the classic version due to its generality.

To answer **RQ1**, we measure (a) the *size of partition*, (b) the *failure and success rates* and (c) the *accumulated reward* during learning. Being offline, our approach is hard to compare with online methods, since the different parameters may affect the results. Therefore, we separate the comparison with offline and online algorithms. For offline algorithms, we first find the number of abstract states using SymPar and partition the state space using tile coding accordingly (i.e., the number of tiles is set to the smallest square number greater than the number of parts in SymPar's partition). Then, we use standard Q-learning for these partitions, and compare their performance. For online algorithms, we compute the running time for SymPar and its learning process, run CAT-RL for the same amount of time, and compare their performance. Obviously, if the agent observes a failing state, the episode stops. This decreases the running time. Finally, we compare the accumulated reward for SymPar with well-known algorithms DQN [31], A2C [30], PPO [40], using the Stable-Baselines3 implementations[3] [38]. These comparisons are done for two complementary cases: (1) randomly selected states and (2) states that are less likely to be chosen by random selection. The latter are identified by SymPar's partition. We sample states from different parts obtained by SymPar and evaluate the learning process by measuring the accumulated reward.

To answer **RQ2**, we create different learning problems with various partitioning granularities by changing the search depth for the symbolic execution. We then compare the maximum accumulated reward of the learned policy to gain an understanding of the learning performance for the given abstraction.

To answer **RQ3**, we compare the number of parts when increasing the state space of problems.

---

[3] https://github.com/DLR-RM/stable-baselines3

	SymPar					Tile Coding					CAT-RL			
	$\|\mathcal{S}\|$	Succ	Fail	T_{out}	Opt	$\|\mathcal{S}\|$	Succ	Fail	T_{out}	Opt	$\|\mathcal{S}\|$	Succ	Fail	T_{out}
	(#)	(%)	(%)	(%)	(%)	(#)	(%)	(%)	(%)	(%)	(#)	(%)	(%)	(%)
SM	33	74.9	<0.1	25.0	5.0	10^4	6.0	7.1	86.9	0.0	154	63.0	5.0	32.0
MAN	130	5.8	82.6	11.6	0.0	10^4	0.0	99.6	0.4	0.0	620	0.0	74.7	25.3
WW 1	73	18.4	0.0	81.6	2.1	8^4	9.6	0.0	90.4	0.0	157	2.7	0.0	97.3
WW 2	52	37.3	22.9	39.8	4.2	64	19.1	33.2	47.7	0.0	22	14.5	30.2	55.3
Nav	51	13.2	4.8	82.0	<0.1	64	0.0	0.0	100.0	0.0	100	1.7	1.5	96.8
BC	81	89.1	10.9	0.0	29.8	81	82.0	18.0	0.0	14.9	127	34.0	66.0	0.0
MC	70	82.2	0.0	17.8	61.3	81	59.4	0.0	40.6	14.7	16	78.7	0.0	21.3
RW	184	61.2	11.1	27.7	44.0	196	6.5	5.1	88.4	<0.1	52	41.8	31.8	26.4

Table 1. Partitions size and learning performance. Discrete cases above bar, continuous below. **SM**, **MAN**, **WW 1**, **WW 2**, **Nav**, **BC**, **MC**, **RW**, respectively, stand for Simple Maze, Multi-Agent Navigation, Wumpus World 1, Wumpus World 2, Navigation, Braking Car, Mountain Car, Random Walk.

To answer **RQ4**, we select five random parts from the partition obtained by SymPar, and five random concrete states from each part. Then, we feed the concrete states as initial states to RL, and compute the accumulated reward using the policy obtained from a trained model, assuming the training converged to the optimal policy. This way we can check how different the concrete states are with regard to performance.

Test Problems. The **Navigation** problem with a room (continuous) size of 10×10. The **Simple Maze** is a discrete environment (100×100) including blocks, goal and trap, in which a robot tries to find the shortest and safest route to the goal state [43]. **Braking Car** describes a car moving towards an obstacle with a given velocity and distance. The goal is to stop the car to avoid a crash with minimum braking pressure [47]. The **Multi-Agent Navigation** environment (10×10 grid) contains two agents attempting to find safe routes to a goal location. They must arrive to the goal position at the same time [42]. The **Mountain Car** aims to learn how to obtain enough momentum to move up a steep slope [32]. The **Random Walk** in continuous space is an agent with noisy actions on an infinite line [43]. The agent aims to avoid a hole and reach the goal region. **Wumpus World** [39] is a grid world (1: 64×64, 2: 16×16) in which the agent should avoid holes and find the gold.

6   Results

6.1   RQ1: Partition Size

Table 1 shows that SymPar consistently outperforms both tile coding (offline) and CAT-RL (online) on discrete state space cases in terms of success and failure rates, and reduces number of timeouts ($\mathbf{T_{out}}$) during learning in majority of cases. Also, the agents using SymPar partitions show better performance in terms of the percentage of episodes during the learning in which they achieve the maximum accumulated reward in comparison to tile coding partitions (**Opt**), cf. Tbl. 1. Note that in Tbl. 1, the size of partitions is substantially biased in favour of tiling. Nevertheless, SymPar enables better learning. In Tbl. 1, CAT-RL obtains smaller partitions for **WW2**, **MC**, and **RW** in the same amount of time as SymPar. However, the results for CAT-RL show worse learning performance in comparison to SymPar for these cases as demonstrated by failure and success rates (reporting **Opt** is not supported by the available CAT-RL implementations, and would require a modification of that method). The small partition size in CAT-RL can be explained by its operational mechanism, which involves initialising the agent from a small set. This approach prevents divergence and ensures the number of parts remains constant. Subsequently, CAT-RL implements a policy, aiming to identify the goal state and partitions based on the observations it gathers. Hence, in scenarios where the initial states are not limited and the policies are not goal-oriented, the number of parts will increase. For instance, we have evaluated CAT-RL for mountain car in scenarios where exploration is unrestricted, and the number of parts for a given number of episodes has increased to 302. For the other test problems, SymPar achieves better results than CAT-RL in both the partition size and learning performance.

For randomly selected states, the three left plots in Fig. 8, show that the agents trained by SymPar obtain a better normalized cumulative reward and subsequently converge faster to a better policy than the best competing approaches. The three right plots in the figure show the accumulated reward when starting from unlikely states (small parts) for the best competing approaches. Here, we expect to observe a good policy from algorithms that capture the dynamics of environment. Interestingly, the online technique CAT-RL struggles when dealing with large sets of initial states. This can be seen in, e.g., the training for Braking Car, where each episode introduces new positions and velocities.

6.2 RQ2: Granularity vs Learning

The plots in Fig. 9 shows that a higher granularity of partitions yields a higher accumulated reward achieved with the optimal policy. To be more specific, increasing the depth of search for symbolic execution would result in additional constraints on each PC, consequently a finer partition. Then, given sufficient repetition of RL algorithms, finer partitions can yield a better policy for each part, due to a reduction in the variance of optimal policies across states in the part. This results in a higher accumulated reward when both partitions are evaluated for the same states.

The plots in Fig. 10 show the shapes of partitions obtained by SymPar for Braking Car and Simple Maze. The first plot represents different parts with different colors. Notably, the green and purple parts depict partition expressions that contain a non-linear relation between the components of the state space (position and velocity). Besides, close to the x-axis, narrow parts are discernible,

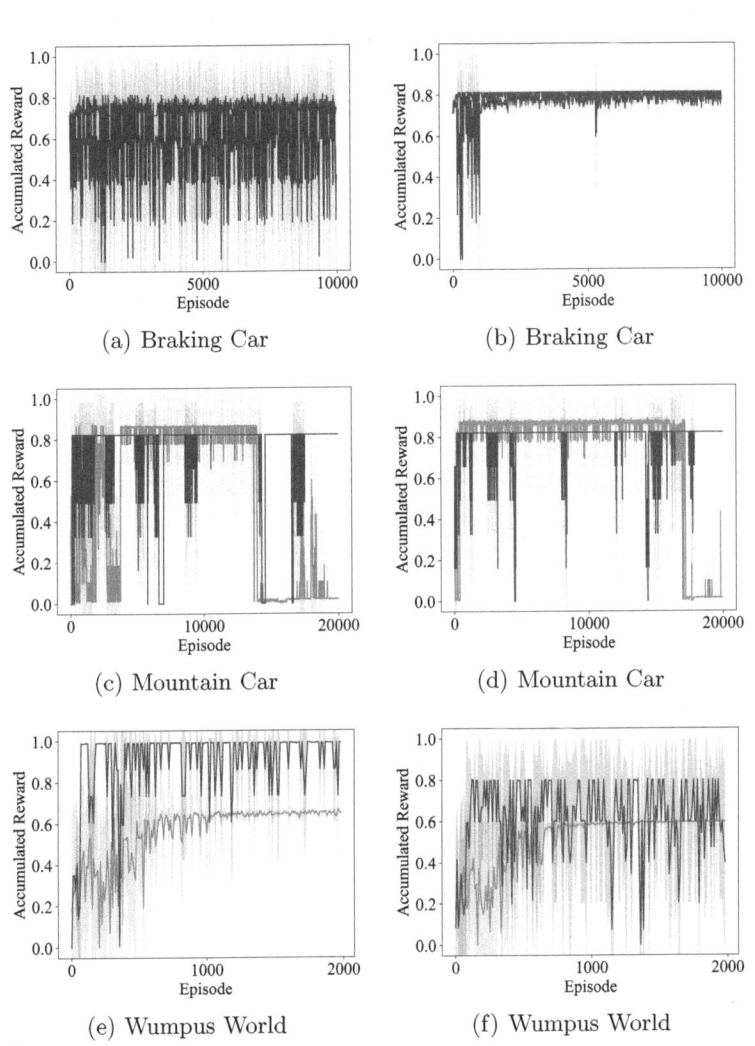

Fig. 8. Normalized cumulative reward per episode while evaluating ten random states (Left), and less likely states (Right). The best approach for each case is shown.

depicted in yellow and pink. To illustrate the partitions obtained for Simple Maze, the expressions are translated into a 10×10 grid. The maze used for Fig. 10(b) differs from the one before, by including additional obstacles in the environment. These two visualizations shed light on the intricacies of state space partitioning and hint at the logical explainability of the partitions obtained by SymPar.

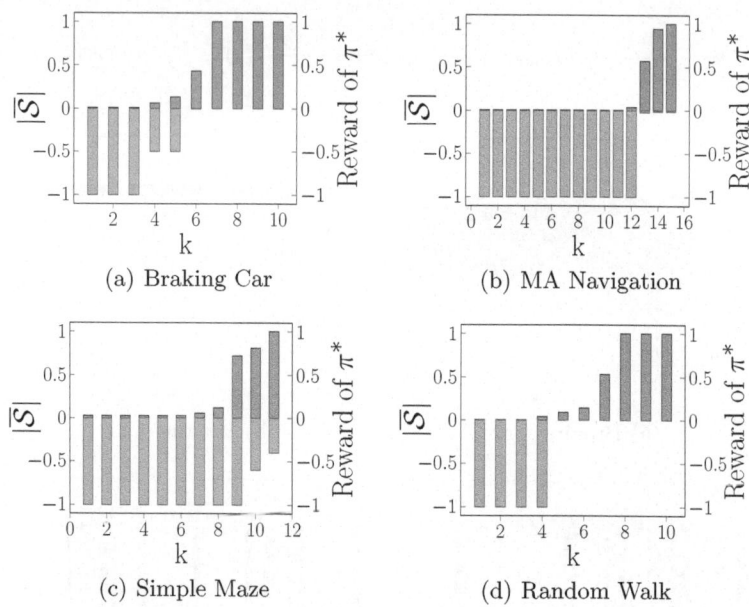

Fig. 9. Normalized granularity of states and its performance for symbolic execution with search depth k.

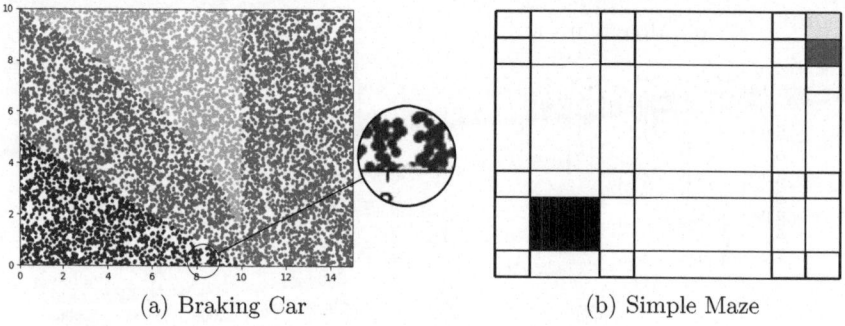

Fig. 10. Partitions with SymPar for the Braking Car and Simple Maze.

6.3   RQ3: Scalability

Table 2 shows that the number of parts in SymPar partitions is independent of the size of the state space. However, this does not imply the universal applicability of the same partition across different sizes. The conditions specified within the partitions are size-dependent. Consequently, when analyzing environments with different sizes for a given problem, running SymPar is necessary to ensure the appropriate partition, even though the total number of parts remains the same.

	$|\bar{\mathcal{S}}|$	$|\mathcal{S}|$		$|\bar{\mathcal{S}}|$	$|\mathcal{S}|$		$|\bar{\mathcal{S}}|$	$|\mathcal{S}|$
Simple Maze	10×10	33	**Wumpus World**	64×64	73	**Navigation**	10×10	51
	$10^2\times10^2$	33		$10^2\times10^2$	73		$10^2\times10^2$	51
	$10^3\times10^3$	33		$10^3\times10^3$	73		$10^3\times10^3$	51

Table 2. Size of state space and partition for test problems.

	$\mathcal{P}_1$	$\mathcal{P}_2$	$\mathcal{P}_3$	$\mathcal{P}_4$	$\mathcal{P}_5$
BC	$-0.05\pm0.0\%$	$-0.01\pm0.0\%$	$-0.5\pm0.0\%$	$-10.0\pm0.0\%$	$-10.01\pm0.0\%$
MC	$996.1\pm0.1\%$	$975.5\pm0.2\%$	$979.04\pm0.2\%$	$986.7\pm0.2\%$	$981.6\pm0.2\%$
WW 1	$486.8\pm0.3\%$	$490.0\pm0.2\%$	$477.6\pm0.2\%$	$475.0\pm0.0\%$	$495.8\pm0.1\%$

Table 3. Assessment of similarity of concrete states within parts. **BC, MC, WW 1,** respectively, stand for Braking Car, Mountain Car, Wumpus World 1.

	Off	Auto	Dyn	NonL	NarrP	SInd
SymPar	✓	✓	✓	✓	✓	✓
CAT-RL	✗	✓	✓	✗	✗	✗
Tiling	✓	✗	✗	✗	✗	✗

Table 4. Capabilities and properties.

6.4 RQ4: Partitioning as an Abstraction

Table 3 presents the variance in accumulated rewards for concrete states across various parts. The findings demonstrate a notable consistency in accumulated rewards among states within the same part, indicating minimal divergence. This is particularly evident when the mean and normalized standard deviation are compared, which demonstrates that the standard deviation is considerably smaller in relation to the mean accumulated reward.

Summary. Our experiments show distinct advantages of SymPar over the other approaches, cf. Tbl. 4. It is an offline (**Off**) automated (**Auto**) approach, which captures the dynamics of the environment (**Dyn**), and maps the nonlinear relation between components of the state into their representation (**NonL**). SymPar can detect narrow parts (**NarrP**) without excessive sampling and generates a logical partition that is independent of the specific size of the state space (**SInd**). This comprehensive comparison underscores the robust capabilities of SymPar across various dimensions, positioning it as a versatile and powerful approach compared to CAT-RL and Tile Coding.

Threats to Internal Validity. The data produced in response to RQ1 and RQ2 may be incorrectly interpreted as suggesting existence of a correlation between the size of partitions and the effectiveness of learning. No such obvious correlation exists: too small, too large, and incorrectly selected partitions hamper learning.

We cannot claim any such correlation. We merely report the size of the partitions and the performance of learning for the selected cases.

While we study the impact of the state space size on SymPar (RQ3), one should remember that there is no strong relationship between the size and the complexity of the state space. In general, the complexity (the branching of the environment model) has a dominant effect on the performance of symbolic execution.

We assumed that two states are similar if they have yield similar accumulated reward in the obtained policy (RQ4). First, note that we have no guarantee that the used policy is optimal, although the plots suggest convergence. Second, a more precise, but also more expensive, alternative would be to compute the optimal policy for each of the two states separately (taking them out of partitions). This could lead to higher and different reward values. However, even this would not guarantee the reliability of the estimated state values, as the hypothetical optimal accumulated reward requires representing the optimal policy precisely for all reachable states, which is infeasible in a continuous state space with a probabilistic environment.

Threats to External Validity. The results of experiments are inherently not generalizable, given that we use a finite set of cases. However, the selected cases do cover a range of situations: discrete and continuous state spaces, deterministic and non-deterministic environments, as well as single- and multi-agent environments.

Technical Details. The implementation of SymPar (will be publicly available upon the acceptance) uses Symbolic PathFinder[4] [36] as its symbolic executor, Z3[5] [34] as its main SMT-Solver and the SMT-solver DReal[6] [14] to handle non-linear functions such as trigonometric functions.

7   Discussion and Limitations

SymPar is not limited to reinforcement learning. Theoretically, it could be applied with traditional solving techniques for MDPs. However, this would require efficient methods for extracting MDP models from simulator code.

SymPar uses environments that are implemented as programs, so they are formally specified. This may suggest that one can obtain the policies analytically, not through (statistical) RL. However, many problems exist which we can formulate as programs, but those semantics are too complex to handle with precise analytical methods by solving the derived MDPs. For example, consider an autonomous drone delivery system in an urban setting that needs to transport packages efficiently, while avoiding static (buildings) and dynamic (other drones) obstacles. The urban environment can be modeled with precise geometry and established laws of physics that govern drone flight dynamics. Weather predictions and obstacle patterns can frequently be pre-simulated. Despite the availability of an exact

---

[4] https://github.com/SymbolicPathFinder
[5] https://github.com/Z3Prover/z3
[6] https://github.com/dreal/dreal4

environment model, reinforcement learning remains the preferred solution due to its ability to scale to this complexity, which analytical methods cannot [7,19,24].

Simulations often rely on simplifying assumptions to make them computationally feasible. If these assumptions abstract from critical details, the simulations might not be fully transparent or interpretable. Even in these cases, the efficacy of SymPar in achieving effective partitions, and the capacity of RL to identify optimal policies, remains valid. While we did not undertake a direct experiment for this scenario, the experiments for RQ2 can serve as a surrogate evidence. Limiting the depth of search for symbolic execution may generate a coarser partition than from a fully analyzed the program, which while not exactly the same, is similar to using a more abstract program for partitioning. These experiments indicate that if a simplified model of the environment is used, SymPar could still generate a partition that can be used for more realistic environment models.

In concurrency theory, lumping or bisimulation minimization is sometimes used as a partitioning technique. Note that bisimulation minimization is presently not possible for environment models expressed as computer programs. We would need symbolic bisimulation-minimization methods. Also, note that bisimulation induces a finer partitioning than we need: it puts in a single equivalence class all states that are externally indistinguishable, while we only need to unify states that share the same optimal action in one step. In contrast, symbolic execution performs a mixed syntactic-semantic decomposition of the input state space by means of path conditions. This process is mainly driven by the syntax of the program, yet it is semantically informed via the branch conditions. The obtained partition might be unsound from the bisimulation perspective, but it tends to produce coarser partitions.

SymPar analyzes single step executions of the environment. There are however problems where the interesting behaviors are observed only over a sequence of decisions. For example, the dynamics of Cart Pole [43] is described by a continuous formula over its position and velocity along with the angle and angular velocity of the pole. There is, in fact, no interesting explicit branching—the path conditions found by symbolic execution are trivial. SymPar is better suited for problems with explicit branching in the environment dynamics. At the same time, excessive branching can hamper its efficiency. In these cases, choosing a reasonable depth may achieve a partition that is sufficiently good while controlling its size (Fig. 9).

8   Conclusion

SymPar is a new generic and automatic offline method for partitioning state spaces in reinforcement learning based on a symbolic analysis of the environment's dynamics. In contrast to related work, SymPar's partitions effectively capture the semantics of the environment. SymPar accommodates non-linear environmental behaviors by using adaptive partition shapes, instead of rectangular tiles. Our experiments demonstrate that SymPar improves state space coverage with respect to environmental behavior and allows reinforcement learning to better handle with sparse rewards. However, since SymPar analyzes the simulator of the environment, it is sensitive to the implementation of the environment model.

The performance of the underlying tools, including the symbolic executor and SMT solvers, also affect the effectiveness of SymPar for complex simulators with long execution paths. In the future, we would like to address these limitations and consider using symbolic execution also for online partitioning.

Acknowledgment. This work was partially funded by DIREC (Digital Research Centre Denmark), a collaboration between the eight Danish universities and the Alexandra Institute supported by the Innovation Fund Denmark.

Data Availability Statement. The source code of SymPar, the benchmark items, the evaluation results and instructions for reproduction are available online via DOI 10.5281/zenodo.14620119.

References

1. Adelt, J., Herber, P., Niehage, M., Remke, A.: Towards safe and resilient hybrid systems in the presence of learning and uncertainty. In: Proc. 11th Intl. Symposium on Leveraging Applications of Formal Methods, Verification and Validation. Verification Principles (ISoLA 2022). Lecture Notes in Computer Science, vol. 13701, pp. 299–319. Springer (2022). https://doi.org/10.1007/978-3-031-19849-6_18
2. Ahrendt, W., Beckert, B., Bubel, R., Hähnle, R., Schmitt, P.H., Ulbrich, M. (eds.): Deductive Software Verification - The KeY Book - From Theory to Practice, Lecture Notes in Computer Science, vol. 10001. Springer (2016). https://doi.org/10.1007/978-3-319-49812-6
3. Akrour, R., Veiga, F., Peters, J., Neumann, G.: Regularizing reinforcement learning with state abstraction. In: Proc. Intl. Conf. on Intelligent Robots and Systems (IROS). pp. 534–539. IEEE (2018)
4. Albus, J.S.: Brains, behavior, and robotics. BYTE Books (1981)
5. de Boer, F.S., Bonsangue, M.M.: Symbolic execution formally explained. Formal Aspects Comput. **33**(4-5), 617–636 (2021). https://doi.org/10.1007/S00165-020-00527-Y
6. Cadar, C., Dunbar, D., Engler, D.R.: KLEE: unassisted and automatic generation of high-coverage tests for complex systems programs. In: Proc. 8th Symposium on Operating Systems Design and Implementation (OSDI 2008). pp. 209–224. USENIX Association (2008), http://www.usenix.org/events/osdi08/tech/full_papers/cadar/cadar.pdf
7. Chen, X., Wang, H., Li, Z., Ding, W., Dang, F., Wu, C., Chen, X.: Deliversense: Efficient delivery drone scheduling for crowdsensing with deep reinforcement learning. In: Adjunct Proceedings of the 2022 ACM International Joint Conference on Pervasive and Ubiquitous Computing and the 2022 ACM International Symposium on Wearable Computers. pp. 403–408 (2022)
8. Clarke, L.A.: A program testing system. In: Proc. 1976 Annual Conf. pp. 488–491. ACM (1976). https://doi.org/10.1145/800191.805647
9. Dadvar, M., Nayyar, R.K., Srivastava, S.: Conditional abstraction trees for sample-efficient reinforcement learning. In: Proc. 39th Conf. on Uncertainty in Artificial Intelligence. Proc. Machine Learning Research, vol. 216, pp. 485–495. PMLR (2023)
10. Davey, B.A., Priestley, H.A.: Introduction to lattices and order. Cambridge University Press, Cambridge (1990), http://www.worldcat.org/search?qt=worldcat_org_all&q=0521367662

11. Ferns, N., Panangaden, P., Precup, D.: Metrics for finite Markov decision processes. In: UAI. vol. 4, pp. 162–169 (2004)
12. Ferns, N., Panangaden, P., Precup, D.: Bisimulation metrics for continuous Markov decision processes. SIAM Journal on Computing **40**(6), 1662–1714 (2011)
13. Fulton, N., Platzer, A.: Safe reinforcement learning via formal methods: Toward safe control through proof and learning. In: Proc. 32nd Conf. on Artificial Intelligence (AAAI-18). pp. 6485–6492. AAAI Press (2018). https://doi.org/10.1609/AAAI. V32I1.12107
14. Gao, S., Kong, S., Clarke, E.M.: dReal: An SMT solver for nonlinear theories over the reals. In: Proc. 24th Intl. Conf. on Automated Deduction (CADE-24). Lecture Notes in Computer Science, vol. 7898, pp. 208–214. Springer (2013). https://doi.org/10.1007/978-3-642-38574-2_14
15. Ghaffari, M., Afsharchi, M.: Learning to shift load under uncertain production in the smart grid. Intl. Transactions on Electrical Energy Systems **31**(2), e12748 (2021)
16. Giunchiglia, F., Walsh, T.: A theory of abstraction. Artificial intelligence **57**(2-3), 323–389 (1992)
17. Jaeger, M., Jensen, P.G., Larsen, K.G., Legay, A., Sedwards, S., Taankvist, J.H.: Teaching Stratego to play ball: Optimal synthesis for continuous space MDPs. In: Proc. 17th Intl. Symposium on Automated Technology for Verification and Analysis (ATVA 2019). Lecture Notes in Computer Science, vol. 11781, pp. 81–97. Springer (2019). https://doi.org/10.1007/978-3-030-31784-3_5
18. Jansson, A.D.: Discretization and representation of a complex environment for on-policy reinforcement learning for obstacle avoidance for simulated autonomous mobile agents. In: Proc. 7th Intl. Congress on Information and Communication Technology. Lecture Notes in Networks and Systems, vol. 464, pp. 461–476. Springer (2023)
19. Jevtić, Ð., Miljković, Z., Petrović, M., Jokić, A.: Reinforcement learning-based collision avoidance for uav. In: 2023 10th International Conference on Electrical, Electronic and Computing Engineering (IcETRAN). pp. 1–6. IEEE (2023)
20. Jin, P., Tian, J., Zhi, D., Wen, X., Zhang, M.: Trainify: A CEGAR-driven training and verification framework for safe deep reinforcement learning. In: Proc. 34th Intl. Conf. on Computer Aided Verification (CAV 2022). Lecture Notes in Computer Science, vol. 13371, pp. 193–218. Springer (2022). https://doi.org/10.1007/978-3-031-13185-1_10
21. King, J.C.: Symbolic execution and program testing. Communications of the ACM **19**(7), 385–394 (1976)
22. Kober, J., Bagnell, J.A., Peters, J.: Reinforcement learning in robotics: A survey. The Intl. Journal of Robotics Research **32**(11), 1238–1274 (2013)
23. Kozen, D.: Semantics of probabilistic programs. In: Proc. 20th Annual Symposium on Foundations of Computer Science (SFCS 1979). pp. 101–114. IEEE Computer Society (1979). https://doi.org/10.1109/SFCS.1979.38
24. Kretchmara, R.M., Young, P.M., Anderson, C.W., Hittle, D.C., Anderson, M.L., Delnero, C.C.: Robust reinforcement learning control. In: Proceedings of the 2001 American Control Conference.(Cat. No. 01CH37148). vol. 2, pp. 902–907. IEEE (2001)
25. Lanzi, P.L., Loiacono, D., Wilson, S.W., Goldberg, D.E.: Classifier prediction based on tile coding. In: Proc. Genetic and Evolutionary Computation Conf. (GECCO 2006). pp. 1497–1504. ACM (2006). https://doi.org/10.1145/1143997.1144242
26. Lee, I.S., Lau, H.Y.: Adaptive state space partitioning for reinforcement learning. Engineering applications of artificial intelligence **17**(6), 577–588 (2004)

27. Madumal, P., Miller, T., Sonenberg, L., Vetere, F.: Explainable reinforcement learning through a causal lens. In: Proc. 34th Conf. on Artificial Intelligence (AAAI 2020). pp. 2493–2500. AAAI Press (2020). https://doi.org/10.1609/AAAI.V34I03.5631

28. Mavridis, C.N., Baras, J.S.: Vector quantization for adaptive state aggregation in reinforcement learning. In: 2021 American Control Conf. (ACC). pp. 2187–2192. IEEE (2021)

29. Michie, D., Chambers, R.A.: Boxes: An experiment in adaptive control. Machine intelligence **2**(2), 137–152 (1968)

30. Mnih, V., Badia, A.P., Mirza, M., Graves, A., Lillicrap, T.P., Harley, T., Silver, D., Kavukcuoglu, K.: Asynchronous methods for deep reinforcement learning. In: Proc. 33nd Intl. Conf. on Machine Learning (ICML 2016). JMLR Workshop and Conf. Proceedings, vol. 48, pp. 1928–1937. JMLR.org (2016), http://proceedings.mlr.press/v48/mniha16.html

31. Mnih, V., Kavukcuoglu, K., Silver, D., Graves, A., Antonoglou, I., Wierstra, D., Riedmiller, M.: Playing Atari with deep reinforcement learning. arXiv preprint arXiv:1312.5602 (2013)

32. Moore, A.W.: Efficient memory-based learning for robot control. Ph.D. thesis, University of Cambridge, UK (1990). https://doi.org/10.1.1.17.2654

33. Moore, A.W.: Variable resolution dynamic programming: Efficiently learning action maps in multivariate real-valued state-spaces. In: Machine Learning Proceedings 1991, pp. 333–337. Elsevier (1991)

34. de Moura, L.M., Bjørner, N.S.: Z3: an efficient SMT solver. In: Proc. 14th Intl. Conf. on Tools and Algorithms for the Construction and Analysis of Systems (TACAS 2008). Lecture Notes in Computer Science, vol. 4963, pp. 337–340. Springer (2008). https://doi.org/10.1007/978-3-540-78800-3_24

35. Nicol, S., Chadès, I.: Which states matter? an application of an intelligent discretization method to solve a continuous POMDP in conservation biology. PloS one **7**(2), e28993 (2012)

36. Pasareanu, C.S., Visser, W., Bushnell, D.H., Geldenhuys, J., Mehlitz, P.C., Rungta, N.: Symbolic PathFinder: integrating symbolic execution with model checking for Java bytecode analysis. Autom. Softw. Eng. **20**(3), 391–425 (2013). https://doi.org/10.1007/S10515-013-0122-2

37. Puiutta, E., Veith, E.M.S.P.: Explainable reinforcement learning: A survey. In: Proc. 4th Intl. Cross-Domain Conf. (CD-MAKE 2020). Lecture Notes in Computer Science, vol. 12279, pp. 77–95. Springer (2020). https://doi.org/10.1007/978-3-030-57321-8_5

38. Raffin, A., Hill, A., Ernestus, M., Gleave, A., Kanervisto, A., Dormann, N.: Stable baselines3 (2019), https://stable-baselines3.readthedocs.io/

39. Russell, S.J., Norvig, P.: Artificial intelligence a modern approach. London (2010)

40. Schulman, J., Wolski, F., Dhariwal, P., Radford, A., Klimov, O.: Proximal policy optimization algorithms. arXiv preprint arXiv:1707.06347 (2017)

41. Seipp, J., Helmert, M.: Counterexample-guided cartesian abstraction refinement for classical planning. Journal of Artificial Intelligence Research **62**, 535–577 (2018)

42. Sharon, G., Stern, R., Felner, A., Sturtevant, N.R.: Conflict-based search for optimal multi-agent pathfinding. Artificial Intelligence **219**, 40–66 (2015)

43. Sutton, R.S., Barto, A.G.: Reinforcement Learning: An Introduction. The MIT Press, 2nd edn. (2018)

44. Szita, I.: Reinforcement learning in games. In: Reinforcement Learning, Adaptation, Learning, and Optimization, vol. 12, pp. 539–577. Springer (2012). https://doi.org/10.1007/978-3-642-27645-3_17

45. Tran, H.D., Cai, F., Diego, M.L., Musau, P., Johnson, T.T., Koutsoukos, X.: Safety verification of cyber-physical systems with reinforcement learning control. ACM Transactions on Embedded Computing Systems (TECS) **18**(5s), 1–22 (2019)

46. Uther, W.T.B., Veloso, M.M.: Tree based discretization for continuous state space reinforcement learning. In: Proc. 15th National Conf. on Artificial Intelligence and Tenth Innovative Applications of Artificial Intelligence Conf. (AAAI 98, IAAI 98). pp. 769–774. AAAI Press / The MIT Press (1998), http://www.aaai.org/Library/AAAI/1998/aaai98-109.php

47. Varshosaz, M., Ghaffari, M., Johnsen, E.B., Wąsowski, A.: Formal specification and testing for reinforcement learning. Proc. ACM Program. Lang. **7**(ICFP) (aug 2023). https://doi.org/10.1145/3607835

48. Verdier, C.F., Babuška, R., Shyrokau, B., Mazo, M.: Near optimal control with reachability and safety guarantees. IFAC-PapersOnLine **52**(11), 230–235 (2019). https://doi.org/10.1016/j.ifacol.2019.09.146

49. Visser, W., Pasareanu, C.S., Pelánek, R.: Test input generation for java containers using state matching. In: Pollock, L.L., Pezzè, M. (eds.) Proceedings of the ACM/SIGSOFT International Symposium on Software Testing and Analysis, ISSTA 2006, Portland, Maine, USA, July 17-20, 2006. pp. 37–48. ACM (2006). https://doi.org/10.1145/1146238.1146243

50. Voogd, E., Johnsen, E.B., Silva, A., Susag, Z.J., Wąsowski, A.: Symbolic semantics for probabilistic programs. In: Proc. 20th Intl. Conf. on Quantitative Evaluation of Systems (QEST 2023). Lecture Notes in Computer Science, vol. 14287, pp. 329–345. Springer (2023). https://doi.org/10.1007/978-3-031-43835-6_23

51. Vyetrenko, S., Xu, S.: Risk-sensitive compact decision trees for autonomous execution in presence of simulated market response. arXiv preprint arXiv:1906.02312 (2019). https://doi.org/10.48550/ARXIV.1906.02312

52. Wei, H., Corder, K., Decker, K.: Q-learning acceleration via state-space partitioning. In: Proc. 17th Intl. Conf. on Machine Learning and Applications (ICMLA 2018). pp. 293–298. IEEE (2018)

53. Whiteson, S.: Adaptive Representations for Reinforcement Learning, Studies in Computational Intelligence, vol. 291. Springer (2010). https://doi.org/10.1007/978-3-642-13932-1

54. Yu, C., Liu, J., Nemati, S., Yin, G.: Reinforcement learning in healthcare: A survey. ACM Computing Surveys (CSUR) **55**(1), 1–36 (2021)

55. Zelvelder, A.E., Westberg, M., Främling, K.: Assessing explainability in reinforcement learning. In: Proc. Third Intl. Workshop on Explainable and Transparent AI and Multi-Agent Systems (EXTRAAMAS 2021). Lecture Notes in Computer Science, vol. 12688, pp. 223–240. Springer (2021). https://doi.org/10.1007/978-3-030-82017-6_14

Formal Architectural Patterns
for Adaptive Robotic Software

James Baxter[1]([✉])[ID], Bert van Acker[2][ID],
Morten Kristensen[3][ID], Thomas Wright[3][ID], Ana Cavalcanti[1][ID],
and Cláudio Gomes[3][ID]

[1] University of York, York, UK
james.baxter@york.ac.uk
[2] University of Antwerp, Antwerp, Belgium
[3] Aarhus University, Aarhus, Denmark

Abstract. It is often the case that a robot must adapt to unexpected changes in its environment. It is, however, important that these changes can be demonstrated to maintain the safe operation of the robot. The adaptive systems community has developed the MAPE-K pattern as a widely recognised conceptual architecture. We propose extending MAPE-K to incorporate runtime verification, resulting in an architecture we call MAPLE-K. In this paper, we capture and formalise both the MAPE-K and MAPLE-K architectures using a domain-specific language. Additionally, we provide support for translation from architectural models to software models and code to facilitate the deployment of verified applications. MAPE-K is rarely maintained at the implementation level, but our work ensures traceability between the code and its design, enabling the use of architectural information to verify the correctness of the software.

Keywords: adaptive systems · robotics · formal modelling

1 Introduction

It is essential that robots behave safely, as they can cause damage to property or harm to humans nearby. A particular challenge is the possibility of unexpected changes in the environment. These may include the appearance of obstacles, sensor readings outside the range the robot can handle, or changes to the robot's body, such as failures. In all these cases, the robot must be able to adapt in a way that maintains safe and effective operation wherever possible.

The most common pattern for the development of software capable of adapting to unexpected changes is the MAPE-K architecture, where the system is overseen by a manager component. A widely accepted view of MAPE-K is that the manager proceeds in a cycle of four steps: monitoring inputs to detect anomalies; analysing the anomaly to determine its nature; planning to adapt the system; and executing the plan by signalling to the managed system to implement it. These four components form the "MAPE" of the MAPE-K, pattern and they are supported by a Knowledge Base (the "K"), through which information is shared between steps and across iterations of the cycle.

A. Boronat and G. Fraser (Eds.): FASE 2025, LNCS 15693, pp.145–165, 2025.
https://doi.org/10.1007/978-3-031-90900-9_8

In the RoboSAPIENS project [18], we propose an extension of MAPE-K called MAPLE-K, which incorporates an additional legitimisation step to ensure that adaptations maintain the safe operation of the robot. This extra step checks that the plan produced (in the planning step) is safe before it is executed. It is useful to have legitimisation as a separate step, since safety cannot always be guaranteed during the formulation of the plan. In particular, neural networks may be used in the analysis or planning steps for greater adaptability, but neural networks cannot always ensure compliance with safety requirements so the legitimisation cannot be performed by a neural network. It is thus important that the planning and legitimisation steps be considered separately, since they may adopt different approaches. The planning step may also itself be adapted by a further MAPE-K or MAPLE-K component, whereas safety requirements would not permit the legitimate step to be adapted.

Additionally, we propose that the conceptual elements of MAPLE-K should also be applied at the implementation level. While MAPE-K is widely used to plan the structure of software, the pattern is often not reflected in the implementation. This jeopardises traceability between the deployment and the design of the code and hinders the compositional verification of adaptations.

This loss of traceability can be avoided through a Model-Driven Engineering (MDE) approach, where architectural patterns are reflected in system models, which form the basis for implementation. The connection is strengthened by automated transformation from the model to code.

The RoboStar framework [11] is a family of domain-specific languages for robotics, with support for verification via automated generation of formal semantics from models. In particular, RoboChart is used to describe software designs. RoboChart [19] models represent software components and their connections, describing behaviour via timed state machines or neural networks. Through transformation, RoboChart models can be validated and converted into code.

Another RoboStar language, RoboArch [7], supports the modelling of architectural designs. RoboArch embeds a layered approach to software architecture and allows the definition of layers using patterns that describe their internal structure. Automatic translation from RoboArch architectural models into RoboChart sketches ensures that architectural designs are reflected in the design models, from which formal verification and code generation are possible. The translation formalises the RoboArch architectural models.

Architecture and Analysis Description Language (AADL) [5,13] provides standardized notations for specifying hardware and software components of a system and their interactions. It can be used to describe the architecture in the detail required for deployment as well as its implementation.

In the work presented here, we propose the process for the development of robotic software shown in Fig. 1. A developer starts with a high-level model of the architecture of a system in RoboArch and generates a corresponding sketch in RoboChart, possibly enriching it with application-specific logic. This provides support for formal verification of the architecture. We then propose an approach to transform the RoboChart model into a corresponding AADL model, enabling

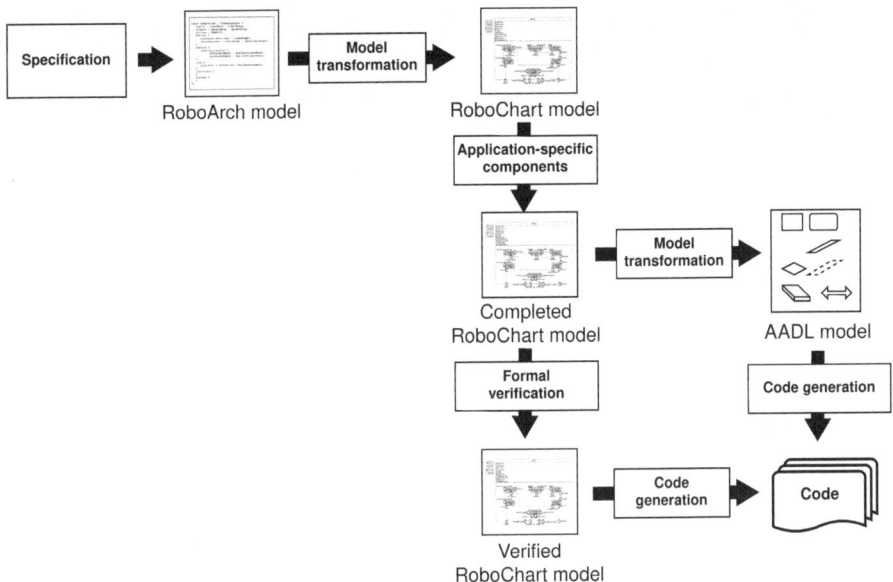

Fig. 1: RoboChart and AADL model-based development process

the development of a deployment model, annotating it with deployment-specific properties, and generating code skeletons for the interface and infrastructure code of each component. Using the code skeletons, the behaviour (the "application code") can be written in the chosen programming language or obtained automatically from RoboChart as well. The auto-generated code skeletons are aligned with the AADL/RoboArch architectures, ensuring that throughout this process the MAPLE-K loop itself, and particularly the Legitimate component, can be modelled, verified, and maintained all the way down to the code level. In this case, legitimisation can take advantage of the high-level structure of the RoboArch model to reason about the adaptations. Although our approach makes use of the particular notations of RoboArch, RoboChart and AADL, it demonstrates this more general process for development of software following a MAPLE-K pattern, transforming from higher-level specification notations to lower-level models and code.

In this paper, we contribute to the design of open-ended self-adaptive systems that require certification by presenting extensions of RoboArch and AADL to capture MAPLE-K architectures, with the traditional MAPE-K architecture as a special case. We also present a mapping from RoboChart to AADL, allowing a RoboArch and RoboChart design architecture to be translated into deployment. We demonstrate our approach using a robot that navigates through a space, avoiding obstacles, and adapting to faults and occlusions in its LiDAR sensor.

Next, in Section 2, we discuss related work on modelling MAPE-K. In Section 3, we describe RoboArch, RoboChart, and AADL. We present our model of MAPLE-K in RoboArch and RoboChart in Section 4, and in AADL in Section 5. We then discuss our mapping from RoboChart to AADL in Section 6. Our example is the subject of Section 7. Finally, we conclude in Section 8.

2   Related Work

The MAPE-K conceptual architecture was first introduced by IBM, as outlined in the seminal work of Kephart et al. [17] and further detailed in [16]. Over the years, several variations have been proposed [4,20,9,6].

In the context of MDE, several works align with our goal of formalising architectures based on MAPE-K loops, albeit with very different approaches and applications. For instance, Arcaini et al. [4] model self-adaptive systems as multi-agent systems, representing both the managed system and the managing subsystem as interacting agents. Their model utilises multi-agent ASMs (Abstract State Machines) within the ASMETA framework [1], which supports formal techniques for validating and verifying adaptation scenarios. This approach provides feedback on the correctness of adaptation logic during system design.

Camilli et al. [10] introduce a formal framework for modelling and analysing self-adaptive systems with decentralised adaptation control using Petri nets. Their framework supports the validation and verification of the MAPE-K components, demonstrated through a self-optimising cluster management system.

Finally, Weyns et al. [22] contribute an end-to-end approach for engineering self-adaptive systems, addressing design, deployment, runtime adaptation, and evolution. Their tool uses timed automata and runtime statistical model checking, validated through an IoT application. The approach provides: correctness guarantees for the feedback loop with respect to properties preserved throughout the execution of formally verified models; efficient selection of adaptation options that meet accuracy and confidence requirements; and support for on-the-fly changes to adaptation goals and updates to verified models.

What distinguishes our work is the creation of a pathway from high-level, albeit formal, descriptions of architectures based on MAPLE-K to deployment architectures. In this way, developers can: (1) describe architectures using accessible notation; (2) verify properties, potentially involving timing; and (3) use the same architecture for deployment, preserving both properties and structure.

3   Preliminaries

In this section, we first present RoboArch and its translation to RoboChart in Section 3.1. Afterwards, in Section 3.2, we describe AADL.

3.1   RoboArch and RoboChart

As noted, RoboArch architectures are layered, a structure widely used in robotics. These layered architectures usually have a control layer at the lowest level, communicating directly with the robot, followed by an executive layer, which carries

```
system ObstacleAvoidance          layer Application {
                                     inputs= eventReply:Events,  ...;
datatype Velocities {                outputs= activate:Skills, deactivate:Skills, ...;
   linear:real                    } ;
   angular:real                   layer MoveAndSense: ControlLayer {
}                                    requires Motors
                                     uses Sense
interface Motors {
   move(vel: Velocities)             inputs= activate:Skills, deactivate:Skills, ...;
}                                    outputs= eventReply:Events,  ...;
                                     pattern= ReactiveSkills;
interface Sense {                    ...
   event proximity: int           } ;
}
                                  connections=
robotic platform PuckRobot {      Application on activate to MoveAndSense on activate,
   provides Motors                Application on deactivate to MoveAndSense on deactivate,
   uses Sense                     ...
}                                 MoveAndSense on eventReply to Application on eventReply,
                                  MoveAndSense on activeSkills to Application on activeSkills,
                                  ...
                                  PuckRobot on proximity to MoveAndSense on proximity;
```

Fig. 2: An example of a RoboArch model

out sequences of actions, and a planning layer at the highest level, which makes high-level decisions. Each layer can have a pattern describing its internal architecture, and uses events and operations to communicate with other layers and the robot. We describe RoboArch via the example of an obstacle avoidance robot. In Fig. 2, we describe the architecture of its software as a system called ObstacleAvoidance. We note that RoboArch is a textual language. Future work could define a graphical notation for RoboArch as a profile of SysML block diagrams.

RoboArch uses the type system of the formal modelling notation Z [23]. New types can be declared to be used in specifying the data flow in the architecture. Here, we define a record datatype Velocities, with two real fields.

RoboArch distinguishes communication between layers and communication with the robot. Communication between layers uses input and output events only. Communication with the robot is specified by a robotic platform, declaring (via interfaces) events and operations that describe services of the platform used by the software. A RoboArch architecture is platform independent. Here, we declare two interfaces: Motors, defining an operation, and Sense, defining an event. These are declared in a robotic platform PuckRobot. With the uses keyword we indicate that the platform has points of interaction via the events of the declared interface. Operations, on the other hand, are services provided by the platform, so the provides keyword declares interfaces with operations. Events may be inputs, outputs, or both, depending on the the robotic firmware and API.

The declaration of each layer may give a pre-defined type: a ControlLayer, ExecutiveLayer or PlanningLayer, each with its own restrictions following a commonly used architectural definition. A layer without a type is generic, allowing alternative structures to be defined. Here, we define two layers: a generic layer called Application, and a ControlLayer, called MoveAndSense.

Each layer declares `inputs` and `outputs`: events that may have types, such as `Skills` and `Events` (both of which come from the layer's pattern). A `ControlLayer` additionally `uses` or `requires` the same interfaces as the robotic platform, since it is intended to coordinate communication with the robot.

A layer can have a `pattern`. In our example, `MoveAndSense` uses the pattern `ReactiveSkills` [8]. Declaration of a pattern establishes the additional information required to specify the architecture. We omit details in Fig. 2.

After the layers, `connections` are defined between the events of the layers and robotic platform, ensuring a strict layering discipline is maintained. For example, here the `activate` and `deactivate` outputs for the `Application` layer are connected to the corresponding inputs in the `MoveAndSense` layer to activate and deactivate skills. Similarly, the `proximity` event from the `PuckRobot` robotic platform is connected to the `MoveAndSense` layer.

RoboChart, in contrast to RoboArch, is a diagrammatic notation for software design, and gives semantics to RoboArch. A RoboChart model is a module, containing a robotic platform declaring variables, operations and events, and one or more controllers, with connections between their events. A controller in turn either contains one or more state machines describing its behaviour, or is defined by an artificial neural network, and may require interfaces from the robotic platform or declare local variables and operations. Fig. 6 shows an example of a RoboChart controller containing several state machines. A state machine, such as the one shown in Fig. 8, defines states and transitions between them, and may also declare local variables or require interfaces. Each state can have statements it executes, and may also have nested states and transitions. In addition to modules, controllers and state machines, a RoboChart model may also define types and interfaces, such as those in Fig. 7. We describe further features of RoboChart used in models generated from RoboArch as needed. A full account of RoboChart can be found in [19].

3.2 AADL

AADL is a prominent language for MDE that provides standardized notations for specifying the architectural representation of a system. A supporting toolkit, Open Source Architectural Tool Environment (OSATE) [12], is available. It is an industry standard under the Society of Automotive Engineering (SAE).

AADL is a highly extensible language which allows for enhancing models with additional details through a set of standard properties and annexes. Properties refine component definitions and establish hierarchical connections across the system. Larger, more specialized extensions are defined in separate annexes.

RA2DL (Reconfiguration Architecture Analysis and Design Language) [3] is an extension of AADL designed to address the challenges of dynamic reconfiguration in system architectures. Unlike standard AADL, which focuses on modeling static architectures, RA2DL introduces constructs for handling reconfigurable components, allowing systems to adapt at runtime.

Research by [14] has shown how AADL can be combined with UPPAAL to verify timing constraints. The work in [15] presents the formal verification of

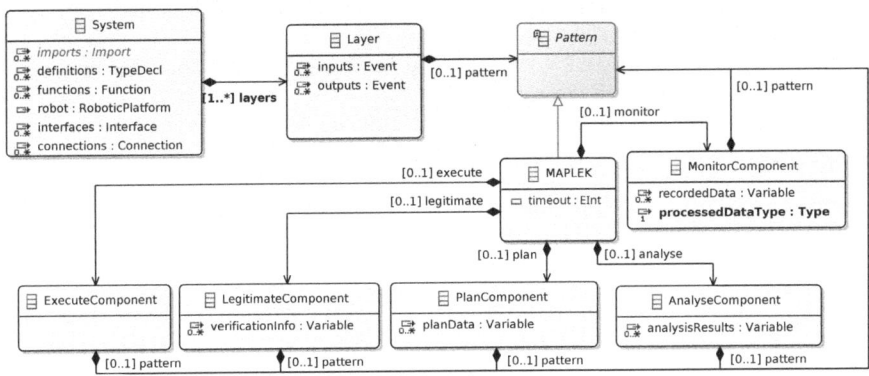

Fig. 3: Part of the RoboArch metamodel showing the MAPLE-K pattern

safety and liveness properties of an AADL model by transformation to Event-B. We carry out verification at the more abstract RoboArch and RoboChart levels, and use transformation to AADL to ensure properties are preserved.

4   MAPLE-K in RoboArch

Here, we present our extension of RoboArch to support MAPE-K and MAPLE-K architectures (Section 4.1), and give its semantics in RoboChart (Section 4.2).

4.1   Metamodel and well-formedness conditions

We have extended the RoboArch metamodel to introduce a pattern for MAPLE-K flexible enough to handle several variations, including the standard MAPE-K pattern. Fig. 3 shows the metamodel for the new pattern for MAPLE-K.

The top level of a RoboArch architecture is an instance of the class System in Fig. 3. It has one or more layers: instances of Layer. A layer may have a pattern represented by a subclass of Pattern. MAPLEK is our new subclass, which can be used for a PlanningLayer set above the layers of the managed system.

MAPLEK has components representing each of the five steps of the MAPLE-K loop: monitor, analyse, plan, legitimate and execute, each with its own type: MonitorComponent, AnalyseComponent, PlanComponent, LegitimateComponent and ExecuteComponent. These components are optional, leading to variations on the pattern. For example, omitting the monitor is a common variation where analysis is performed on raw input data from the managed system. Omitting the legitimate component yields the traditional MAPE-K pattern.

The inputs of the Layer from the managed system in the layer below are connected to the monitor component. Similarly, the outputs of the Layer are the outputs from the execute component to the managed system.

MK1 A Layer that has a pattern of type MAPLEK must be a GenericLayer or PlanningLayer.

MK2 An instance MAPLEK must have at least one of the components monitor, analyse, plan, execute.

MK3 If an instance of MAPLEK has a legitimate component, then it must have plan and execute components.

Fig. 4: The well-formedness conditions for MAPLEK

Each of the components has its own parameters, and can have their own pattern, allowing further variations on a MAPLE-K pattern to be defined. All of the components, except ExecuteComponent, have attributes recording a list of declarations for Variables within the knowledge base to which they can write. For MonitorComponent, these variables, in recordedData, record the monitored data. AnalyseComponent records analysisResults with information computed from the analysis that needs to be used in the plan or legitimate components. PlanComponent records planData, with information on the plan created, such as configuration values or a series of commands. LegitimateComponent records verificationInfo, giving an account of why a plan did or did not pass verification; such information can be used in replanning or passed as part of execution of the plan.

MonitorComponent also contains a type declaration processedDataType, indicating the type of the data output from the monitor to the analyse component. This may, for example, collect inputs from the managed system (possibly received at different times), or result from a filtering or error correcting operation.

In addition to its metamodel, RoboArch has well-formedness conditions that identify valid instances of its metamodel. These conditions further formalise the architectures captured in the metamodel, for which we can provide a formal semantics. A full account of existing well-formedness conditions is in [7]. For a MAPLEK pattern, the extra well-formedness conditions are shown in Fig. 4.

MK1 restricts the types of layer that can use a MAPLEK pattern, since MAPLE-K is intended to go above the layers of the managed system and PlanningLayers are the topmost layer types. By allowing for a GenericLayer to use MAPLEK, however, we cater for its use in an architecture where, for instance, we just separate the MAPLE-K loop and the managed system.

MK2 and **MK3** restrict the components that can be omitted. **MK2** ensures that there is at least one component to handle the inputs and outputs. We note that legitimate is not included in **MK2**, since it must receive a plan, reporting back if it is rejected or accepted. **MK3** captures this by requiring plan and execute components to be defined whenever legitimate is.

The metamodel for RoboArch underlies its textual representation shown in Fig. 2. We have defined a textual representation for the new MAPLEK pattern, an example of which can be seen in Fig. 5, which shows a layer of the application discussed later in Section 7, with the types it uses. It declares datatypes for each of the types used for the input and output events of the layer, and then declares the Adaptation layer, which declares its pattern as MAPLE-K.

```
datatype SpinConfig {
    commands: Seq(SpinCommand)
    period: int
}

datatype SpinCommand {
    angleVelocity: real
    duration: real
}

datatype LidarRange {
    ...
}

datatype BoolLidarMask {
    values: Seq(boolean)
    baseAngle: real
}

datatype ProbLidarMask {
    values: Seq(real)
    baseAngle: real
}
```

```
layer Adaptation : PlanningLayer {
    inputs = lidarData : LidarRange;
    outputs = spinConfig : SpinConfig;
    pattern = MAPLE-K;
    monitor {
        processed_data_type = LidarRange;
        recorded_data = lidarScans : Seq(LidarRange);
    }
    analyse {
        analysis_results =
            boolLidarMasks : Seq(BoolLidarMask),
            probLidarMasks : Seq(ProbLidarMask);
    }
    plan {
        plan_data = directions: Seq(SpinCommand);
    }
    legitimate {
    }
    execute {
    }
};
```

Fig. 5: An example of of a MAPLE-K pattern in a RoboArch model

With the definition of MAPLE-K as a pattern, the components of a MAPLE-K loop can be declared in their own blocks within the layer. The monitor component specifies a processed_data_type, corresponding to processedDataType in the metamodel, and declares a list of recorded_data variables, corresponding to recordedData in the metamodel. Similarly, analyse declares a list of analysis_results variables, and plan declares a list of plan_data variables. For the legitimate component, no variables are required in this example since this application uses a default safe plan if the legitimate rejects the original plan. The component execute declares no variables (although it may have its own Pattern), but it is included because it does need to be implemented.

Definition of additional patterns for each of the components is ongoing work.

4.2 Formalisation in RoboChart

As noted, RoboArch models can be automatically translated to a sketch of a RoboChart model; each layer is translated to a RoboChart controller. The metamodel and well-formedness conditions formalise the structural aspects of the architecture. The translation to RoboChart formalises the behavioural aspects.

To give an overview of how we capture the behaviour of a MAPLE-K architecture, and, in particular, when all components are present, we show in Fig. 6 the controller for the MAPLEK layer Adaptation in Fig. 5. As shown, each MAPLEK component is represented by a state machine. The connections between them reflect the control flow of the MAPLE-K loop, with the types of the events based on the types of the Variables, in the pattern definitions. The definitions of the state machine capture the control flow of its associated component.

The six state machines of the Adaptation controller are included by reference and explained in the sequel. The state machine named Monitor receives inputs from the managed system and sends on processed data via an event processedData. The inputs are those declared in the RoboArch model, in this case lidarData

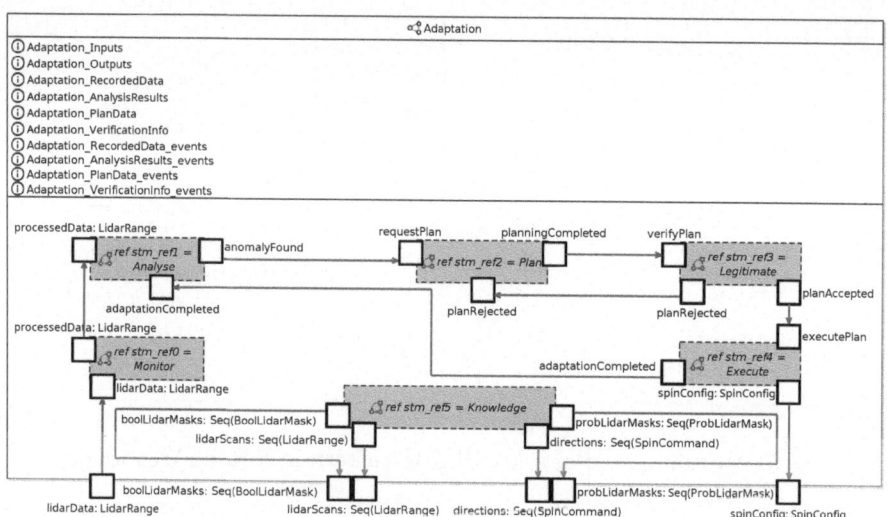

Fig. 6: The RoboChart controller generated for the `Adaptation` layer in Fig. 5

of type LidarRange, representing data from a lidar device detecting objects in the surroundings. The processedData event also has the type LidarRange, since that is the processed_data_type provided in Fig. 5.

Analyse receives the processedData from Monitor and analyses it, signalling via an anomalyFound event if an anomaly is found. This event is connected to the requestPlan event of the state machine, Plan.

The Plan state machine creates a plan to adapt to the anomaly, and signals to the Legitimate state machine on the planningCompleted event. Legitimate receives the planningCompleted event as the verifyPlan event, and performs verification and validation on the plan, signalling either planRejected back to the Plan state machine or planAccepted to the machine for the Execute component.

Execute receives planAccepted via executePlan and communicates with the managed system via output events, signalling via adaptationCompleted when it has finished. As with the input events, the output events are those declared in the RoboArch model: spinConfig of type SpinConfig, representing instructions for the robot to rotate as it moves to mitigate against occlusions of the LiDAR.

The knowledge base itself is represented as variables in interfaces and shared among the controller's state machines. In RoboChart, controllers and state machines declare the variables that they use. The declarations of the interfaces for Adaptation are the top of its block in Fig. 6, and their definitions are in Fig. 7.

The name of each interface is prefixed with the name of the controller, to ensure the names are unique when there is more than one MAPLE-K layer. The first two of interfaces, Adaptation_Inputs and Adaptation_Outputs, define the input and output events, lidarData and spinConfig in our case. The next four interfaces (RecordedData, AnalysisResults, PlanData, VerificationInfo) declare variables that form the knowledge base. The definition of each interface comes

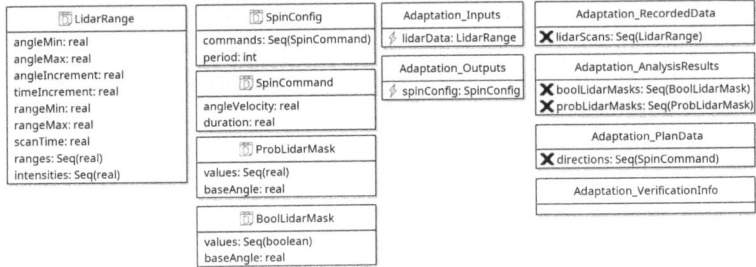

Fig. 7: The RoboChart interfaces and types generated for the example in Fig. 5

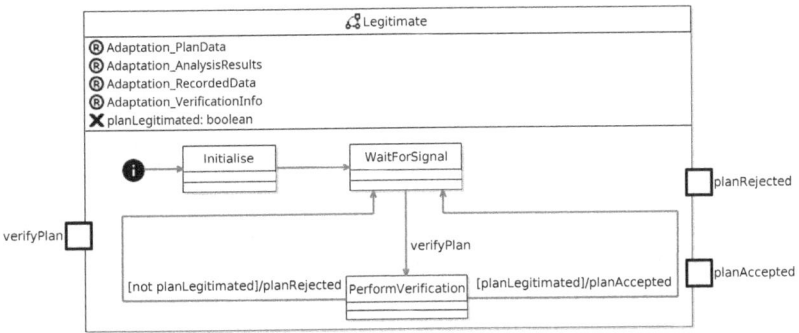

Fig. 8: An example of the Legitimate state machine generated for Fig. 5

from the variables in the components of the RoboArch model. VerificationInfo contains no variables, since the legitimate block in Fig. 5 contains no variables. Fig. 7 also shows the type definitions on the left.

The machine Knowledge communicates values from the knowledge base to the managed system. This supports an enhancement to the MAPLE-K architecture, where the managed system, or an extra layer between the MAPLEK layer and the managed system, performs additional validation of the outputs passed to it using data from the knowledge base. This is a trustworthiness checker. The final four interfaces declared in the controller Adaptation declare events for each variable. Their simple definitions are omitted here, the full model is in [2].

As an example of one of the state machines generated for the MAPLEK pattern, we present Legitimate for our example in Fig. 8. At the top, the declarations of interfaces indicate that Legitimate requires all variables of the controller. It needs access to the PlanData to check if it is safe, the RecordedData and AnalysisResults as supporting data for its checks, and the VerificationInfo to store more details on the outcome of the checks. Legitimate also declares a local boolean variable planLegitimated used to indicate whether the checks are successful.

The body of a state machine automatically generated from a RoboArch model consists of a set of states and transitions between them that give the skeleton of the state machine that the developer can extend with application-specific guards and actions. Each state can contain statements or a nested state machine, so such additions can be made without changing its structure.

The initial junction (black circle with an i) indicates Initialise as the initial state of Legitimate, where any required initialisation can be performed, and then enters a state WaitForSignal, where it waits for a verifyPlan event. After it occurs, Legitimate enters PerformVerification, where application-specific verification and validation are performed, with the verdict recorded in planLegitimated.

This variable is used in the guards of the transitions out of PerformVerification. If planLegitimated is true, planAccepted is output to signal the plan is accepted and can begin being executed. Otherwise, planRejected is output, to signal that a new plan should be created to replace it. In either case, Legitimate enters WaitForSignal afterwards, waiting for the next request to verify a plan.

The control flow just described embeds a parallel execution of the MAPLE-K components. It is possible to analyse for a new anomaly while one is already being handled. The definition of Analyse allows application-specific logic to choose what to do with new data that comes from the monitor. Plan can also use a new anomaly coming in (disregarding the legitimate result for any plan already sent for verification). An alternative semantics defines a sequential behavioural model. In this version, events of one machine are used to trigger another, which provides for compositional reasoning since each state machine can be considered separately. The less complex sequential semantics may be sufficient for simpler systems, so offering both is beneficial.

The RoboArch and even the RoboChart models give a high-level account of MAPLE-K. Next, we describe our realisation model of MAPLE-K in AADL.

5   MAPLE-K in AADL

The primary goal of our AADL models is to generate software skeletons for each of the MAPLE-K components, ensuring they conform to the RoboArch architecture. This guarantees compatibility with our implementation of an adaptive platform providing data storage and communication services, for example, while preserving the MAPLE-K pattern throughout the implementation.

The MAPLE-K pattern is modeled as a constellation of components communicating via the knowledge component through messages. Every component is modeled as an *AADL process*, defining its inputs and outputs, and its platform-independent implementation where its internal structure is defined. Messages passed between components are modeled using *AADL ports*.

An *AADL thread* is used to model any internal (user) functions (that is, callback). The model of a component also contains a state machine, modeled as *AADL modes and mode transitions*. For each element (that is, threads, subprograms, connections, ports, and so on) it is possible to define in which mode it is active, defining a specific workflow (that is, initialisation procedure and internal function activation). In AADL each transition has to be triggered by the occurrence of an event (that is, when a new message is received).

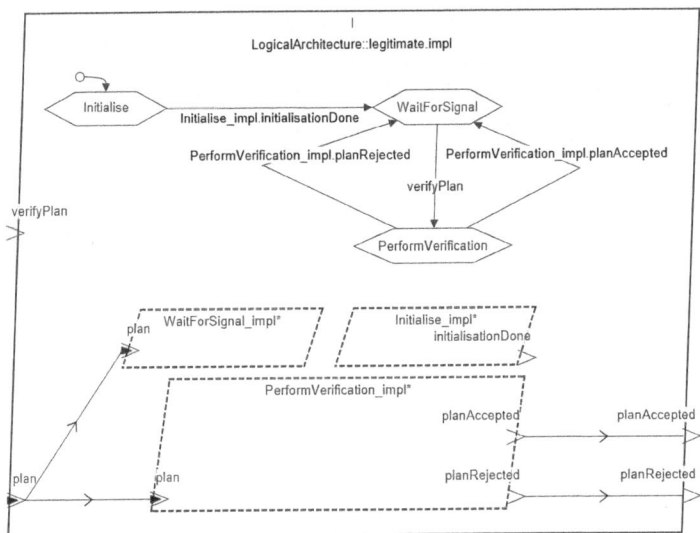

Fig. 9: Graphical representation of the Legitimate component in AADL

A graphical representation of the Legitimate component[4], shown in Fig. 9, presents its state machine with its states and transitions, represented as *AADL modes (hexagons)* and *mode transitions (arrows)*. Additionally, an *AADL thread (dotted parallelogram)* is included, which is executed within the corresponding state. For instance, in the *PerformVerification* state, the *PerformVerification_impl* thread is executed. The internal and external interface ports of the Legitimate component, whether event- or data-based, are depicted as *AADL event (open arrows)* ports and *AADL event data (open filled arrows)* ports.

As mentioned before, the global structure of AADL models is generated from the RoboChart models arising from RoboArch architectures, providing a foundational description for system design. Users, however, have the flexibility to extend these models. They can add threads to handle aspects of the deployment.

Before code generation from our AADL models, we need to specify how the software is deployed on the hardware. Fig. 10 shows the hardware setup for our example. At the top level, it shows a TurtleBot 4 robot connected via Wireless LAN (WLAN) to a companion computer with a mission processor modeled as a single core Intel Xeon, which allows for complex software components such as the MAPLE-K loop to be executed on a more powerful system, while making use of smaller and less powerful robot hardware. The TurtleBot 4 contains a Raspberry Pi 4B, modeled as four Cortex-A72 processors (quad core) and a firmware processor, internally connected via WLAN. The processors, depicted as an *AADL processor (cuboid)*, are able to execute software elements (threads) and can communicate, for instance, via a wireless connection, depicted as an *AADL*

---

[4] Full AADL textual models for this and other components can be found in [2]

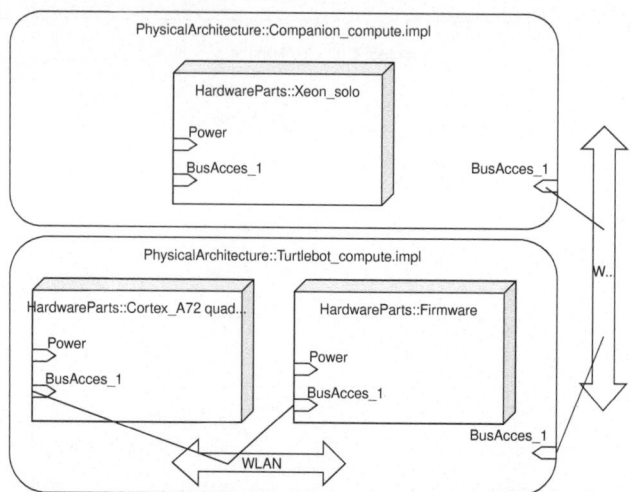

Fig. 10: Graphical representation of compute hardware of the Turtlebot 4.

bus (double sided arrow). The Raspberry Pi executes the software onboard the Turtlebot, while the firmware processor executes built-in code for managing the hardware components of the robot.

We can bind the software components to the appropriate physical (execution) hardware using property associations of one of two categories:

- **Actual_Processor_Binding:** fixed processor allocation
- **Allowed_Processor_Binding:** flexible processor allocation, which permits scheduling tools to assign the threads to processors.

Binding properties are added to the implementation model, including the application model (components like that in Fig. 8) and the hardware model (such as that in Fig. 10) as subcomponents. From them, different analyses can be performed using OSATE, such as *Resource budget and allocation analysis* or *bus load analysis,* for instance. These are complementary to the analyses that can be carried out using RoboChart, which focus on behavioural properties.

From the implementation model, interface and infrastructure code can be generated for integration of MAPLE-K components in existing software platforms. Ours is customised for trustworthy self-adaptive robotics applications.

This auto-generation step does not generate code for the software component's application logic; it only generates infrastructure code for "gluing together" the software components within a given software architecture. Code for the application logic can be generated from RoboChart.

For the infrastructure code, our platform supports multiple programming languages, including Python and C/C++, as well as various interfacing protocols, such as MQTT, Redis, and ROS2. We also support containerisation (that is, Docker), ensuring consistent behaviour across different execution environments,

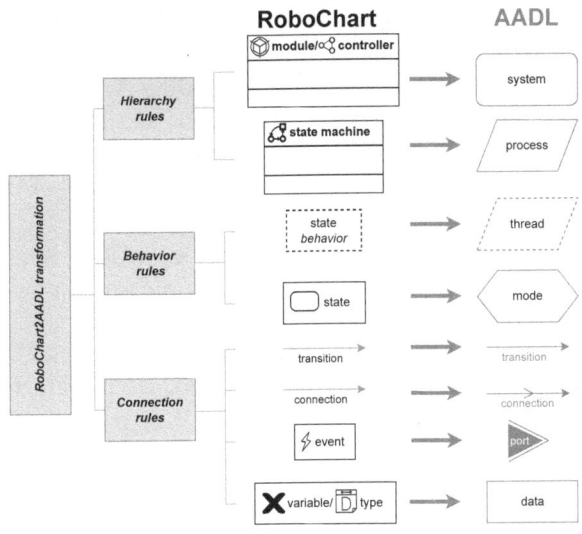

Fig. 11: High-level view of the *RoboChart2AADL* transformation

regardless of the underlying hardware or OS. This is facilitated by the following AADL extension points:

- **Programming language property:** AADL processes can be annotated to indicate which programming language will be used for the component.
- **Containerisation property:** AADL processes can be annotated to indicate the use of containerisation.
- **Interface protocol property:** AADL connections can be annotated to specify the interface protocol[5].

6   From RoboChart to AADL

Our work integrates formal verification in an MDE process based on the RoboChart and AADL languages. In this section, we define the *RoboChart2AADL* model transformation from a RoboChart model into an AADL model based on the proposed RoboChart (Section 4) and AADL (Section 5) MAPLE-K encodings.

Model transformation plays a crucial role in MDE for modeling, optimisation, and analysis. It involves generating a target model using information from a source model. The *RoboChart2AADL* transformation is described by correspondence rules between RoboChart and AADL, shown graphically in Fig. 11.

Overall, a RoboChart module or controller is mapped to an AADL system, containing a collection of AADL processes: one for each RoboChart state machine (hierarchy rules in Fig. 11). For each machine, the behaviour rules from

---

[5] Each MAPLE-K component can have different interface protocols.

Fig. 11 are applied exhaustively. With the connection rules, each RoboChart state is mapped to an AADL mode, with the internal behaviour of the RoboChart state, defined by actions or further machines for composite states, represented by an AADL thread executed within the corresponding AADL mode. RoboChart transitions are mapped to AADL mode transitions and RoboChart connections to AADL connections. Finally, RoboChart events correspond to ports in AADL, and variables to data. In what follows, we present the details of these mappings.

Hierarchy rules These are concerned with the RoboChart module, controller, and state machine elements. In RoboChart, a module is a top-level element that encapsulates a robotic platform and controllers.

When translated, a RoboChart module is mapped to an AADL system, with each controller mapped to a nested system. Each state machine within a RoboChart controller is represented as an AADL process, which serves as the execution environment for the corresponding functionality. This mapping ensures that the hierarchical structure of RoboChart model is preserved in the AADL model, preserving the system-level architecture and component interactions.

Behaviour rules The behaviour rules concern the RoboChart *state* element.

In RoboChart, a state serves a dual role within the state machine. First, it represents a primary component of the state machine, namely the state itself, and second, it encapsulates the behaviour executed by that state. To align with AADL, this dual representation is mapped accordingly.

The RoboChart state directly maps to an AADL mode, representing the static aspect of the state and capturing its presence within the component. On the other hand, the dynamic behaviour associated with the RoboChart state is mapped to an AADL thread. This thread is executed within the corresponding AADL mode and defines the internal behaviour during the mode's execution. Thus, we create a clear and accurate representation in the AADL model while preserving the essential semantics of the RoboChart state machine.

Connection rules The connection rules are concerned with the RoboChart connection, event and variable elements. In RoboChart, events serve two primary purposes: they can be used as triggers for transitions between RoboChart states and they can carry data between RoboChart controllers and state machines. RoboChart connections between events define how components within the system communicate and transition between different operational modes.

When translating to AADL, the transitions triggered by events in RoboChart are mapped onto AADL mode transitions. They facilitate the dynamic switching between AADL modes, reflecting the event-driven behaviour of RoboChart state transitions. For RoboChart transitions without event triggers, events are added to trigger the corresponding AADL transitions.

RoboChart connections link state machines and controllers via events. They are mapped to various types of AADL ports, depending on what is communicated. An AADL event port is used for event-based communication without data

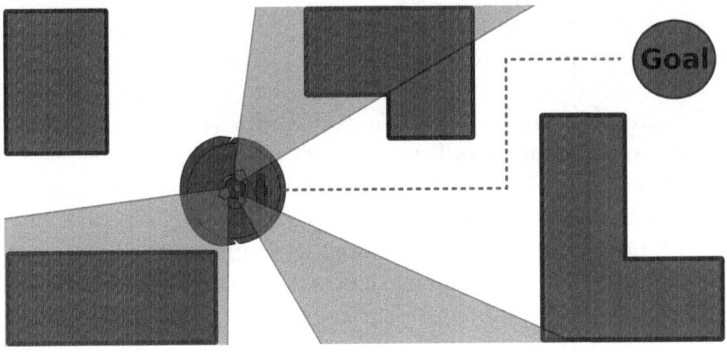

Fig. 12: The TurtleBot 4 navigating past obstacles with LiDAR occlusion

exchange. An AADL data port is used for data-based communications. Finally, an AADL event data port handles both event signaling and data transmission.

Lastly, variables and types in RoboChart, which represent information manipulated in states and transitions, are directly mapped onto AADL data. The flow of data between components is represented using connections between AADL data ports, as said above. This mapping ensures that the data structure and flow within RoboChart are accurately reflected in the AADL model.

7   Architecture deployment experience

To demonstrate our work, we present our experience implementing our self-adaptive robot using a TurtleBot 4 in a navigation scenario. The code is available in [2]. Below, we present the scenario (Section 7.1), the implementation (Section 7.2), and the results of tests in simulation and deployment (Section 7.3).

7.1   Self-adaptive navigation scenario description

We consider the task of navigating the robot through an environment with obstacles. The TurtleBot4 robot uses the ROS2 Nav2 stack performing navigation tasks based on data from its onboard 2D LiDAR sensor. During navigation, the LiDAR sensor may experience occlusion from various forms of persistent debris attached to the robot's frame or the LiDAR scanner itself (Fig. 12). This can lead to the robot's perception of the environment being obstructed, causing navigation decisions to be based on incomplete or outdated maps of the environment. Adaptation is used to handle these unexpected situations, with the robot moving around to cope with its obstructed vision.

7.2   Implementing the MAPLE-K architecture

Associated with an AADL model for an architecture based on MAPLE-K, we have template Python code for each of the MAPLE-K components and runtime code implementing our customised adaptive platform. The control flow of the overall MAPLE-K architectural pattern is implemented via the adaptive platform and does not need to be provided manually.

The adaptive platform provides a general-purpose communication interface with backends for different middleware, which we can choose between based on the hardware platform. In our example, we communicate with the TurtleBot 4 hardware platform via ROS2 messages conforming to the AADL ports of our model corresponding to the interfaces from Fig. 7 (including receiving and representing the LiDAR data in the knowledge base). Future work will automatically generate sketches of platform-dependent code based on the AADL ports.

The adaptive platform provides code that may even obviate the need to program entire MAPE-K components. For our example, the Monitor and Execute are fully handled because they just record and pass data onwards: for Analysis in the case of the Monitor, and to the managed system, in the case of Execute. This is a simple pattern that can be automatically generated from RoboArch and embedded in AADL and match the adaptive platform.

Future work will integrate code generated from RoboChart into ROS2, dealing with communication facilities of RoboChart using ROS publish/subscribe mechanisms. So we have developed code for classes to represent application-specific data types used within the knowledge base (namely the Boolean and probabilistic LiDAR occlusion masks and the sequence of SpinCommands making up the plan). We have also completed the template code realising the Analyse, Plan, and Legitimate components of the MAPLE-K loop.

In the Analysis, the probabilistic LiDAR mask is updated as a sliding window averaged over occlusions from the last n LiDAR scans to estimate the probability of occlusion whilst the Boolean LiDAR mask gives boolean judgements. The Plan component finds a minimal sequence of SpinCommands that allows the robot to completely observe the occluded regions recorded in the LiDAR mask.

Finally, the managed system for our example needed to be extended to support adaptation via the SpinCommands. Our work assumes that the managed system is adaptable, and we needed to extend it to make sure that this is the case. We also implemented an additional ROS2 node for faking LiDAR occlusions, making it possible to test adaptations in simulation.

7.3   Simulation and Validation

We have validated the RoboArch, RoboChart, and AADL MAPLE-K loop via a combination of Gazebo simulations and physical testing on the TurtleBot 4 robot. In simulation, we have considered a range of mocked occlusion scenarios, and then deployed the code to test against real LiDAR occlusions.

We have found that the architecture is effectively able to provide the desired self-adaptive functionality to detect LiDAR occlusions and to modify the robot's movement in response. This enabled the robot to navigate effectively (at reduced speed) in many scenarios with high degrees of LiDAR occlusion.

Physical testing revealed issues not present in simulation. First, noisy LiDAR data can cause small transient occlusions to be detected, leading to unnecessary spinning. Second, the TurtleBot 4's LiDAR sensor driver deviates from the ROS2 specifications, making it difficult to distinguish LiDAR occlusions from objects outside of the sensor range. Both issues are caused by the gap in existing simulations of the LiDAR in ROS2, and they can solved by platform-dependent data validation without changing code that is automatically generated.

8 Conclusions

We have presented our approach to modelling, verifying, and implementing adaptive robotic systems using the MAPLE-K pattern. Our work formalises MAPLE-K in RoboArch, providing support for platform-independent architectural modelling and translation to RoboChart for formal analysis and verification. The verified RoboChart model can be mapped onto an AADL model, which is enriched to describe a particular platform for deployment. From AADL and RoboChart, an implementation can be developed via automatic code generation.

We have demonstrated this approach using the example of a navigation robot that can adapt to occlusions in its LiDAR sensor. In future work, we will consider additional case studies, extending the architectural patterns as required. We will also further develop the navigation case study to apply it to more complex scenarios and provide for additional cases of adaptation.

Our work offers a complete pathway from architectural modelling through to code. With the use of our software platform for implementing adaptive, trustworthy systems, we can preserve the structure and concepts of RoboArch high-level MAPLE-K (or MAPE-K as a special case) models at the code level. A major line of future work involves using this traceability for compositional reasoning about adaptive systems. The semantic model of RoboChart is based on CSP process algebra [21], whose constructs are compositional with respect to refinement. Since the structure of the model's components is preserved in the code, we can utilise this compositionality to reason about changes in the code.

Acknowledgements Funding is provided by the Royal Academy of Engineering under Grant No CiET1718/45, the UKRI (UK Research and Innovation Council) under Grants No EP/R025479/1 and EP/V026801/1, and by EU Horizon project RoboSAPIENS under agreement number 101133807.

References

1. The ASMETA toolset website, https://asmeta.github.io/
2. RoboArch, AADL and Turtlebot code (October 2024), https://drive.google.com/file/d/1GafWyNsXQt7fX67SVfNrPbNTnvLXY9Tg
3. Adaili, F., Mosbahi, O., Khalgui, M., Bouzefrane, S.: Ra2dl: New flexible solution for adaptive aadl-based control components. In: 2015 International Conference on Pervasive and Embedded Computing and Communication Systems (PECCS). pp. 247–258 (2015)

4. Arcaini, P., Riccobene, E., Scandurra, P.: Modeling and Analyzing MAPE-K Feedback Loops for Self-Adaptation. In: 2015 IEEE/ACM 10th International Symposium on Software Engineering for Adaptive and Self-Managing Systems. pp. 13–23. IEEE, Florence, Italy (May 2015). https://doi.org/10.1109/SEAMS.2015.10

5. AS5506A, S.: Architecture analysis and design language (aadl) version 2.0. SAE: Warrendale, PA, USA (2009)

6. Bagheri, M., Sirjani, M., Movaghar, A., Lee, E.A.: Coordinated actor model of self-adaptive track-based traffic control systems. The Journal of Systems & Software **143**(September 2017), 116–139 (2018). https://doi.org/10.1016/j.jss.2018.05.034

7. Barnett, W., Cavalcanti, A.L.C., Miyazawa, A.: Architectural Modelling for Robotics: RoboArch and the CorteX example. Frontiers of Robotics and AI (2022). https://doi.org/10.3389/frobt.2022.991637

8. Bonasso, R.P., Firby, R.J., Gat, E., Kortenkamp, D., Miller, D.P., Slack, M.G.: Experiences with an architecture for intelligent, reactive agents. Journal of Experimental and Theoretical Artificial Intelligence **9**(2-3), 237–256 (1997)

9. Bruni, R., Corradini, A., Gadducci, F., Lluch Lafuente, A., Vandin, A.: A conceptual framework for adaptation. vol. 7212 LNCS, pp. 240–254 (2012). https://doi.org/10.1007/978-3-642-28872-2_17

10. Camilli, M., Bellettini, C., Capra, L.: A high-level petri net-based formal model of Distributed Self-adaptive Systems (2018). https://doi.org/10.1145/3241403.3241445

11. Cavalcanti, A.L.C., Barnett, W., Baxter, J., Carvalho, G., Filho, M.C., Miyazawa, A., Ribeiro, P., Sampaio, A.C.A.: RoboStar Technology: A Roboticist's Toolbox for Combined Proof, Simulation, and Testing, pp. 249–293. Springer International Publishing (2021). https://doi.org/10.1007/978-3-030-66494-7_9, papers/CBBCFMRS21.pdf

12. Feiler, P.: Open source aadl tool environment (osate). In: AADL Workshop, paris. pp. 1–40 (2004)

13. Feiler, P.H., Gluch, D.P.: Model-based engineering with AADL: an introduction to the SAE architecture analysis & design language. Addison-Wesley (2012)

14. Goncalves, F.S., Pereira, D., Tovar, E., Becker, L.B.: Formal verification of aadl models using uppaal. In: 2017 VII Brazilian Symposium on Computing Systems Engineering (SBESC). pp. 117–124. IEEE (2017)

15. Hadad, A.S.A., Ma, C., Ahmed, A.A.O.: Formal verification of aadl models by event-b. IEEE Access **8**, 72814–72834 (2020)

16. IBM: An architectural blueprint for autonomic computing. Tech. rep. (2005)

17. Kephart, J., Chess, D.: The vision of autonomic computing. Computer **36**(1), 41–50 (Jan 2003). https://doi.org/10.1109/MC.2003.1160055

18. Larsen, P.G., Ali, S., Behrens, R., Cavalcanti, A., Gomes, C., Li, G., De Meulenaere, P., Olsen, M.L., Passalis, N., Peyrucain, T., et al.: Robotic safe adaptation in unprecedented situations: the robosapiens project. Research Directions: Cyber-Physical Systems **2**, e4 (2024). https://doi.org/10.1017/cbp.2024.4

19. Miyazawa, A., Ribeiro, P., Li, W., Cavalcanti, A.L.C., Timmis, J., Woodcock, J.C.P.: RoboChart: modelling and verification of the functional behaviour of robotic applications. Software & Systems Modeling **18**(5), 3097–3149 (2019). https://doi.org/doi.org/10.1007/s10270-018-00710-z, rdcu.be/bh7dI

20. Portocarrero, J., Delicato, F., Pires, P., Batista, T.: Reference architecture for self-adaptive management in wireless sensor networks. vol. 8779 LNAI, pp. 110–120 (2014). https://doi.org/10.1007/978-3-319-11298-5_12

21. Roscoe, A.W.: Understanding Concurrent Systems. Texts in Computer Science, Springer (2011)
22. Weyns, D., Iftikhar, U.: ActivFORMS: A Formally Founded Model-based Approach to Engineer Self-adaptive Systems. ACM Transactions on Software Engineering and Methodology **32**(1) (2023). https://doi.org/10.1145/3522585
23. Woodcock, J.C.P., Davies, J.: Using Z - Specification, Refinement, and Proof. Prentice-Hall (1996)

RoboScene: Notation for Formal Verification of Human-Robot Interaction

Holly Hendry[1]([✉])[ID], Ana Cavalcanti[1][ID],
Cade McCall[2][ID], and Mark Chattington[3]

[1] Department of Computer Science, University of York, York, UK
[2] Department of Psychology, University of York, York, UK
{holly.hendry,ana.cavalcanti,cade.mccall,mark.chattington}@york.ac.uk
[3] Thales Research, Technology and Innovation, Reading, RG2 6GF, UK

Abstract. Proving properties about robotic systems with humans-in-the-loop relies on assumptions about human behaviour. Existing technologies require expertise not reasonably expected from psychologists and human-factors engineers, for instance. A user-needs analysis of industrial design techniques for human-robot interaction has identified a lack of standardised approach. We present RoboScene, a notation based on UML sequence diagrams that can be used to capture assumptions derived from human-factors artefacts, through novel constructs enabling consideration of stakeholders with different traits. We describe a tock-CSP semantics for RoboScene, and show how we can connect (mathematically) RoboScene diagrams to platform-independent software models. This is applied in the context of a Human-Centered Engineering process, demonstrated via an industrial case study.

Keywords: RoboStar · Sequence diagrams · CSP · HCE

1 Introduction

Currently, capturing assumptions for mathematical reasoning about human behaviours when interacting with a robotic system requires expert knowledge that many stakeholders do not normally have [25,4,24]. Psychologists, human-factors engineers, and experts in human-robot interaction (HRI) in general are best placed to provide the data for human behaviour and interaction models, but the communication with those capable of generating formal models poses challenges. Cross-discipline communication should be facilitated without loss of precision.

Many recognise the importance of formal reasoning about HRI, and significant progress has been made on modelling and verification. Pioneer works model the human as a black-box deterministic input into the system [10], or obtain by (manual) translation a mathematical model of human-behaviour for verification from an accessible notation [2]. In addition, the pioneering works do not always consider connections with models for the robotic platform and operational scenarios [33,34] that play a key role in system-level reasoning.

A. Boronat and G. Fraser (Eds.): FASE 2025, LNCS 15693, pp.166–187, 2025.
https://doi.org/10.1007/978-3-031-90900-9_9

In this paper, we present RoboScene, a UML-based notation, accessible, with minimal training, to human-behaviour experts, that can be used to capture assumptions about human behaviour. RoboScene diagrams can be connected to models of system software, hardware, and the operational scenario to create a model with a system-level view. RoboScene can be used to generate automatically a mathematical process-algebraic model for verification of the entire system. With RoboScene, we can capture assumptions about humans as nondeterministic timed interactions with the robot or environmental elements.

In designing RoboScene, we have started with a user-needs analysis (UNA) to confirm the need and identify the requirements for a notation to capture human behaviour [16]. RoboScene is the notation we have designed to address these requirements. We present the RoboScene's metamodel and semantics in tock-CSP [32,1], a timed variant of CSP [18]. We demonstrate the use of RoboScene, via a search-and-rescue (SAR) drone example, and work from a Hierarchical Task Analysis (HTA) [37], carried out by Thales, to create RoboScene and RoboChart models. We follow an (automated) engineering process enabled by RoboScene, also described here. In doing this, we identify gaps in the HTA and prove properties about the time taken to complete a search.

We present our work in the context of the RoboStar framework [7], which includes domain-specific notations [5,6,38] and tools for robotics. In particular, we use RoboChart [27] to describe platform-independent models of control software. With RoboScene and RoboChart, we give an accessible and holistic account of a robotic-system design and explore properties and consequences of human behaviours at an early stage of development. RoboScene, however, is an independent novel notation that can be used in connection with models written in other notations. RoboScene is independent of the RoboStar framework, but connects well with it via their common process-algebraic foundations.

RoboScene adopts the structure of UML sequence diagrams, but includes novel constructs. RoboScene diagrams use a notion of capability, and actors to represent human stakeholders, the robotic platform, or other interaction devices. The capabilities of the platform are used to connect the assumptions in the sequence diagram and a software model. Groups of diagrams enable the definition of related assumptions for different human traits, such as "tired" or "untrained". A construct is also available to represent human decisions. Finally, time constructs allow the definition of assumptions about ranges of reaction times.

Our contributions are as follows: **(1)** RoboScene, a notation for modelling expected user behaviour accessible to various stakeholders; **(2)** mathematical semantics for RoboScene; **(3)** a technique to prove properties of a system that depend on human interaction; and **(4)** the description and demonstration of a process to use RoboScene through an industrial case study.

Next, we present related work. Section 3 summarises the UNA used to design RoboScene whose proposed use in an engineering process is defined in Section 4. RoboScene is described in Section 5, and formalised in Section 6. We demonstrate use of RoboScene in Section 7. We conclude and propose future work in Section 8.

2   Related work

In this section, we briefly describe three formal approaches to reason about HRI, and works that formalise UML-like sequence diagrams. In all cases, either there is no support for a notation that facilitates communication, or for verification involving key aspects of human behaviour: time and data exchange.

We single out three state-of-the art approaches to reason about HRI. PVSio-web [25] is an environment for user testing of PVS [30] models. IVY [4] is a textual notation that uses action-logic for modelling of human interaction and behaviour. In both cases, the creation of models requires specialist knowledge. The CIRCUS [24] component HAMSTERS provides a graphical interface for creating an HTA-like user task tree, but has no associated verification approach.

In terms of formal UML-like sequence diagrams, RoboCert [38] is a notation for defining and proving properties of RoboChart models and their components. RoboCert does not cater for human input and some of its constructs (such as parallel and alt) are not in accordance with the UML semantics.

Several works cater for manual [19,39,13,22] or automatic [20,28,36,29,11,35] generation of mathematical models, like we do, but do not cover timed constructs and reasoning, and some consider a restricted or modified set of UML constructs. Both [8] and [23] model these constructs, but do not cater for nondeterministic time specification in their sequence diagrams, and as such do not provide an opportunity to model human decision-making with respect to time.

3   User-Needs Analysis

To understand HRI design and verification techniques used in industry, we have undertaken 14 semi-structured interviews of industry professionals, across a variety of sectors, working in roles at different stages of the robotics-development lifecycle. Interviewees included human factors engineers, UX designers, software engineers, researchers, and technical directors [16].

UML sequence diagrams have been identified as a basis for the study due to their usability and existing use base across the robotics-development lifecycle. Their standardisation and documentation increase usability, and Kutar [21] indicates that these diagrams can be understood by those with little knowledge of the notation. To validate use of these diagrams, the interviews questioned the methods, tools, and standards used during design, how designers think about the human component of HRI, and the use of UML.

Through qualitative thematic and content analysis [3] of the interview transcripts, we have identified the need, and requirements, for a standardised notation to capture human behaviour that can facilitate effective communication. RoboScene is the notation we have designed to address these requirements.

Internal, external, and construct threats to validity have been considered. For instance, we have mitigated selection bias by ensuring no two participants had the same role and affiliation. We have addressed the risk of over representation via participant variety. We have also improved reliability by the interviewing researcher doing the initial encoding of the transcripts.

4   Modelling approach

Communication between robotic-system designers, identified through the analysis of the interviews as a key requirement, is facilitated through the approach described in Fig 1. The process begins with a model of the robotic system as defined by an expert on the human component; in our example this is a Hierarchical Task Analysis (HTA) [37] provided by a human-factors engineer.

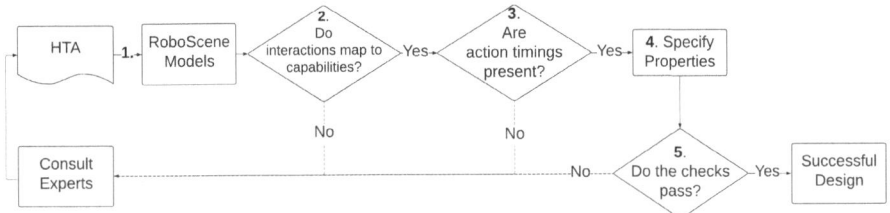

Fig. 1. Modelling flow for SAR example

HTA is a well-known notation and technique [37], with support provided by several tools [26]. In ongoing work, we are defining a metamodel for a version of HTA that is appropriate for use with RoboScene, and are defining a technique to extract RoboScene models from HTA. As we generate models of user scenarios in RoboScene we can handle large and complex HTAs. Here, we consider the HTA just as an informal source of information to write RoboScene models.

The next step of the process is the creation of HRI models using RoboScene. Validating the RoboScene model, in terms of how interactions are carried out using the capabilities of the robot and of information on timings for human actors, requires communication with domain experts in the case of an issue. These experts include software engineers, roboticists, hardware engineers, human-factors engineers, and maybe even prospective users. Issues of time may be addressed by additional computational capacity or improved interfaces, for example. So, our work is complementary to those in HCI concerned with identifying and improving the design of human-robot interfaces.

The process is iterative, and finishes when the design meets the properties. All steps except (5) are manual; our work presented here automates (5).

5   RoboScene

RoboScene addresses the requirements identified in the study described in Section 3. This is achieved by novel constructs to capture HRI scenarios: groups of sequence diagrams per scenario of use, a notion of traits for actors, memory (holding variables) to capture information exchange, time constructs to capture reaction times, and nondeterminism to capture uncertainty or time ranges. Moreover, self-directed messages are used to capture decisions. Here, we describe the metamodel of RoboScene (Section 5.1) and then present examples (Section 5.2).

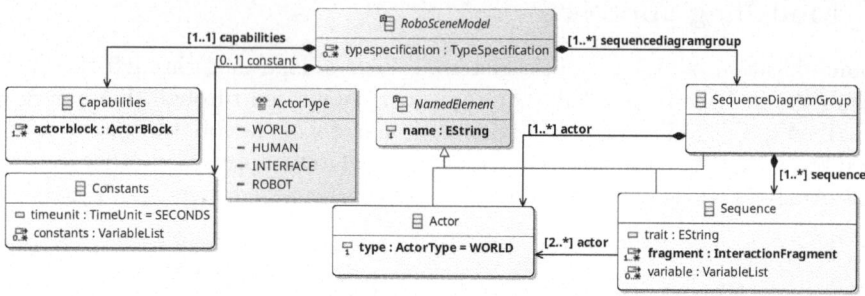

Fig. 2. An excerpt of the RoboScene metamodel

5.1   Metamodel

The RoboScene metamodel, sketched in Figure 2 and fully defined in [17], represents a RoboSceneModel via four attributes. It has exactly one declaration of a capabilities block, one or more sequencediagramgroups, and optional constants and typespecifications. The capabilities can include one or more actorblocks. An actorblock consists of exactly one actor, any number of variables, and any number of ins and outs corresponding to the lifeline events of the actor. An actor has a name and a type, set to WORLD as default. The sequencediagramgroups have a name, one or more actors, and one or more sequence diagrams. A sequence has a name, two or more actors, and one or more fragments, like in UML, but also optionally includes a trait and variables. Moreover, RoboScene has additional forms of fragments for wait and deadline.

Well-formedness conditions identify the valid instances of the RoboScene metamodel for which we can give semantics. These can be found at [17].

5.2   RoboScene overview

Figure 3 shows a small example inspired by our case study: it includes 7 capabilities, 3 actors, and 7 fragments. The full case study, developed in an industrial setting, has 32 capabilities, 5 actors, and 105 fragments [17]. In Figure 3, we give some Constants, Capabilities, and one diagram. Further examples of RoboScene sequence diagrams can be seen in Figures 4, 5, 6, 7 and 16.

Capabilities are variables, events, or operations, representing the actors possible interactions used in their lifelines. Capabilities declarations are grouped in blocks by actors. Variables (var) record inputs or outputs of messages for later use in any lifeline. The lifeline for the actor that declares the variable has write access to it; the others have only read access. Figure 3 shows three actors. For a Pilot, for instance, we have two variables status and statusOk.

Events and operations are declared to specify incoming (in) or outgoing (out) messages, respectively, for the lifelines of their actors. A declaration defines the source or target of the message. A message is a communication, possibly passing data, resulting in action on the source (events) or target (operations). For

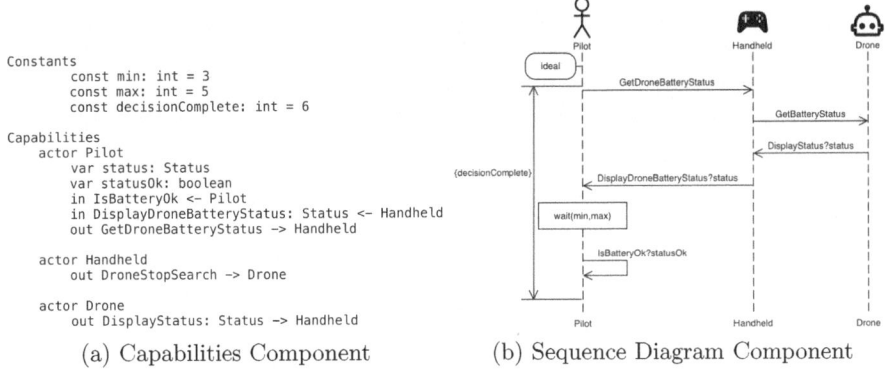

(a) Capabilities Component   (b) Sequence Diagram Component

Fig. 3. RoboScene model of a simple drone system

instance, for the Pilot, DisplayDroneBatteryStatus is an incoming message from the Handheld; GetDroneBatteryStatus is outgoing to the Handheld.

Each group of sequence diagrams can represent a scenario of interaction between humans and robotic devices, such as nominal and off-nominal (failure) paths. Inside a group, diagrams can reflect different traits of the humans. In our full example, we have one diagram capturing the interactions and times for the Pilot when fatigued, and another, for when attentive. For a given scenario, we may have sequence diagrams for all possible combinations of traits. These RoboScene elements facilitate accurate representation of user stories and scenarios.

A scenario has several elements of interest. The first is the robot (which might be specified, for example, by a RoboChart model [27]); this is an actor of type robot. RoboScene can deal with multiple robot actors, although our verification approach presented in Section 7 is for a single-robot.

Each relevant input device, providing an interface to a robot, can be represented by an actor. In our example, we have the drone, represented by a robot actor, and a handheld device through which most interactions with a human happen. Since the handheld impacts on reaction times of the human and the robot, which transmit information through it, we need to model it as an interface.

Like a robot, an interface can be defined by, and connected to, another behavioural model, or be just an abstraction reflecting the management of the interaction flow. This choice might be influenced by the knowledge of the device software and the properties of interest. When using third-party software, we can create software models to record, for example, just response times.

In our example, we model the handheld in RoboChart as a buffer to store and pass data to and from the robot. Such a simple behaviour could be captured in RoboScene itself, but use of a RoboChart software model indicates that the times are a feature of the handheld, not of a particular scenario.

Every scenario can have at most one world actor, which represents entities that participate in the system but we do not need to represent individually. For our example, in Figure 16, this includes the weather forecast agency, an external SAR management system, and the missing person call, among others.

The final type of actor is human. We can include multiple human actors to capture different roles of humans: for example, tele-operators, such as the Pilot and the Operator actors in our example, those interacting as a user, for instance, the missing person in our example, or just passers by.

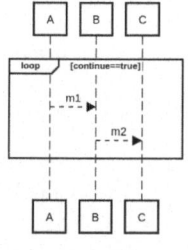

UML constructs are defined as fragments in the meta-model and used to define the system flow. Communication between actors is via the UML message construct, which defines a sender and receiver for all data and events. Typically, interactions with robots are asynchronous, so RoboScene covers only this type of message. In our example, for instance, the human does not require the agreement of the handheld to request the drone battery status (although the request may be ignored) nor does the handheld require agreement of the human to display this status. Where synchronicity is required, we can use a protocol. In our example, we model both call and response messages (see Figure 3b).

Fig. 4. Loop

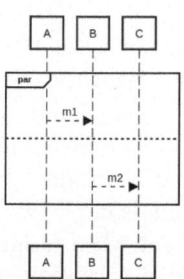

As already mentioned, we use self-directed messages of human actors to capture decision making. This message can be used to represent an input from the human, which can take time, and be recorded for later use in guards and messages. In Figure 3b, the Pilot's final message is IsBatteryOK?statusOk representing that a decision about the battery status is made by the Pilot and recorded in the variable statusOk.

Fig. 5. Parallel

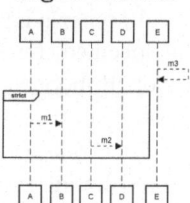

To model nondeterminism through the system flow, RoboScene includes the UML constructs loop (see Figure 4 for an example), alt and opt. Each fragment can be guarded by an expression, perhaps using a human decision-making variable, or remain unguarded and entirely nondeterministic.

Fig. 6. Strict

The par construct enables parallel execution of lifelines fragments divided in threads. The sequential flow is maintained within a thread, but across threads it is relaxed. For example, without the par, in Figure 5 m1 has to come before m2, but with the par this restriction is lifted. This adds further nondeterminism and some freedom of action for actors.

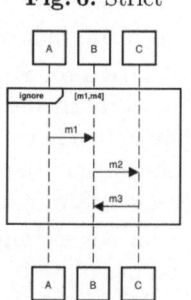

In contrast to par, a strict fragment sequentially orders all its contained fragments, even across disconnected lifelines. For the sequence diagram in Figure 6, for instance, it ensures that m1 happens before m2; without the strict, that order is unconstrained. The order of messages outside the strict is

Fig. 7. Ignore

unaffected; m3 in Figure 6, for example, can take place before, after, or between m1 and m2.

The ignore and consider fragments define which interactions are included in system traces. Messages are ignored or considered dependent on the fragment parameter list, regardless of whether those messages are present in the fragment block. For instance, for the diagram in Figure 7, traces do not include messages m1 or m4, the latter not actually occurring in the body of the ignore anyway.

To capture passage of time, RoboScene includes a wait construct defining a specific value, or minimum and maximum values for a nondeterministic waiting period. An example in Figure 3b is on the Pilot lifeline. Nondeterminism more accurately represents a human's interaction with a system, as humans are inherently variable, and even those trained will react within a margin of precision.

RoboScene also includes a deadline construct to restrict the time of a sequence of interactions: it ensures that every actor involved in the constrained interactions responds quickly enough. In our example, a deadline wraps (with a vertical bidirectional arrow) all interactions within the diagram, defining that they can take at most decisionComplete time units.

Next, we describe the formal semantics of RoboScene.

6   Formalisation

We now give a brief introduction to CSP and tock-CSP (Section 6.1), and an overview of the tock-CSP semantics of RoboScene (Section 6.2). The semantics are presented as rules that are the basis for automatic translation of RoboScene models to tock-CSP; an example is provided in Section 6.3.

6.1   CSP and *tock*-CSP

CSP is a process algebraic notation for modelling concurrent systems. Processes and channels are the key constructs of CSP, used to model systems, their components, and their interactions. Processes define possible interactions and passage of time as a sequence of events. Channels are used to define events representing interactions with possible communication of values.

As said, we use tock-CSP [32,1], a timed variant of CSP that provides the special event *tock* for the representation of the passage of a time unit. Table 1 summarises the tock-CSP operators used in this paper.

6.2   Overview of Semantics

The overall structure of the RoboScene semantics is outlined, using an informal notation of blocks for processes and || for parallel composition, in Figure 8. A RoboScene model, (1) in Figure 8, is given semantics as a collection of tock-CSP processes, one for each sequence diagram, defined over channels representing messages and variables corresponding to the Capabilities used in the diagram. For instance, for our drone, the process defines the allowed interactions over channels representing statusOk and DisplayBatteryStatus, among others.

Operator	Meaning		Operator	Meaning
$tock$	Passage of one time unit		$P \mathbin{\raise.3ex\hbox{$\scriptstyle;$}} Q$	Sequential composition
$Skip$	Termination		$g \& P$	Guarding
$e \to P$	Timed event prefixing		$P \;\|\|\; Q$	Interleaving parallel
$wait\ t$	Delay of t time units		$P[\![c \leftarrow d]\!]$	Renaming
$P \blacktriangleright t$	Deadline; at most t $tocks$ can pass within P		$P\ [\![X]\!]\ Q$	Time-synchronising parallel composition
$P \sqcap Q$	Internal choice		$\mu P \bullet f(P)$	Recursive function
$P \mathbin{\Box} Q$	External choice		$P \setminus X$	Hiding

Table 1. *Tock*-CSP rules used in the RoboScene semantics

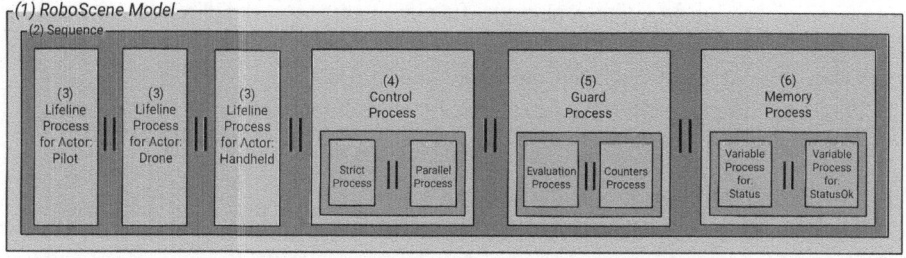

Fig. 8. Pictoral informal representation of the semantic structure of RoboScene

In Figure 8, we show the structure of a process for a sequence diagram, (2). For our example, that process is in Figure 9. It is, at the core, a parallel composition of processes that capture the behaviour of each of the lifelines. In tock-CSP, $P[\![cs]\!]Q$ is the parallel composition of processes P and Q synchronising on the events in the set cs and interleaving on the others.

Lifeline processes, (3), specify the interactions of a lifeline via a sequential composition of processes defining the interactions of fragments. In our example, the lifeline processes are $lifeline(Pilot)$, $lifeline(Handheld)$, and $lifeline(Drone)$. In Figure 10, we present $lifeline(Pilot)$ for the Pilot lifeline, defined by a single deadline fragment, and so a single process $deadline(Pilot)$ with a deadline given by the constant $decisionComplete$. The fragment process $deadline(Pilot)$ is in turn a sequential composition of fragment processes: one for each message and for the wait. Sequential composition is defined through $\mathbin{\raise.3ex\hbox{$\scriptstyle;$}}$ and timed event prefixing $\to$. A final control event $terminate$ just signals the end of the lifeline.

Lifeline processes synchronise on the intersections of what we define as their alphabets: the sets of channels representing the capabilities of their actors. In Figure 9, we have alphabets $alpha(Pilot)$, $alpha(Handheld)$, and $alpha(Drone)$. In $alpha(Pilot)$, we have, for instance, the channel $GetDroneBatteryStatus$.

The semantics of a message fragment is a prefixing on the channel for the message; for the fragment with GetDroneBatteryStatus, see the process in Figure 10. If a value is communicated, then the corresponding variable is also set.

$$BatteryCheck = \left(\left(\left(\left(\left(\begin{array}{c} lifeline(Pilot) \\ [\![\, alpha(Pilot) \cap alpha(Handheld) \,]\!] \\ lifeline(Handheld) \end{array} \right) \\ [\![\, ((alpha(Pilot) \cup alpha(Handheld)) \cap alpha(Drone) \,]\!] \\ lifeline(Drone) \\ [\![\, \{terminate, par, str\} \,]\!] \\ Control \\ [\![\, \{loop, alt, guard, terminate\} \,]\!] \\ Guard \\ [\![\, sharedVars \cup \{terminate\} \,]\!] \\ Memory \\ \setminus \{loop, alt, par, str, guard\} \cup sharedVars \end{array} \right) \right) \right) \right) \right)$$

Fig. 9. This tock-CSP process, called *BatteryCheck*, results from the application of a rule to translate the `Sequence` in Figure 3. That rule is defined using rules to translate `Actor`, `VariableList` and `InteractionFragment` constructs.

$lifeline(Pilot) = deadline(Pilot) \blacktriangleright decisionComplete$

$deadline(Pilot) = GetDroneBatteryStatus \rightarrow DisplayDroneBatteryStatus?status \rightarrow setStatus!status \rightarrow$
$(\sqcap x : \{min .. max\} \bullet wait(x)) \, \fatsemi \, IsBatteryOk?statusOk \rightarrow setStatusOk!statusOk \rightarrow terminate \rightarrow SKIP$

Fig. 10. Process for the Pilot lifeline in Figure 3, generated by the rule for `Sequence`, defined using rules for `Actor`, `VariableList`, and `InteractionFragment`.

For instance, for DisplayDroneBatteryStatus?status, the fragment process in Figure 10 uses $setStatus!status$ to record the input value in the memory process.

The wait fragment is defined using the tock-CSP wait construct, and nondeterminism, if applicable. In our example, the fragment wait(min,max) is a nondeterministic choice (operator $\sqcap$) of values x between min and max to define a $wait(x)$. Just like for deadlines, there is direct rendering in tock-CSP.

The control flow of a lifeline, however, can be affected by control fragments. So, Control and Guard processes, (4) and (5) in Figure 8, synchronise with the lifeline processes through additional control channels to define the valid sequences of interactions. As our example has no Control nor Guarded elements, their corresponding processes are ready to engage in the terminate event immediately.

In general, however, the Control process gives semantics to strict and par fragments. *Control* composes in parallel Strict and Parallel processes, which themselves compose processes for each strict and par fragment in the diagram. The lifeline processes communicate with *Control*, via events $str.ID\_STR$ and $par.ID\_PAR$, to pass across the control of its flow while inside a strict or par fragment. Each fragment is numbered and the event communicates an identifier, for instance, x in $str.ID\_STR.x$, for each control fragment.

The *Parallel* process for the par in Figure 5 is shown in Figure 11. We also show the definition of the lifeline process for A, which immediately uses $par.ID\_PAR.1$ to pass control to *Parallel* before terminating, since A has no other fragment. *Parallel* accepts events $par?ID\_PAR.x$ for all values of x; in our example, only 1 is used. For each identifier there is a guarded ($\&$) choice ($\Box$) of an interleave ($|||$) of processes for the parallel threads. In our example, there are similar thread processes $parallel\_1\_1$ and $parallel\_1\_2$. The definition of a

$A = par.ID\_PAR.1 \rightarrow terminate \rightarrow Skip$

$Parallel = par?ID\_PAR.x \rightarrow ((x == 1)\&(parallel\_1\_1 \mid\mid\mid parallel\_1\_2)) \, \S \, Parallel$
$\qquad\qquad \Box \; terminate \rightarrow Skip$

Fig. 11. Process for a Par fragment is generated by our rules.

$A = loop\_A\_1 \, \S \, terminate \rightarrow Skip$

$loop\_A\_1 = loop!ID\_LOOP.1 \rightarrow guard.ID\_LOOP.1.1?x \rightarrow \begin{pmatrix} (x)\&(m1 \rightarrow loop\_A\_1) \\ \Box \\ (not(x))\&(SKIP) \end{pmatrix}$

$Evaluation = reset\_counters \, \S \, guards\_response$

$guards\_response = loop?ID\_LOOP.id \rightarrow$
$\begin{pmatrix} \begin{pmatrix} (id == 1)\& \\ \begin{pmatrix} getcontinue?continue \rightarrow getCount.ID\_LOOP.1?x \rightarrow \\ \begin{pmatrix} not(continue == true)\& \\ (setCount.ID\_LOOP.1!0 \rightarrow Skip \, \S \, guard.ID\_LOOP.1.1!false \rightarrow Skip) \end{pmatrix} \\ \Box \ldots \end{pmatrix} \end{pmatrix} \end{pmatrix} \, \S \, guards\_response$
$\Box \; terminate \rightarrow Skip$

Fig. 12. Process for a Loop fragment generated by our rules.

thread process is similar to that for a sequence diagram matching the fragments in the thread, but without a memory or a guard process. To ensure that *Parallel* terminates when the lifeline processes do, *terminate* is offered in choice.

The definition of *Strict* is very similar to that of *Parallel* shown in Figure 11.

The loop, alt, and opt fragments determine the control flow based on the evaluation of guards (entry conditions). The processes for these fragments are captured in the lifeline processes, using the Guard process to evaluate their entry conditions and synchronising those evaluations as needed. Figure 12 shows the semantics for the diagram in Figure 4. The semantics for alt and opt are similar.

For the lifeline A, the process uses a loop process, $loop\_A\_1$, to capture its participation in a loop fragment. The definition of a loop process starts with an event $loop!ID\_LOOP.x$, where x is the identifier of the loop; 1 in our example. That event signals to the guard process the requirement to evaluate the entry condition. The processes for all lifelines involved in the loop synchronise on that event, so evaluation happens only when all lifelines are ready to enter the loop. After that, all lifelines receive the result of the evaluation via a *guard* event. With that result, the loop process decides ($\Box$) whether to iterate or finish ($SKIP$). The semantics in the case of an iteration is that of the fragment of the lifeline inside the loop (just $m1$ in the example), followed by a recursive call to the *loop* process.

Guard is a parallel composition of Evaluation and Counters processes. *Counters* handles counter variables to keep track of the number of times a loop is executed. To enable model checking, we limit the number of times that every loop can iterate. The *Evaluation* process resets the counters (process $reset\_counters$) and proceeds as defined by $guards\_response$, which composes processes for each of the guards of the loop, alt and opt fragments.

The $guards\_response$ process gets from the memory process the values for the variables used in the guard conditions, preventing potential inconsistencies

$$A = ignore\_A\_1 \, \S \, terminate \rightarrow Skip$$

$$ignore\_A\_1 = (m1) \setminus \{m1, m4\}$$

Fig. 13. Process for an Ignore fragment generated by our rules.

$$[\![\text{rsm} : \texttt{RoboSceneModel}]\!]_M \mathrel{\widehat{=}} [\![\text{rsm.constant}]\!]_{CO} \; [\![\text{rsm.caps}]\!]_C \; [\![\text{rsm.seqdgrmgrps}]\!]_{SDG} \; [\![\text{rsm.types}]\!]_{TY}$$

$$[\![\text{s} : \texttt{Sequence}]\!]_S \mathrel{\widehat{=}} ((((\underset{a \,:\, \text{actors}(a_1, ..., a_n)}{\big\|} \bullet \; \text{alpha}(a) \circ \text{lifeline}(a))$$
$$\|[\; \overline{\{str, par, terminate\}} \;]\| \; Control(\text{parFrags}, \text{strFrags}))$$
$$\|[\; \{alt, opt, loop, guard, terminate\} \;]\| \; Guard(\text{altFrags}, \text{loopFrags}, \text{optFrags}))$$
$$\|[\; sharedVars \cup \{terminate\} \;]\| \; Memory) \setminus \{alt, opt, loop, guard, str, par\}$$

$\cdots$

$\underline{\text{where}}$ actors = s.actor $\underline{\text{and}}$ parFrags = $\underline{\text{par}}$(s.fragment) $\cdots$

Fig. 14. RoboScene CSP rules for a `Sequence`

arising if each lifeline evaluates the condition separately. In the example, for guard 1 ($id == 1$), *getcontinue* and *getCount.ID_LOOP*.1 are used. Afterwards, a choice ($\Box$), based on the result of the evaluation of the guard, defines the value communicated via the *guard* event. In Figure 4, A uses guard condition continue==true, so in *guards_response*, if *not*(*continue* == *true*) holds, *guard* communicates *false*. Other choices are omitted in Figure 12.

The semantics for the ignore fragment in Figure 7 is in Figure 13. *A* uses the process *ignore_A_1* to capture *A*'s interactions within the ignore fragment, but with the channels for the fragment parameters $\{m1, m4\}$ hidden ($\setminus$). For consider fragments, the same process is used but the hidden set is the set of all possible interactions in the diagram minus the parameter set.

To capture the semantics of a diagram, we also have a memory process, (6), composing in parallel processes that record the values of the variables. This is a standard way of modelling state in CSP. Each variable in the Capabilities ActorBlocks is defined by a pair of *get* and *set* channels and a process that uses these channels to provide and update the value of the variable.

The Memory process (see Figure 9) synchronises with all processes on the variable *get* and *set* channels, which is included in the set *sharedVars* and hidden. Synchronisation occurs in all variable processes on *terminate*.

Next, we explain how the semantics of RoboScene models is formalised.

6.3 Formalisation

We have defined 41 semantic rules that map RoboScene models to tock-CSP; they can be found at [17]. They are the basis for automatic translation from RoboScene to tock-CSP. The rules use multiple typefaces to differentiate between references to the metamodel, a metanotation, variable names, and *CSP terms*.

The top rule defines the function $[\![\_]\!]_M$, which maps a `RoboSceneModel` to a collection of channel and type declarations, and process definitions. It is shown in Figure 14. The channel and type declarations are defined by rules for

`Capabilities`, `Constants`, and `TypeSpecifications`, whose simple definitions are omitted. The channels declared are those mentioned in the previous section. The processes are defined by the rule for a function $[\![\_]\!]_{SDG}$ for groups of sequence diagrams. This rule uses the function $[\![\_]\!]_S$ shown in Figure 14.

With $[\![s : \texttt{Sequence}]\!]_S$, we get a tock-CSP process for a sequence diagram s. The first part of this process is the parallelium of lifeline processes, $\overline{\text{lifeline}(a)}$, for each actor, a, in s.actor over the alphabets, $\overline{\text{alpha}(a)}$, of these actors.

This in turn is put in parallel with the $\overline{Control()}$ process which, as previously explained, manages all **parallel** and **strict** fragments through channels *par* and *str*, respectively, and these channels are used to synchronise between the $\overline{\text{lifeline}(a)}$ processes and $Control()$. Similarly, the **alt**, **opt**, and **loop** fragments are managed by the $Guard()$ process which uses *alt*, *opt*, *loop* and *guard* channels to synchronise with the lifeline(a) processes, using the *guard* channel to evaluate all fragment guards. The parallel composition of $\overline{\text{lifeline}(a)}$s, $Control()$ and $Guard()$ is then synchronised with the *Memory* process over the alphabet of all accessible variables, *sharedVars*. All processes are synchronised on the special channel *terminate* to ensure that they all successfully conclude when the sequence ends. The channels *alt, opt, loop, guard, str, par* are considered internal events and as such are hidden, $\backslash\ \{\}$, within the sequence diagram process. Within the $\underline{\text{where}}$ statement, $\underline{par}$ is a syntactic filtering function that defines the set of fragments in s.fragment that are of the particular type `ParFragment` representing parallel fragments in the metamodel. Similar comments apply to $\underline{\text{strFrags}}$, $\underline{\text{altFrags}}$, $\underline{\text{loopFrags}}$ and $\underline{\text{optFrags}}$, for the other forms of fragments.

Omitted in Figure 14, as $\cdots$, but found at [17], are the definitions of: processes for $\underline{\text{lifeline}(a)}$, *Control* and *Guard*; and the channels and datatypes defined for UML constructs; and, actor alphabets, *alpha(a)*.

Next, we describe how we have used the calculated semantics.

7   Verification

Here, we use a search-and-rescue UAV system, used in the field in the UK [15], to demonstrate the application of RoboScene. We present the needed software models for the UAV system (Section 7.1). We then present the RoboScene model obtained from an HTA (Section 7.2), specify and check properties of interest using RoboCert (Section 7.3), and report our results (Section 7.4).

7.1   Software Models

As RoboScene is intended for providing scenario models and guiding training, in a way usable by human-behaviour experts, it does not model the control software. For system-level verification we need comprehensive software and hardware models. We can connect these models to RoboScene models using capabilities.

RoboChart [27] is a notation to describe platform-independent behaviour of robotics software. In contrast to RoboScene, RoboChart defines complete behavioural models, not scenarios, with human-interaction abstracted via inputs

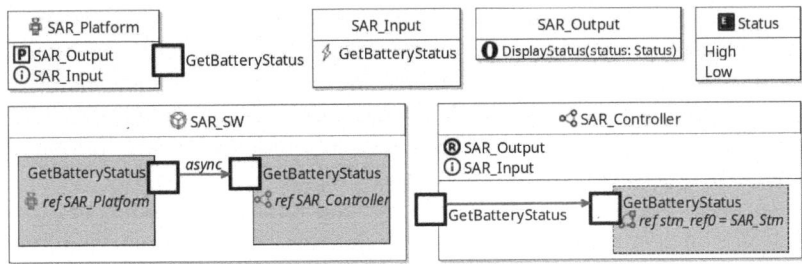

Fig. 15. RoboChart model of a simple drone

or outputs. RoboChart can be used to define design models for code generation, test generation, and verification of software properties, such as deadlock freedom.

RoboChart A brief overview of RoboChart is given here via a simplified version of our example. We describe just the RoboChart features needed to explain its joint use with RoboScene. The models for the full case study are available [17].

RoboChart models are modules characterised by an abstraction for the robotic platform defining services required by the software events and operations. The behaviour of a module is defined by one or more parallel controllers. Each controller is defined by one or more state machines also in parallel.

The RoboChart model for a simple drone software can be seen in part in Figure 15. The module is defined by the block labelled SAR_SW; it connects the robotic-platform block SAR_Platform with a single controller block, SAR_Controller. The blocks inside SAR_SW are references (keyword *ref*) to definitions outside. The simplified drone has a single event GetBatteryStatus as input: an abstraction declared in an interface called SAR_Input for a mechanism to receive commands. A single operation DisplayStatus declared in an interface SAR_Output is an abstraction for a light providing information about the battery. A call to DisplayStatus takes an argument of type Status: either High or Low. The definition of SAR_Platform declares the interfaces SAR_Input and SAR_Output.

SAR_Controller uses GetBatteryStatus and DisplayStatus (and so declares the interfaces). SAR_SW passes on the input from SAR_Platform to SAR_Controller, asynchronously. SAR_Controller in turn passes it on to a simple state machine SAR_Stm, omitted here. It just defines that DisplayStatus is called in response to an input GetBatteryStatus, after a certain amount of time.

The capabilities of the robotic platform provide potential links to a RoboScene model. These capabilities define the points of interaction available in the robot, so it is via them that a human can observe, affect, or be affected by the robot. For our example, the messages to and from the Drone in Figure 3 match the services of SAR_Platform in Figure 15.

Connecting RoboScene and RoboChart models To capture the behaviour of the entire system in the scenario defined by a RoboScene diagram, we can compose the processes for the RoboScene and the RoboChart models in parallel. Optionally, to capture the behaviour of any additional devices, such as a handheld, we may define RoboChart models for them as well. For instance, for our SAR example, we have been advised to define a RoboChart model for the handheld to capture the time delay for communication between with the handheld and the actual drone. In this case, two RoboChart processes are composed. The parallel composition can be generated automatically based on the definition of the correspondence between capabilities of the diagrammatic models.

Synchronisation between the RoboScene and RoboChart models must reflect the way in which their capabilities are connected. For example, in Figure 3a we see that Handheld has a capability GetBatteryStatus, which is an output to the Drone. GetBatteryStatus is in the platform for the Drone RoboChart model, Figure 15, as an event and is an operation in the Handheld RoboChart model (available at [17]). The scenario captured in the RoboScene Model in Figure 3b controls the flow between the Handheld and the Drone using the GetBatteryStatus capability. In tock-CSP, renaming of the channels representing RoboChart platform capabilities in the RoboChart semantics, to their corresponding channels in our RoboScene semantics, establishes the required connection in the parallelism. For example, *GetBatteryStatusCall*, representing Handheld operation calls, is renamed to *GetBatteryStatus*, representing the Drone event.

7.2   Search-and-Rescue Drone Human-Interaction Model

Our example is from a research study that observed the Brecon Beacons search-and-rescue team utilising a UAV [15]. All information has been captured in a HTA [37], provided as a document defining tasks identified during the analysis. These tasks are associated with data recorded by the analyst: times, humans, and devices, or systems. The HTA, recorded in a spreadsheet, contains 121 tasks, each with fields for device, hardware, software, user, external communication source, time estimates, time windows, and more. We show here how we can use RoboScene to add value to this work with the process in Figure 1.

Step 1 in our workflow can be achieved by traversing the paths of the HTA, and ensuring they are covered within the RoboScene model. This scenario traversal is best achieved through a DFS, to cover all the subtasks of a task in the HTA.

A RoboScene group of sequence diagrams captures a single scenario, rather than the entire HTA. In our example, available in [17], we cover the path for the Area Search. This has led to a group of three sequence diagrams representing the "ideal" users (Figure 16), an operator under pressure, and a fatigued operator. The sequence diagrams for the latter two traits are available at [17].

To create the RoboScene model, we first define actors, for the humans and devices, and capabilities to represent the tasks assigned to these actors. Figure 16 sketches the very large model of our example, showing some capabilities, and part of the end flow of one of the diagrams. The complete model has 32 capabilities, one group, with three diagrams; the one sketched has 35 fragments. The generated tock-CSP semantics (53 processes) is at [17].

We have five RoboScene actors: a UAV (of type robot), a handheld controller (interface), a Pilot (human), an Operator (human), and all further ex-

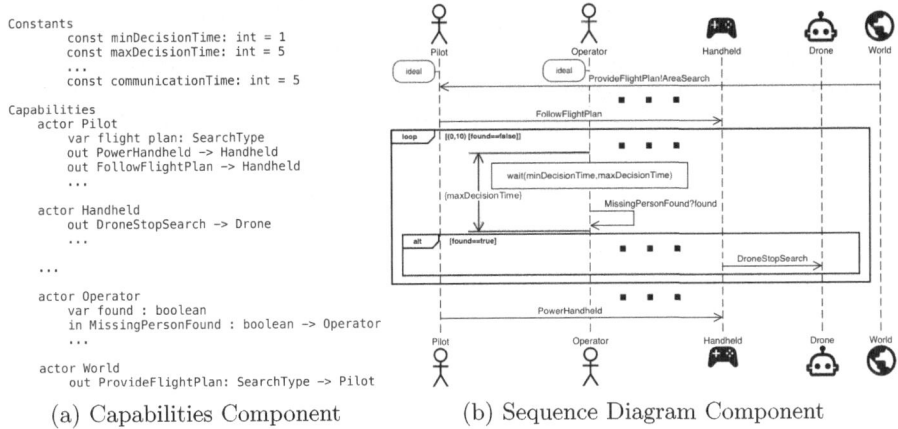

Fig. 16. RoboScene model of a search-and-rescue UAV system

ternal organisations (world). The diagram in Figure 16b is for the "ideal" Pilot and Operator. A tired Operator might make mistakes, but with experience and training the fatigue of the operator may only be present as slower reaction and decision times [31]. This is captured by an increase on the minDecisionTime and maxDecisionTime for the operator when determining if a missing person has been found, and the time taken to communicate the found status. For an Operator under pressure, reaction times are quickened and the likelihood of erroneous behaviour is increased due to the skipping of tasks [12]. Erroneous behaviour may also come from the incorrect identification of the missing person. All this can be captured through (non)deterministic choice using alt or opt fragments.

Step 2 can highlight issues in the HTA, whose development is entirely informal. The first possible issue is that some of the tasks may not map to capabilities of the software. This reveals an inconsistency between the system analysis and the robot design that needs to be resolved. The second potential issue is that some necessary interactions between system actors may be missing. This indicates that the analysis has failed to require proper use of the robot. To address these issues, the human-factor engineers and roboticists need to give input.

In our example, the HTA had a task "set return to home", which did not map to any capability of the Drone. The experts indicated that we needed to model the Handheld with a InputHomeCoordinate capability, matching "set return to home". The Handheld records that information and uses it to control the Drone.

The Handheld model primarily defines a buffer but has a notion of time passing, including specific communication times that occur between the receiving and subsequent sending of data. It can be found in full at [17].

We also had in the HTA a task "initiate matrix search programme", which did not match any capability of the Drone. In that case, the human-factors team decided to expand the HTA. Many such issues have been identified.

Step 3 is concerned with lack of timing information for the HTA actions and human decisions. Obtaining this information may require studies, for example, identifying expected response times by providing users with simulations. For our example, the HTA did not record the decision-making times. To resolve that, we have worked with a human-factors engineer who, reflecting the unpredictability of human behaviour, provided nondeterministic timings to be modelled.

All of these problems have been due to a combination of missing data and ambiguity in the textual descriptions of the HTA. This does raise the question of whether a HTA is an appropriate source for a RoboScene diagram, but provided the analysis is complete, and has times recorded, then it is well-positioned.

7.3 Properties To Prove

RoboScene models support verification of safety and time properties using tock-CSP traces refinement. With that, we can, for instance, determine whether a task is, or is not, started or completed within a predicted time frame.

Trace refinement verifies whether specific execution paths exist by traversing through the model. Before specifying properties and checking them, however, we can provide an extensive collection of trace examples to the experts. These provide a basis for a detailed discussion of the common understanding of the model among the human-factors team, engineers, and verifiers. This can be done for each group of sequence diagrams, allowing in addition a preliminary analysis of the impact of the human traits on the system.

Step 4 The RoboCert [38] notation provides a sequence-diagram based approach for property definition, enabling those without expertise in formal methods to specify properties. Like RoboScene, it has a semantics defined in tock-CSP, and so it is convenient for verification using a CSP model checker [14].

As an example, we define a property via the diagram AreaSearchTimedProperty, partially seen in Figure 17, to verify that, once the flight plan is initiated, the area search completes within 170 time units. In AreaSearchTimedProperty, we require that first a sequence of events (omitted but indicated via ... in Figure 17) occurs, starting with ProvideFlightPlan and ending in FollowFlightPlan, then any event can occur, specified by any (*) until, but the event DroneStopSearch must be encountered within 170 time units. This is defined by the the vertical line enclosing the stated interactions with a deadline range of {0..170}. The lifeline continues with a number of events before concluding with PowerHandheld.

A RoboCert assertion using AreaSearchTimedProperty requires traces refinement, $\sqsubseteq_T$, by the SAR system (composing the RoboScene and RoboChart models). This assertion checks that the set of possible traces within the SAR system is a subset of those defined by AreaSearchTimedProperty.

Step 5 On checking AreaSearchTimedProperty, it fails and the counterexample demonstrates that at least 170+1 time steps could occur after FollowFlightPlan and before DroneStopSearch occurs. This has been identified as being due to missing constraints on the passage of time throughout the RoboChart model. As

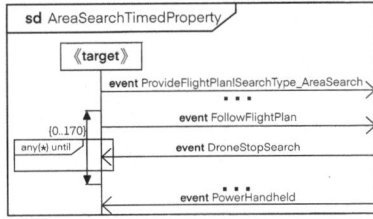

Fig. 17. RoboCert property for the Search-and-Rescue Drone

such, we have consulted domain experts and updated our RoboChart model to record the deadlines for the software response. This has resulted in the successful check of AreaSearchTimedProperty for all diagrams.

If a property of interest is concerned with a specific trace, we can also use a RoboCert assertion to check that it is possible for the system. This type of property can also be used to ensure specific traces are not possible, such as a failure trace. Finally, we can include an indication of expected time.

A trace can define specific amounts of time between events. For traces where these times correlate to the lower bound expectations from the "ideal" Pilot and Operator, the verification succeeds for the diagram whose trait is "ideal". The diagram for the Operator under pressure also passes these checks, since the upper bound for reaction time of the Operator in this case is the lower bound of the "ideal" case. Finally, the reaction time for the "fatigued" Operator has a minimum bound exceeding that of the "ideal"; so the check fails for that diagram.

7.4   Discussion

The process in Figure 1 is a systematic approach to creation and analysis of RoboScene models from a HTA source. It can be applied to other artefacts (such as a Circus [24] model), provided they specify the human actions and timings. The essential component of this flow is the experts consultation. To enable accurate model creation, through communication between human-behaviour experts and software engineers, use of RoboScene has proved key.

Verification failure suggests one of the following: inaccurate software modelling, missing or malformed RoboScene source data, incorrect mapping between the software and RoboScene models, or expectation of human interaction that does not align with that needed to satisfy the requirement. All these kinds of issues have been encountered and addressed as part of our industrial case study. These issues are symptoms of the communication difficulties between human-factors and software experts. Including them in the RoboScene model-creation process decreases the likelihood of these issues lingering during development.

Wrong expectations regarding human interaction with the system can indicate that a redesign of the robot is needed. Alternatively, the account of human interactions in RoboScene may be unrealistic and require further user testing, through simulation, prototyping, or analysis of users of an existing system. The timings defined for human reaction need checking separately for validity.

Not featured in this case study are hardware and operational scenario models. Including these robotic system models can identify further potential failure cases unique to HRI, such as unexpected weather events during a UAV flight.

A verified design that satisfies the properties of interest has successful property checks for all diagrams of a RoboScene model. These proofs are evidence that can potentially be used in a safety case. The expectations on human interaction can also inform training mechanisms for future users.

8　Conclusion

Through an industrial case study, we have presented RoboScene, a notation to capture assumptions for mathematical timed reasoning about human-robot interaction. RoboScene formalises UML 2.0 sequence diagram constructs and, unlike other approaches [19,20,22,13,9,8,23], adds the ability to capture (non-deterministic) time properties within the modelled user scenarios. Use of RoboScene requires no knowledge of a mathematical notation, making it accessible to various stakeholders. RoboScene enables cross-discipline communication between human-factors and software experts without the loss of precision.

The UML constructs, Assert and Neg are not included in RoboScene as they are concerned with trace validation, which is handled by RoboCert [38]. The constructs break and critical are also not included since we can use, respectively, an alt construct and loop guard, or alt and strict constructs, to express the same behaviour. Similarly, synchronous messages can be achieved through defining an asynchronous message as a response. Finally, as the standard flow within all sequence diagrams corresponds to weak sequencing, the omitted seq construct can be replicated through exiting and reentering the containing strict constructs.

Future work Evaluation through an additional industrial case study is the next step in our work. Quantitively comparing the impact of RoboScene relative to traditional methods and usability testing, with human-factors and software engineers, are planned to take place during the case study. To overcome the scalability concerns with the use of model checking, the RoboStar team is investing in support of theorem proving using Isabelle. Additionally, RoboScene diagrams can be used as a source to define runtime verifiers that can flag when assumptions about human behaviours are violated.

Acknowledgments. We would like to acknowledge the participants of the UNA. The work is funded by the UK EPSRC Grants EP/R025479/1, and EP/V026801/2, by the Royal Academy of Engineering Grants No CiET1719/45 and IF2122\183, and by a Thales EPSRC iCASE Grant EP/W522296/1, Award No 2605294.

Disclosure of Interests. The authors have no competing interests to declare that are relevant to the content of this article.

References

1. Baxter, J., Ribeiro, P., Cavalcanti, A.L.C.: Sound reasoning in tock-CSP. Acta Informatica **59**, 125–162 (2022). https://doi.org/10.1007/s00236-020-00394-3
2. Bolton, M., Bass, E.: A Method for the Formal Verification of Human-interactive Systems. Proc. of the HFES Annual Meeting **52**, 764–768 (11 2009)
3. Braun, V., Clarke, V.: Using thematic analysis in psychology. Qualitative Research in Psychology **3**, 77–101 (01 2006)
4. Campos, J.: IVY Workbench, http://ivy.di.uminho.pt/
5. Cavalcanti, A., Baxter, J., Hierons, R., Lefticaru, R.: Testing robots using CSP (September 2019), https://eprints.whiterose.ac.uk/150135/
6. Cavalcanti, A.: Modelling and Verification of Robotic Platforms for Simulation Using RoboStar Technology, pp. 3–5. Springer International Publishing (05 2020)
7. Cavalcanti, A., Barnett, W., Baxter, J., Carvalho, G., Filho, M.C., Miyazawa, A., Ribeiro, P., Sampaio, A.: RoboStar Technology: A Roboticist's Toolbox for Combined Proof, Simulation, and Testing. Software Engineering for Robotics (2020)
8. Chen, X., Mallet, F., Liu, X.: Formally Verifying Sequence Diagrams for Safety Critical Systems. In: TASE 2020. pp. 217–224 (2020)
9. Chen, Z., Zhenhua, D.: Specification and Verification of UML2.0 Sequence Diagrams Using Event Deterministic Finite Automata. In: SSIRI-C 2011. pp. 41–46 (2011)
10. Choi, B., Park, J., Park, C.H.: Formal Verification for Human-Robot Interaction in Medical Environments. In: HRI '21 Companion. pp. 181–185 (03 2021)
11. Cunha, E., Custodio, M., Rocha, H., Barreto, R.: Formal Verification of UML Sequence Diagrams in the Embedded Systems Context. In: SBESC 2011. pp. 39–45 (2011)
12. Donkin, C., Little, D.R., Houpt, J.W.: Assessing the speed–accuracy trade-off effect on the capacity of information processing. J Exp Psychol Hum Percept Perform **40**(3), 1183–1202 (Mar 2014)
13. Ejnioui, A., Otero, C.E., Qureshi, A.A.: Formal semantics of interactions in sequence diagrams for embedded software. In: 2013 ICOS. pp. 106–111 (2013)
14. Gibson-Robinson, T., Armstrong, P., Boulgakov, A., Roscoe, A.W.: FDR3 - A Modern Refinement Checker for CSP. In: Tools and Algorithms for the Construction and Analysis of Systems. pp. 187–201 (2014)
15. Hart, S., Steane, V., Bullock, S., Noyes, J.M.: Understanding human decision-making when controlling UAVs in a search and rescue application. In: IHIET 2022: Artificial Intelligence & Future Applications. AHFE International (2022)
16. Hendry, H., Cavalcanti, A., McCall, C., Chattington, M.: Modelling of Human Behaviour in Robotic Systems, https://robostar.cs.york.ac.uk/publications/reports/Human_Behaviour_in_RS.pdf, Working Paper/Draft
17. Hendry, H., Cavalcanti, A., McCall, C., Chattington, M.: RoboScene Materials, https://github.com/UoY-RoboStar/RoboScene
18. Hoare, C.: Communicating Sequential Process. CACM **21**, 666–677 (08 1978)
19. Jacobs, J., Simpson, A.: On a Process Algebraic Representation of Sequence Diagrams. In: Canal, C., Idani, A. (eds.) Software Engineering and Formal Methods. pp. 71–85. Springer International Publishing (2015)
20. Kaizu, T., Isobe, Y., Suzuki, M.: Refinement and Verification of Sequence Diagrams Using the Process Algebra CSP. IEICE Trans. Fundam. Electron. Commun. Comput. Sci. **96-A**, 495–504 (2013)

21. Kutar, M., Britton, C., Barker, T.: A Comparison of Empirical Study and Cognitive Dimensions Analysis in the Evaluation of UML Diagrams. In: Proc. of the 14th Workshop of the PPIG (01 2002)
22. Li, X., Liu, Z., Jifeng, H.: A formal semantics of UML sequence diagram. In: 2004 ASWEC Proc. pp. 168–177 (2004)
23. Lima, V., Talhi, C., Mouheb, D., Debbabi, M., Wang, L., Pourzandi, M.: Formal Verification and Validation of UML 2.0 Sequence Diagrams using Source and Destination of Messages. Electr. Notes Theor. Comput. Sci. **254**, 143–160 (10 2009)
24. Martinie, C., Navarre, D., Palanque, P., Barboni, E., Pottier, G., Winckler, M.: Circus Tool Suite, https://www.irit.fr/recherches/ICS/softwares/circus/
25. Masci, P., Oladimeji, P.: PVSio-web, http://www.pvsioweb.org
26. Microsoft Corporation: Microsoft visio (2024), https://products.office.com/en/visio/flowchart-software
27. Miyazawa, A., Ribeiro, P., Li, W., Cavalcanti, A., Timmis, J., Woodcock, J.: RoboChart: modelling and verification of the functional behaviour of robotic applications. Software & Systems Modeling **18**, 1–53 (10 2019)
28. Muram, F.U., Tran, H., Zdun, U.: A model checking based approach for containment checking of uml sequence diagrams. In: 2016 23rd Asia-Pacific Software Engineering Conference (APSEC). pp. 73–80 (2016). https://doi.org/10.1109/APSEC.2016.021
29. do Nascimento, F.A.M., da Silva Oliveira, M.F., Wagner, F.R.: Using MDE for the Formal Verification of Embedded Systems Modeled by UML Sequence Diagrams. In: SBCCI'09. SBCCI '09, ACM, New York, NY, USA (2009)
30. Owre, S., Rushby, J., Shankar, N.: PVS: A Prototype Verification System. In: Kapur, D. (ed.) Automated Deduction—CADE-11. vol. 607, pp. 748–752. Springer, Berlin, Heidelberg (02 2001)
31. Román, C.A.F., DeLuca, J., Yao, B., Genova, H.M., Wylie, G.R.: Signal Detection Theory as a Novel Tool to Understand Cognitive Fatigue in Individuals With Multiple Sclerosis. Front Behav Neurosci **16**, 828566 (Mar 2022)
32. Roscoe, A.W.: The Theory and Practice of Concurrency. Prentice-Hall Series in Computer Science, Prentice-Hall (1998)
33. Sadigh, D., Driggs-Campbell, K., Puggelli, A., Li, W., Shia, V., Bajcsy, R., Vincentelli, A., Sastry, S., Seshia, S.: Data-Driven Probabilistic Modeling and Verification of Human Driver Behavior. In: AAAI Spring Symposium. pp. 55–61 (03 2014)
34. Sadigh, D., Sastry, S., Seshia, S., Dragan, A.: Planning for Autonomous Cars that Leverage Effects on Human Actions. In: Robotics: Science and Systems (06 2016)
35. Saputra, A.B., Basuki, T.A., Tirtawangsa, J.: Transformation of UML 2.0 sequence diagram into Coloured Petri Nets. In: 2014 ICAICTA. pp. 243–248 (2014)
36. Shen, H., Robinson, M., Niu, J.: A Logical Framework for Sequence Diagram with Combined Fragments (2011), https://api.semanticscholar.org/CorpusID:8677948
37. Shepherd, A.: HTA as a framework for task analysis. Ergonomics **41**, 1537–52 (12 1998)
38. Windsor, M., Cavalcanti, A.: RoboCert: Property Specification in Robotics. In: Riesco, A., Zhang, M. (eds.) Formal Methods and Software Engineering. pp. 386–403. Springer (2022)
39. Zafar, N.: Formal Specification and Verification of Few Combined Fragments of UML Sequence Diagram. Arabian Journal for Science and Engineering **41** (02 2016)

Stochastic Timed Graph Transformation Systems

Sven Schneider$^{(\boxtimes)}$, Maria Maximova , and Holger Giese

Hasso Plattner Institute, University of Potsdam, Potsdam, Germany
{sven.schneider,maria.maximova,holger.giese}@hpi.de

Abstract. The correct operation of safety-critical distributed embedded systems is crucial. Following a model-driven approach, the relevant system aspects must be captured and rigorous ideally fully-automatic analysis of (probabilistic) timed safety properties must be supported. Probabilistic Timed Graph Transformation Systems (PTGTSs) support the modeling of such systems and analysis of such properties via model checking or simulation. However, they only support the modeling of probabilistic choice with a fixed numbers of outcomes and non-deterministic timing delays via timing constraints limiting applicability (descriptive expressiveness) and usefulness (precision of analysis results).

To remedy this drawback of PTGTSs, we (a) extend PTGTSs to Stochastic Timed Graph Transformation Systems (STGTSs) integrating discrete/continuous random variables to capture stochastic behavior and (b) outline an adaptation of PTGTS model checking for STGTSs to enable analysis w.r.t. probabilistic timed safety properties. Relying on a running example in which shuttles navigating on a track topology must avoid derailing, we exemplify STGTS support for modeling and analysis.

Keywords: cyber-physical systems · model-driven engineering · system analysis · model checking · stochastic processes · reliability

1 Introduction

Large-scale distributed embedded real-time systems often encompass complex coordinating behavior or spatial movement of numerous interacting agents. Such agents behave according to timing constraints and may exhibit probabilistic behavior and stochastic failures. The analysis of whether such systems and their agents adhere to given specifications describing admissible or desired system behavior is crucial in safety-critical environments. An abundance of model-driven approaches has been applied in the past for designing, understanding, and improving the behavior of such systems in domains such as automotive or railway transportation. These approaches rely on adequate modeling formalisms that define system states and steps by capturing the relevant system aspects at a desired level of abstraction (omitting certain details) benefiting from a suitable descriptive expressiveness (to achieve acceptable applicability) while enabling at the same time an ideally fully-automatic analysis of desired behavioral properties (to enable the derivation of useful insights on the system behavior).

© The Author(s) 2025
A. Boronat and G. Fraser (Eds.): FASE 2025, LNCS 15693, pp.188–213, 2025.
https://doi.org/10.1007/978-3-031-90900-9_10

For example, in the embedded real-time RailCab [66, 52, 54] system, shuttles navigate on a large-scale track segment topology where driving behavior is restricted by installed traffic lights ordering shuttle deceleration and local maneuver coordination using shuttle-to-shuttle communication. The resolution of non-determinism determines *which* shuttle performs the next step, *where* that shuttle navigates to for alternative successor track segments, and *when* that shuttle navigates to the next track segment. Timing constraints model the shuttles' speeds based on their driving modes. Probabilistic choice models whether intershuttle communication attempts and traffic light observation on pass-by fail. To concisely exemplify the novel modeling capabilities of STGTS, we consider a simple variant of this system (detailed in section 4) with reduced probabilistic and structural behavior in which one shuttle approaches a construction site preceded by two traffic lights. As a stochastic behavior not be previously modeled, we consider stochastic failures of traffic lights exhibiting sudden complete failures.

In the past, attributed graphs as a universal visual comprehensive modeling language have been used to model system states allowing to capture global system information, local actor states, and the communication architecture between actors and physical components with great flexibility, while not imposing domain-specific language-based restrictions. Therefore, attributed graphs are employed in many contexts such as UML-based system design [61] and graph databases [58, 2, 69]. The Turing complete formalism of Graph Transformation Systems (GTSs) [21] then relies on rules to describe viable steps among graph-based states in terms of local graph structure modifications and attribute reassignments. GTSs have been extended to Probabilistic Timed Graph Transformation Systems (PTGTSs) [52] integrating clock-based timing constraints as in Timed Automata (TA) [1] using lower and upper time bounds as well as discrete probabilistic choice as in Probabilistic Automata (PA) [72] among a fixed set of outcomes. Non-determinism in PTGTSs originates (in line with the running example) from *which* rule is applied, *where* it is applied in the graph, and *when* it is applied. Quantitative analysis of PTGTSs w.r.t. probabilistic timed reachability/safety properties delivers a worst-case to best-case probability interval of probabilities for different resolutions of non-determinism. For our running example, we note that the stochastic failures cannot be modeled adequately using PTGTSs because the only way to model such failures using PTGTSs is to permanently permit the non-deterministic occurrence of such failures, which precludes the derivation of meaningful quantitative results using analysis.

A deficiency of PTGTSs as a modeling formalism is its lacking support for stochastic behavior. Regarding time, the PTGTS support for clock-based timing constraints has proven useful in many domains (including their use in TA and Probabilistic Timed Automata (PTA) [48]). However, continuous distributions would be needed to model probabilistically distributed delays governing, e.g., arrival times or stochastic failures (e.g., malfunctioning hardware affecting system operation). Regarding choice, PTGTS supports probabilistic choice among a fixed number of outcomes enabling the modeling of, e.g., probabilistic failures on demand. However, discrete distributions governing probabilistic choice among a statically unknown, large, or largely varying number of outcomes would be needed to model, e.g., some probabilistic distributed consensus algorithms where pseudo-random number generators are used to generate uniformly distributed integers from 1 to the number n of processes.

In this paper, to resolve this modeling deficiency of PTGTSs w.r.t. stochastic behavior, we introduce Stochastic Timed Graph Transformation Systems (STGTSs) (as an extension of PTGTSs) by providing its formal syntax and concrete semantics. STGTSs support the modeling of not only *structure dynamics*, *timed behavior*, and *probabilistic behavior* but also of *stochastic behavior* because, in STGTSs, rules are additionally equipped with information on how stochastic discrete/continuous variables are to be probabilistically sampled using Cumulative Distribution Functions (CDFs), following loosely the extension of PTA into Stochastic Timed Automata (STA) [14]. To derive model checking for STGTSs w.r.t. best-case/worst-case probabilistic timed reachability/safety properties, we adapt the existing PTGTS model checking approach to the STGTS extension incorporating stochastic discrete/continuous variables, their sampling, and usage in timing constraints. We exemplify the novel STGTSs modeling capabilities and the model checking approach using our running example.

This paper is structured as follows. In section 2, we discuss related work regarding model-driven analysis of (embedded) systems. In section 3, we present preliminaries and notation. In section 4, we introduce STGTSs and present the STGTS model for our running example. In section 5, we discuss a model checking approach for STGTSs based on our running example STGTS. Finally, in section 6, we conclude the paper and provide an outlook on future work.

2 Related Work

In the past, GTSs [21] have been extended with concepts of time, probabilism, and stochastics along the lines of different automata formalisms into which these graph-based formalisms can be translated to enable their analysis using automata-based techniques: *(a)* Timed Graph Transformation Systems (TGTSs) [59, 12] extend GTSs by including timing constraints based on clocks, guards, invariants, and clock resets along the lines of TA [1], *(b)* Probabilistic Graph Transformation Systems (PGTSs) [44, 46] extend GTSs by allowing steps to have different effects each associated with a probability value along the lines of PA or Markov Decision Processes (MDPs) [65, 72], *(c)* PTGTSs [52, 50, 51] combine TGTSs and PGTSs along the lines of PTA [47, 48], *(d)* Interval Probabilistic Timed Graph Transformation Systems (IPTGTSs) [56, 55] extend PTGTSs by supporting a non-deterministic specification of probabilities for cases where probabilities can only be estimated along the lines of Interval Probabilistic Timed Automata (IPTA) [77, 43], *(e)* Stochastic Graph Transformation Systems (SGTSs) [34, 35, 49] extend GTSs by supporting exponentially distributed delay modeling along the lines of Continuous Time Markov Chains (CTMCs) [60, 22, 41, 5, 7, 6], and *(f)* Hybrid Graph Transformation Systems (HGTSs) [25, 10, 11, 9] extend GTSs by supporting differential equations for delay modeling along the lines of Hybrid Automata (HA) [37]. Note that SGTSs and CTMCs are *deterministic* (all steps compete based on their exponential distributions) while TGTSs, PTGTSs, and IPTGTSs are non-deterministic (adversaries are used to resolve the non-determinism between timed and discrete steps). Other variants of GTS with time where each step consumes a specified amount of time (instead of using TA-like clock handling) have been considered in [27, 28, 71].

Analysis for these graph-based formalisms is often obtained by translating them into their automata counterparts and applying model checking tools such as PRISM [64, 47, 48, 46, 43, 16], UPPAAL [74], KRONOS [45, 17, 15], and the MODEST toolset [57, 30, 14] on the resulting automata.

We focus on probabilistic timed reachability properties to express quantitative safety properties because further formulas, e.g., of Probabilistic Timed Computation Tree Logic (PTCTL) [48, 47] are not supported by model checkers due to the computational complexity of the required model checking algorithms.

Note that an abundance of graph-based analysis approaches for varying properties have been developed in, e.g., [21, 63, 20, 53, 54, 71, 70] and are supported by graph-based tools such as GROOVE [26, 24, 39], AUGUR2 [4, 42], HENSHIN [36, 3, 52], AUTOGRAPH, and the PTGTS-simulator [79, 78].

STA [14] and Stochastic Hybrid Automata (SHA) [30] support the modeling of delay distributions using CDFs and differential equations via the compositional programming languages MODEST and HMODEST [57, 30, 14, 33]. However, they lack domain specific support for high-level operations such as GT (attributed graphs can capture many relevant kinds of system states and their domain specific adaptations more naturally (simpler, more concise, and with fewer model steps) compared to the C programming language like data structures of, e.g., MODEST). Similarly, e.g., UML Statecharts providing hierarchical modeling have been extended with probabilistic and stochastic capabilities in [40, 38] also supporting a translation into MODEST. Analysis support for STA and SHA is very limited as of now and the authors instead state the goal of integrating sensible modeling capabilities first (obtaining MODEST and HMODEST) to then develop/integrate analysis tools on that common ground. Besides simulation and the simple subclass case of PTA [32, 31] relying on standard PTA model checking using PRISM, analysis of STA has only been derived by approximating STA using PTA [23, 29], which also means that full model-checking support is not yet available for STA. In fact, we note that STGTSs model checking as discussed later on is not supported by existing STA analysis approaches.

3   Preliminaries

For a partial function $f : A \rightharpoonup B$, support$(f) = \{a \in A \mid \exists b.\ f(a) = b\}$ and range$(f) = \{b \in B \mid \exists a.\ f(a) = b\}$. For injective functions $f_1 : A \hookrightarrow B$ and $f_2 : A \hookrightarrow C$, $\Delta(f_1, f_2) = f_2 \circ f_1^{-1} = \{(b, c) \mid \exists a.\ f_1(a) = b \wedge f_2(a) = c\} : B \rightharpoonup C$.

Graphs: We consider typed attributed graphs (such as the graph G_1 in Figure 1c (left)), which are typed over a type graph (such as the one in Figure 1a) relying on a variation of symbolic graphs [62] from [71]. To capture the graph

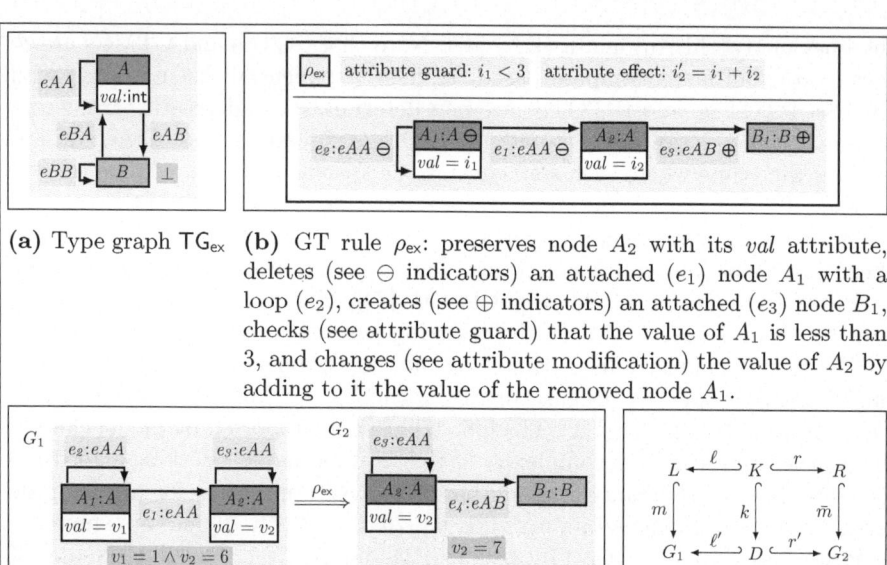

(a) Type graph TG_{ex} **(b)** GT rule ρ_{ex}: preserves node A_2 with its *val* attribute, deletes (see $\ominus$ indicators) an attached (e_1) node A_1 with a loop (e_2), creates (see $\oplus$ indicators) an attached (e_3) node B_1, checks (see attribute guard) that the value of A_1 is less than 3, and changes (see attribute modification) the value of A_2 by adding to it the value of the removed node A_1.

(c) A GT step using the rule ρ_{ex} from Figure 1b   **(d)** A DPO diagram for a GT step

Fig. 1. An example of a GT step as an application of a GT rule

attribution, Attribute Conditions (ACs) over a many sorted first-order attribute logic are used for which we denote the set of all ACs with (free) variables from X of sort s as $\mathsf{AC}(s, X)$. In a graph G, each attribute is connected to a unique variable from $\mathsf{vars}(G)$ and their values are captured using an AC $\mathsf{ac}(G)$ from $\mathsf{AC}(\mathsf{bool}, \mathsf{vars}(G))$ such as $\mathsf{ac}(G_1) = (v_1 = 1 \wedge v_2 = 6)$ in Figure 1c. In a graph G to be transformed, each attribute/variable is restricted by $\mathsf{ac}(G)$ to at most one value (for GTS to exactly one value but in section 4 certain kinds of variables are not restricted) resulting in a (partial) valuation $\mathsf{val}(G) : \mathsf{vars}(G) \rightharpoonup D$ where D is the union of data sets across all sorts. An injective graph morphism $m : H \hookrightarrow G$ matches an occurrence of a graph H in a graph G and must satisfy that $\mathsf{ac}(G)$ implies $m(\mathsf{ac}(H))$. For example, if $\mathsf{ac}(H) = (x \geq 2)$, $\mathsf{ac}(G) = (y = 4)$, and m matches the variable x to variable y, then $y = 4$ must imply $m(x \geq 2) = (y \geq 2)$, which is the case. Type graphs such as TG_{ex} in Figure 1a have the AC $\bot$ (false) thereby not restricting attribute values in typed graphs.

Graph Transformation (GT): A GT step from a graph G_1 to a graph G_2 (see Figure 1c for an example) is obtained by applying a GT rule $\rho = (\ell : K \hookrightarrow L, r : K \hookrightarrow R, \gamma)$ for a match $m : L \hookrightarrow G_1$ (see [21, 71] for technical details), written $(G_1, (\rho, m), G_2) \in \mathsf{GTsteps}$. Intuitively, the rule morphisms ℓ and r model that the elements in K are preserved, the elements in $L - \ell(K)$ are deleted, and the elements in $R - r(K)$ are created (see Figure 1b for an example GT rule in which we use an integrated notation where $\ominus$ and $\oplus$ indicate the elements to be deleted and created). The graphs L, K, and R have the AC $\top$ (true) thereby not imposing restrictions on matches: instead, the AC γ specifies how values of variables are related between G_1 and G_2 using the variables from L and R in unprimed and primed form (in Figure 1b, we split the AC $i_1 < 3 \wedge i_2' = i_1 + i_2$ into an attribute guard and an attribute effect for readability). While the AC of a graph essentially represents a valuation for all attributes (a partial valuation later on), the use of ACs is required to express attribute modifications in rules as well as to state properties on graphs as exemplified later on. Technically, the structural changes of a GT step are constructed using a Double Pushout (DPO) diagram (see Figure 1d) and we therefore also write $(G_1, (\rho, m, k, \bar{m}, \ell', r'), G_2) \in$ GTsteps when further morphisms from this diagram are to be referred to. To ease presentation, we consider graphs up to isomorphism: for GT steps, this means that we assume that $(G_1, \kappa, G_2), (G_3, \kappa', G_4) \in$ GTsteps implies that G_i and G_j are equal when they are isomorphic ($i, j \in \{1, 2, 3, 4\}$); during state space generation, derived steps can easily be manipulated to satisfy this requirement when an isomorphism between inequal graphs would be observed.

Clock-based Timing Constraints: PTA [47] and PTGTSs [52, 50, 51] employ clocks and Clock Constraints (CCs) thereon, as introduced for TA [1], to model possible timed steps (i.e., delays) between discrete steps. For a set of clock variables X, CCs $\psi \in$ CC$(X) \subseteq$ AC(bool, X) are finite conjunctions of clock comparisons of the form $c_1 \sim r$ and $c_1 - c_2 \sim r$ where $c_1, c_2 \in X$, $\sim \in \{<, >, \leq, \geq\}$, and $r \in \mathbf{R}_0^+ \cup \{\infty\}$.[1] Moreover, Extended Clock Constraints (ECCs) $\psi \in$ ECC$(X, Y) \subseteq$ AC(bool, $X \cup Y$) are ACs that can be simplified to CCs from CC(X) after substituting all non-clock variables in $Y - X$. Clock valuations $vc : X \rightarrow \mathbf{R}_0^+$ satisfy CCs ψ, written $vc \models \psi$, as expected. For a clock valuation vc and a set of clocks X', $vc[X' := 0]$ is the clock valuation mapping the clocks from X' to 0 and all other clocks according to vc. For a clock valuation vc and a duration $\delta \in \mathbf{R}_0^+$, $vc + \delta$ is the clock valuation mapping each clock x to $vc(x) + \delta$.

Probability Foundations: We recall standard notions and notations (see, e.g., [73, 19]). If Ω is a set, $\mathcal{F} \subseteq 2^\Omega$, $\Omega \in \mathcal{F}$, and $\mathcal{F}$ is closed under countable union and complement w.r.t. Ω, then $\mathcal{F}$ is a σ-algebra on Ω and $(\Omega, \mathcal{F})$ is a measurable space with measurable sets $\mathcal{F}$. If $(\Omega, \mathcal{O})$ is a topological space (such as the euclidean topology $(\mathbf{R}^n, \mathcal{O})$ using open sets/balls or the discrete topology $(\Omega, 2^\Omega)$), then $\mathcal{B}(\Omega) = \sigma(\mathcal{O})$ denotes the smallest σ-algebra on Ω containing $\mathcal{O}$ and is called Borel σ-algebra. The extended reals $\overline{\mathbf{R}}$ are given by $\mathbf{R} \cup \{\infty, -\infty\}$. If $(\Omega, \mathcal{F})$ is a measurable space, $\mu : \mathcal{F} \rightarrow \overline{\mathbf{R}}$, $\mu(x) \geq 0$, $\mu(\emptyset) = 0$, and $\mu(\bigcup x_i) = \sum \mu(x_i)$ for all countably many disjoint sets x_i, then μ is a measure on $(\Omega, \mathcal{F})$ and $(\Omega, \mathcal{F}, \mu)$ is a measure space. If $(\Omega, \mathcal{F}, P)$ is a measure space and $P(\Omega) = 1$, then P is a probability measure and $(\Omega, \mathcal{F}, P)$ is a probability space. If $(\Omega_1, \mathcal{F}_1)$ and $(\Omega_2, \mathcal{F}_2)$ are measurable spaces, $f : \Omega_1 \rightarrow \Omega_2$, $f^{-1}(X) \in \mathcal{F}_1$ for each $X \in \mathcal{F}_2$, then f is a measurable function $f : (\Omega_1, \mathcal{F}_1) \rightarrow (\Omega_2, \mathcal{F}_2)$. If $(\Omega_1, \mathcal{F}_1, \mu)$ is a measure space, $X : (\Omega_1, \mathcal{F}_1) \rightarrow (\Omega_2, \mathcal{F}_2)$ is a measurable function, $X_*(\mu) : \mathcal{F}_2 \rightarrow \overline{\mathbf{R}}$, and $X_*(\mu) = \mu \circ X^{-1}$, then $X_*(\mu)$ is the pushforward measure of μ. If $(\Omega_1, \mathcal{F}_1, P)$

---

[1] Using $r \in \mathbf{R}_0^+ \cup \{\infty\}$ in CCs is required because we compare clocks to real-valued stochastic continuous variables later leading to such CCs in the symbolic semantics.

is a probability space, $X : (\Omega_1, \mathcal{F}_1) \rightarrow (\Omega_2, \mathcal{F}_2)$ is a measurable function, then X is an $(\Omega_2, \mathcal{F}_2)$-valued random variable and $X_*(P)$ is a probability measure and the distribution of X; $X_*(P)(S)$ and $X_*(P)(\{s\})$ are written $P(X \in S)$ and $P(X = s)$; discrete random variables have countable image $X(\Omega_1)$ and random variables use $(\Omega_2, \mathcal{F}_2) = (\mathbf{R}, \mathcal{B}(\mathbf{R}))$. If $X : (\Omega_1, \mathcal{F}_1) \rightarrow (\Omega_2, \mathcal{F}_2)$ is a discrete random variable, $p_X : \Omega_2 \rightarrow \overline{\mathbf{R}}$, and $p_X(x) = P(X = x)$, then p_X is the Probability Mass Function (PMF) of X (p_X distributes the joint probability of 1 across the countable outcomes of X). If $X : (\Omega_1, \mathcal{F}_1) \rightarrow (\mathbf{R}, \mathcal{B}(\mathbf{R}))$ is a random variable, $F_X : \mathbf{R} \rightarrow \overline{\mathbf{R}}$, and $F_X(x) = P(X \in (-\infty, x])$ (also written $P(X \leq x)$), then F_X is the CDF of X ($F_X(x)$ is the probability of a value of at most x); if F_X is absolutely continuous then there is a unique f satisfying $f(x) = \mathrm{d}F(x)/\mathrm{d}x$ called the Probability Density Function (PDF) of X.

The Sierpiński-Dynkin's π-λ theorem [19, Theorem A.1.5] implies the unique existence of a probability measure $P(F)$ for a CDF F; this allows us to switch from CDFs to probability measures as needed. The Hahn-Kolmogorov (or Carathéodory's extension) theorem [19, Theorem A.1.1] for σ-finite probability spaces (which is the case here since we assume probability measures based on real-valued random variables), implies the unique existence of a product (probability) measure $\prod \mathbf{P}$ of n (probability) measures $\mathbf{P}_i$ (where the Borel operator $\mathcal{B}$ distributes over countable products: $\prod_I \mathcal{B}(\mathbf{R}) = \mathcal{B}(\prod_I \mathbf{R})$); this allows to measure multiple random variables at once (when multiple CDFs are sampled in a single STGTS step later on). We use $\mathsf{Prob}(\Sigma)$ to denote the set of all probability measures on $(\Sigma, \mathcal{B}(\Sigma))$; later, Σ is the set of all system states.

Discrete/Continuous Probabilistic Choice: To model discrete probabilistic behavior including (pseudo)random number generation, we employ PMFs for choosing probabilistically from a finite set of outcomes. In general, discrete distributions and PMFs also support the case of non-finite countably many outcomes with non-zero probabilities but this would yield non-finite branching in the symbolic semantics in section 5, preventing model checking, and has no practical relevance for the modeling of finite-state finite-software embedded systems.

To model continuous probabilistic behavior, we employ parameterized CDFs to capture the likelihood for possible delay intervals.

Timed Probabilistic Transition Systems (TPTSs): We capture the semantics of STGTSs in terms of their induced TPTSs later on in section 4 (cf. [76, 30]). A TPTS T consists of a set of states $\mathsf{states}(T)$, a unique start state $\mathsf{start}(T) \in \mathsf{states}(T)$, a set of events (step labels) $\mathsf{events}(T)$ containing $\mathbf{R}^+$, a probabilistic step relation $\mathsf{steps}(T) \subseteq \mathsf{states}(T) \times \mathsf{events}(T) \times \mathsf{Prob}(\mathsf{states}(T))$, a set of state Atomic Propositions (APs) $\mathsf{aps}(T)$, and a state labeling function $\mathsf{lab}(T) : \mathsf{states}(T) \rightarrow 2^{\mathsf{aps}(T)}$.

Timed Probabilistic Reachability Properties: TPTSs induced by STGTSs are to be analyzed w.r.t. timed probabilistic reachability/safety properties. Different resolutions of non-determinism result in minimal/maximal probabilities for timed reachability capturing best and worst cases.

Definition 1 (Min/Max Probabilistic Timed Reachability Problems).
Evaluate $\mathcal{P}_{op=?}(\mathsf{F}_{\sim c}\, ap)$ for a TPTS T with $op \in \{\min, \max\}$, $\sim\, \in \{\leq, <\}$, $c \in$

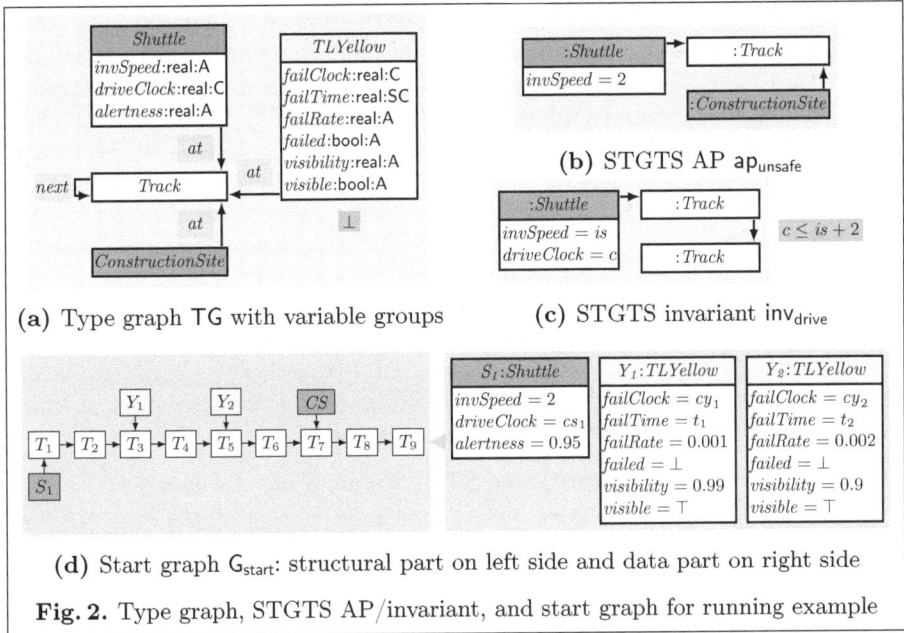

(a) Type graph TG with variable groups

(b) STGTS AP ap_{unsafe}

(c) STGTS invariant inv_{drive}

(d) Start graph G_{start}: structural part on left side and data part on right side

Fig. 2. Type graph, STGTS AP/invariant, and start graph for running example

$\mathbf{N} \cup \{\infty\}$, and $ap \in aps(T)$ to obtain the infimal/supremal probability (depending on op) over all adversaries to reach some ap-labeled state at time $t \sim c$.

This problem is solved for a PTGTS (i.e., STGTSs without stochastic variables) by translating it into a PTA and then applying the PRISM model checker [52]. In section 5, we adapt this model checking procedure for general STGTSs.

4 Stochastic Timed Graph Transformation Systems

We introduce the syntax of STGTSs in terms of their components in subsection 4.1 and define the concrete STGTSs semantics in terms of the induced TPTSs in subsection 4.2.

4.1 Syntax of Stochastic Timed Graph Transformation Systems

Each STGTS employs a type graph and contains a single start graph (for our running example, see again Figure 2). In our running example, the shuttle S_1 initially drives fast on the track topology and will reach the construction site at track T_7 with that speed unless the shuttle navigator observes one of the two traffic lights Y_1 or Y_2 decreasing the shuttle speed. However, both traffic lights may exhibit technical failure before the shuttle reaches them making their observation impossible. Also, the shuttle navigator may still fail to observe a functional traffic light based on his alertness and the traffic lights visibility.

For STGTSs, we assign to each variable of the type graph one variable group from $\{A, C, SC, SD\}$. For the running example, this assignment is given behind the sort in Figure 2a for each variable. Group A contains the attribute variables for storing regular attribute values of arbitrary sort, group C contains the clock variables for measuring durations of sort real, group SC contains the stochastic continuous variables for storing sampled continuous values of sort real such as time points, and group SD contains the stochastic discrete variables for storing sampled discrete values of sort real such as numbers of a pseudo-random number generator, which may be simply integer values when using, e.g., the discrete uniform distribution. The variables $vars(G)$ of a typed graph G are split into $varsA(G)$, $varsC(G)$, $varsSC(G)$, and $varsSD(G)$ accordingly. Also, we use $varsS(G)$ for all stochastic variables $varsSC(G) \cup varsSD(G)$ together.

STGTS states contain a graph and valuations for its clock variables, stochastic continuous variables, and stochastic discrete variables.

Definition 2 (STGTS State). *An STGTS state s has 4 components.*
- $graph(s) = G$ *is a finite graph.*
- $valC(s) : varsC(G) \rightarrow \mathbf{R}_0^+$ *maps the clock variables to non-negative reals.*
- $valSC(s) : varsSC(G) \rightarrow \mathbf{R}$ *maps the stochastic continuous variables to reals.*
- $valSD(s) : varsSD(G) \rightarrow \mathbf{R}$ *maps the stochastic discrete variables to reals.*

Moreover, we define the following three abbreviations.
- $valA(s)$ *is the restriction of the valuation $val(G)$ (see section 3) to $varsA(G)$,*
- $val(s)$ *is the joint valuation $valC(s) \cup valSC(s) \cup valSD(s) \cup valA(s)$, and*
- $s + \delta$ *is the time advanced STGTS state obtained from s by changing $valC(s)$ to $valC(s) + \delta$ and keeping the other components unchanged.*

In STGTS states, the three valuations are captured outside the graph (as opposed to the valuation for the attribute variables, which is recorded as an AC in the graph) to simplify the definition of concrete/symbolic semantics; in particular, our integration of structural GT-behavior with timed and stochastic behavior ensures that (especially discrete) STGTS steps can only read/write the clock and stochastic variables in the desired restricted way. The start state of an STGTS consists of the start graph and the three valuations mapping all (real-valued) variables to 0.

STGTS invariants state clock constraints based on graph patterns; the states of an STGTS S are those STGTS states satisfying all STGTS invariants of S. Most commonly, STGTS invariants provide upper bounds such as $c \leq r$ to prevent the progress of time when the clock c reaches r to enforce the occurrence of a discrete step at that time (if the progress of time is prevented while no discrete step is enabled, the state is in a time lock and an STGTS with such a state being reachable is invalid). Technically, STGTS invariants are pairs of a graph I and an ECC $\psi \in ECC(varsC(I), vars(I))$ (ranging over all variables) and are satisfied by an STGTS state s when for every match $m : I \hookrightarrow graph(s)$, ψ is satisfied in the sense that $val(s)(m(\psi))$ is equivalent to $\top$. In principle, STGTS invariants can also be used to rule out discrete steps based on structurally forbidden patterns using $\psi = \top$ but, in our experience, this results in a more complex STGTS with degraded separation of concerns with the threat of unexpectedly prevented steps. For our running example, all STGTS invariants are of the form (I, ψ) where I is the left hand side graphs of some STGTS rule; we therefore provide the ECCs ψ alongside the corresponding STGTS rules later on. For now, we refer to Figure 2c to provide the STGTS invariant $\mathsf{inv}_{\mathsf{drive}}$ expressing that shuttles must advance to the next track within $is + 2$ time units for which the duration that a shuttle is on its current track is measured using the clock $driveClock = c$. This STGTS invariant is satisfied by the start state s (see again Figure 2d for the start graph) because the shuttle is 0 time units on its current track (due to $\mathsf{valC}(s)(cs_1) = 0$) while it may be up to 4 time units on that track (due to the STGTS invariant requiring $cs_1 \leq 2 + 2$ using the $invSpeed$ attribute of the shuttle). Technically, for $\mathsf{inv}_{\mathsf{drive}} = (I, \psi)$ and the only existing match $m : I \hookrightarrow \mathsf{G}_{\mathsf{start}}$, we obtain the ECC $m(\psi) = (cs_1 \leq is_1 + 2)$ (assuming that is_1 is the variable attached to the $invSpeed$ attribute of the shuttle S_1 with value 2) and then $\mathsf{val}(s)(m(\psi)) = (0 \leq 2 + 2) \equiv \top$.

STGTS APs are given by graphs; in the concrete semantics, each state s is labeled with the STGTS APs A for which a match $m : A \hookrightarrow \mathsf{graph}(s)$ exists. In contrast to STGTS invariants, STGTS APs may not depend on clock/stochastic variables as a consequence of how the model checking algorithm from section 5 operates on the symbolic semantics. Also note that if $\mathsf{ac}(A)$ refers to such a clock/stochastic variable, m cannot be a match as its implication check cannot be satisfied because G does not record a value for such variables. In our running example, we employ the STGTS AP $\mathsf{ap}_{\mathsf{unsafe}}$ from Figure 2b capturing states where a fast shuttle (advancing every 2 to 4 time units to the next track) is at a construction site.

To clarify our assumptions on and handling of distributions in STGTSs, we rely on a Distribution Structure (DS) capturing the required information for each supported distribution (such as whether it is a discrete/continuous distribution, its parameters, and requirements on these parameters). For each distribution, we hereby only assume oracles allowing to apply the distributions PMF/CDF and to generate random variates (i.e., sample random variables) and thereby abstract from whether the CDF must be approximated for CDFs without closed form (such as for the normal distribution) or which sampling technique is employed.

Definition 3 (Distribution Structure (DS)). *A DS Γ has 7 components.*
- $\mathsf{dist}(\Gamma) = D$ *is a set of (symbols for) distributions.*
- $\mathsf{kind}(\Gamma)(d) \in \{\mathsf{d}, \mathsf{c}\}$ *defines for each $d \in D$ its discrete/continuous kind.*
- $\mathsf{varsP}(\Gamma) = P$ *is a set of parameter variables.*
- $\mathsf{param}(\Gamma)(d) \in 2^P \times \mathsf{AC}(\mathsf{bool}, P)$ *defines for each $d \in D$ its set p of parameter variables and an AC γ restricting instantiations of p. For $\mathsf{param}(\Gamma)(d) = (p, \gamma)$ and $v : p \to \mathbf{R}$, we write $v \in \langle \mathsf{param}(\Gamma)(d) \rangle$ when v satisfies γ.*
- $\mathsf{pmf}(\Gamma, d, v)$ *for $d \in D$ with $\mathsf{kind}(\Gamma)(d) = \mathsf{d}$ and $v \in \langle \mathsf{param}(\Gamma)(d) \rangle$ is the PMF p_X of a $d(v)$-distributed random variable X returning for some value $x \in \mathbf{R}$ the probability $p \in [0, 1]$ that X takes the value x.*
- $\mathsf{cdf}(\Gamma, d, v)$ *for $d \in D$ with $\mathsf{kind}(\Gamma)(d) = \mathsf{c}$ and $v \in \langle \mathsf{param}(\Gamma)(d) \rangle$ is the CDF F_X of a $d(v)$-distributed random variable X returning for some value $x \in \mathbf{R}$ the probability $p \in [0, 1]$ that X takes a value in $(-\infty, x]$.*

- sample(Γ, d, v) *for* $d \in D$ *and* $v \in \langle$param$(\Gamma)(d)\rangle$ *returns a random variate for a $d(v)$-distributed random variable X whenever it is used.*

Subsequently, we assume a fixed DS Γ containing, e.g., the distributions dist$(\Gamma) =$ {exp, normal, uniformC, weibull, uniformD, bernoulli, binomial} for the exponential, normal, (continuous) uniform, Weibull, (discrete) uniform, bernoulli, and binomial distribution. For example, for the exponential distribution, we include $\lambda \in$ varsP(Γ) and param(Γ)(exp) $= (\{\lambda\}, \lambda > 0)$. Clearly, distribution convolutions such as $X \sim Y + 2 \times Z$ where $Y \sim$ exp(2) and $Z \sim$ exp(4) are exponentially distributed (for this particular case, see [75]) or bathtub distributions combining multiple Weibull distributions [68, p. 614] (allowing to express decreasing, constant, and increasing failure rates across a components life span) from reliability/deterioration engineering [67, 8] may be (a) included explicitly in Γ (when oracles for their CDF/PMF and sampling can be provided) or (b) obtained by combining sampled values for the underlying distributions at use time. To simplify analysis, option (a) appears advantageous for non-trivial convolutions.

STGTS rules describe how discrete steps between STGTS states are to be derived. Each STGTS rule contains a set of underlying GT rules leading to (usually) different STGTS states; they have a common left hand side graph L implying that these GT rules are all applicable based on just one match m from L into the graph of the current STGTS state. Each of these GT rules is equipped with a weight expression based on the attribute and stochastic discrete variables, which express relative probabilities among each other.[2] The STGTS rules also contain a clock guard given by an ECC that must be satisfied for the STGTS rule to be applicable (the guard is simplified to a CC by substituting all variables by values except for the clock variables and applying trivial simplification).[3] The STGTS rules also capture for each underlying GT rule ρ the clocks (from the right hand side of ρ) that must be reset to 0 when applying ρ. To capture the novel sampling of stochastic continuous/discrete variables, the STGTS rule also provides for such variables (from the right hand side of ρ), based on the assumed DS, the distributions and their parameters (given by ACs over the attribute variables of L) to be used using a map stoch(σ).[4] Note that not all stochastic continuous/discrete variables must be (re)sampled in each step meaning that stoch$(\sigma)(\rho)$ is a partial map and that precisely the parameters of

---

[2] varsC(L) and varsS(L) are excluded to make the probabilistic aspect independent from the clock-based and stochastic timing aspect.

[3] The guard is not just a CC over the clock variables of L to allow that attributes store, e.g., the speed of a shuttle while also stating CCs based on that shuttle speed. Also, the stochastic continuous variables must be allowed in clock guards to model urgent rules in which components fail. Also, only for the symbolic semantics, we need to ensure that the guard can be simplified to a CC; for the concrete semantics, we just need to evaluate it to a Boolean after substituting all its variables.

[4] varsC(L) and varsS(L) are excluded as concrete parameter variables to make the probabilistic aspect independent from the clock-based timing and to prevent sampling based on sampled values, which should rather be implemented using further convoluted distributions in the DS.

the chosen distribution must be instantiated (leading to the partial map of type varsP(Γ) $\rightharpoonup$ AC(real, varsA(L))). Lastly, each STGTS rule is equipped with a priority from $\mathbf{N}$ meaning that it is only applicable when no other STGTS rule is applicable with a higher priority.

Definition 4 (STGTS Rule). *An STGTS rule σ has 7 components.*

- lhs(σ) = L *is a graph (a common left-hand side to be matched).*
- rules(σ) *is a finite non-empty set of GT rules ρ with* lhs(ρ) = L *where* lhs(ρ) *is the left-hand side graph of ρ.*
- weight(σ)(ρ) $\in$ AC(real, varsA(L) $\cup$ varsSD(L)) *assigns a probability weight expression to each underlying GT rule $\rho \in$ rules(σ) using only attributes variables and stochastic discrete variables of L.*
- guard(σ) $\in$ ECC(varsC(L), vars(L)) *is a guard defined as an ECC over the variables from the left-hand side graph L.*
- reset(σ)(ρ) $\subseteq$ varsC(rhs(ρ)) *identifies the clocks to be reset for each underlying GT rule $\rho \in$ rules(σ) where* rhs(ρ) *is the right-hand side graph of ρ.*
- stoch(σ)(ρ) : varsS(rhs(ρ)) $\rightharpoonup$ (dist(Γ) $\times$ (varsP(Γ) $\rightharpoonup$ AC(real, varsA(L)))) *assigns to each underlying GT rule $\rho \in$ rules(σ) and to some stochastic variables $x \in$ rhs(ρ) available after application of ρ a stochastic assignment (d, i) containing the distribution $d \in$ dist(Γ) to be used and an instantiation map i mapping arguments of d to an AC over attribute variables of L where* kind(Γ)(d) = c *iff $x \in$ varsSC(rhs(ρ)) (ensures that only continuous/discrete distributions are used for stochastic continuous/discrete variables) and* param(Γ)(d) = (p, γ) *implies* support(i) = p *(ensures that the arguments of d are instantiated).*
- prio(σ) $\in \mathbf{N}$ *is the priority assigned to σ.*

For our running example, see Figure 3 for the STGTS rules and their described behavior where trivial components are omitted. For simplicity, we employ exponential distributions to model the failures of traffic lights while, e.g., Weibull or bathtub distributions could be more adequate if domain knowledge on the used hardware components would be available.

An STGTS then collects the components presented so far. For our running example, see Figure 2 and Figure 3 for these components.

Definition 5 (STGTS). *An STGTS S has 4 components.*

- start(S) *is a finite start graph.*
- rules(S) *is a finite set of STGTS rules.*
- invs(S) *is a finite set of STGTS invariants.*
- aps(S) *is a finite set of STGTS APs.*

Moreover, states(S) *contains the* invs(S)-*satisfying STGTS states of S (i.e., $s \in$* states(S) *iff for all $(I, \psi) \in$ invs(S) and $m : I \hookrightarrow$ graph(s),* val(s) $\circ m \models \psi$*).*

4.2   Semantics of Stochastic Timed Graph Transformation Systems

We now introduce the STGTS (single) step relation based on which we then define the TPTS induced by an STGTS subsequently. As for all modeling formalisms based on clocks as used in TA, STGTSs define (a) timed steps where

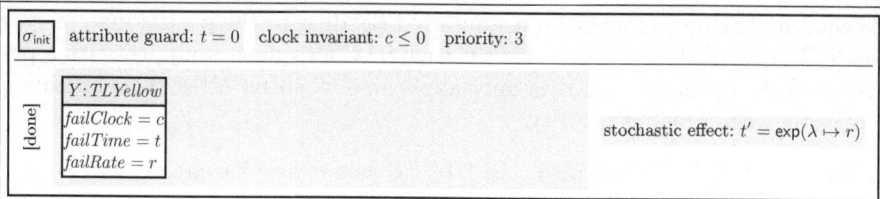

(a) STGTS rule σ_{init}: this rule is applied first (highest priority and $failTime = t$ is 0 in the start graph and $c \leq 0$ ensures that no time may elapse beforehand); it samples t using the exponential distribution with the rate parameter provided by Y.

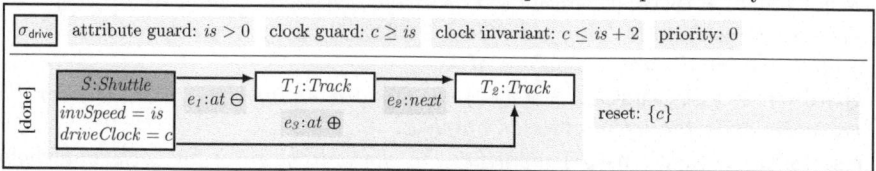

(b) STGTS rule σ_{drive}: this rule advances a non-halted ($invSpeed = is > 0$) shuttle to the next track after it has been on the current track for is to $is + 2$ time units as measured using c, which is therefore reset.

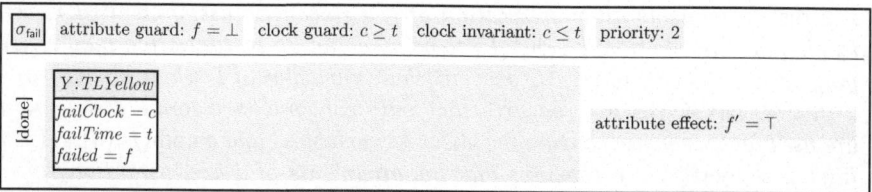

(c) STGTS rule σ_{fail}: this rule urgently sets a traffic light into failed mode when its $failClock = c$ has reached the $failTime = t$.

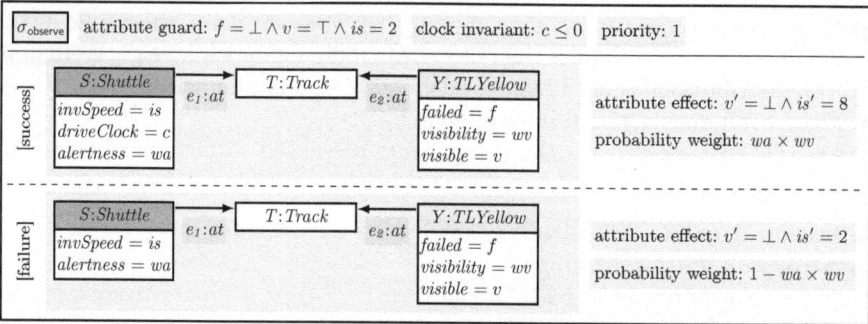

(d) STGTS rule σ_{observe}: this rule is applied once (changing $visible = v$ to $\bot$) when a fast (requiring $invSpeed = is = 2$) shuttle S reaches a track T with a non-failed ($failed = f = \bot$) traffic light Y. In its fixed probabilistic outcomes, $invSpeed = is$ is either changed to 8 (indicating slow down) or kept at 2. The probability weight for successfully observing the traffic light slowing down is given by the product of the probability of the shuttle navigator to observe a traffic light and the visibility of the traffic light; since this probability weight is a probability already, we simply assign the remaining probability to the other outcome as a weight.

Fig. 3. The STGTS rules for our running example.

only time elapses adding the same delay to all clock variables and (b) discrete steps where clocks may be reset but where, with more technical effort, the other components of the STGTS states may be adapted. We note that the step relation operates only on the states of the given STGTS, requiring that all STGTS invariants are satisfied, which also holds for the states implicitly traversed during a timed step. For the discrete steps, we consider six construction steps in the following definition. Step (1): this step entails a standard GT step applying one GT rule of the STGTS rule; but the valuation of the stochastic discrete variables has to be temporarily added to the graph to enable their usage. Step (2): as for PTGTSs, the clock guard is checked and the resulting clock valuation is obtained by preserving clock values (along the morphisms of the GT step) and setting all created clocks and clocks to be reset to 0. Step (3): the resulting valuation of stochastic discrete variables is obtained by adapting it, similarly to clock variables, along the morphisms of the GT step, setting created stochastic discrete variables to 0, and sampling the specified stochastic discrete variables using the DS according to the given distribution and its evaluated arguments (also checking the admissibility of those parameters using the constraints in the DS). Also, the CDF (belonging to the PMF) as well as the sampling reassignments are recorded in the step label (F and sr) for the subsequent definition of the induced TPTS. Step (4): this step is analogous to the previous but for the stochastic continuous variables. Step (5): we check that all GT rules of the STGT rule are applicable for the given match (thereby checking also the STGTS invariants) with a weight from $\mathbf{R}_0^+$ and that the sum of all weights is in $\mathbf{R}^+$ to be able to obtain a PMF from these weights. Step (6): as for PTGTSs, we rule out the applicability of an STGTS rule with higher priority.

Definition 6 (STGTS Step). *An STGTS S defines timed and discrete steps.*

- *Timed Step:* $(s, \delta, s + \delta) \in \mathsf{steps}(S)$ *where* $s \in \mathsf{states}(S)$ *and* $\delta \in \mathbf{R}^+$, *if*
  ○ *Clock Invariants:* $(s + \delta') \in \mathsf{states}(S)$ *for each delay* $\delta' \in [0, \delta]$.
- *Discrete Step:* $(s_1, (\sigma, m, \rho, pw, F, sr), s_2) \in \mathsf{steps}(S)$ *where* $s_1, s_2 \in \mathsf{states}(S)$ *are STGTS states,* $\sigma \in \mathsf{rules}(S)$ *is an STGTS rule,* $m : \mathsf{lhs}(\sigma) \hookrightarrow \mathsf{graph}(s_1)$ *is a match, and* $\rho \in \mathsf{rules}(\sigma)$ *is a GT rule of* σ, *if all following items are satisfied.*
  (1) Attributed Graph Transformation (Using Stochastic Discrete Variables):
  ○ $(G_1, (\rho, m, k, \bar{m}, \ell', r'), G_2) \in \mathsf{GTsteps}$ *where* G_1 *is obtained from* $\mathsf{graph}(s_1)$ *by adding* $\mathsf{valSD}(s_1)$ *to* $\mathsf{ac}(\mathsf{graph}(s_1))$ *and* $\mathsf{graph}(s_2)$ *is obtained from* G_2 *by restricting* $\mathsf{ac}(G_2)$ *to* $\mathsf{varsA}(G_2)$.[5]
  (2) Clock Guards, Resets, and Invariants:
  ○ $\mathsf{val}(s_1) \models \mathsf{guard}(\sigma)$ *(i.e., the clock guard of the STGTS rule σ is satisfied),*
  ○ *for* $c \in \mathsf{varsC}(s_2)$, *if* $c \in \bar{m}(\mathsf{reset}(\sigma)(\rho))$ *(i.e., c is reset), then* $\mathsf{valC}(s_2)(c) = 0$, *elseif* $c \in \mathsf{varsC}(s_2) - \mathsf{range}(r')$ *(i.e., c is created), then* $\mathsf{valC}(s_2)(c) = 0$, *else (i.e., c is preserved)* $\mathsf{valC}(s_2)(c) = \mathsf{valC}(s_1)(\Delta(r', \ell')(c))$.
  (3) Sampling of Stochastic Discrete Variables:

---

[5] That is, $\mathsf{val}(G_1)(x)$ is $\mathsf{val}(\mathsf{graph}(s_1))(x)$ for $x \in \mathsf{varsA}(G_1)$, $\mathsf{valSD}(s_1)(x)$ for $x \in \mathsf{varsSD}(G_1)$, and undefined otherwise. Also, $\mathsf{val}(\mathsf{graph}(s_2))(x)$ is $\mathsf{val}(G_2)(x)$ for $x \in \mathsf{varsA}(G_2)$ and undefined otherwise.

○ *for* $x \in \text{varsSD}(s_2)$, *if* $x \in \bar{m}(\text{support}(\text{stoch}(\sigma)(\rho)))$ *(i.e.,* x *is sampled),* *then* $\text{valSD}(s_2)(x) = \theta$ *(see next item for* θ*), elseif* $x \in \text{varsSD}(s_2) - \text{range}(r')$ *(i.e.,* x *is created), then* $\text{valSD}(s_2)(x) = 0$*, else (i.e.,* x *is preserved)* $\text{valSD}(s_2)(x) = \text{valSD}(s_1)(\Delta(r', \ell')(x))$.

○ *(Sampling of* θ*)* *If* $x \in \bar{m}(\text{support}(\text{stoch}(\sigma)(\rho)))$*, there are* y*,* d*, and* v' *satisfying* $x = \bar{m}(y)$ *and* $\text{stoch}(\sigma)(\rho)(y) = (d, v')$*; we abbreviate* $v'' = \text{valA}(s_1) \circ m \circ v'$ *as the valuated parameters of* d*; if* $v'' \in \langle \text{param}(\Gamma)(d) \rangle$*, we sample* $\theta = \text{sample}(\Gamma, d, v'')$ *and derive no step otherwise. Also, the partial maps* F *and* sr *with domain* $\text{varsS}(s_2)$ *map* x *to (the CDF belonging to)* $\text{pmf}(\Gamma, d, v'')$ *and* θ *as sampling record.*

(4) Sampling of Stochastic Continuous Variables:

○ *(analogously to stochastic discrete variable sampling)*

(5) Derivability of all Probabilistic Outcomes:

○ $pw = \text{val}(s_1)(m(\text{weight}(\sigma)(\rho))) \geq 0$ *is the valuated probability weight.*

○ *For all* $\rho' \in \text{rules}(\sigma)$ *there is* $(s_1, (\sigma, m, \rho', \_, \_, \_), \_) \in \text{steps}(S)$.

○ *For some* ρ' *there is* $(s_1, (\sigma, m, \rho', pw', \_, \_), \_) \in \text{steps}(S)$ *with* $pw' > 0$.

(6) Restriction to Highest Priority Steps:

○ *If there is some* $\sigma' \in \text{rules}(S)$ *with* $(s_1, (\sigma', \_, \_, \_, \_, \_), \_) \in \text{steps}(S)$*, then* $\text{prio}(\sigma') \leq \text{prio}(\sigma)$.

We now define the semantics of STGTSs in terms of their induced TPTSs. Besides formally capturing the start state discussed above, this definition entails the aggregation of steps from $\text{steps}(S)$ that belong to the same probabilistic decision (defined by source state s_1, STGTS rule σ, and match m) into steps of the resulting TPTS. Firstly, considering the case without sampling of stochastic variables, the probability to reach a certain state is defined using the probability weights of the GT rules of σ when being evaluated using m: to obtain a PMF from these weights, we construct a *probability weight map* $w : Y \twoheadrightarrow \mathbf{R}_0^+$ that assigns a weight $w(y) > 0$ to some $y \in Y$; this map induces the unique PMF $p : Y \twoheadrightarrow \mathbf{R}$ with $p(y) = w(y) / \sum_{y \in Y} w(y)$. Based on this PMF p, for a possible outcome $o \in \text{states}(S)$, we add up the probabilities $p(\rho)$ assigned to GT rules ρ of σ that lead to the outcome o (for cases where the same outcome o is obtained for multiple GT rules). Secondly, when extending this consideration to the sampling of stochastic variables, we note that the probability of a single outcome is 0, which is why CDFs capture the probabilities of *sets* of outcomes $O \subseteq \text{states}(S)$. Focusing on a single GT rule ρ, we consider all steps for s_1, σ, m, and ρ differing in how stochastic variables are sampled and obtain the $n(\rho)$ many variables $\boldsymbol{x}(\rho)$ sampled for ρ and the CDFs $\boldsymbol{F}(\rho)$ used for that sampling, which correspond to probability measures $\boldsymbol{P}(\rho)$. Filtering the given set O to those states that can be reached using these steps, we obtain a set of assignments for the sampled variables. We note that the resulting probability measure from $\text{Prob}(\text{states}(T))$ (to obtain a TPTS) is obtained as the convex combination using p from above of the product measures obtained from each $\boldsymbol{P}(\rho)$.[6]

---

[6] If $p : Y \twoheadrightarrow \mathbf{R}$ is a PMF, $(\mathbf{R}^{n(y)}, \mathcal{B}(\mathbf{R}^{n(y)}), P(y))$ are probability spaces (for $y \in Y$), and $X(y) : (\mathbf{R}^{n(y)}, \mathcal{B}(\mathbf{R}^{n(y)})) \twoheadrightarrow (\Omega, \mathcal{F})$ are random variables (for $y \in Y$), then

Definition 7 (TPTS Induced by STGTS). *Each STGTS S induces a unique* TPTS T *as follows.*

- states(T) *is the smallest subset of* states(S) *such that* steps(T) *and* start(T) *below are well-defined.*
- start$(T) = ($start$(S), \mathbf{0}, \mathbf{0}, \mathbf{0})$ *where* $\mathbf{0}$ *maps each argument to* 0.
- events(T) *is the smallest set containing* $\mathbf{R}^+$ *and tuples* (σ, m) *where* $\sigma \in$ rules(S) *and* m *is a match such that* steps(T) *below is well-defined.*
- $(s_1, a, \mathcal{P}) \in$ steps(T), *if one of the two following cases applies.*
  ○ *Timed Step: if all following items are satisfied.*
  ▷ $(s_1, a, s_2) \in$ steps(S) *is a timed step of* S.
  ▷ $\mathcal{P}(\{s_2\}) = 1$.
  ○ *Discrete Step: if all following items are satisfied.*
  ▷ $a = (\sigma, m) \in$ events(T) *is a partial step label.*
  ▷ $\mathcal{P}(O) = \sum_{\rho \in \mathsf{rules}(\sigma)} p(\rho) \times X(\rho)_*(P(\rho))(O)$ *for which we define* p, X, *and* P.
  ▷ steps(ρ) *contains all* $(s_1, (\sigma, m, \rho, pw, F, sr_j), s_{2,j}) \in$ steps(S). *These steps agree in* pw, F, *and* graph$(s_{2,j})$. *Requiring that* steps(ρ) *is not empty implies that all GT rules* ρ *of* σ *have been applied successfully (which may fail due to dangling edges, STGTS invariant violation, or unsatisfiable attribute change requirements), we denote* pw *and* F *for a fixed* ρ *by* pw(ρ) *and* F(ρ).
  ▷ p *is the unique PMF induced by the probability weight map* pw(ρ).
  ▷ $\boldsymbol{x}(\rho) = (x_1, \dots, x_{n(\rho)})$ *is an ordering of the* $n(\rho) \in \mathbf{N}$ *sampled stochastic continuous/discrete variables* $x_i \in$ support$($F$(\rho))$ *contained in* graph$(s_{2,j})$.
  ▷ $\boldsymbol{F}(\rho) = (F_1, \dots, F_{n(\rho)})$ *is the corresponding list of CDFs used to sample the variables* $\boldsymbol{x}(\rho)$ *defined by* $F_i =$ F$(\rho)(x_i)$.
  ▷ $\boldsymbol{P}(\rho) = (P_1, \dots, P_{n(\rho)})$ *is the corresponding list of probability measures obtained from the CDFs* $\boldsymbol{F}(\rho)$ *defined by* $P_i = P(F_i)$.
  ▷ $P(\rho) = \prod \boldsymbol{P}(\rho)$ *is the product measure of the* $n(\rho)$ *probability measures* $\boldsymbol{P}(\rho)$ *(see section 3).*
  ▷ $X(\rho) : \mathbf{R}^{n(\rho)} \rightharpoonup$ states(S) *maps* $\boldsymbol{r} = (r_1, \dots, r_{n(\rho)})$ *to the* $s_{2,j}$ *where* $\forall 1 \leq i \leq n(\rho)$. $sr_j(x_i) = r_i$.[7]
- aps$(T) =$ aps(S).
- lab$(T)(s) = \{A \in$ aps$(T) \mid \exists m : A \hookrightarrow$ graph$(s)\}$.

5   Model Checking Approach

PTGTS model checking support w.r.t. probabilistic timed reachability/safety properties has been obtained by constructing a symbolic PTGTS state space on which standard PTA model checking algorithms can be applied. We now outline an extension of this approach for the setting of STGTSs omitting a formal definition due to space restrictions. While STGTSs and STA have different semantics

---

$(\Omega, \mathcal{F}, \mathcal{P})$ is a probability space with $\mathcal{P}(O) = \sum_{y \in Y} p(y) \times X(y)_*(P(y))(O)$ where $X(y)_*(P(y))$ is the pushforward measure of $P(y)$ (see section 3).

[7] Note that sr_j and $s_{2,j}$ are bound together by being in a single step in steps(ρ) defined above and that $s_{2,j}$ is unique because the different $s_{2,j}$ only vary in how the stochastic variables are sampled.

due to the STGTS use of priorities and invariants and the STA use of urgent steps to enable compositional modeling, we conjecture that our STGTS model checking approach can also be adapted to STA for which only sampling based analysis exists (essentially flattening the stochastic distributions to probabilistic PTA steps exists).

Model checking requires the construction of a state space with finitely many states. However, STGTS employ (a) real valued clocks that are changed using timed steps of varying length[8] and (b) real-valued stochastic continuous variables changed using sampling steps. Both, (a) and (b), result in infinitely many states and steps where even single states are exited by infinitely many steps (infinite branching). Consequently, we require the construction of a symbolic state space (based on symbolic states and symbolic steps between them) in which these two notions are captured symbolically aggregating enough possibilities together such that a finite symbolic state space is obtained for which model checking can be applied equivalently w.r.t. the original properties to be analyzed.

First, for real-valued clocks, this problem has been solved in TA, PTA, as well as PTGTS model checking based on the zone-abstraction (see [47, 48, 52]). In particular, symbolic states (G, ψ) contain a CC $\psi \in CC(X)$ called zone and represent all concrete states (G, vc) with clock valuations $vc : X \rightarrow \mathbf{R}_0^+$ for which vc satisfies ψ. Zones can easily be compared because they can be uniquely represented using finite Difference Bound Matrices (DBMs) [18, 13]. Discrete and (symbolic) timed steps are then always applied in tandem when constructing symbolic state spaces using this zone-abstraction and the effects of clock guards, resets, and invariants are applied based on standard DBM operations. The syntax of CCs and their usage in guards and invariants (as introduced for TA) ensures that concrete states represented by symbolic states have the same subsequent behavior. Lastly, this zone-abstraction results in a finite equivalent symbolic state space for TA, PTA, and PTGTS (when the set of reachable graphs is finite).

For probabilistic formalisms (such as PTA, PTGTSs, and now STGTSs) using the zone-abstraction for constructing a finite symbolic state space, we note that model checking must be performed backwards from the target states specified in the property to be analyzed. Thereby, symbolic states are constructed backwards from the target applying discrete and timed steps in tandem deriving weakest preconditions.[9] In particular, backward analysis is required to check which successor states (G_i, ψ_i) each symbolically representing the paths starting in them do not contradict each other: for example, for a clock x, a continuation

---

[8] Despite time being deterministic (which is even stated as a requirement for TPTS in [76, 30]) there are infinitely many defined timed steps.

[9] For PTGTSs and now STGTSs, we first identify all reachable graphs and the steps between them by constructing a (symbolic) forward state space and then restrict the symbolic backward state space to use only discrete steps from this (symbolic) forward state space. Hereby, we also apply sampling of the discrete stochastic variables (assuming a small number of results) while we may consider approaches to also handle their sampling symbolically in the future. This construction of the (symbolic) forward state space is not necessary for TA and PTA because locations and steps are provided explicitly upfront for them.

from one successor may require $x \leq 1$ while the continuation from another successor requires $2 \leq x$ making them incompatible. During backward analysis, all such subsequent constraints are propagated backwards enabling the analysis of compatibility when needed.

Second, as our core extension of PTGTS model checking to STGTS model checking, we need to capture real-valued stochastic continuous variables symbolically, which are sampled in discrete steps and are used in the evaluation of clock guards of later discrete steps. We note that stochastic continuous variables would not be a challenge when their sampling and the usage of that sampling would always occur in single discrete STGTS steps (thereby the stochastic sampling would have only a local effect on step derivation). Instead, the STGTS semantics allows to execute sampling in one step also when the sampled values are not used immediately for clock guard evaluation, which we call eager sampling. For our running example, this is of course required to sample a *failTime* for the traffic lights, which will fail based on that *failTime* later on. During symbolic backward state space generation and model checking, when constructing a step backwards from a state s, we replace each stochastic continuous variable t that occurs in a clock guard ψ by a clock counterpart t_c and employ the TA-based zone-abstraction to then propagate the adapted clock guard $\psi' = \psi\{t_c/t\}$ obtained by replacing t by t_c backwards. During this backward propagation, we infer lower and upper bounds $a \leq t_c \leq b$ for t_c along the way based on the STGTS invariants applicable on intermediate states and guards of applied steps. Such restrictions of the clock t_c indirectly restrict the possible samplings of t that could lead to the state s from which we started the backward propagation of restrictions. Also, if a sampled continuous stochastic variable is used in multiple continuation paths of a (probabilistic) step, the mechanism discussed above for CCs readily evaluates their compatibility. Finally, when the sampling step for the continuous stochastic variable t is reached, unrestricted sampling of t (in the defined forward semantics) can be replaced by applying the CDF on the restriction given by an interval $a \leq t_c \leq b$ specified for t_c in the CC of the reached symbolic state.

The following exemplary application of our model checking approach demonstrates that sampling can be replaced by CDF applications during model checking once the relevant arguments for the CDFs have been derived via backward propagation.

See Figure 3 where the rule σ_{init} samples a duration for a stochastic continuous variable also resetting a clock to measure that duration and where σ_{fail} checks in its guard and invariant whether that duration has elapsed already (i.e., *failClock* is the proposed clock to be associated with the stochastic continuous variable *failTime*). STGTS symbolic state space generation reveals that, due to its speed of 2 to 4 time units per track, the shuttle is at the traffic lights at times $X \in [4, 8]$ and $Y \in [8, 16]$ depending on how non-determinism is resolved and the traffic lights have failed until time t with probabilities $P(X \leq t) = 1 - e^{-0.001 \times t}$ and $P(Y \leq t) = 1 - e^{-0.002 \times t}$. To obtain best-case/worst-case probabilities, non-determinism would let the shuttle reach these traffic lights at the lower/upper borders of these intervals. For the best-case, we obtain the minimal probability for derailing at track T_7 reaching the construction site there with *invSpeed* of 2 of $(P(X \leq 4) + P(X > 4) \times (1 - 0.95 \times 0.99)) \times (P(Y \leq 8) + P(Y > 8) \times (1 - 0.95 \times 0.9)) \approx 1.6 \times 10^{-4}$ given by the product of not slowing down twice where (for $r \in \{4, 8\}$) $P(X \leq r)$ checks for the probability of reaching the traffic light after it has failed and $P(X > r) \times (1 - 0.95 \times p)$ (for $p \in \{0.99, 0.9\}$) is the probability of reaching the traffic light before it has failed but the navigator not observing it based on alertness and limited visibility. Lastly, we report the worst-case probability 4.2×10^{-4}.

This exemplary analysis for our running example already indicates that backward model checking indeed needs to accumulate constraints on stochastic variables (by determining duration intervals for the additional clocks t_c for the stochastic variables t from the CC of the current state). For the example, the two clocks measuring the time since sampling are constrained to the intervals $[4, 8]$ and $[8, 16]$ as required. These constraints are then probabilistically evaluated by applying the CDFs when reaching the sampling steps for the stochastic continuous variables t to minimize/maximize the resulting probability.

6 Conclusion and Future Work

We extended the formalism of PTGTSs to STGTSs to obtain a high-level description language for the modeling and analysis of complex distributed embedded probabilistic real-time systems with stochastic behavior where CDFs are sampled to capture in particular pseudo-random number generators and stochastic delays. This extension thereby improves the modeling capabilities as exemplified in our running example featuring stochastic failures. Moreover, we outlined a model checking approach for STGTSs w.r.t. worst-case/best-case probabilistic timed reachability properties based on prior work on PTGTSs.

As future work, we plan to formalize, implement, and evaluate the outlined model checking algorithm for an extension of our running example featuring shuttle convoy establishment from [52] with more complex structural behavior thereby also enabling analysis for those STA that can be encoded into STGTSs. Moreover, we plan to employ standard CDF sampling techniques to extend an already existing PTGTS simulator for large-scale systems to STGTSs.

References

[1] R. Alur and D. L. Dill. "A Theory of Timed Automata". In: *Theor. Comput. Sci.* 126.2 (1994), pp. 183–235. DOI: 10.1016/0304-3975(94)90010-8.

[2] Amazon. *Neptune.* URL: https://aws.amazon.com/neptune/.

[3] T. Arendt, E. Biermann, S. Jurack, C. Krause, and G. Taentzer. "Henshin: Advanced Concepts and Tools for In-Place EMF Model Transformations". In: *Model Driven Engineering Languages and Systems - 13th International Conference, MODELS 2010, Oslo, Norway, October 3-8, 2010, Proceedings, Part I.* Ed. by D. C. Petriu, N. Rouquette, and Ø. Haugen. Vol. 6394. Lecture Notes in Computer Science. Springer, 2010, pp. 121–135. ISBN: 978-3-642-16144-5. DOI: 10.1007/978-3-642-16145-2_9.

[4] *Augur 2.* Universität Duisburg-Essen. 2008. URL: https://www.ti.inf.uni-due.de/en/research/tools/augur2.

[5] A. Aziz, K. Sanwal, V. Singhal, and R. K. Brayton. "Model-checking continous-time Markov chains". In: *ACM Trans. Comput. Log.* 1.1 (2000), pp. 162–170. DOI: 10.1145/343369.343402.

[6] C. Baier, B. R. Haverkort, H. Hermanns, and J. Katoen. "Model Checking Continuous-Time Markov Chains by Transient Analysis". In: *Computer Aided Verification, 12th International Conference, CAV 2000, Chicago, IL, USA, July 15-19, 2000, Proceedings.* Ed. by E. A. Emerson and A. P. Sistla. Vol. 1855. Lecture Notes in Computer Science. Springer, 2000, pp. 358–372. DOI: 10.1007/10722167_28.

[7] C. Baier, B. R. Haverkort, H. Hermanns, and J. Katoen. "Model-Checking Algorithms for Continuous-Time Markov Chains". In: *IEEE Trans. Software Eng.* 29.6 (2003), pp. 524–541. DOI: 10.1109/TSE.2003.1205180.

[8] M. Bebbington, C. Lai, and R. Zitikis. "Useful periods for lifetime distributions with bathtub shaped hazard rate functions". In: *IEEE Trans. Reliab.* 55.2 (2006), pp. 245–251. DOI: 10.1109/TR.2001.874943.

[9] B. Becker. "Architectural modelling and verification of open service-oriented systems of systems". PhD thesis. Hasso Plattner Institute, University of Potsdam, 2014. URL: http://nbn-resolving.de/urn:nbn:de:kobv:517-opus-70158.

[10] B. Becker and H. Giese. *Cyber-Physical Systems with Dynamic Structure: Towards Modeling and Verification of Inductive Invariants.* Tech. rep. 64. Hasso Plattner Institute, University of Potsdam, 2012. URL: https://nbn-resolving.org/urn:nbn:de:kobv:517-opus-62437.

[11] B. Becker and H. Giese. *Modeling and Verifying Dynamic Evolving Service-Oriented Architectures.* Tech. rep. 75. Hasso Plattner Institute, University of Potsdam, 2013. URL: https://nbn-resolving.org/urn:nbn:de:kobv:517-opus-65112.

[12] B. Becker and H. Giese. "On Safe Service-Oriented Real-Time Coordination for Autonomous Vehicles". In: *11th IEEE International Symposium on Object-Oriented Real-Time Distributed Computing (ISORC 2008), 5-7 May 2008, Orlando, Florida, USA.* IEEE Computer Society, 2008, pp. 203–210. ISBN: 978-0-7695-3132-8. DOI: 10.1109/ISORC.2008.13. URL: https://ieeexplore.ieee.org/xpl/mostRecentIssue.jsp?punumber=4519543.

[13] J. Bengtsson and W. Yi. "Timed Automata: Semantics, Algorithms and Tools". In: *Lectures on Concurrency and Petri Nets, Advances in Petri Nets [This tutorial volume originates from the 4th Advanced Course on Petri Nets, ACPN 2003, held in Eichstätt, Germany in September 2003. In addition to lectures*

given at ACPN 2003, additional chapters have been commissioned]. Ed. by J. Desel, W. Reisig, and G. Rozenberg. Vol. 3098. Lecture Notes in Computer Science. Springer, 2003, pp. 87–124. DOI: 10.1007/978-3-540-27755-2_3.

[14]   H. C. Bohnenkamp, P. R. D'Argenio, H. Hermanns, and J. Katoen. "MODEST: A Compositional Modeling Formalism for Hard and Softly Timed Systems". In: *IEEE Trans. Software Eng.* 32.10 (2006), pp. 812–830. DOI: 10.1109/TSE.2006. 104.

[15]   M. Bozga, C. Daws, O. Maler, A. Olivero, S. Tripakis, and S. Yovine. "Kronos: A Model-Checking Tool for Real-Time Systems". In: *Computer Aided Verification, 10th International Conference, CAV '98, Vancouver, BC, Canada, June 28 - July 2, 1998, Proceedings*. Ed. by A. J. Hu and M. Y. Vardi. Vol. 1427. Lecture Notes in Computer Science. Springer, 1998, pp. 546–550. DOI: 10.1007/BFb0028779.

[16]   Christian Krause. *IPTA edition of PRISM*. https://www.hpi.uni-potsdam.de/giese/public/mdelab/2011/06/08/ipta-edition-of-prism/. Hasso Plattner Institute at the University of Potsdam, 2011.

[17]   C. Daws, A. Olivero, S. Tripakis, and S. Yovine. "The Tool KRONOS". In: *Hybrid Systems III: Verification and Control, Proceedings of the DIMACS/SYCON Workshop on Verification and Control of Hybrid Systems, October 22-25, 1995, Ruttgers University, New Brunswick, NJ, USA*. Ed. by R. Alur, T. A. Henzinger, and E. D. Sontag. Vol. 1066. Lecture Notes in Computer Science. Springer, 1995, pp. 208–219. ISBN: 3-540-61155-X. DOI: 10.1007/BFb0020947.

[18]   D. L. Dill. "Timing Assumptions and Verification of Finite-State Concurrent Systems". In: *Automatic Verification Methods for Finite State Systems, International Workshop, Grenoble, France, June 12-14, 1989, Proceedings*. Ed. by J. Sifakis. Vol. 407. Lecture Notes in Computer Science. Springer, 1989, pp. 197–212. DOI: 10.1007/3-540-52148-8_17.

[19]   R. Durrett. *Probability: Theory and Examples (Cambridge Series in Statistical and Probabilistic Mathematics)*. 5th ed. Vol. 49. Cambridge New York, NY: Cambridge University Press, 2019. ISBN: 978-1-108-47368-2.

[20]   J. Dyck and H. Giese. "k-Inductive Invariant Checking for Graph Transformation Systems". In: *Graph Transformation - 10th International Conference, ICGT 2017, Held as Part of STAF 2017, Marburg, Germany, July 18-19, 2017, Proceedings*. Ed. by J. de Lara and D. Plump. Vol. 10373. Lecture Notes in Computer Science. Springer, 2017, pp. 142–158. ISBN: 978-3-319-61469-4. DOI: 10.1007/978-3-319-61470-0_9.

[21]   H. Ehrig, K. Ehrig, U. Prange, and G. Taentzer. *Fundamentals of Algebraic Graph Transformation*. Monographs in Theoretical Computer Science. An EATCS Series. Springer, 2006. ISBN: 978-3-540-31187-4. DOI: 10.1007/3-540-31188-2.

[22]   W. Feller. *An introduction to probability theory and its applications, Volume 1*. Wiley, 1968. ISBN: 978-0471257080.

[23]   M. Fränzle, E. M. Hahn, H. Hermanns, N. Wolovick, and L. Zhang. "Measurability and safety verification for stochastic hybrid systems". In: *Proceedings of the 14th ACM International Conference on Hybrid Systems: Computation and Control, HSCC 2011, Chicago, IL, USA, April 12-14, 2011*. Ed. by M. Caccamo, E. Frazzoli, and R. Grosu. ACM, 2011, pp. 43–52. DOI: 10.1145/1967701.1967710.

[24]   A. H. Ghamarian, M. de Mol, A. Rensink, E. Zambon, and M. Zimakova. "Modelling and analysis using GROOVE". In: *Int. J. Softw. Tools Technol. Transf.* 14.1 (2012), pp. 15–40. DOI: 10.1007/s10009-011-0186-x.

[25]   H. Giese. "Modeling and Verification of Cooperative Self-adaptive Mechatronic Systems". In: *Reliable Systems on Unreliable Networked Platforms - 12th Mon-*

terey Workshop 2005, Laguna Beach, CA, USA, September 22-24, 2005. Revised Selected Papers. Ed. by F. Kordon and J. Sztipanovits. Vol. 4322. Lecture Notes in Computer Science. Springer, 2005, pp. 258–280. ISBN: 978-3-540-71155-1. DOI: 10.1007/978-3-540-71156-8_14.

[26]   GROOVE Team. *Graphs for Object-Oriented Verification (GROOVE).* https://groove.cs.utwente.nl. University of Twente, 2011.

[27]   S. Gyapay, R. Heckel, and D. Varró. "Graph Transformation with Time: Causality and Logical Clocks". In: *Graph Transformation, First International Conference, ICGT 2002, Barcelona, Spain, October 7-12, 2002, Proceedings.* Ed. by A. Corradini, H. Ehrig, H. Kreowski, and G. Rozenberg. Vol. 2505. Lecture Notes in Computer Science. Springer, 2002, pp. 120–134. DOI: 10.1007/3-540-45832-8_11.

[28]   S. Gyapay, D. Varró, and R. Heckel. "Graph Transformation with Time". In: *Fundam. Inform.* 58.1 (2003), pp. 1–22. URL: https://content.iospress.com/articles/fundamenta-informaticae/fi58-1-02.

[29]   E. M. Hahn, A. Hartmanns, and H. Hermanns. "Reachability and Reward Checking for Stochastic Timed Automata". In: *Electron. Commun. Eur. Assoc. Softw. Sci. Technol.* 70 (2014). DOI: 10.14279/tuj.eceasst.70.968.

[30]   E. M. Hahn, A. Hartmanns, H. Hermanns, and J. Katoen. "A compositional modelling and analysis framework for stochastic hybrid systems". In: *Formal Methods Syst. Des.* 43.2 (2013), pp. 191–232. DOI: 10.1007/s10703-012-0167-z.

[31]   A. Hartmanns. "Model-Checking and Simulation for Stochastic Timed Systems". In: *Formal Methods for Components and Objects - 9th International Symposium, FMCO 2010, Graz, Austria, November 29 - December 1, 2010. Revised Papers.* Ed. by B. K. Aichernig, F. S. de Boer, and M. M. Bonsangue. Vol. 6957. Lecture Notes in Computer Science. Springer, 2010, pp. 372–391. DOI: 10.1007/978-3-642-25271-6_20.

[32]   A. Hartmanns and H. Hermanns. "A Modest Approach to Checking Probabilistic Timed Automata". In: *QEST 2009, Sixth International Conference on the Quantitative Evaluation of Systems, Budapest, Hungary, 13-16 September 2009.* IEEE Computer Society, 2009, pp. 187–196. DOI: 10.1109/QEST.2009.41.

[33]   A. Hartmanns and H. Hermanns. "The Modest Toolset: An Integrated Environment for Quantitative Modelling and Verification". In: *Tools and Algorithms for the Construction and Analysis of Systems - 20th International Conference, TACAS 2014, Held as Part of the European Joint Conferences on Theory and Practice of Software, ETAPS 2014, Grenoble, France, April 5-13, 2014. Proceedings.* Ed. by E. Ábrahám and K. Havelund. Vol. 8413. Lecture Notes in Computer Science. Springer, 2014, pp. 593–598. DOI: 10.1007/978-3-642-54862-8_51.

[34]   R. Heckel, G. Lajios, and S. Menge. "Stochastic Graph Transformation Systems". In: *ICGT 2004.* Ed. by H. Ehrig, G. Engels, F. Parisi-Presicce, and G. Rozenberg. Vol. 3256. LNCS. Springer, 2004, pp. 210–225. DOI: 10.1007/978-3-540-30203-2_16.

[35]   R. Heckel, G. Lajios, and S. Menge. "Stochastic Graph Transformation Systems". In: *Fundam. Inform.* 74.1 (2006), pp. 63–84. URL: https://content.iospress.com/articles/fundamenta-informaticae/fi74-1-04.

[36]   Henshin Team. *Henshin.* https://www.eclipse.org/henshin/. 2021.

[37]   T. A. Henzinger. "The Theory of Hybrid Automata". In: *Verification of Digital and Hybrid Systems.* Ed. by M. K. Inan and R. P. Kurshan. Berlin, Heidelberg: Springer Berlin Heidelberg, 2000, pp. 265–292. ISBN: 978-3-642-59615-5. DOI: 10.1007/978-3-642-59615-5_13.

[38]   H. Hermanns, D. N. Jansen, and Y. S. Usenko. "From StoCharts to MoDeST: a comparative reliability analysis of train radio communications". In: *Proceedings of the Fifth International Workshop on Software and Performance, WOSP 2005, Palma, Illes Balears, Spain, July 12-14, 2005.* ACM, 2005, pp. 13–23. DOI: 10. 1145/1071021.1071023.

[39]   E. Jakumeit, S. Buchwald, D. Wagelaar, L. Dan, Á. Hegedüs, M. Herrmanns-dörfer, T. Horn, E. Kalnina, C. Krause, K. Lano, M. Lepper, A. Rensink, L. M. Rose, S. Wätzoldt, and S. Mazanek. "A survey and comparison of transformation tools based on the transformation tool contest". In: *Sci. Comput. Program.* 85 (2014), pp. 41–99. DOI: 10.1016/j.scico.2013.10.009.

[40]   D. N. Jansen, H. Hermanns, and J. Katoen. "A Probabilistic Extension of UML Statecharts". In: *Formal Techniques in Real-Time and Fault-Tolerant Systems, 7th International Symposium, FTRTFT 2002, Co-sponsored by IFIP WG 2.2, Oldenburg, Germany, September 9-12, 2002, Proceedings.* Ed. by W. Damm and E. Olderog. Vol. 2469. Lecture Notes in Computer Science. Springer, 2002, pp. 355–374. DOI: 10.1007/3-540-45739-9_21.

[41]   J. Katoen, M. Z. Kwiatkowska, G. Norman, and D. Parker. "Faster and Symbolic CTMC Model Checking". In: *Process Algebra and Probabilistic Methods, Performance Modeling and Verification: Joint International Workshop, PAPM-PROBMIV 2001, Aachen, Germany, September 12-14, 2001, Proceedings.* Ed. by L. de Alfaro and S. Gilmore. Vol. 2165. Lecture Notes in Computer Science. Springer, 2001, pp. 23–38. DOI: 10.1007/3-540-44804-7_2.

[42]   B. König and V. Kozioura. "Augur 2—A New Version of a Tool for the Analysis of Graph Transformation Systems". In: *ENTCS* 211 (2008), pp. 201–210. DOI: 10.1016/j.entcs.2008.04.042.

[43]   C. Krause and H. Giese. "Model Checking Probabilistic Real-Time Properties for Service-Oriented Systems with Service Level Agreements". In: *Proceedings 13th International Workshop on Verification of Infinite-State Systems, INFIN-ITY 2011, Taipei, Taiwan, 10th October 2011.* Ed. by F. Yu and C. Wang. Vol. 73. EPTCS. 2011, pp. 64–78. DOI: 10.4204/EPTCS.73.8.

[44]   C. Krause and H. Giese. "Probabilistic Graph Transformation Systems". In: *Graph Transformations - 6th International Conference, ICGT 2012, Bremen, Germany, September 24-29, 2012. Proceedings.* Ed. by H. Ehrig, G. Engels, H. Kreowski, and G. Rozenberg. Vol. 7562. Lecture Notes in Computer Science. Springer, 2012, pp. 311–325. ISBN: 978-3-642-33653-9. DOI: 10.1007/978-3-642-33654-6_21.

[45]   Kronos Team. *Kronos.* https://www-verimag.imag.fr/DIST-TOOLS/TEMPO/kronos/. 2002.

[46]   M. Z. Kwiatkowska, G. Norman, and D. Parker. "PRISM 4.0: Verification of Probabilistic Real-Time Systems". In: *Computer Aided Verification - 23rd International Conference, CAV 2011, Snowbird, UT, USA, July 14-20, 2011. Proceedings.* Ed. by G. Gopalakrishnan and S. Qadeer. Vol. 6806. Lecture Notes in Computer Science. Springer, 2011, pp. 585–591. ISBN: 978-3-642-22109-5. DOI: 10.1007/978-3-642-22110-1_47.

[47]   M. Z. Kwiatkowska, G. Norman, R. Segala, and J. Sproston. "Automatic verification of real-time systems with discrete probability distributions". In: *Theor. Comput. Sci.* 282.1 (2002), pp. 101–150. DOI: 10.1016/S0304-3975(01)00046-9.

[48]   M. Z. Kwiatkowska, G. Norman, J. Sproston, and F. Wang. "Symbolic Model Checking for Probabilistic Timed Automata". In: *Formal Techniques, Modelling and Analysis of Timed and Fault-Tolerant Systems, Joint International Confer-*

ences on Formal Modelling and Analysis of Timed Systems, FORMATS 2004 and Formal Techniques in Real-Time and Fault-Tolerant Systems, FTRTFT 2004, Grenoble, France, September 22-24, 2004, Proceedings. Ed. by Y. Lakhnech and S. Yovine. Vol. 3253. Lecture Notes in Computer Science. Springer, 2004, pp. 293–308. ISBN: 3-540-23167-6. DOI: 10.1007/978-3-540-30206-3_21.

[49] J. de Lara, E. Guerra, A. Boronat, R. Heckel, and P. Torrini. "Domain-specific discrete event modelling and simulation using graph transformation". In: Softw. Syst. Model. 13.1 (2014), pp. 209–238. DOI: 10.1007/s10270-012-0242-3.

[50] M. Maximova, H. Giese, and C. Krause. "Probabilistic Timed Graph Transformation Systems". In: Graph Transformation - 10th International Conference, ICGT 2017, Held as Part of STAF 2017, Marburg, Germany, July 18-19, 2017, Proceedings. Ed. by J. de Lara and D. Plump. Vol. 10373. Lecture Notes in Computer Science. Springer, 2017, pp. 159–175. ISBN: 978-3-319-61469-4. DOI: 10.1007/978-3-319-61470-0_10.

[51] M. Maximova, H. Giese, and C. Krause. Probabilistic timed graph transformation systems. Tech. rep. 118. Potsdam, Germany: Hasso Plattner Institute at the University of Potsdam, 2017.

[52] M. Maximova, H. Giese, and C. Krause. "Probabilistic timed graph transformation systems". In: J. Log. Algebr. Meth. Program. 101 (2018), pp. 110–131. DOI: 10.1016/j.jlamp.2018.09.003.

[53] M. Maximova, S. Schneider, and H. Giese. "Compositional Analysis of Probabilistic Timed Graph Transformation Systems". In: Fundamental Approaches to Software Engineering - 24th International Conference, FASE 2021, Held as Part of the European Joint Conferences on Theory and Practice of Software, ETAPS 2021, Luxembourg City, Luxembourg, March 27 - April 1, 2021, Proceedings. Ed. by E. Guerra and M. Stoelinga. Vol. 12649. Lecture Notes in Computer Science. Springer, 2021, pp. 196–217. DOI: 10.1007/978-3-030-71500-7_10.

[54] M. Maximova, S. Schneider, and H. Giese. "Compositional Analysis of Probabilistic Timed Graph Transformation Systems". In: Form. Asp. Comput. (Nov. 2022). Just Accepted. ISSN: 0934-5043. DOI: 10.1145/3572782.

[55] M. Maximova, S. Schneider, and H. Giese. Interval Probabilistic Timed Graph Transformation Systems. Tech. rep. 134. Hasso Plattner Institute, University of Potsdam, 2021. DOI: 10.25932/publishup-51289.

[56] M. Maximova, S. Schneider, and H. Giese. "Interval Probabilistic Timed Graph Transformation Systems". In: Graph Transformation - 14th International Conference, ICGT 2021, Held as Part of STAF 2021, Virtual Event, June 24-25, 2021, Proceedings. Ed. by F. Gadducci and T. Kehrer. Vol. 12741. Lecture Notes in Computer Science. Springer, 2021, pp. 221–239. DOI: 10.1007/978-3-030-78946-6_12.

[57] Modest Team. The Modest Toolset. https://www.modestchecker.net/. Universiteit Twente, 2023.

[58] Neo4J Team. Neo4J. URL: https://neo4j.com/.

[59] S. Neumann. "Modellierung und Verifikation zeitbehafteter Graphtransformationssysteme mittels GROOVE". MA thesis. University of Paderborn, 2007.

[60] J. R. Norris. Markov Chains. Cambridge Series in Statistical and Probabilistic Mathematics. Cambridge University Press, 1997. DOI: 10.1017/CBO9780511810633.

[61] OMG. Unified Modeling Language. 2017. URL: https://www.omg.org/spec/UML/.

[62] F. Orejas. "Symbolic graphs for attributed graph constraints". In: *J. Symb. Comput.* 46.3 (2011), pp. 294–315. DOI: `10.1016/j.jsc.2010.09.009`.

[63] K. Pennemann. "Development of correct graph transformation systems". URN: `urn:nbn:de:gbv:715-oops-9483`. PhD thesis. University of Oldenburg, Germany, 2009. URL: `https://oops.uni-oldenburg.de/884/`.

[64] PRISM Team. *PRISM Probabilistic Model Checker.* `https://www.prismmodelchecker.org/`. 2023.

[65] M. O. Rabin. "Probabilistic Automata". In: *Information and Control* 6.3 (1963), pp. 230–245. DOI: `10.1016/S0019-9958(63)90290-0`.

[66] *RailCab Project.* URL: `https://www.hni.uni-paderborn.de/cim/projekte/railcab`.

[67] M. Rausand. *Reliability of Safety-Critical Systems.* Hoboken, New Jersey: John Wiley & Sons, Ltd, 2014. ISBN: 978-1-118-11272-4. DOI: `10.1002/9781118776353`.

[68] S. M. Ross. *Introduction to Probability Models.* London, United Kingdom: Elsevier, Academic Press, 2019. ISBN: 978-0-12-814346-9.

[69] SAP. *Hana.* URL: `https://www.sap.com/products/technology-platform/hana.html`.

[70] S. Schneider, M. Maximova, and H. Giese. "Probabilistic Metric Temporal Graph Logic". In: *Graph Transformation - 15th International Conference, ICGT 2022, Held as Part of STAF 2022, Nantes, France, July 7-8, 2022, Proceedings.* Ed. by N. Behr and D. Strüber. Vol. 13349. Lecture Notes in Computer Science. Springer, 2022, pp. 58–76. DOI: `10.1007/978-3-031-09843-7_4`.

[71] S. Schneider, M. Maximova, L. Sakizloglou, and H. Giese. "Formal testing of timed graph transformation systems using metric temporal graph logic". In: *Int. J. Softw. Tools Technol. Transf.* 23.3 (2021), pp. 411–488. DOI: `10.1007/s10009-020-00585-w`.

[72] R. Segala. "Modeling and verification of randomized distributed real-time systems". PhD thesis. Massachusetts Institute of Technology, Cambridge, MA, USA, 1995. URL: `https://hdl.handle.net/1721.1/36560`.

[73] A. N. Shiryaev. *Probability-1.* 3rd ed. Title Graduate Texts in Mathematics. Springer New York, NY. DOI: `10.1007/978-0-387-72206-1`.

[74] UPPAAL Team. *UPPAAL.* `https://uppaal.org/`. Department of Information Technology at Uppsala University, Sweden and Department of Computer Science at Aalborg University, Denmark, 2021.

[75] G. P. Yanev. "Exponential and Hypoexponential Distributions: Some Characterizations". In: *Mathematics* 8.12 (2020). ISSN: 2227-7390. DOI: `10.3390/math8122207`.

[76] W. Yi. "Real-Time Behaviour of Asynchronous Agents". In: *CONCUR '90, Theories of Concurrency: Unification and Extension, Amsterdam, The Netherlands, August 27-30, 1990, Proceedings.* Ed. by J. C. M. Baeten and J. W. Klop. Vol. 458. Lecture Notes in Computer Science. Springer, 1990, pp. 502–520. DOI: `10.1007/BFb0039080`.

[77] J. Zhang, J. Zhao, Z. Huang, and Z. Cao. "Model Checking Interval Probabilistic Timed Automata". In: *2009 First International Conference on Information Science and Engineering.* 2009, pp. 4936–4940. DOI: `10.1109/ICISE.2009.749`.

[78] C. Zöllner, M. Barkowsky, M. Maximova, and H. Giese. "On the Complexity of Simulating Probabilistic Timed Graph Transformation Systems". In: *Graph Transformation - 14th International Conference, ICGT 2021, Held as Part of STAF 2021, Virtual Event, June 24-25, 2021, Proceedings.* Ed. by F. Gadducci

and T. Kehrer. Vol. 12741. Lecture Notes in Computer Science. Springer, 2021, pp. 262–279. DOI: 10.1007/978-3-030-78946-6_14.

[79]   C. Zöllner, M. Barkowsky, M. Maximova, M. Schneider, and H. Giese. "A Simulator for Probabilistic Timed Graph Transformation Systems with Complex Large-Scale Topologies". In: *Graph Transformation - 13th International Conference, ICGT 2020, Held as Part of STAF 2020, Bergen, Norway, June 25-26, 2020, Proceedings*. Ed. by F. Gadducci and T. Kehrer. Vol. 12150. Lecture Notes in Computer Science. Springer, 2020, pp. 325–334. DOI: 10.1007/978-3-030-51372-6_20.

Prove your Colorings: Formal Verification of Cache Coloring of Bao Hypervisor

Axel Ferréol [ID], Laurent Corbin [ID], and Nikolai Kosmatov[(✉)] [ID]

Thales Research & Technology, Palaiseau, France
{axel.ferreol,laurent.corbin,nikolai.kosmatov}@thalesgroup.com

Abstract. Hypervisors allow sharing of computing resources between applications—possibly of various levels of criticality—that makes them increasingly relevant for modern embedded systems. In this context, memory isolation properties (including low-level cache isolation) are essential to guarantee. This paper presents a case study on formal verification of the cache coloring mechanism implemented in the Bao hypervisor. It proposes an original technique for coloring memory pages and assigning to each virtual machine only pages of certain colors, aimed to provide strong isolation guarantees. The implementation presents several challenges for formal verification, such as bit-level operations, complex arithmetic operations, multiple levels of nested loops, and linked lists. We identify two subtle bugs in the existing implementation breaking the expected guarantees, and propose bug fixes. We provide formal specification for the key functions of the mechanism and verify their (fixed) version in the Frama-C verification platform with a few lemmas proved in the Coq proof assistant. We present our specification choices, verification approach and obtained results. Finally, we outline possible optimizations of the current implementation.

Keywords: deductive verification, Frama-C, cache coloring, Bao hypervisor, memory pages, Coq.

1 Introduction

Hypervisors allow a host system to support multiple guest systems (*virtual machines*, or VMs) by virtually sharing its resources, such as memory and processing. Already intensively used in some domains (e.g. cloud infrastructures), hypervisors become highly relevant today for *critical embedded systems* due to an increasing number of necessary functions and features. Numerous functions have already been added to embedded systems, such as driver assistance or sensor management, and more functions need to be integrated today, for example, artificial intelligence (AI) solutions for mission-critical systems, or further entertainment and connectivity features. In many contexts, it is not possible to add more hardware because of size, weight and cost constraints. To enable this integration, it is necessary to share the same hardware between several functions (or systems), often with different levels of criticality. It can be achieved thanks to virtualization, when each system runs on a separate VM.

© The Author(s) 2025
A. Boronat and G. Fraser (Eds.): FASE 2025, LNCS 15693, pp.214–235, 2025.
https://doi.org/10.1007/978-3-031-90900-9_11

Hardware resources can be shared by the hypervisor in two ways: (i) *time sharing:* each VM has access to all resources in turn, i.e. VMs are scheduled; (ii) *partitioning:* each VM has access only to the part of resources dedicated to it. Time sharing requires a more complex and resource-hungry hypervisor, due to the scheduling function. That is why partitioning-based hypervisors (called *static hypervisors*) are more widely used in embedded systems. Static hypervisors allocate all hardware resources to VMs during the hypervisor start-up, so that each resource is allocated to only one VM. In addition, each VM has direct access to its resources, without interception by the hypervisor, which is particularly important for real-time systems. Thus, a static hypervisor seems to be an ideal solution for mixed-criticality systems.

However, some resources must be shared, such as *processor last-level cache* (LLC), which is by definition shared between several cores, each one possibly running a different VM. To tackle this problem, some static hypervisors implement *cache coloring*. The main idea is to split cache—without specific hardware—into several areas, each associated with a color. A color can then be associated with a VM, so that the data of memory pages used by this VM can be stored only in the cache area of the same color. The underlying implementation becomes more complex and highly critical, and its correctness is essential to guarantee.

The purpose of this work is formal verification of the cache coloring mechanism implemented in Bao [1,37], an open-source static hypervisor used in embedded systems. While it proposes an elegant optimized implementation, its code is also challenging for formal verification because it contains non-trivial logic, bit-level operations, complex arithmetic operations, multiple levels of nested loops, and linked lists. During this case study, we identified two subtle bugs[1] in the existing implementation breaking the expected guarantees, and proposed bug fixes[2]. We provide formal specification for the key functions of the mechanism and verify their (fixed) version in the **Frama-C** verification platform [31,10,33]. The proof requires carefully chosen predicates, ghost code, non-trivial loop invariants and lemmas. Some proof goals are not proved by automatic solvers: we prove them interactively (in **Frama-C** or in the **Coq** proof assistant [40,13]). We present our specification choices, verification approach and obtained results, and outline possible further optimizations of the current code.

Contributions. The contributions of this work include:

- a pedagogical presentation of the cache coloring mechanism of Bao;
- an identification of some subtle bugs in its implementation and proposals of bug fixes, as well as suggestions of possible further optimizations;
- formal specification and verification of a subset of (fixed) real-life code of this mechanism in **Frama-C**, publicly available via a companion artifact [27];
- an overview of key specification choices, verification solutions and results.

---

[1] present in the code since 2020 (commit d840da).

[2] Shortly before the final submission of this paper, the authors reported the bugs and the suggested fixes to Bao developers, who integrated the proposed fixes into the code (commit ee73f7e in the Bao repository [1] on January 6, 2025).

In a broader sense, this work promotes rigorous software engineering approaches, contributes to an empirical evaluation of modern verification tools, and enriches the record of successful formal verification case studies for critical real-life code in industrially relevant contexts.

Outline. Section 2 presents Frama-C. Bao and cache coloring are described in Sect. 3. The considered implementation is presented in Sect. 4. Section 5 presents the bugs, suggested fixes and optimizations. Section 6 describes key specification choices, verification solutions and results. Finally, Sect. 7 provides some related work and concludes the paper.

2   Frama-C Verification Platform

Frama-C [31,10,33] is an open-source verification platform for C code. It offers various plugins along with a kernel providing basic services for source-code parsing and analysis. The program under analysis can be annotated in ACSL (ANSI/ISO C Specification Language) [11,33], a formal specification language for C, that allows users to express functional properties of programs in the form of *annotations*, such as assertions or function contracts, written in special comments `/*@...*/` and `//@...` . A function contract includes pre- and postconditions (resp., **requires** and **ensures** clauses) expressing properties that must hold, resp., before and after a call to the function. It also includes an **assigns** clause listing (non-local) variables and memory locations that the function is allowed to modify. The **terminates** `\true` clause specifies that the function must terminate. Users can add *ghost code*, used only for verification purposes and written in annotations `/*@ ghost ... */`. Ghost code can also contain annotations, written in special comments `/@...@/` and `//@...` . ACSL offers built-in predicates and logic functions to express frequent properties such as pointer validity or memory separation, and provides different ways to define new predicates and logic functions. As it is often done, in this document some ACSL notation (e.g. `\forall`, `integer`, `==>`, `<=`, `!=`) is pretty-printed (resp., as $\forall$, $\mathbb{Z}$, $\Rightarrow$, $\leq$, $\neq$).

Frama-C offers a deductive verification plugin called Wp [33] . Given a C program annotated in ACSL, Wp generates the corresponding *proof obligations* (also called *proof goals* or *verification conditions*) that can be proved either by Wp itself, or (through the Why3 platform [28]) by SMT solvers [20,14,9] or an interactive proof assistant like Coq [40,13]. To ensure the absence of runtime errors (RTE), Wp can automatically add necessary assertions and try to prove them as well. In this work, we chose to use Frama-C/Wp due to its capacity to perform deductive verification of industrial C code with successful verification case studies [23] and the fact that it is currently the only tool for C source code verification recognized by ANSSI, the French Common Criteria certification body, as an acceptable formal verification technique for the highest certification levels EAL6–EAL7 [24].

3   The Bao Hypervisor and Cache Coloring

The cache issue. Caches in modern CPUs are organized in levels: each core has a first-level cache, and the data in these caches are replicated in (possibly several levels of) higher-level caches until last-level cache (LLC), shared by all cores. While data from a given page is always stored in the same cache area, the memory-to-cache mapping is not bijective: data from different memory addresses can end up being stored in the same cache area. This reduces isolation guarantees and can potentially increase the risk of (e.g. side-channel) attacks. Moreover, memory addresses mapped to the same cache set compete for space. If a VM running on one core frequently accesses a large amount of data, it can monopolize the shared cache, slowing down other VMs running on nearby cores. This is a serious issue for real-time applications. To prevent this, the hypervisor must ensure that memory pages assigned to different VMs do not overlap in cache.

Cache coloring. Cache coloring is a technique that assigns colors to memory pages such that pages of the same color compete for the same cache sets, while pages of different colors do not compete for the same cache sets. In essence, cache coloring segments the main memory based on cache segmentation. The minimum number of colors is one (i.e., no cache coloring), and the maximum is determined by the number of cache sets of the different caches.

When a hypervisor assigns a unique color to each virtual machine—meaning a VM is loaded exclusively on pages of its color that have not been allocated to other VMs—it ensures that: (i) VMs cannot access each other's data since they reside on separate pages in memory; (ii) VMs do not compete for the same cache sets because their data is stored in cache sets of different colors. Thereby, cache coloring is essential for memory isolation.

Bao. Bao [1,37] is a lightweight open-source static hypervisor specifically designed for embedded systems and real-time applications. It focuses on providing strong isolation between VMs and ensuring real-time guarantees, being thus particularly well-suited for environments where both performance and reliability are critical. Bao elegantly implements a general version of cache coloring where the uniqueness property can be relaxed, that is, each VM accepts a subset of colors. It is crucial to ensure correctness of this implementation, that makes it a highly relevant target for formal verification.

4   Implementation of Cache Coloring in Bao

This section presents an overview of the cache coloring mechanism in the Bao hypervisor (see the real-life code in [1]), and a simplified version of its key functions (given in Fig. 3). Several syntactical changes were realized to make the real-life code more compact and clearer for the paper. The only semantic change is the removal of lock and unlock instructions (in the beginning and the end of function pp_next_clr) used to prevent concurrent modifications of a page pool and page allocation statuses, which are classic and orthogonal to our main scope. The semantics of other instructions (with all real-life code optimizations and bit-level operations) was carefully preserved.

4.1   Overview of the Implementation

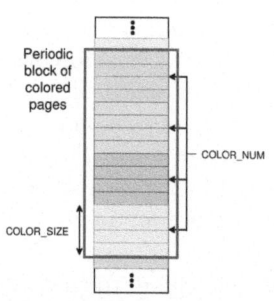

Fig. 1. The main memory layout in Bao with cache coloring, where the periodic block of colors is repeated to engender the coloring of pages for the whole memory.

When the option to use cache coloring is activated, Bao calculates during the boot the number of colors allowed by the hardware. Then, it attributes to every page a single color depending on the page number, so that its data is mapped to a cache area of the same color. COLOR_SIZE denotes the number of contiguous pages of the same color in memory, while COLOR_NUM represents the number of different colors in memory. In other words, pages are colored into the same color by consecutive groups of COLOR_SIZE pages, and the colors of the groups follow a constant sequence that loops every COLOR_NUM groups. Thus, the main memory is colored following a specific pattern—a periodic block of COLOR_NUM*COLOR_SIZE pages—as illustrated in Fig. 1 (where both constants are equal to 4, so the block contains 16 pages).

In a configuration file, for each VM, the user specifies a set of (possibly several) acceptable colors for pages where the VM will be loaded. When loading a VM, Bao maps the VM's address space into free pages of acceptable colors.

1	Page p7
0	Page p6
0	Page p5
0	Page p4
1	Page p3
0	Page p2
0	Page p1
1	Page p0

0 free page   1 allocated page

Fig. 2. Example of a pool of memory pages where COLOR_SIZE equals to 1 and COLOR_NUM equals to 2.

The allocation of suitably-colored pages is handled by function pp_alloc_clr (detailed below). It searches for a set $\{p_1, \ldots, p_n\}$ of a required number n of free consecutive pages of acceptable colors $c_1, \ldots, c_k$. To formalize these requirements for selected pages, it is convenient to introduce the notion of a *pset* (pronounced as *p-set*).

A set of pages $\{p_1, \ldots, p_n\}$ is called a *pset* of n pages for acceptable colors $c_1, \ldots, c_k$ if: (i) each page p_i in the set has one of the acceptable colors $c_1, \ldots, c_k$; (ii) the pages of the set are (colorwise) consecutive, that is, there does not exist a non-selected page of an acceptable color between two selected ones (notice that there may exist a non-selected page between two selected pages if its color is not acceptable). We say that the pset is *free* if in addition: (iii) each page p_i in the set is free. We say that the pset is *in* (or *inside*) a pool of pages if: (iv) each page p_i belongs to the pool.

In this terminology, function pp_alloc_clr searches for *a free pset of a given size* n *for given acceptable colors* $c_1, \ldots, c_k$ *inside a given pool of pages*. When the conditions are clear from the context, we may drop them and just say "a (free) pset".

For example, in the pool of 8 pages shown in Fig. 2, the set $\{p_2, p_4, p_6\}$ forms a free pset of size 3 for the yellow color; the set $\{p_1, p_3\}$ does not form a free pset of size 2 for the blue color (since p_3 is not free); while $\{p_1, p_5\}$ is not a pset of size 2 for the blue color, as (ii) fails (page p_3 is in-between).

Bao developers chose to search only for consecutive pages because it simplifies the process for other functions to access the newly allocated pages: from the starting page of a pset of size n, function pp_next_clr is iteratively called n times to obtain the first page of an acceptable color (that should return the starting page itself), then the second page of an acceptable color, and so forth (as it will be shown on lines 62–65 in Fig. 3).

Functions bitmap_get and bitmap_set are used, resp., to read and to write the allocation status of a page (allocated if nonzero or free if zero) from a bitmap, in which each bit represents the status of a page.

4.2 Basic Type Definitions and Constants

Lines 2–22 of Fig. 3 define basic types and constants used in the code. P_SIZE denotes the size of a memory page (in bytes). COLOR_NUM and COLOR_SIZE were presented above. CELL_SIZE defines the number of bits in an array cell of type u32, which will be used for a compact storage of bits in a bitmap (defined as an array of type u32*).

The page_pool structure (lines 5–11) represents a *pool of pages*, that is, a contiguous memory area, starting at the page address base and containing size pages. Each page is marked as free or allocated using the corresponding bit in bitmap. For heuristic purposes, the field last records the page that follows the last page of the last allocated pset. Field node is used (in higher-level functions) to link several pools into a linked list. Some other fields unrelated to the scope of this work were removed in this paper for simplicity (but this simplification does not impact the proof results).

A set of colors is encoded as a 64-bit unsigned integer, called a *vector* of colors, in which the i-th bit is set if the i-th color is authorized. The ppages structure (lines 12–16) is used to store a pset, described by the first page's address base, the number of pages num_pages and the vector of acceptable colors colors.

4.3 Implementation of pp_next_clr

Function pp_next_clr (see Fig. 3, lines 23–29) looks for a first suitably-colored page starting from a given page. This function takes as arguments the address of a base page base, an offset from (in terms of page numbers with respect to the base page) of the starting page of the search, and a color vector colors indicating the acceptable colors. It returns the offset (again, in terms of page numbers with respect to the base page) of the first page whose color is one of the acceptable colors specified in the color vector. Notice that while the base page base is given by its address, the starting page and the returned page are identified by their page number offsets (with respect to the number of the base page) and not their address offsets. The page number of the base page with address base is

```
 1  #include <limits.h>
 2  typedef unsigned char  u8;
 3  typedef unsigned int   u32;
 4  typedef unsigned long  u64;
 5  typedef struct page_pool {
 6    struct page_pool *node;
 7    u64 base;
 8    u64 size;
 9    u64 last;
10    u32 *bitmap;
11  } page_pool;
```

```
12  typedef struct {
13    u64 base;
14    u64 num_pages;
15    u64 colors;
16  } ppages;
17  #define P_SIZE (0x1000)
18  #define CELL_SIZE (sizeof(u32) * 8)
19  u64 COLOR_NUM;
20  u64 COLOR_SIZE;
21  #define P_NB(addr) ((addr)/P_SIZE)
22  #define P_NB_MAX (1UL << 52)
```

```
23  u64 pp_next_clr(u64 base, u64 from, u64 colors){
24    u64 clr_offset = (base / P_SIZE) % (COLOR_NUM * COLOR_SIZE);
25    u64 index = from;
26    while (!(((colors >> ((clr_offset + index) / COLOR_SIZE % COLOR_NUM)) & 1))
27      index++;
28    return index;
29  }
30
31  u32 bitmap_get(u32 *map, u64 bit){
32    return (map[bit / CELL_SIZE] & (1U << (bit % CELL_SIZE))) ? 1U : 0U;
33  }
34
35  void bitmap_set(u32 *map, u64 bit){
36    map[bit / CELL_SIZE] |= 1U << (bit % CELL_SIZE);
37  }
38
39  u8 pp_alloc_clr(page_pool *pool, u64 n, u64 colors, ppages *ppages){
40    u64 allocated = 0;
41    u64 first_index = 0;
42    u8  ok = 0;
43    ppages->colors = colors;
44    ppages->num_pages = 0;
45    u64 index = pp_next_clr(pool->base, pool->last, colors);
46    u64 top = pool->size;
47    for (u64 i = 0; i < 2 ∧ !ok; i++){
48      while ((allocated < n) ∧ (index < top)){
49        allocated = 0;
50        while ((index < top) ∧ bitmap_get(pool->bitmap, index))
51          index = pp_next_clr(pool->base, ++index, colors);
52        first_index = index;
53        while ((index<top)∧(bitmap_get(pool->bitmap,index)==0)∧(allocated<n)){
54          allocated++;
55          index = pp_next_clr(pool->base, ++index, colors);
56        }
57        index++;                    // FIX: remove this line
58      }
59      if (allocated == n){
60        ppages->num_pages = n;
61        ppages->base = pool->base + (first_index * P_SIZE);
62        for (u64 j = 0; j < n; j++){
63          first_index = pp_next_clr(pool->base, first_index, colors);
64          bitmap_set(pool->bitmap, first_index++);
65        }
66        pool->last = first_index;
67        ok = 1;
68        break;
69      }
70      else {
71        index = 0;                  // FIX: replace this line by the next one
72        // index = pp_next_clr(pool->base, 0, colors);
73      }
74    }
75    return ok;
76  }
```

Fig. 3. Simplified code of the cache coloring mechanism in Bao.

base / P_SIZE, while the starting page defined by the number offset from has page number base / P_SIZE + from and address base + from * P_SIZE.

Calculation of the color of a page. In Bao, the cache coloring mechanism defines the color of a page with page number PNum through the formula:

$$\text{PNum / COLOR\_SIZE \% COLOR\_NUM.} \qquad \text{(A)}$$

The function keeps track of the offset of the current candidate page in the variable index, initialized to from, see line 25. The page number of the current page is base / P_SIZE + index and its color is naturally calculated as:

$$\text{(base / P\_SIZE + index) / COLOR\_SIZE \% COLOR\_NUM.} \qquad \text{(B)}$$

However, since the function frequently calculates this formula, it performs an optimization to calculate the color as[3]:

$$\text{(clr\_offset + index) / COLOR\_SIZE \% COLOR\_NUM,} \qquad \text{(C)}$$

where clr_offset is the (page number) offset of the base page with respect to the beginning of its periodic block of colored pages, defined on line 24.

Going through the pages. To find the next suitably-colored page, the function iterates over the pages (through the loop on lines 26–27), starting from the index from (line 25), each time checking if the color is acceptable using a bit shift of the color vector. The color c is acceptable if and only if !((colors >>c) & 1) (line 26). Once a page with an acceptable color is found, the loop condition fails, and the function returns the offset of the found page on line 28.

Callers always check that the color vector colors contains (hence, accepts) at least one existing color, which ensures the termination of the loop as it will eventually find a page of an acceptable color. Notice that the function does not guarantee that the returned page belongs to the valid range of page indices; this verification is supposed to be done in the upper-level functions.

4.4   Implementation of bitmap_get and bitmap_set

Function bitmap_get (see Fig. 3, lines 31–33) checks the allocation status of pages encoded by a bitmap. It takes two arguments: a bitmap map and a bit number bit, and returns 1 if the bit-th bit is set in map, and 0 otherwise. The bit-th bit is contained in the cell of index bit / CELL_SIZE, at offset bit % CELL_SIZE. This explains the calculation on line 32. Similarly, function bitmap_set (line 35–37) updates the allocation status of a page.

4.5   Implementation of pp_alloc_clr

Function pp_alloc_clr (see Fig. 3, lines 39–76) searches for a given number of free consecutive pages of acceptable colors in a given page pool, that is, a free pset. The function takes four arguments: a pointer to a pool structure pool, the number of pages n, a vector colors of acceptable colors, and a pointer to a physical page structure ppages to store the result of the search. In case of success, it returns (inside the structure) the number of pages n and the address of the first page; otherwise, it sets the number of pages to 0.

---

[3] We show below (in lemma arith_1 in Sect. 6.4) that (B) and (C) are equal.

The variable `index` contains the number offset of the current candidate page (with respect to the base page of the pool). The search proceeds in two phases performed by two iterations of the loop on lines 47–74. During the first phase (`i==0`), it starts by searching the first page of an acceptable color from the page with number offset `last` (cf. line 45). Recall that `last` stores the page that follows the last page of the last pset found by the function. The intuition behind this heuristic is that starting from the `last` page is on average more efficient than starting always from the beginning of the pool, because after several allocations the pages in the beginning of the pool will be more likely to be already allocated. To be exhaustive, the second phase (`i==1`) starts from the beginning (line 71).

In each phase, the loop on lines 48–58 scans for free psets. It stops either when it finds a free pset of size n of acceptable colors or when the current candidate page runs outside the pool (cf. lines 46, 48).

To find such a pset, the function first searches for the first free page of an acceptable color, as shown in the loop on lines 50–51. If the candidate page has already been allocated (line 50), the function moves to the next candidate page of an acceptable color (line 51). The loop continues until it finds a free page of an acceptable color or the current candidate page runs outside the pool.

If the first page is within the pool and free, the loop on lines 53–56 verifies that the next `n-1` consecutive pages of acceptable colors are also within the pool and free. As long as n suitable pages are not yet found, the loop condition checks that the previously found page is free and belongs to the pool (line 53), and the loop body identifies the following page of an acceptable color (line 55). The number of already found pages is maintained in the counter `allocated` (cf. lines 40, 49, 54).

The iteration of the loop on lines 48–58 stops when it has found n pages (that is, a free pset is found) or when the candidate page is outside the pool or allocated. If the candidate page is allocated, the search for a new pset restarts just after the last candidate page, as shown on line 55. (The fixes for lines 57 and 71 are discussed in Sect. 5.)

If the function successfully finds n pages (line 59), it marks these pages as allocated (loop on lines 62–65), updates the number of allocated pages to n (line 60), sets the address of the first page in `ppages` (line 61), updates the address of the last allocated page of the pool (line 66), and, finally, returns.

If the function does not find n pages, it returns with `ppages` containing zero allocated pages, as set initially on line 44. The function always terminates and examines all pages in the pool (at least in the second phase).

5   Bugs, Corrections and Further Optimizations

Bugs and fixes. The current version of `pp_alloc_clr`, contrary to its intended behavior, does not guarantee that the returned set is indeed a free pset of n pages in the pool. In some intricate cases, depending on the status of the pages, the n-th page might be already in use or outside the pool. The first case may break memory isolation, while the second case may cause the VM to crash.

The bugs reside in the selection of the first page of a candidate pset: the function may choose a first page whose color is not acceptable. Indeed, the loop calculating the first page (lines 50–51) only checks that the page is free, without checking its color. This is sufficient for the very first execution or if the loop has already been executed at least once, as a call to pp_next_clr (resp., on line 45 or 51)—to select the new candidate page—guarantees it has an acceptable color.

However, if the function fails to find a pset of size n, it wrongly starts a new search from the page following the last candidate page (see line 57), whose color may be unacceptable. Additionally, during the second phase, the function starts searching from page index 0 (line 71), which might also have an unacceptable color. In these two faulty cases, if the candidate page is free, it will be selected as the first page of a tentative pset (lines 50–52).

To fix these bugs, we should ensure that the first page has an acceptable color before entering the loop. We propose two bug fixes: we remove line 57 and modify line 71 to index=pp_next_clr(pool->base, 0, colors);. These bugs were discovered during the formal specification step, and the fixed version was formally proved with Wp.

Counterexample. To illustrate the first bug, consider the mock pool of Fig. 2 on which pp_alloc_clr is called to find a free pset of size 2 for the blue color with pool->last==p0. The function will succeed and wrongly return (the address of page) p4 in ppages->base as the first page of a pset. Recall (cf. Sect. 4.1) that in higher-level functions the pages are assigned to a VM via consecutive calls to pp_next_clr starting from the first page (like on lines 62–65). The VM will receive pages p5 and p7, the latter being potentially already allocated to another VM! This counterexample (along with another one, due to the second bug) was formally confirmed in Frama-C with the static value analysis plugin Eva [33]. Eva was used to confirm the undesired situation (described with a few ACSL annotations that were proved by Eva) to avoid any risk of misinterpretation of the code. The counterexamples can be found in the companion artifact [27].

Suggestions of optimizations. It would be sufficient for the second phase in the outer loop on lines 47–74 (cf. Sect. 4.5) to perform the search of the first pset page *until* pool->last, instead of uselessly performing a full search until the end of the pool (and re-exploring the pages tried in the first phase). This can be done, for instance, by adding **if** (i==1 $\wedge$ index $\geq$ pool->last) **return** ok; as a second instruction in the body of the loop on lines 50–51. Another optimization can be to perform direct jumps to the first page of the next color without enumerating all pages (as it is done on lines 26–27 in function pp_next_clr, *very frequently called*). This can be realized e.g. with a *precomputed array of jumps*, based on the number offset of the current page inside its periodic block of colors. We plan to submit these and some other suggestions to Bao developers before integrating them into the code under verification.

```
40  predicate ValidCacheCfg = 0 < COLOR_NUM ≤ 64 ∧ 0 < COLOR_SIZE < P_NB_MAX;
41  predicate IsValidPool(page_pool* pool) =
42    \valid(pool) ∧ 0 ≤ P_NB(pool->base) < P_NB_MAX ∧
43    0 ≤ pool->size < P_NB_MAX ∧ 0 ≤ pool->last ≤ pool->size ∧
44    0 ≤ P_NB(pool->base) + pool->size ≤ P_NB_MAX ∧
45    \valid(pool->bitmap + (0..pool->size/CELL_SIZE)) ∧
46    \separated(pool,&(pool->bitmap[0..pool->size/CELL_SIZE]));
47  predicate flatPoolStatus(page_pool* pool) =
48    \valid_read(pool) ∧ \valid_read(pool->bitmap + (0..pool->size/CELL_SIZE)) ∧
49    \valid_read(&gPStatus[P_NB(pool->base)]..(P_NB(pool->base)+pool->size-1)]) ∧
50    ∀ Z idx; 0 ≤ idx < pool->size ⇒
51      (((pool->bitmap[idx/CELL_SIZE] >> (idx%CELL_SIZE)) & 1)⟺
52        gPStatus[P_NB(pool->base) + idx]);
53  predicate flatClrs(u64 colors) = ∀ Z clr; 0 ≤ clr < 64 ⇒
54    (((colors >> clr) & 1) ⟺ gFlatClrs[clr]);
55  predicate IsInClrs(Z clr) = gFlatClrs[clr] ≠ 0;
56  predicate IsNotInClrs(Z clr) = gFlatClrs[clr] == 0;
57  predicate HasClrPages{L1,L2}(u64* PArr, Z p_base, u64 n) =
58    \at(\valid_read(PArr + (0..n-1)),L2) ∧
59    ∀ Z i; 0 ≤ i < n ⇒ IsInClrs{L1}(P_CLR{L1}(p_base + \at(PArr[i],L2)));
60  predicate NoClrPBtw(Z p_base, Z start, Z end) =
61    ∀ Z index; start ≤ index < end ⇒ IsNotInClrs(P_CLR(p_base + index));
62  predicate HasSeqPages{L1,L2}(u64* PArr, Z p_base, u64 n) =
63    \at(\valid_read(PArr + (0..n-1)),L2) ∧
64    ∀ Z i;  1 ≤ i < n ⇒ \at(PArr[i-1],L2) < \at(PArr[i],L2) ∧
65      NoClrPBtw{L1}(p_base,\at(PArr[i-1],L2)+1,\at(PArr[i],L2));
66  predicate HasPagesInPool{L1,L2}(u64* PArr, page_pool* pool, u64 n) =
67    \at(\valid_read(PArr + (0..n-1)),L2) ∧ \at(\valid_read(pool),L1) ∧
68    ∀ Z i; 0 ≤ i < n ⇒ 0 ≤ \at(PArr[i],L2) < \at(pool->size,L1);
69  predicate PSetInPool{L1,L2}(u64* PArr, page_pool* pool, u64 n, u64 colors) =
70    \at(\valid_read(pool),L1) ∧ flatClrs{L1}(colors) ∧
71    HasPagesInPool{L1,L2}(PArr,pool,n) ∧
72    HasClrPages{L1,L2}(PArr,P_NB(\at(pool->base,L1)),n) ∧
73    HasSeqPages{L1,L2}(PArr,P_NB(\at(pool->base,L1)),n);
74  predicate HasFreePages{L1,L2}(u64* PArr, page_pool* pool, u64 n) =
75    \at(\valid_read(PArr + (0..n-1)),L2) ∧
76    ∀ Z i; 0 ≤ i < n ⇒ \at(gPStatus[P_NB(pool->base)+\at(PArr[i],L2)],L1) == 0;
77  predicate HasAllocPages(u64* PArr, page_pool* pool, u64 n) =
78    \valid_read(PArr + (0..n-1)) ∧
79    ∀ Z i; 0 ≤ i < n ⇒ gPStatus[P_NB(pool->base) + PArr[i]] ≠ 0;
```

Fig. 4. Predicates used in the specification of the cache coloring mechanism of Bao.

6   Verification of Cache Coloring

This section presents key specification and verification points and the results of the case study. Its full annotated code can be found in the companion artifact [27]. We mainly focus in the paper on the verification of the key functions presented in Fig. 3. The specified and verified code also includes a simplified version of two higher-level functions (pp_alloc_ppages and mem_map), which were verified to get confidence in consistency of the proposed contracts for the key functions with the expected behavior in the callers. For an easier navigation, unless otherwise stated, the line numbers in the figures and text below are kept as in the full annotated code.

6.1   Basic Predicates and Flattening Invariants

In this case study (cf. Fig. 3, lines 17, 22), we consider a 64-bit implementation with 2^{12}-byte pages and a maximum number of pages of 2^{52}, which aligns with the maximum number of pages supported by most 64-bit architectures. Additionally, we consider 64-bit long color vectors, which sets the maximal number of colors to 64 accordingly, and we do not impose any prior constraints on COLOR_SIZE to ensure compatibility with a wide range of hardware configurations, as specified in the definition of predicate ValidCacheCfg (Fig. 4, line 40).

Predicate IsValidPool (line 41) ensures that pool represents a valid segment of memory, and that its bitmap is sufficiently large to store the status of its pages and does not overlap with the pool structure. Macros P_NB and P_NB_MAX were defined in Fig. 3, lines 21–22.

Earlier verification efforts with Frama-C (e.g. [23]) demonstrated that reasoning on array cells instead of bits makes solvers *more efficient*. We introduce a global companion ghost array u8 gPStatus[P_NB_MAX] to store page allocation statuses, and express the equivalence between a bitmap and the companion array with predicate flatPoolStatus (Fig. 4, line 47). It guarantees that checking the i-th bit in the bitmap is equivalent to checking the i-th cell in gPStatus. A starting letter g (e.g. in gPStatus) indicates a ghost variable name in this work.

Similarly, we introduce a global companion ghost array u8 gFlatClrs[64] to flatten the color vector (unchanged in our scope[4]), and express the equivalence between a color vector and the companion array with predicate flatClrs (line 53), i.e. that checking the i-th bit in color vector clrs is equivalent to checking the i-th cell in gFlatClrs. Maintaining such *flattening invariants* in contracts enables expressing properties on array cells instead of bits.

Predicates IsInClrs and IsNotInClrs (lines 55, 56) state that color clr is, resp., acceptable and unacceptable w.r.t. the color vector encoded in gFlatClrs.

Predicate HasClrPages (line 57) states that array PArr of size n contains page number offsets (with respect to the base page p_base) of pages with acceptable colors. Labels L1 and L2 characterize, resp., the moment of calculation of the color and of reading the cell in PArr. Such a distinction of labels will often be used in predicates below. Logic function P_CLR(PNum) computes the color of a given page as in (A) in Sect. 4.2. Predicate NoClrPBtw (line 60) states that there is no page of an acceptable color with number offset between start and end (excluded) with respect to p_base.

Predicate HasSeqPages (line 62) ensures that page number offsets stored in array PArr of size n are in ascending order, and any other page between them does not have an acceptable color. Predicate HasPagesInPool (line 66) states that page number offsets stored in array PArr of size n are within the memory pool pointed to by pool.

Predicate PSetInPool (line 69) states that the page number offsets stored in array PArr of size n are within the memory pool pointed to by pool, consecutive and of an acceptable color. In other words, array PArr is a pset of size n for colors inside pool.

Predicate HasFreePages (line 74) states that pages with page number offsets stored in array PArr of size n are free according to gPStatus. Likewise, predicate HasAllocPages (line 77) states that those pages are allocated.

---

[4] this is not a limitation for larger scopes: such arrays can be ghost function arguments.

```
144    requires ValidCacheCfg;
145    requires 0 ≤ from < P_NB_MAX;
146    requires flatClrs(colors);
147    requires \valid_read(gFlatClrs + (0..63));
148    requires 0 ≤ gClrValid < COLOR_NUM ∧ IsInClrs(gClrValid);
149    terminates \true;
150    assigns \nothing;
151    ensures flatClrs(colors);
152    ensures clr: IsInClrs(P_CLR(P_NB(base) + \result));
153    ensures cons: NoClrPBtw(P_NB(base),from,\result);
154    ensures bnd: from ≤ \result < from + COLOR_NUM*COLOR_SIZE;
```

Fig. 5. Contract of `pp_next_clr`.

In order to verify the code with the deductive verification plugin Wp of Frama-C, we provide an ACSL specification for each of the considered functions. We overview here the contracts of `pp_next_clr` and `pp_alloc_clr`.

6.2 Specification of `pp_next_clr`

Preconditions. Given the scope of our verification, we bound the range of the page number offset `from` between 0 and 2^{52} (excluded), assuming there can be a single memory pool supporting up to 2^{52} pages (Fig. 5, line 145). We did not need to impose specific constraints on the address `base` since we are considering 12-bit wide pages and 52-bit wide page numbers, so the address is naturally bounded by its type. Predicate `ValidCacheCfg` (line 144) specifies the considered arithmetic constraints. The equivalence between the color vector and the companion array must hold before and after the call (lines 146, 151). Finally, recall that callers ensure that the color vector accepts at least one color (cf. Sect. 4.3). To guarantee termination, we express this constraint on line 148, where the existential property is replaced by a witness—a global ghost variable `gClrValid`—since this value will be used in ghost code inside the function. We preferred this (simple and sufficient) option for our scope to the alternative when a witness has to be found inside the function from an existential precondition.

Postconditions. We express that the function always terminates (line 149) and does not modify the memory (line 150). Finally, we express the functional properties. The returned page has an acceptable color (line 152) and is the closest page with this property to `from`, the starting page of the search (line 153); Line 154 gives an interval of values for the result, a maximum offset being the size of a color block (line 154). This upper bound is tight[5] and suffices to prove the absence of overflows during the update of `index`.

6.3 Specification of `pp_alloc_clr`

Preconditions. The preconditions (omitted in the paper) are relatively natural and mostly similar to those of `pp_next_clr`. An interval of values is specified for the number of allocated pages `n`, and the validity of `ppages` is required. The validity of `pool` and flattening invariants are present both in preconditions and postconditions (the latter on lines 259–261 in Fig. 6).

---

[5] this upper bound is reached for `COLOR_SIZE==1`.

```
258   ensures res:  \result == 0 ∨ \result == 1;
259   ensures fltc: flatClrs(colors);
260   ensures vldp: IsValidPool(pool);
261   ensures fltp: flatPoolStatus(pool);
```

```
264   ensures suc: PSetInPool{Pre,Pre}((u64*)gExistPSet,pool,n,colors) ∧
265     HasFreePages{Pre,Pre}((u64*)gExistPSet,pool,n) ⇒ \result == 1;
266   ensures wit1: \result == 1 ⇒
267     PSetInPool{Pre,Post}((u64*)gFoundPSet,pool,n,colors);
268   ensures wit2: \result == 1 ⇒
269     HasFreePages{Pre,Post}((u64*)gFoundPSet,pool,n);
270   ensures fct1: \result == 1 ⇒
271     PSetInPool{Post,Post}((u64*)gFoundPSet,pool,n,colors);
272   ensures fct2: \result == 1 ⇒ HasAllocPages((u64*)gFoundPSet,pool,n);
273   ensures pps: \result == 1 ⇒  ppages->num_pages == n ∧
274     ppages->base == pool->base + (gFoundPSet[0]*P_SIZE);
```

```
279   ensures ppf: \result == 0 ⇒ ppages->num_pages == 0;
280   ensures ups: \result == 0 ⇒ ∀ ℤ i; 0 ≤ i < P_NB_MAX ⇒
281     \at(gPStatus[i],Pre) == \at(gPStatus[i],Post);
282   ensures upp: \result == 0 ⇒ \at(pool,Pre) == \at(pool,Post) ∧
283     \at(*pool,Pre) == \at(*pool,Post);
```

Fig. 6. Selected postconditions of the contract of `pp_alloc_clr`.

Additionally, we had to add a dozen of explicit *separation clauses* (omitted in the paper) between the arguments and the ghost variables. Some of these separation predicates are likely to become unnecessary in a future version of Frama-C/Wp that will be capable to deduce that the modification of ghost variables cannot impact non-ghost variables, and vice versa.

Postconditions. At the end of the function, there are two possible return values, 0 and 1 (line 258). Other notable postconditions fall into two categories: those for the success case and those for the failure case.

Predicates that hold on success (when the function returns 1) must ensure that subsequent calls in the callers (cf. Sect. 4.1) to `pp_next_clr` starting from the first allocated page—the only page returned in `ppages`—will really return pages of a required pset in the pool (whose pages were *free before the call* and then *marked as allocated* by the function). Since ACSL does not allow using the C function `pp_next_clr` in the specification, we used predicates over the selected pages. We capture these pages by their number offsets (with respect to the starting page of the pool) in a global ghost array u64 `gFoundPSet[P_NB_MAX]`, by adding ghost code into the function. It is another illustration of an *advantageous usage of ghost code artifacts* for the specificaiton.

Precisely, we state that n pages in `gFoundPSet` were free before the call (lines 268–269) and are now allocated (line 272); and constitute a pset of size n for colors (line 270–271). Moreover the `ppages` structure must contain n pages and store the page address corresponding to the first cell of the `gFoundPSet` (line 273–274).

In case of a failure, the function returns 0 (line 279), it has not modified the page status array (lines 280–281) nor the pool (line 282–283).

Specification completeness. The completeness and disjointness of the two cases of the specification was non-trivial to ensure because of the complexity of the calling cases: either there exists a suitable subset of pages—free pset—on entry, or not. As the size of the subset depends on an argument of the function, the conditions involve an undetermined number of pages. Expressing such properties with an undetermined number of quantifiers is not directly allowed in ACSL and would only be possible indirectly (e.g. with a list, an array, or a set). However, since solvers often have issues with complex conditions involving multiple quantifiers, we decided to adopt another, more pragmatic approach.

We decided to represent the existence of a suitable subset of pages through the existence of a witness array containing the number offsets of the pages. Thus, we stated the existence case assumption by giving a witness pset in a global companion ghost array u64 gExistPSet[P_NB_MAX], see lines 264–265. This establishes that the function returns 1 in this case. But this unique implication is not sufficient: the function could still return 0 while a suitable free pset existed *on entry*.

That is why we added another clause (lines 266–267) stating that the companion ghost array gFoundPSet mentioned above—*with its values on exit*—was a suitable pset (of size n with acceptable colors inside pool) *already on entry*. Along with lines 268–269, we deduce a condition similar to that on the left of the implication on lines 264–265.

Recall that the first label indicates when the property is evaluated while the second label indicates at which state the array values are read. Notice that, while the aforementioned clause on lines 270–271 looks similar, strictly speaking, it does not directly state the same property as on lines 266–267, since it considers the property at label **Post** instead of **Pre** (the values of gFoundPSet being, of course, considered at **Post** in both cases as it is computed during the function).

Therefore, we can deduce that the function returns 1 *if and only if* a suitable subset of pages existed *on entry, before the call*. As the function can only return 0 or 1 (line 258), our specification of both cases is complete and disjoint.

We did not use ACSL behaviors because Frama-C would not be capable to prove that behaviors are complete and disjoint for this version of specification. That is why we justify it here with an additional argument, external to Frama-C.

6.4   Selected Aspects and Difficulties of the Proof

The proof required *carefully chosen* predicates, ghost code and ghost variables, loop invariants, assertions and lemmas. The predicates, ghost variables and our approach to ensure the *completeness of the specification* of pp_alloc_clr were presented above. A companion ghost model and flattening invariants helped to efficiently deal with *bit-level operations*. This section presents some other selected aspects and verification choices.

Termination of pp_next_clr. To prove termination, we compute (in ghost code) an upper bound for the number offset index using the witness color gClrValid. We distinguish two cases of relative position of the starting page in its periodic

```
337    loop invariant I3_ex:
338        PSetInPool{Pre,Pre}((u64*)gExistPSet,pool,n,colors) ∧
339        HasFreePages{Pre,Pre}((u64*)gExistPSet,pool,n) ∧
340        i == 1 ∧ allocated < n ⇒ index ≤ gExistPSet[0];
```

```
371    loop invariant I1_ex:
372        PSetInPool{Pre,Pre}((u64*)gExistPSet,pool,n,colors) ∧
373        HasFreePages{Pre,Pre}((u64*)gExistPSet,pool,n) ∧
374        i == 1 ∧ allocated < n ∧ gExistPSet[0] ≤ index ⇒
375        (∃ ℤ i; 0 ≤ i ≤ allocated ∧ gExistPSet[i] == index);
```

Fig. 7. Loop invariants for the loops on lines 48–58 (above) and lines 53–56 (below) of pp_alloc_clr (in Fig. 3), used to prove the success when a pset exists on entry.

```
120    lemma arith_1: ∀ ℤ a,b,c,d; 0 ≤ a ∧ 0 ≤ b ∧ 0 < c ∧ 0 < d ⇒
121        ((a+b)/c)%d == ((a+b%(c*d))/c)%d;
```

Fig. 8. One of the four arithmetic lemmas used in the proof of pp_next_clr.

color block: either its color lies before the existing acceptable color gClrValid or after it in (in the latter case, the upper bound is in the next color block).

Proof of pp_alloc_clr. With three levels of nested loops, a significant number of carefully chosen loop invariants was necessary. For instance, to prove that the function finds a pset in case there exists a suitable pset in the pool (lines 264–265), we have to ensure that if such a pset exists in the pool, then it is located in the part of the pool the function has not explored so far. Thus, if the function fails to find such a pset after going through the entire pool, then the existing pset must be located outside the memory, which is contradictory. Due to the structure of the function, we express this property in the main loop and then recursively in the nested loops to have it preserved. Figure 7 shows the invariants for two of them. We constrain only the second phase since it runs—in the current version—a full search from the beginning of the pool, that explains the condition i==1. The second invariant is relatively tricky. Indeed, the loop on lines 53–56 in Fig. 3—that attempts to complete a previously identified first page to a full pset—may possibly find the witness pset pExistPSet or another existing pset starting before it. To address this, we adjust the loop invariant by stating that *we did not miss the witness pset* pExistPSet: if the current candidate page is greater or equal to the first page of pExistPSet, then it lies inside it (line 375).

Arithmetic lemmas. As page colors are computed with modulo and division operations, reasoning about them involves such arithmetic operations. The solvers we used were unable to handle them directly. To address this issue, we introduced four arithmetic lemmas, and had to prove three of them in Coq (see the companion artifact [27] for Coq proof scripts). One lemma, proving the equivalence of (B) and (C) (see Sect. 4.3), is shown in Fig. 8.

Separation issues and Frama-C's memory model. The need for additional separation clauses (in particular, between ghost and non-ghost variables) was already mentioned in Sect. 6.3. In many parts of the code, we also encountered difficulties in proving the preservation of seemingly trivial properties through assignments. These difficulties stem from the memory model used in Frama-C/Wp, where pointers are treated as indices within arrays, where cells correspond to the pointed values. Consequently, properties involving pointers in ACSL are translated into properties over arrays in Wp. When a pointed value is modified, the whole array is seen as possibly modified, making proofs non-trivial for solvers. To prove such properties, we often had to manually create proof scripts in Wp to demonstrate that the pointed values used in predicates remain unchanged through assignments. This process introduced a significant specification and verification overhead making the verification process more complex to maintain.

Semantic lemmas. To show the preservation of the PSetInPool predicate between two program points despite the modification of some variables, a preservation lemma was necessary (lemma PSetInPool_preserved in the companion artifact [27]). While the idea is well-known, a very careful formulation with four labels was necessary since each predicate has two labels. Moreover, its proof required a manually crafted proof script in Wp with carefully selected tactics.

Function pp_next_clr must ensure that the pages of the found free pset eventually become allocated. This task is handled in the loop on lines 62–65 in Fig. 3, which iterates through the found page indices and marks them as allocated. However, the function moves to the next page of the pset by calculating it through a call to pp_next_clr. To ensure that the function gets the same page indices as that of the free pset found earlier, another interesting lemma (lemma unique_next_clr_page in the companion artifact [27]) was necessary.

Linked lists. During the verification of higher-level function pp_alloc_ppages, which looks for a free pset of a given size in a set of pools *represented by a linked list of pools* (as mentioned in Sect. 4.2), an additional difficulty was related to linked lists. Indeed, contrary to simple linked lists, in our case list nodes contain several data fields and pointers to external arrays. Broadly inspired by previous work [15,36,16], this issue was solved using a companion ghost array containing the addresses of the nodes of the linked list and by defining and maintaining a suitable linking predicate, which establishes the link between them. Detailed specifications are available in the companion artifact [27].

Unstable proof scripts in Wp. During the last stages of the case study, we discovered an issue in Frama-C/Wp related to proof scripts. A created script, which leads to a successful proof at the time of its creation, fails with error messages during the proof replay. Presumably, this comes from a different degree of proof goal simplifications during the script creation and the proof replay, resulting in slight differences in the proof goal. This issue has been reported to the Wp team.

6.5   Proof Statistics

This verification case study took approximately three months of intensive work, including understanding the implementation, formal specification, verification, detecting and fixing the bugs, readability improvements and restructuring of the specification for the paper. Formal verification was, initially, carried out on the four key functions: `pp_next_clr`, `bitmap_get`, `bitmap_set` and `pp_alloc_clr`. To ensure the relevance of the proposed contracts, formal specification and verification for simplified versions of two upper-level functions, `mem_alloc_ppages` and `mem_map`, were realized as well, focusing on the mapping of colored pages (and excluding other behavior e.g. when cache coloring is deactivated). The former one searches for a pset in a linked list of pools, while the latter calls the former to assign a pset of pages to a VM. They are not detailed in the paper, but the annotated code is available in the companion artifact [27]. *The claim that formal verification is complete can be demonstrated with the artifact.*

The specified functions total, approximately, 100 lines of C code and 600 lines of ACSL. ACSL annotations include ghost code (20 lines), predicates (100 lines), contracts (455 lines), assertions (30 lines), and lemmas (25 lines).

The proof goals include function contracts, assertions, lemmas, the absence of run-time errors, smoke tests (to detect potential specification inconsistencies), and memory hypotheses made by Wp's typed memory model; they result in 463 proof goals and 60 extra goals for smoke tests; that is, 523 in total.

The proof was carried out with Frama-C v.29.0 and Why3 1.7.2, with the external solvers Alt-Ergo 2.5.4, CVC5 1.0.9 and Z3 4.8.12 (run in that order), and the proof assistant Coq 8.18.0. The proofs were run on a desktop computer running Ubuntu 22.04.5 LTS, with an Intel® Core™ i5-1145G7 CPU @ 2.60 GHz, featuring 4 cores 8 threads, with 32 GB RAM. We ran Frama-C/Wp with options `-wp-par=8` and `-wp-timeout=40`.

The full proof takes approx. 5 minutes. All smoke tests passed. Over the 523 goals[6], around 1% (6) were discharged by control-flow analysis; around 83% of the goals (433) were proved by automatic solvers: the internal simplifier engine Qed of Wp handled around 53% of the goals (277) in an average time of 146ms per goal, then Alt-Ergo discharged around 28% of the goals (147) in an average time of 110ms, CVC5 covered around 5% of the goals (26) in an average time of 725ms, Z3 proved 2% of the goals (9) in an average time of 1.4s. Around 11% of the goals (55) were achieved through proof scripts in Wp, while less than 1% of the goals (3) were proved in Coq. At the end of the case study, when the authors were used to proof contexts, the scripts in Wp required around 5 hours to be fully re-created manually, which was often necessary after code and specification updates. The proof scripts in Coq required a couple of hours to be created manually (and did not need to be re-created after the first attempt).

7   Conclusion and Future Work

Related work. A number of hypervisors are in use today. Some are used in IT infrastructures (e.g cloud) for their flexibility and dynamic resource management such as Xen [6], VMWare [4] or KVM [3]. Others are better suited to critical

---

[6] The per-solver results are given as an indication of a possible proof run, can vary and should not be used to compare solvers or draw any conclusions about their relative efficiency; our purpose was to reach a full proof and not to compare the solvers.

embedded systems such as Xen Dom0-less [5], Jailhouse [2] or Xtratum [7]. In this case, it is the *static resource sharing property* that is exploited. The use of hypervisors in critical embedded systems requires a high level of confidence in resource allocation, and particularly in maintaining *isolation between VMs*. Formal verification has been applied to provide high confidence in some resource allocation systems, such as ProvenCore [17] ans seL4 [32]. To the best of our knowledge, formal verification of cache coloring has never been addressed in previous work.

More generally, this work is related to other verification case studies on real-life code and empirical evaluations of verification tools [29]. Among other examples, the KeY tool was used for verification of several libraries and applications in Java [22,12]. Verification of a traffic tunnel control system [38] was realized with VerCors [8]. Verification for a real-world avionics example [25] and for security properties [23] provided useful feedback on using Frama-C. SPARK was used in the verification of a TCP Stack [19] and complex datastructures [26]. Verification of the Hyper-V hypervisor with VCC [34] highlighted some issues specific to hypervisor verification. Deductive verification of smart contracts [18] was realized with Dafny [35]. Several case studies [39] were performed using VeriFast [30]. Each new case study contributes to enhance verification tools by identifying their limitations and to push further the frontiers of what is achievable for formal verification.

Conclusion. This paper has presented a formal verification case study for an original, industrially relevant and security-critical target—the cache coloring in Bao. We have given its pedagogical presentation and emphasized main aspects of its verification with Frama-C. The target code is very elegant but challenging for deductive verification (containing bit-level operations, non-trivial logic, complex arithmetic operations, multiple nested loops, linked lists). This case study contributes to a better understanding of the capacities of modern deductive verifiers. It also allowed us to identify and fix two bugs in the target code, to suggest its further optimizations, and to discover a minor issue in the verification tool.

Future work. Future work includes the verification of optimized versions of cache coloring and a larger verification of critical parts of the Bao hypervisor, with a long-term goal to reach a highly optimized, provably correct static hypervisor ensuring strong isolation properties and suitable for modern embedded systems. Another work direction is to enhance automatic proof script generation [21].

Data availability statement. The companion artifact [27] contains the annotated code, counterexamples and a virtual machine (with all necessary tools installed), ready to reproduce the proof.

Acknowledgment. Part of this work was supported by ANR (grants ANR-22-CE39-0014, ANR-22-CE25-0018). We warmly thank Téo Bernier for his valuable advice and help, Allan Blanchard, Loïc Correnson and Frédéric Loulergue for fruitful discussions, the whole Frama-C team for their support, and the anonymous referees for helpful comments.

References

1. Bao project, https://github.com/bao-project/bao-hypervisor
2. Jailhouse hypervisor, https://github.com/siemens/jailhouse
3. KVM hypervisor, https://linux-kvm.org/page/Main_Page
4. VmWare hypervisor, https://www.vmware.com
5. Xen   Dom0-less   hypervisor,   https://xenproject.org/2019/12/16/ true-static-partitioning-with-xen-dom0-less/
6. Xen project, https://xenproject.org
7. XtratuM hypervisor, https://www.fentiss.com/xtratum/
8. Armborst, L., Bos, P., van den Haak, L.B., Huisman, M., Rubbens, R., Sakar, Ö., Tasche, P.: The VerCors verifier: A progress report. In: Proc. of the 36th International Conference on Computer Aided Verification (CAV 2024). LNCS, vol. 14682, pp. 3–18. Springer (2024). https://doi.org/10.1007/978-3-031-65630-9_1
9. Barbosa, H., Barrett, C.W., Brain, M., Kremer, G., Lachnitt, H., Mann, M., Mohamed, A., Mohamed, M., Niemetz, A., Nötzli, A., Ozdemir, A., Preiner, M., Reynolds, A., Sheng, Y., Tinelli, C., Zohar, Y.: cvc5: A versatile and industrial-strength SMT solver. In: Proc. of the 28th International Conference on Tools and Algorithms for the Construction and Analysis of Systems (TACAS 2022). LNCS, vol. 13243, pp. 415–442. Springer (2022). https://doi.org/10.1007/978-3-030-99524-9_24
10. Baudin, P., Bobot, F., Bühler, D., Correnson, L., Kirchner, F., Kosmatov, N., Maroneze, A., Perrelle, V., Prevosto, V., Signoles, J., Williams, N.: The dogged pursuit of bug-free C programs: the Frama-C software analysis platform. Commun. ACM 64(8), 56–68 (2021). https://doi.org/10.1145/3470569
11. Baudin, P., Cuoq, P., Filliâtre, J.C., Marché, C., Monate, B., Moy, Y., Prevosto, V.: ACSL: ANSI/ISO C Specification Language, http://frama-c.com/acsl.html
12. Beckert, B., Sanders, P., Ulbrich, M., Wiesler, J., Witt, S.: Formally verifying an efficient sorter. In: Proc. of the 30th International Conference on Tools and Algorithms for the Construction and Analysis of Systems (TACAS 2024). LNCS, vol. 14570, pp. 268–287. Springer (2024). https://doi.org/10.1007/978-3-031-57246-3_15
13. Bertot, Y., Castéran, P. (eds.): Interactive Theorem Proving and Program Development: Coq'Art: The Calculus of Inductive Constructions. Texts in Theoretical Computer Science. An EATCS Series, Springer (2004)
14. Bjørner, N.S.: Z3 and SMT in industrial R&D. In: Proc. of the 22nd International Symposium on Formal Methods (FM 2018). LNCS, vol. 10951, pp. 675–678. Springer (2018). https://doi.org/10.1007/978-3-319-95582-7_44
15. Blanchard, A., Kosmatov, N., Loulergue, F.: Ghosts for lists: A critical module of Contiki verified in Frama-C. In: Proc. of the 10th NASA Formal Methods Symposium (NFM 2018). LNCS, vol. 10811, pp. 37–53. Springer (2018)
16. Blanchard, A., Kosmatov, N., Loulergue, F.: Logic against ghosts: Comparison of two proof approaches for a list module. In: Proc. of the 34th Annual ACM/SIGAPP Symposium on Applied Computing, Software Verification and Testing Track (SAC-SVT 2019). pp. 2186–2195. ACM (2019). https://doi.org/10.1145/3297280.3297495
17. Bolignano, P.: Formal models and verification of memory management in a hypervisor. Ph.D. thesis, Université de Rennes ; Prove & Run (May 2017), https://theses.hal.science/tel-01637937

18. Cassez, F., Fuller, J., Quiles, H.M.A.: Deductive verification of smart contracts with Dafny. In: Proc. of the 27th International Conference on Formal Methods for Industrial Critical Systems (FMICS 2022). LNCS, vol. 13487, pp. 50–66. Springer (2022). https://doi.org/10.1007/978-3-031-15008-1_5

19. Cluzel, G., Georgiou, K., Moy, Y., Zeller, C.: Layered formal verification of a TCP stack. In: Proc. of the IEEE Secure Development Conference (SecDev 2021). pp. 86–93. IEEE (2021). https://doi.org/10.1109/SecDev51306.2021.00028

20. Conchon, S., Coquereau, A., Iguernlala, M., Mebsout, A.: Alt-Ergo 2.2. In: SMT Workshop: International Workshop on Satisfiability Modulo Theories (2018), https://hal.inria.fr/hal-01960203

21. Correnson, L., Blanchard, A., Djoudi, A., Kosmatov, N.: Automate where automation fails: Proof strategies for Frama-C/WP. In: Proc. of the 30th International Conference on Tools and Algorithms for the Construction and Analysis of Systems (TACAS 2024), Held as Part of the European Joint Conferences on Theory and Practice of Software (ETAPS 2024). LNCS, vol. 14570, pp. 331–339. Springer (Apr 2024). https://doi.org/10.1007/978-3-031-57246-3_18

22. de Boer, M., de Gouw, S., Klamroth, J., Jung, C., Ulbrich, M., Weigl, A.: Formal specification and verification of JDK's identity hash map implementation. Formal Aspects Comput. 35(3), 18:1–18:26 (2023). https://doi.org/10.1145/3594729

23. Djoudi, A., Hána, M., Kosmatov, N.: Formal Verification of a JavaCard Virtual Machine with Frama-C. In: Proc. of the 24th International Symposium on Formal Methods (FM 2021). LNCS, vol. 13047, pp. 427–444. Springer (2021). https://doi.org/10.1007/978-3-030-90870-6_23

24. Djoudi, A., Hána, M., Kosmatov, N., Kříženecký, M., Ohayon, F., Mouy, P., Fontaine, A., Féliot, D.: A bottom-up formal verification approach for common criteria certification: Application to JavaCard virtual machine. In: Proc. of the 11th European Congress on Embedded Real-Time Systems (ERTS 2022) (Jun 2022)

25. Dordowsky, F.: An experimental study using ACSL and Frama-C to formulate and verify low-level requirements from a DO-178C compliant avionics project. Electronic Proceedings in Theoretical Computer Science 187, 28–41 (2015). https://doi.org/10.4204/EPTCS.187.3

26. Dross, C., Moy, Y.: Auto-active proof of red-black trees in SPARK. In: Proc. of the 9th International Symposium on NASA Formal Methods (NFM 2017). LNCS, vol. 10227, pp. 68–83 (2017). https://doi.org/10.1007/978-3-319-57288-8_5

27. Ferréol, A., Corbin, L., Kosmatov, N.: Prove your colorings: Formal verification of cache coloring of Bao hypervisor. Companion artifact for the paper submitted to FASE 2025 (2025). https://doi.org/10.5281/zenodo.14616331

28. Filliâtre, J.C., Paskevich, A.: Why3 - where programs meet provers. In: Proc. of the 22nd European Symposium on Programming (ESOP 2013). LNCS, vol. 7792, pp. 125–128. Springer (2013)

29. Hähnle, R., Huisman, M.: Deductive software verification: From pen-and-paper proofs to industrial tools. In: Computing and Software Science – State of the Art and Perspectives, LNCS, vol. 10000, pp. 345–373. Springer (2019). https://doi.org/10.1007/978-3-319-91908-9_18

30. Jacobs, B., Smans, J., Philippaerts, P., Vogels, F., Penninckx, W., Piessens, F.: VeriFast: A powerful, sound, predictable, fast verifier for C and Java. In: Proc. of the Third International Symposium on NASA Formal Methods (NFM 2011). LNCS, vol. 6617, pp. 41–55. Springer (2011). https://doi.org/10.1007/978-3-642-20398-5_4

31. Kirchner, F., Kosmatov, N., Prevosto, V., Signoles, J., Yakobowski, B.: Frama-C: A software analysis perspective. Formal Asp. Comput. **27**(3), 573–609 (2015). https://doi.org/10.1007/s00165-014-0326-7

32. Klein, G., Elphinstone, K., Heiser, G., Andronick, J., Cock, D., Derrin, P., Elka-duwe, D., Engelhardt, K., Kolanski, R., Norrish, M., Sewell, T., Tuch, H., Win-wood, S.: seL4: formal verification of an OS kernel. In: Proc. of the 22nd ACM Symposium on Operating Systems Principles (SOSP 2009). pp. 207–220. ACM (2009). https://doi.org/10.1145/1629575.1629596

33. Kosmatov, N., Prevosto, V., Signoles, J. (eds.): Guide to Software Verification with Frama-C. Core Components, Usages, and Applications. Computer Science Foundations and Applied Logic Book Series, Springer (2024). https://doi.org/10.1007/978-3-031-55608-1

34. Leinenbach, D., Santen, T.: Verifying the microsoft Hyper-V hypervisor with VCC. In: Proc. of the Second World Congres on Formal Methods (FM 2009). LNCS, vol. 5850, pp. 806–809. Springer (2009). https://doi.org/10.1007/978-3-642-05089-3_51

35. Leino, K.R.M.: Program Proofs. The MIT Press (2023)

36. Loulergue, F., Blanchard, A., Kosmatov, N.: Ghosts for lists: from axiomatic to executable specifications. In: Proc. of the 12th International Conference on Tests and Proofs (TAP 2018). LNCS, vol. 10889, pp. 177–184. Springer (2018). https://doi.org/10.1007/978-3-319-92994-1_11

37. Martins, J., Tavares, A., Solieri, M., Bertogna, M., Pinto, S.: Bao: A lightweight static partitioning hypervisor for modern multi-core embedded systems. In: Work-shop on Next Generation Real-Time Embedded Systems (NG-RES 2020). Open Access Series in Informatics (OASIcs), vol. 77, pp. 3:1–3:14. Schloss Dagstuhl – Leibniz-Zentrum für Informatik (2020). https://doi.org/10.4230/OASIcs.NG-RES.2020.3

38. Oortwijn, W., Huisman, M.: Formal verification of an industrial safety-critical traffic tunnel control system. In: Proc. of the 15th International Conference on Integrated Formal Methods (IFM 2019). LNCS, vol. 11918, pp. 418–436. Springer (2019). https://doi.org/10.1007/978-3-030-34968-4_23

39. Philippaerts, P., Mühlberg, J., Penninckx, W., Smans, J., Jacobs, B., Piessens, F.: Software verification with VeriFast: Industrial case studies. Sci. Comput. Program. **82**, 77–97 (2014). https://doi.org/10.1016/J.SCICO.2013.01.006

40. The Coq Development Team: The Coq proof assistant. http://coq.inria.fr,

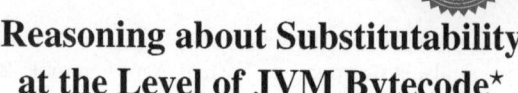

Reasoning about Substitutability at the Level of JVM Bytecode*

Marco Paganoni[1(✉)] and Carlo A. Furia[1]

Software Institute, USI Università della Svizzera italiana, Lugano, Switzerland
marco.paganoni@usi.ch
https://www.bugcounting.net

Abstract. Subtyping in object-oriented languages is widely based on Liskov's substitution principle, which offers static correctness guarantees of type safety while abstracting implementation details. Unfortunately, the type systems of languages like Java cannot statically enforce full behavioral substitutability, and in fact there are numerous examples of libraries some of whose components are related by inheritance but not substitutable (for example, because they do not implement "optional" operations).

In this paper, we present a novel approach to precisely specify and reason about substitutability in JVM languages. A distinctive feature of our approach is that it targets JVM bytecode, as opposed to a program's source code, as it is based on the BYTEBACK deductive verifier. To support reasoning about substitutability, we extended BYTEBACK with ghost specifications, a (restricted) form of class invariants, and substitutability-preserving specification inheritance (precondition weakening and postcondition strengthening). Equipped with these features, BYTE-BACK can now reason precisely about behavioral substitutability violations in a way that is applicable to realistic examples (such as with optional operations of Java's List interface). Our experiments also demonstrate that BYTEBACK can analyze substitutability in programs written in a combination of JVM languages, including multi-language code where Scala or Kotlin code interacts with Java libraries.

1 Introduction

Since Liskov and Wing's influential work [17], behavioral *substitutability* is a widely accepted, fundamental requirement of types related by subtyping—especially relevant for object-oriented programming [20]. Informally, a type T is substitutable for another type S if replacing an instance of S with an instance of T does not break the behavior of the code using it. Thus, a type system that can statically check substitutability combines correctness guarantees (absence of behavioral incompatibility errors) with flexibility (transparently switching between different implementations through polymorphism). This is why most modern statically typed object-oriented languages are designed with type systems that enforce substitutability.

Unfortunately, other features of a programming language may still allow developers to bypass a type system's static checks and introduce subtypes that are not truly substitutable. Take the example of Java: the overriding of a method m in a class D that inherits

---

* Work partially supported by SNF grant 200021-207919 (LastMile).

A. Boronat and G. Fraser (Eds.): FASE 2025, LNCS 15693, pp.236–256, 2025.
https://doi.org/10.1007/978-3-031-90900-9_12

from another class C can simply throw an UnsupportedOperation exception; then, D is not substitutable for C, because the call o.m() terminates normally if o is an instance of C, and exceptionally if it is an instance of D—even though D is a subtype of C because they are related by inheritance. This substitutability-breaking pattern is not merely a theoretical possibility: there is empirical evidence that it is (deliberately) adopted in popular Java libraries to selectively enable or disable inherited operations [27,18,19].

In this paper, we introduce an approach to model behavioral substitutability constraints within a deductive verification framework, which we use to precisely reason about the behavior of programs involving these features. We develop our approach on top of our BYTEBACK verifier [23,22], which works on JVM bytecode. Extending BYTE-BACK makes our approach applicable to different languages that run on the JVM, such as (any versions) of Java, as well as (subsets of) Scala and Kotlin. This capability is especially relevant when verifying Scala or Kotlin programs that *use* Java libraries with optional operations, such as in Sec. 2's capsule example; using our approach, we are able to consistently check substitutability violations (or to prove their absence) even in multi-language programs.

To support reasoning about substitutability, we extend BYTEBACK with three specification features, which we present in detail in Sec. 3: *i*) Ghost specification predicates, which we use as "flags" denoting whether a certain operation is or is not available; *ii*) A (restricted) form of class invariants, which specify, in each concrete class, which specification predicates hold; *iii*) Substitutability-preserving specification inheritance (precondition weakening and postcondition strengthening), which propagates the information about available operations through the inheritance hierarchy.

While these specification features are fairly standard in source-level deductive verifiers for object-oriented languages (for example, JML-based verifiers such as KeY [1] and OpenJML [6] support them), they become considerably more challenging to implement at the level of bytecode—in a way that is applicable to multi-language programs, and without access to any source code of clients or libraries. As we discuss in Sec. 3.6, our approach relies on mechanisms to "attach" a specification to existing classes in the system, as well as to correctly propagate such attached specifications to other classes that are related by inheritance.

The extension of BYTEBACK described in the present paper is, to our knowledge, the first deductive verification technique that can reason about behavioral properties of programs combining different JVM languages. Even when applied to single-language programs, working at the level of bytecode has the advantage of handling robustly any versions of Java (and other JVM languages); in contrast, as we discuss in Sec. 5, source-level deductive verifiers usually only support older versions of Java. Another distinguishing capability of our approach is verifying programs that use complex libraries (such as the JDK) by directly analyzing the compiled bytecode, without need to build or access the libraries' source code. Sec. 4 discusses several experiments that demonstrate these capabilities on benchmark examples in Java, Kotlin, and Scala.

Contributions and positioning. In summary, the paper makes the following contributions: *i*) Specification features to express substitutability properties on top of the type system of JVM languages; *ii*) A verification technique based on these specification features; *iii*) An implementation of the verification technique built on top of the BYTEBACK verifier [23]; *iv*) An experimental evaluation with 22 programs involving unsupported operations in Java, Kotlin, and Scala; *v*) For reproducibility, our version of BYTEBACK and all experimental artifacts are available in a replication package [24].

While our implementation is based on BYTEBACK's previous instances [23,22], this paper's contributions substantially extend our previous work with specification and verification features necessary to reason about behavioral substitutability, and with a newly engineered implementation that makes them applicable to single- and multi-language bytecode programs. For simplicity, "BYTEBACK" will refer to the new verification technique, and its implementation, described in the rest of this paper—unless we explicitly point out that we are referring to earlier work.

```
List<Integer> ml = new ArrayList<Integer>();
// valid call: ml is mutable
ml.add(42);
```

```
List<Integer> il = List.of(1, 2);
// invalid call: il is immutable
il.add(42);
```

(a) The second call to method add is accepted by the Java compiler, but results in an exception at runtime because List.of returns an immutable List.

```
val bi: Buffer[Int] = java.util.List.of(1, 2).asScala
// invalid call: bi is immutable
bi.append(42)
```

(b) The call to method append is accepted by the Scala compiler, but results in an exception at runtime because Java's List.of returns an immutable List, but asScala converts all instances of List to instances of mutable Buffer.

```
@Attach(java.util.List)
interface ListSpec<T> {

@NoState @Behavior
boolean is_mutable();

@Raise(UnsupportedOperationException.class, when =¬is_mutable())
@Return(when = is_mutable())
boolean add(T element);

@Abstract
@Ensure( ¬result.is_mutable())
static <E> List<E> of(E e1, E e2)
{ return null; }

}
```

(c) An excerpt of BYTEBACK's specification of java.util.List.

```
@Attach(java.util.ArrayList)
@Invariant(Ghost.of(
  ListSpec.class, this
).is_mutable())
public class ArrayListSpec<T> {
  // ...
```

```
@Attach(java.util.LinkedList)
@Invariant(Ghost.of(
  ListSpec.class, this
).is_mutable())
public class LinkedListSpec<T> {
  // ...
}
```

(d) Class invariants of java.util's ArrayList and LinkedList.

```
@Require(Ghost.of(classOf[ListSpec[A]], this).is_mutable())
@Return
def asScalaBufferConverter[A](l: java.util.List[A]): AsScala[Buffer[A]]
```

(e) An excerpt of BYTEBACK's specification of Scala's asScalaBufferConverter, called by asScala to convert a Java List to a mutable Scala Buffer.

Fig. 1: An example of behavioral substitutability errors that are uncaught by the Java and Scala type systems, which can be precisely analyzed with this paper's deductive verification technique. The annotations use a simplified BBlib syntax, similar to the one used in previous work on BYTEBACK [23,22].

2   Motivating Example

The best-known example of Java libraries that violate behavioral substitutability is probably that of java.util's collections—in particular, interface List. Operations such as add are denoted *optional*, and hence some concrete classes inheriting from List may choose not to implement those operations, or to implement them only for a restricted set of valid inputs.

Fig. 1a shows a snippet of Java code that incurs this issue. First, there is a call of add on target ml, which is an instance of ArrayList. Since ArrayList is a subtype of List that implements all optional operations, the call ml.add(42) returns without errors. Then, there is a call of add on target il, which is an instance of List returned by static method List.of. As explained by the JDK's documentation, List.of always returns *immutable* lists;[a] therefore, the call il.add(42) fails with an UnsupportedOperation exception. However, the compiler accepts this code because, according to the type system's rules, every instance of List should support method add.

Fig. 1b demonstrates the same kind of problem in Scala code that uses Java data structures. Scala's library function asScala converts instances of java.util.List to instances of mutable.Buffer; this is usually sound, because Java lists are generally mutable. However, List.of actually returns an immutable list, which asScala simply wraps around; hence, calling modification operations, such as append, on instance bi of Buffer results in an exception at runtime. Even though Scala's own collection library has been carefully designed to avoid such behavioral substitutability problems, Scala code may still indirectly suffer from the limitations of Java's collections design.

To round off this brief diagnosis of the problem, we observe that the issue with using methods such as List.of is twofold: *i*) first, this method returns instances of List where some operations are not available (breaking List's behavioral interface); *ii*) second, there is no type[1] corresponding to an immutable variant of List that we can explicitly convert List.of's output to.

Specifying substitutability. Fig. 1 outlines how our approach supports precisely specifying different behavioral variants of List. Fig. 1c shows how we equip type List with a behavioral specification predicate is_mutable(), which returns **true** iff the current instance of List is indeed modifiable. Since we do not have access to the source code of List, BYTEBACK provides the @Attach annotation to augment any compiled class in the system with specification elements. Method is_mutable() is marked with BYTE-BACK annotations @Behavior (it is used for behavioral specifications, and hence any of its implementations must be side-effect free) and @NoState (its value does not depend on the current instance of List's state, since a list cannot become immutable after it is initialized).

After provisioning predicate is_mutable(), we can use it to specify any other members of List: Fig. 1c shows the specification of methods add and of.[2] For add, the specification says that it returns normally when is_mutable() is true, and with an exception when is_mutable() is false. For of, the specification says that it returns an instance **result** of List for which is_mutable() does not hold—which is how we specify that List.of returns unmodifiable lists. Since Java does not allow **static abstract** methods, we provide a dummy implementation of **static** method List.of, but the @Abstract annotation instructs BYTEBACK to effectively ignore it.

---

[1] While there is a class ImmutableCollections in the JDK,[b] it is not part of the public API, and hence it is inaccessible to clients.

[2] For simplicity, we only show the two-argument variant of List.of.

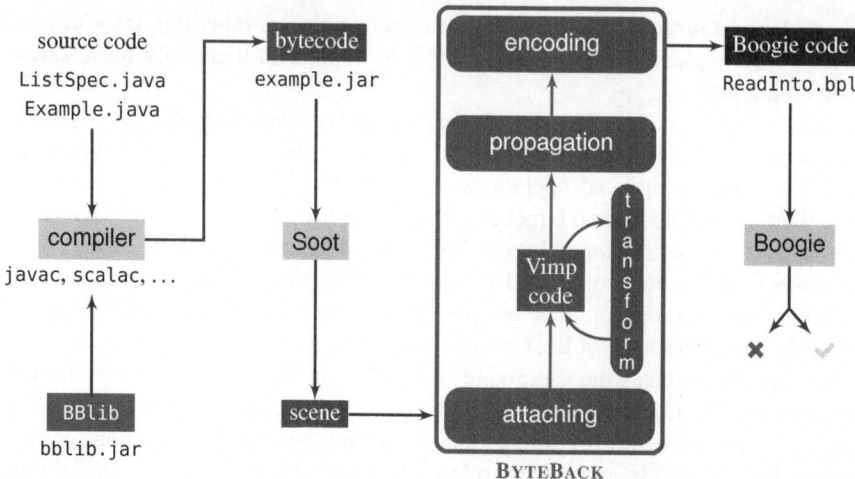

Fig. 2: An overview of BYTEBACK's verification workflow.

Fig. 1d lists other specifications that use is_mutable(). Precisely, we equip concrete classes ArrayList and LinkedList—both subclasses of List—with a class @Invariant: is_mutable() always holds for their instances. The syntax of these class invariants is somewhat cumbersome, as it uses a utility method Ghost.of that we designed as part of this paper's contributions. Since specification predicates such as is_mutable() are only supplied during BYTEBACK's analysis—after the Java program under verification has been compiled into bytecode—we cannot rely on Java's standard inheritance mechanisms to propagate specification elements to subclasses. Instead, BYTEBACK deploys a custom specification propagation algorithm, which weaves usages of Ghost.of into the type hierarchy during analysis. In Fig. 1d, Ghost.of is used to equip **this** (the current instance of ArrayList or LinkedList) with predicate is_mutable() declared in ListSpec.

Fig. 1e uses is_mutable() to specify a precondition for asScalaBufferConverter, to which asScala delegates the conversion of a Java List to a Scala mutable Buffer. Using in Scala the same mechanisms seen in ArrayList's specification, Fig. 1e states that only mutable Java lists can be converted to mutable Scala buffers.

Verifying substitutability. Equipped with Fig. 1c and Fig. 1d's specifications, BYTE-BACK can reason precisely about Fig. 1a's example. Thanks to ArrayList's class invariant, it knows that ml.add(42) terminates normally; thanks to List.of's postcondition, it knows that il.add(42) terminates by throwing an UnsupportedOperation exception—which may or may not be correct behavior, depending of whether the surrounding code expects that exception. BYTEBACK also issues a verification error for Fig. 1b's example: the call to asScala violates Fig. 1e's precondition, and hence it is invalid.

3   How BYTEBACK Specifies and Verifies Substitutability

Fig. 2 overviews how the deductive verification technique described in this paper works. Since our contributions is built atop BYTEBACK, the overall workflow remains similar to the one introduced in BYTEBACK's previous work [23,22]—with some important differences that we outline in Sec. 3.1 and Sec. 3.5 and describe in greater detail in the other subsections.

3.1 BYTEBACK Specification: Overview

Users of BYTEBACK add specifications the source code by means of BBlib—BYTE-BACK's source-level annotation library. Sec. 3.2 summarizes the core annotations provided by BBlib (such as pre- and postconditions), as well as those that are especially geared towards the present paper (such as class invariants). A key novel feature are *attached* specifications: users can list specification elements in separate *ghost* classes, and instruct BYTEBACK to weave them into the project under verification's implementation. Sec. 3.3 describes this mechanism, which is especially useful to supply specifications for components whose source code is not available (including system libraries). In an object-oriented language, subtyping is connected to class inheritance; correspondingly, Sec. 3.4 describes how BBlib's specifications are also *inherited*, following rules that are consistent with behavioral subtyping (i.e., precondition weakening and postcondition strengthening).

3.2 BBlib Specification Elements

BBlib annotations include all fundamental behavioral specification elements; since they were introduced in the previous work on BYTEBACK, we only summarize them here to make the paper self contained. *Method* specification elements include preconditions (@Require) and postconditions (@Ensure), as well as annotations to specify exceptional vs. normal behavior: @Raise(E, when = c) specifies a method that throws an exception of class E when it is called on an object where condition c holds; conversely, @Return(when = c) specifies a method that returns normally when it is called on an object where condition c holds. For example, Fig. 1c specifies that method List.add terminates normally if **this**.is_mutable() holds, and with an UnsupportedOperation exception otherwise.

Method *bodies* may include generic assertions (assertion(c) leads to a verification error iff c does not hold when execution reaches it), assumptions (assumption(c) ignores all executions where c does not hold), and loop invariants (invariant(c) captures the fundamental inductive property of the loop where it appears).

Class-level specifications use annotation @Invariant(c), which asserts that property c must hold for all instances of the specified class. For instance, Fig. 1d annotates class ArrayList with the invariant ℓ.is_mutable(), which every object ℓ of class ArrayList must satisfy. Such support for *class invariants* has been introduced in BYTEBACK only recently, as it is necessary to reason about substitutability. Nevertheless, BYTEBACK's class invariants are still limited in expressiveness: a class C with @Invariant(I) is simply equivalent to annotating every method of C with a "free"[3] precondition I and a (regular) postcondition I, and every constructor of C with a postcondition I. This simple class invariant semantics is sufficient for this paper's purposes, but it falls short of a full-fledged invariant *methodology* [15,16,28,5,12,26], which should support temporary violations of the class invariant (for example, by pri-

---

[3] A *free* precondition is an assumption about a method's pre-state.

vate methods), as well as expressing invariants that depend on the state of multiple objects.

BBlib expresses specification *predicates* as methods marked with @Behavior. BYTE-BACK checks that every method m equipped with such annotation can be expressed as a purely logic predicate: *i*) m must return a **boolean**, *ii*) have a signature consistent with m, *iii*) be pure and aggregable,[4] and *iv*) only call other @Behavior methods. Annotation @Behavior generalizes the @Predicate annotation used in previous work [23,22], since @Behavior also allows recursive calls in a behavior method body. Other annotations further constrain what a behavior method can predicate over. By default, a behavior method b used to specify a method m has access to m's arguments (possibly including its returned value, if m does not return **void**), as well as to the current object's state (e.g., through its fields). If b is annotated with @NoState, it cannot depend on the object state directly. Conversely, if b is annotated with @TwoState, it can also access the current object's *pre-state* (the state just before executing m). Thus, @TwoState behaviors are used in postconditions, where they relate the post-state to the pre-state. On the other hand, @NoState behaviors are useful to specify properties that hold "absolutely", such as is_mutable() in Fig. 1c: an instance of List is either mutable or immutable, and cannot change this property without being explicitly converted into a new object. Thus, annotation @NoState is especially useful for behavioral substitutability properties like those we reason about in this paper; declaring them as @NoState simplifies framing, since BYTEBACK only needs to check that their definitions do not refer to the object state.

3.3 Attached and Ghost Specifications

In previous work, all BBlib annotations had to be introduced in the source code of the element they refer to; for example, a method m's postcondition had to appear just before m's declaration in the program. This mechanism is limiting in all cases where we do not have access to a program's source code, or we simply do not want to alter it in any way. Fig. 1's example is a representative instance of this scenario: even if we had access to the source code of the JDK's collections library, recompiling them just to introduce a handful of specification elements would be practically very inconvenient. In this work, we introduce the *attaching* mechanism, which enables users to add specifications to any element of the program under verification, regardless of whether they have access to its source code.

Attached specifications. A class S annotated with @Attach(C) instructs BYTEBACK to apply all specification features introduced in S to class C. Precisely, the specification of any method m in S whose signature matches that of a method with the same name in C is used as specification of m in C. The attaching mechanism is compositional: users can attach multiple specification classes to the same class C—each specifying only a part of C's interface. If C includes some source-level specification of its own, users can selectively keep some of them, while overriding (or adding) the specifications of other methods. Take the example of Fig. 1c: specification class ListSpec only provides specifications for methods add and of in List. An "attached" specification class may

---

[4] Intuitively, "aggregable" means that it does not translate to branching instructions in bytecode; see previous work on BYTEBACK for a precise definition [22].

also include additional methods, typically to introduce predicates and other specification elements—such as method `is_mutable()` in Fig. 1c's attached specification class `ListSpec`.

Ghost specifications. *Ghost* code denotes code that is introduced only for the purpose of expressing a specification (or other annotations needed for deductive verification purposes) [9]. The term "ghost" was chosen because it suggests that it could be removed without having any effects on the program's behavior. According to this definition, all `BBlib` annotations are ghost code; however, in this paper we will use the term "ghost specification" in a stricter sense to denote only *attached* specifications. The distinction matters for BYTEBACK because an attached specification, unlike a regular source-level specification, is not processed by the compiler consistently with its intended semantics. In particular, ghost specifications are not propagated by inheritance because the compiler does not know that they refer to methods in a different class from where they are declared. To work around this limitation, we equipped `BBlib` with the `Ghost.of` operator, which provide a means to link elements of ghost specifications introduced in different attached specification classes. Fig. 1d shows examples of using `Ghost.of` to specify the class invariants of `ArrayList` and `LinkedList`: `Ghost.of(ListSpec.class, this).is_mutable()` refers to specification predicate `is_mutable()`, introduced in specification class `ListSpec`, and evaluated on an instance `this` of the specified classes `ArrayList` and `LinkedList`. During analysis, BYTEBACK will first weave `is_mutable()` into `List`, propagate it to its subtypes `ArrayList` and `LinkedList`, and finally rewrite the `Ghost.of` annotation so that it correctly refers to this attached method `is_mutable()`.

`@Invariant(`I_A`)`
`class A {`
 	
`@Require(`P_A`)`
`@Ensure(`Q_A`)`
S `m()`
 	
`}`
	`@Invariant(`j_B`)`
	`class B extends A {`
	
	`@Override`
	`@Require(`r_B`)`
	`@Ensure(`e_B`)`
	S `m()`
	
	`}`
		`@InvariantOnly(`I_C`)`
		`class C extends A {`
		
		`@Override`
		`@RequireOnly(`P_C`)`
		`@EnsureOnly(`Q_C`)`
		S `m()`
		
		`}`

Fig. 3: Three classes A, B, and C related by inheritance, and their specifications.

3.4 Specification Inheritance

Behavioral substitutability constrains how the specification of a method can change between classes that are related by inheritance [20]. Consider two classes A and B such that B is a subclass of A; a method m is defined in A and overridden in B; P_A and Q_A denote A.m's pre- and postcondition.

precondition weakening: B.m's precondition P_B must be weaker or as strong as P_A; in formulas: $P_A \implies P_B$.

postcondition strengthening: B.m's postcondition Q_B must be stronger or as strong as Q_A; in formulas: $Q_B \implies Q_A$.

As it is customary in behavioral specification languages [10], BYTEBACK interprets pre- and postcondition annotations in a way that enforces such overriding constraints. Fig. 3 shows classes A and B as above, whose methods m are annotated with BBlib's @Require and @Ensure, which define the following pre- and postconditions:

- B.m's precondition P_B is the disjunction $P_A \lor r_B$; since $P_A \implies P_A \lor r_B$, this is a weakening of A.m's precondition.
- B.m's postcondition Q_B is the conjunction $Q_A \land e_B$; since $Q_A \land e_B \implies Q_A$, this is a strengthening of A.m's postcondition.

When more freedom in the definition of the specification of overridden methods is needed, BBlib offers annotations @RequireOnly and @EnsureOnly, also demonstrated in Fig. 3's class C: C.m's precondition is just P_C, and C.m's postcondition is just Q_C as declared. When verifying a program annotated with @RequireOnly or @EnsureOnly, BYTEBACK generates additional explicit verification conditions that check that all the @RequireOnlys introduce weaker formulas, and the @EnsureOnlys introduce stronger formulas. In Fig. 3's example, BYTEBACK would check that formulas $P_A \implies P_C$ and $Q_C \implies Q_A$ are valid.

Finally, the inheritance of class invariants is consistent with their semantics (discussed in Sec. 3.2): the class invariant I_B of a class B inheriting from A must be stronger or as strong as A's class invariant I_A. The @Invariant annotation enforces this constraint by taking the conjunction of all declared invariants: in Fig. 3, class B's class invariant I_B is $I_A \land j_B$, which is a strengthening of I_A. Similarly to pre- and postconditions, annotation @InvariantOnly declares a full class invariant explicitly, and checks that it is indeed a strengthening during verification. In Fig. 3, the class invariant of class C is literally I_C, but BYTEBACK will check that $I_C \implies I_A$ holds.

3.5   BYTEBACK Verification: Overview

BYTEBACK's verification process inputs a project's bytecode, usually packed in a .jar file that includes all compiled source code and BBlib annotations in several classes. BYTEBACK queries Soot [13,11]'s *scene* object to extract static information about the bytecode under analysis, and to ultimately translate the input program's semantics into the intermediate verification language Boogie [3]. To this end, BYTEBACK first performs *attaching* (described in Sec. 3.6): it weaves the specification elements supplied in separate classes into the source code they refer to. Then, as outlined in Sec. 3.7, BYTEBACK performs a series of incremental, mostly *local* transformations of each method's bytecode, which explicitly model the program's behavior—such as the modular semantics of method calls, or the exceptional control flow. These transformations work on the Vimp intermediate representation: an extension with specification features of Soot's Jimple readable bytecode representation [22]. Since specifications are provided as BBlib annotations (possibly even in separate classes, using the @Attach mechanism), they are not available, in general, down the inheritance hierarchy, since the compiler is not aware of their intended semantics. Therefore, BYTEBACK also takes care of explicitly *propagating* specifications according to inheritance from the Vimp methods where they were explicitly introduced (see Sec. 3.8). After all these transformations, BYTEBACK finally *encodes* the ensemble Vimp components into a *Boogie program* that faithfully encodes the semantics of the input program and its specification. BYTEBACK's output Boogie program can be verified with the Boogie intermediate verifier to determine whether the input JVM program is correct.

`@Attach(A)`		`@Invariant(`I_{ASpec}`)`
`@Invariant(`I_{ASpec}`)`	`abstract class` A {	`abstract class` A {
`abstract class` ASpec {		`@Require(`P_{ASpec}`)`
		`@Ensure(`Q_{ASpec}`)`
`@Require(`P_{ASpec}`)`	`abstract` S m();	S m() { /* ... */ }
`@Ensure(`Q_{ASpec}`)`		
S m() { /* ... */ }	`@Require(`P_{A}`)`	`@Require(`P_{A}`)`
	S n() { /* ... */ }	S n() { /* ... */ }
`@Behavior`		
`abstract boolean` f();		`@Behavior`
		`abstract boolean` f();
}	}	}

(a) Attached specification class ASpec.   (b) Partially specified class A.   (c) Class A after attaching ASpec to it.

Fig. 4: An example of how attaching works in BYTEBACK. Empty padding added for clarity.

3.6   Attaching

By querying Soot's scene for the program under analysis, BYTEBACK retrieves all sorts of information about classes, their inheritance relation, their member declarations and implementations, and so on. BYTEBACK first processes each class S annotated with `@Attach(`C`)`, and copies the specification elements from S to C. If an element specified in S already has a specification in C, the attaching process replaces C's specification with S's. Attaching can also be used to replace *implementations*: if a method is declared as **abstract** in C but is given an implementation in S, the attaching process copies this implementation into C. Fig. 4 shows an example of attaching: class A in Fig. 4b includes an abstract method m and a concrete method n; the latter is annotated with a precondition P_{A}. The process of attaching Fig. 4a's class ASpec to A produces what shown in Fig. 4c: now, A includes a class invariant and a specification predicate f; in contrast, attaching does not modify method n or its specification, since n is not declared in ASpec; finally, method m gets the specification declared in ASpec, as well as its implementation.

Attaching can also target the parts of a program that are only available as external libraries, without access to their implementation. In such cases, attaching equips a library with a specification, which BYTEBACK then uses to reason about client code that uses that library. For example, Fig. 1d equips library class ArrayList with a class invariant; BYTEBACK does not have access to ArrayList's implementation, but can still use this class invariant as a property of every instance of ArrayList used in the program under verification.

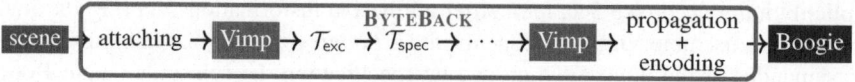

Fig. 5: BYTEBACK incrementally transform Vimp code to encode the semantics of bytecode instructions and specifications.

3.7 Vimp-level Transformations

After attaching, BYTEBACK performs a series of transformations to all components of the program under verification, incrementally taking care of modeling a different aspect of a program in a form suitable for verification. For example, there are transformations to model the exceptional control flow, to process specification expressions, to translate bytecode instructions, and to handle loop invariants. Fig. 5 outlines the first two local transformations: $\mathcal{T}_{exc}$ expresses the implicit exceptional control flow as an explicit control flow; $\mathcal{T}_{spec}$ "aggregates" BBlib specification expressions, so that they can be encoded as pure logic expressions suitable for usage as specification constructs.

All these transformations use the Vimp bytecode representation as an intermediate format, which they use to incrementally encode the semantics of the input program and its specification in a form that is amenable to deductive verification. Vimp was introduced in previous work [22]; in the present paper, we further extended it to accommodate a broader range of features that are needed for verification (in particular, a heap model and background axioms). As a result, the final encoding of Vimp into the Boogie intermediate verification language is even simpler than in previous versions of BYTE-BACK; relying on Vimp even more extensively also has the advantage that if we need to revise or extend the transformations (for example, to support a new construct with a different semantics), retaining a consistent Boogie encoding would be straightforward in many cases. Thus, we expect that our Vimp revision will also be useful to develop future extensions of BYTEBACK.

Ghost inlining. We introduced two new Vimp transformations to handle some of the features introduced in this paper. One is invariant instantiation, which we describe in Sec. 3.8 because it is applied after specification propagation. The other is ghost inlining, which handles all calls to specification method Ghost.of described in Sec. 3.3. For every call Ghost.of(cls, obj)—where cls is a **class** object representing the class where the referenced specification element was declared, and obj is a reference to an object to which the specification should be applied—BYTEBACK first checks that class cls is attached to a class of type compatible with obj's type. If that's the case, it simply replaces the whole Ghost.of(cls, obj) with obj. For example, consider again Fig. 1d's class invariant: Ghost.of(ListSpec.**class**, **this**).is_mutable(); after attaching, this class invariant annotates class ArrayList. When it processes this annotation, BYTEBACK checks that ListSpec is attached to (i.e., provides a specification for) List, and **this** is of type ArrayList—one of List's subtypes; thus, it simply rewrites the class invariant as **this**.is_mutable(). Writing directly **this**.is_mutable() as class invariant of ArrayList would have been rejected by the compiler: is_mutable() is only available in List and its subclasses *after* attaching. Thus, BYTEBACK provides the dummy method `Ghost.of`, which is accepted by the compiler and then rewritten by ghost inlining.

Algorithm 1 Specification Propagation

---

procedure PROPAGATE(DAG)
  for $C \in$ TOPOLOGICALSORT(DAG) **do**   ▷ *For every class C in inheritance order*
    for $B: C \longrightarrow B$ **do**   ▷ *For every direct supertype B of C*
      if $\neg$ONLY(I_c) **then**   ▷ *If C's invariant was not an @InvariantOnly*
        INV(C) ← INV(B) ∧ INV(C)   ▷ *Conjoin B's and C's invariants*
      for $m \in$ OVERRIDES(C) **do**   ▷ *For every method m that C overrides*
        if $\neg$ONLY($P_{c.m}$) **then**   ▷ *If $C.m$'s precondition was not a @RequireOnly*
                             ▷ *Disjoin $B.m$'s and $C.m$'s preconditions*
          PRE($C.m$) ← PRE($C.m$) ∨ PRE($B.m$)
        if $\neg$ONLY($Q_{c.m}$) **then**   ▷ *If $C.m$'s postcondition was not an @EnsureOnly*
                             ▷ *Conjoin $B.m$'s and $C.m$'s postconditions*
          POST($C.m$) ← POST($C.m$) ∧ POST($B.m$)

procedure TOPOLOGICALSORT(DAG)
  $S \leftarrow [\,]$ ▷ *S store the list of classes in DAG sorted by subtyping*
  for $R \in$ ROOTS(DAG) **do**   ▷ *For every root class R*
    $P \leftarrow [R]$ ▷ *Initialize stack P of classes to process*
    while $P \neq \emptyset$ **do**
      $C \leftarrow P.$POP( )   ▷ *C is the next class to process*
      $S.$APPEND(C)   ▷ *Add C to the end of the sorted list of classes*
      for $D: D \longrightarrow C$ **do**   ▷ *For each direct subtype of C*
        ▷ *If D is not already sorted, and all direct supertypes of D are already sorted*
        if $D \notin S \land \forall T: (D \longrightarrow T) \Longrightarrow (T \in S)$ **then**
          $P.$PUSH(D)   ▷ *Process D next*
  return S

3.8   Specification Propagation

The Vimp transformations outlined in Sec. 3.7 are mostly *local* to each method. Before producing a Boogie program, BYTEBACK needs to *propagate* the specification elements of classes (class invariants) and methods (pre- and postconditions) according to the inheritance hierarchy of the program. In fact, BYTEBACK cannot rely on the compiler to propagate BBlib specifications, because specifications are given as BBlib annotations, whose semantics the compiler ignores. Besides, even if the compiler could propagate specifications given at the source-code level, it would still not be able to process *attached* specifications, which are declared in a separate class.

Algorithm 1 presents BYTEBACK's specification propagation algorithm. The algorithm's input is a directed acyclic graph (DAG) that represents the overall inheritance hierarchy among classes/types; henceforth, $C \longrightarrow B$ denotes that class C is a child (heir, direct descendant) subclass of B in such graph. Since Java (as well as other JVM languages) supports a form of multiple inheritance via **interface**s, inheritance is not simply a tree but a DAG, which may have multiple roots (while all classes inherit from `java.lang.Object`, interfaces can only inherit from other interfaces). First, BYTEBACK uses topological sorting to produce a total ordering of all classes that respects the partial inheritance order (procedure TOPOLOGICALSORT in Algorithm 1). Then, the main procedure PROPAGATE goes through the sorted list of classes (from supertypes to subtypes). For every class C, it defines its class invariant as the conjunction of C's explicitly declared class invariant and the invariants of all direct superclasses of C. Similarly, for every method m overridden in C, it defines m's precondition (resp. postcondition) as the disjunction (resp. conjunction) of m's explicitly declared precondition (resp. postcondition) in C and the preconditions (resp. postconditions) of m in all direct superclasses of C. In all these cases, if class C's declared class invariant uses `@InvariantOnly`, or m's declared pre-/postcondition in C uses `@RequireOnly`/`@EnsureOnly`, the specification is not propagated from C's superclasses. Instead, BYTEBACK generates additional side verification conditions (not shown in Algorithm 1), checking that the following implications hold:

$$\text{INV}(C) \implies \bigwedge_{B:\, C \longrightarrow\!\!\!\!\triangleright\, B} \text{INV}(B) \tag{1}$$

$$\bigvee_{B:\, C \longrightarrow\!\!\!\!\triangleright\, B} \text{PRE}(B.m) \implies \text{PRE}(C.m) \tag{2}$$

$$\text{POST}(C.m) \implies \bigwedge_{B:\, C \longrightarrow\!\!\!\!\triangleright\, B} \text{POST}(B.m) \tag{3}$$

Invariant instantiation. After specification propagation, BYTEBACK performs an additional Vimp transformation to express the class invariant semantics described in Sec. 3.2; this transformation has to run *after* propagation, because it depends on knowing the full, propagated class invariant of every class. First, every method m of class C with propagated invariant I_C is equipped with a "free" precondition (equivalent to an assumption) I_C and (regular) postcondition I_C; constructors of C are also equipped with the latter. Second, every method `c_in(... C a ...)` with an argument a of type C is equipped with a free precondition a.I_C (i.e., C's invariant holds for a); and every method `C c_out(...)` that returns an object of type C is equipped with a (regular) postcondition `result`.I_C (i.e., C's invariant holds for the returned object). With this encoding, BYTEBACK can reason about every usage of an object of class C according to C's invariant.

4 Experiments

This section describes several verification experiments that demonstrate BYTEBACK's capabilities to reason about substitutability properties of Java data structures used by clients in Java and other JVM languages.

4.1 Experiment Description

Each experiment consists of client code that uses data structure libraries, namely implementations of `java.util`'s List, Set, and Map provided by Java 17's JDK or by Google's Guava.[c] In each experiments, BYTEBACK inputs the client code, together with a basic input/output specification of the data structures' APIs—specified using the `@Attach` mechanism described in the paper. The verification goal is checking that the client code uses the data structures' operations consistently with their specified behavior (as well as with the expected substitutability properties).

#	EXPERIMENT	LANG	BYTEBACK	BOOGIE	SOURCE	BOOGIE	MET	CLS	ANNOTATIONS	
			TIME [s]		SIZE [LOC]				B	A
1	Mutable Lists	J 17	0.69	1.20	449	11 374	61	5	33	4
2	Mutable Sets	J 17	0.51	0.89	451	10 193	58	6	30	5
3	Mutable Maps	J 17	0.52	0.88	469	10 430	64	6	31	5
4	Nonnullable Lists	J 17	0.51	0.80	470	9 571	64	6	36	5
5	Nonnullable Sets	J 17	0.50	0.80	405	9 471	54	5	29	4
6	Nonnullable Maps	J 17	0.51	0.89	427	9 551	60	5	30	4
7	Unmodifiable Lists	J 17	0.54	0.77	450	11 399	61	6	35	5
8	Unmodifiable Sets	J 17	0.52	0.76	384	10 554	51	5	28	4
9	Unmodifiable Maps	J 17	0.62	0.87	405	10 632	57	5	29	4
10	Nonresizeable Lists	J 17	0.70	1.11	413	11 826	55	5	32	4
11	Guava Immutable Lists	J 17	0.72	0.96	390	10 004	56	5	31	4
12	Guava Immutable Sets	J 17	0.51	0.72	348	9 471	48	5	25	4
13	Guava Immutable Maps	J 17	0.52	0.73	374	9 375	54	5	26	4
14	Invariant Strenghtening	J 17	0.45	0.63	66	7 592	7	3	4	0
15	Precondition Weakening	J 17	0.53	0.84	87	7 681	15	3	6	0
16	Postcondition Strengthening	J 17	0.46	0.72	91	7 668	15	3	6	0
17	Lists Conversion	S 2.13	0.73	1.37	349	22 564	55	9	23	7
18	Sets Conversion	S 2.13	0.69	1.31	309	20 292	47	9	17	7
19	Maps Conversion	S 2.13	0.70	1.30	331	20 377	53	9	18	7
20	Lists Conversion	K 1.8	0.81	1.15	457	12 187	65	5	37	3
21	Sets Conversion	K 1.8	0.65	1.11	415	12 263	57	5	31	3
22	Maps Conversion	K 1.8	0.53	0.88	413	9 985	59	5	30	3
	total		12.90	20.67	7 953	254 460	120	1 116	567	86
	average		0.59	0.94	362	11 566	51	5	26	4

Table 1: Experiments demonstrating how BYTEBACK can specify and verify substitutability properties of standard software components. Each row corresponds to an EXPERIMENT, consisting of several pieces of client code that use library components that we specified using the features presented in this paper. For each experiment, the table reports the LANGuage (Java, Scala, and Kotlin) of the client code (all non-Java experiments also use JDK 17 data structures, and hence they are multilingual); the wall-clock time (in seconds) taken by BYTEBACK to produce a Boogie program, and by BOOGIE to verify it; the size (in non-empty lines of code) of the SOURCE program with its annotations, and of the generated BOOGIE program; the number of methods (MET) and classes (CLS) that make up the program and its specification; the number P of specification predicates (@Behavior), and the number A of attached specification classes (@Attach) .

Tab. 1 gives some details about the experiments: out of 22 experiments, 16 are written in Java 17, 3 in Scala 2.13, and 3 in Kotlin 1.8. These are the languages of the verified *client code*, which uses data structure libraries written in Java 17; therefore, the Scala and Kotlin experiments are effectively multi-language, as they involve manipulating Java data structures within a different JVM language. Java experiments 14–16 are different than the others: they are simpler, as they focus on demonstrating BYTE-BACK's support for non-inherited class invariants, pre-, and postconditions defined with @InvariantOnly, @RequireOnly, and @EnsureOnly (discussed in Sec. 3.4).

Data structure properties. Here is a summary of the data structure behavioral properties that we specified in our experiments.

Mutability. A collection is *mutable* if it supports adding and removing elements to it, as well as replacing existing elements; LinkedList and ArrayList are examples of mutable collections. Conversely, a collection is *immutable* if it does not support adding, removing, or replacing its elements; Collections.unmodifiableList is an example of method that returns lists that are immutable. Since adding and removing are *optional* operations of the various collection interfaces, the implementations of methods such as List.add in an immutable collection simply throw an UnsupportedOperation exception (as demonstrated in Sec. 2's example).

Resizeability. A collection is *nonresizeable* if it does not support adding and removing elements to it; conversely, it is *resizeable* if it does support such operations. A mutable data structure is also resizeable; thus, LinkedList and ArrayList are also examples of resizeable collections. In contrast, there exist collections that are nonresizeable but are still modifiable: method Arrays.asList produces an array-backed list whose elements can be replaced, but not added or removed (because its size is fixed to be that of the backing array).

Nullability. With a little abuse of terminology, we call a collection *nullable* if it can store **null** as elements; and *nonnullable* otherwise. Method List.of produces lists that are immutable and nonnullable: passing a **null** value to this method is accepted by the Java compiler but results in a NullPointer exception at runtime.

Java experiments. In the experiments, we equipped the various collection classes with specifications that characterize whether they are mutable, resizeable, and nullable; and their operations with pre- and postconditions that express when they are available (for example, add terminates exceptionally in nonresizeable collections) and the properties of the objects they return. These specification rigorously express the information that is available in the natural-language documentation of the corresponding Java libraries, but is not accurately captured by the (public) types in the actual implementations. As we discussed in Sec. 2, equipping these specifications relies on the *attach* mechanism to annotate libraries whose implementation is not directly available to BYTEBACK. With these annotations, BYTEBACK can precisely verify the expected behavior of client code, such as distinguishing between the List instances in Fig. 1a—one of them is mutable, the other is not.

Scala and Kotlin experiments. The experiments with Scala and Kotlin client code demonstrate how these fine-grained properties of collections interact with the conversion mechanisms these other JVM languages provide to reuse Java collections. Scala and Kotlin have their own collections libraries, designed based on a detailed type hierarchy that properly distinguishes between mutable, immutable, and other kinds of collections. When converting a Java data structure, there is the problem of choosing the most suitable corresponding Scala or Kotlin type. For performance reasons, the utilities in Scala's JavaConverters do not copy the content of a Java data structure into a Scala data structure; instead, they create a *mutable* Scala collection that wraps the Java collection by delegating operations to it. If the underlying Java collection is actually immutable, some operations of the Scala collection will fail with an exception. Short of performing an expensive data-structure copy, the designers of Scala's converters had no way of properly handling such scenarios, given that the information about which Java types correspond to immutable collections is simply not available statically (e.g., List.of returns an instance of a private class) and, even if it were, it would be inconsistent with the type hierarchy.

Kotlin's type system also distinguishes between mutable and immutable collections; thus, if we want to explicitly convert a Java collection to a Kotlin collection, we can choose the most appropriate Kotlin type corresponding to the actual properties of that collection. Even though Kotlin's List and MutableList types both still represent, at the level of bytecode, objects of type java.util.List, the Kotlin compiler can keep track of which operations are allowed on which variant of list. Nevertheless, Kotlin's extensive support for Java interoperability still presents other means of introducing inconsistent behavior when Kotlin code interacts with Java code after compilation. Any Java type can seamlessly be used as a Kotlin type; compatibility rules are designed to be as general as possible—but this generality comes at the expense of soundness in some cases. For example, consider a Java method with an argument lst of type java.util.List that modifies lst (e.g., by removing an element). When the method is called from Kotlin, the compiler accepts any instance of Kotlin's List and MutableList as actual argument; if we pass an instance of immutable List, the method will actually succeed and mutate the list, which is an obvious violation of an immutable list's contract. In all these cases, using BYTEBACK's annotations, we can still reason statically about the precise behavior of different lists or other collections, and hence soundly check that every operation will perform as intended.

4.2 Experiment Results

The experiments ran on a GNU/Linux machine with an Intel Core i9-12950HX CPU (4.9 GHz), running Boogie 2.15.8.0, Z3 4.11.2.0, and Soot 4.3.0. We repeated the execution of the experiments six consecutive times; we report the average wall-clock running time of each experiment over all repetitions except the first one (which we discard to account for possible cold-start delays).

The central columns of Tab. 1 show some statistics about the experiments' results—all of which verified correctly as expected. The encoding time is usually around $2/3$ of a second, and roughly (linearly) proportional to the size of the annotated code; Boogie's verification time is around 1 second per experiment, and also roughly proportional to the number of methods and classes to be verified. The Boogie code produced by BYTE-BACK is more than twice larger for the Scala examples (64 lines of Boogie code per line of source code) compared to the Java and Kotlin examples (27 lines of Boogie per line of source); the difference is explained by the numerous class definitions that are used by the Scala runtime: even though BYTEBACK does not process these system classes' implementations, it still needs to reason about their specifications and signatures, and how they are (indirectly) used by the program under verification. In fact, the Scala examples also required a larger number of @Attached classes to annotate the (implicit) classes used by Scala's converters.

5   Related Work

Empirical evidence of substitutability violations. As mentioned in Sec. 1, substitutability violations in languages like Java are not merely a theoretical possibility. On the one hand, an empirical study of over 200 thousand classes from open-source Java projects found that "almost all" inheritance relations have some subtype use [29]. This evidence confirms that programmers design software that relies on substitutability via subtyping.

On the other hand, there is also abundant, direct or indirect, evidence that substitutability violations occur in practice. An analysis of over 20 million Java classes found that up to 28% of overridden method may introduce exceptional behavior that is incompatible with substitutability [18]; the same study found similar results when investigating other kinds of effects that break substitutability. Applying random testing techniques to detect substitutability violations [27] found that 30% of the analyzed classes (taken from three popular Java libraries) include crashing substitutes, that is subclasses that may lead to a crash (e.g., with an exception) when they replace an instance of the superclass they inherit from. A recent study of exception preconditions (i.e., preconditions that characterize when a method throws an exception) targeting 46 open-source Java projects and several modules of Java 11's JDK [19] found several instances of methods that unconditionally throw an UnsupportedOperation exception, possibly leading to a violation of substitutability.

Static analysis of substitutability. Extended type checkers are tools that enrich a programming language's core type checker with annotations that capture more expressive properties as types. The Checker Framework [25,7][d] augments the Java compiler with several of such extended type annotations, to detect errors such as for null-pointer dereferencing, optional data, out-of-bound index, and so on. While the Checker Framework does not currently include any checker for immutable or nullable collections,[5] it is extensible with new annotations (and some third-party checkers support some form of immutability annotations). The Checker Framework also offers stub files[e]—a mechanism similar to BYTEBACK's @Attach—to annotate libraries whose source code is not available. Of course, an extended type checker like the Checker Framework and a deductive verifier like BYTEBACK have distinct applications: a type checker is a lightweight tool, which statically verifies, with limited annotation effort, specific properties at the public interface of clients and suppliers; in contrast, a deductive verifier can, in principle, verify arbitrarily complex behavioral properties of every code feature, but also usually requires a substantial annotation effort and highly trained users. Besides, the Checker Framework is primarily a source-level tool, and works only for Java code, whereas BYTEBACK targets bytecode, and supports multi-language programs.

Other forms of static analysis may also support custom annotations that express immutability or similar properties, providing a similar usability as an extended type checker. For example, the Infer analyzer [4]'s impurity plugin includes an @Immutable annotation,[f] which can be used to constrain any kind of object to be immutable.

Deductive verification. A comprehensive behavioral specification language such as JML [14] subsumes the specification features that we introduced in this paper. Therefore, deductive verifiers based on JML, such as OpenJML [6] and KeY [2], can fully reason about behavioral substitutability (and its violations) in a similar fashion as BYTEBACK. As in previous work [23,22], our version of BYTEBACK and verifiers such as KeY and OpenJML offer largely complementary strengths and weaknesses: while the latter support a comprehensive set of specification features, and are much more mature tools, BYTEBACK's strengths follow from its unique angle of targeting bytecode-level verification: it seamlessly supports recent versions of Java (in contrast, OpenJML supports mostly Java features up to version 8, and KeY mostly targets a subset of Java 6), and it can also verify programs written in (subsets of) other JVM languages such as Scala and Kotlin, as well as multilingual programs made of components written in different

---

[5] Here, "nullable" means that may include null—see Sec. 4.

languages (such as in Sec. 2's example). The @Attach mechanism introduced in the present paper supports adding annotations to an existing component without access to the source code; OpenJML's specification files[9] provide a similar functionality for a source-level verifier.[6] In all, our contributions to BYTEBACK further demonstrate how bytecode-level deductive verification can be useful, but are not meant as a replacement of the full-fledged deductive verifiers for Java out there.

On a more theoretical level, there has been work on modeling and reasoning about notions of substitutability that are more flexible than Liskov and Wing [17]'s. Examples include lazy behavioral subtyping [8] and behavioral interface subtyping [21]. These contributions are usually only demonstrated on a core object-oriented language with minimal features; mainstream programming languages such as Java are designed based on stricter (and simpler) typing rules, which are more accessible to ordinary programmers.

6 Conclusions

In this paper, we described an extension of our BYTEBACK technique [23,22] to reason about behavioral substitutability properties at the level of JVM bytecode. To this end, we equipped BYTEBACK with capabilities to specify and reason about ghost specification predicates, a simple form of class invariants, specification inheritance, and a mechanism to annotate library components indirectly, without access to their source code. Our experiments demonstrate that this extension can precisely verify programs that use "optional" features of widely used Java libraries (such as immutable vs. mutable collections), even in multi-language program where client code and libraries are written in two different JVM languages.

The most natural continuation of this work would be equipping BYTEBACK with a more expressive class invariant specification methodology, which would support reasoning about behavioral substitutability for more complex multi-object structures.

---

[6] In BYTEBACK, a class specification can be split into multiple @Attached modules, which in turn can augment (or redefine) an existing source-level specification of the same class; furthermore, BYTEBACK's attach mechanism can also redefine *implementations* of a method in another part of the project under analysis. This makes @Attach a somewhat more flexible mechanism than OpenJML's spec files and the Checker Framework's aforementioned stub files, which do not support such a piecemeal specification style and cannot replace implementations.

References

1. Ahrendt, W., Beckert, B., Bruns, D., Bubel, R., Gladisch, C., Grebing, S., Hähnle, R., Hentschel, M., Herda, M., Klebanov, V., Mostowski, W., Scheben, C., Schmitt, P.H., Ulbrich, M.: The KeY platform for verification and analysis of Java programs. In: Giannakopoulou, D., Kroening, D. (eds.) Verified Software: Theories, Tools and Experiments - 6th International Conference, VSTTE 2014, Vienna, Austria, July 17-18, 2014, Revised Selected Papers. Lecture Notes in Computer Science, vol. 8471, pp. 55–71. Springer (2014). https://doi.org/10.1007/978-3-319-12154-3_4, https://doi.org/10.1007/978-3-319-12154-3_4

2. Ahrendt, W., Beckert, B., Bubel, R., Hähnle, R., Schmitt, P.H., Ulbrich, M. (eds.): Deductive Software Verification—The KeY Book, Lecture Notes in Computer Science, vol. 10001. Springer (2016). https://doi.org/10.1007/978-3-319-49812-6, http://dx.doi.org/10.1007/978-3-319-49812-6

3. Barnett, M., Chang, B.E., DeLine, R., Jacobs, B., Leino, K.R.M.: Boogie: A Modular Reusable Verifier for Object-Oriented P rograms. In: de Boer, F.S., Bonsangue, M.M., Graf, S., de Roever, W.P. (eds.) Formal Methods for Components and Objects, 4th International Symposium, FMCO 2005, Amsterdam, The Netherlands, November 1-4, 2005, Revised Lectures. Lecture Notes in Computer Science, vol. 4111, pp. 364–387. Springer (2005). https://doi.org/10.1007/11804192_17, https://doi.org/10.1007/11804192_17

4. Calcagno, C., Distefano, D., Dubreil, J., Gabi, D., Hooimeijer, P., Luca, M., O'Hearn, P.W., Papakonstantinou, I., Purbrick, J., Rodriguez, D.: Moving Fast with Software Verification. In: Havelund, K., Holzmann, G.J., Joshi, R. (eds.) NASA Formal Methods - 7th International Symposium, NFM 2015, Pasadena, CA, USA, April 27-29, 2015, Proceedings. Lecture Notes in Computer Science, vol. 9058, pp. 3–11. Springer (2015). https://doi.org/10.1007/978-3-319-17524-9_1, https://doi.org/10.1007/978-3-319-17524-9_1

5. Cohen, E., Moskal, M., Schulte, W., Tobies, S.: Local verification of global invariants in concurrent programs. In: Proceedings of CAV. pp. 480–494. Lecture Notes in Computer Science, Springer (2010)

6. Cok, D.R.: OpenJML: Software verification for Java 7 using JML, OpenJDK, and Eclipse. In: Dubois, C., Giannakopoulou, D., Méry, D. (eds.) Proceedings 1st Workshop on Formal Integrated Development Environment, F-IDE 2014, Grenoble, France, April 6, 2014. EPTCS, vol. 149, pp. 79–92 (2014). https://doi.org/10.4204/EPTCS.149.8, https://doi.org/10.4204/EPTCS.149.8

7. Dietl, W., Dietzel, S., Ernst, M.D., Muslu, K., Schiller, T.W.: Building and using pluggable type-checkers. In: Taylor, R.N., Gall, H.C., Medvidovic, N. (eds.) Proceedings of the 33rd International Conference on Software Engineering, ICSE 2011, Waikiki, Honolulu , HI, USA, May 21-28, 2011. pp. 681–690. ACM (2011). https://doi.org/10.1145/1985793.1985889, https://doi.org/10.1145/1985793.1985889

8. Dovland, J., Johnsen, E.B., Owe, O., Steffen, M.: Lazy behavioral subtyping. J. Log. Algebraic Methods Program. 79(7), 578–607 (2010). https://doi.org/10.1016/J.JLAP.2010.07.008, https://doi.org/10.1016/j.jlap.2010.07.008

9. Filliâtre, J., Gondelman, L., Paskevich, A.: The spirit of ghost code. Formal Methods Syst. Des. 48(3), 152–174 (2016). https://doi.org/10.1007/S10703-016-0243-X, https://doi.org/10.1007/s10703-016-0243-x

10. Hatcliff, J., Leavens, G.T., Leino, K.R.M., Müller, P., Parkinson, M.J.: Behavioral interface specification languages. ACM Comput. Surv. 44(3), 16:1–16:58 (2012). https://doi.org/10.1145/2187671.2187678, https://doi.org/10.1145/2187671.2187678

11. Karakaya, K., Schott, S., Klauke, J., Bodden, E., Schmidt, M., Luo, L., He, D.: SootUp: A redesign of the Soot static analysis framework. In: Finkbeiner, B., Kovács, L. (eds.) Tools and Algorithms for the Construction and Analysis of Systems - 30th International Conference, TACAS 2024, Held as Part of the European Joint Conferences on Theory and Practice of Software, ETAPS 2024, Luxembourg City, Luxembourg, April 6-11, 2024, Proceedings, Part I. Lecture Notes in Computer Science, vol. 14570, pp. 229–247. Springer (2024). https://doi.org/10.1007/978-3-031-57246-3_13, `https://doi.org/10.1007/978-3-031-5 7246-3_13`

12. Kassios, I.T.: Dynamic frames: Support for framing, dependencies and sharing without restrictions. In: Proceedings of FM. pp. 268–283. Lecture Notes in Computer Science, Springer (2006)

13. Lam, P., Bodden, E., Lhoták, O., Hendren, L.: The Soot framework for Java program analysis: a retrospective. In: Cetus Users and Compiler Infrastructure Workshop (CETUS 2011) (Oct 2011), `https://www.bodden.de/pubs/lblh11soot.pdf`

14. Leavens, G.T., Schmitt, P.H., Yi, J.: The Java Modeling Language (JML) (NII shonan meeting 2013-3). NII Shonan Meet. Rep. **2013** (2013), `https://shonan.nii.ac.jp/seminars/ 016/`

15. Leino, K.R.M., Müller, P.: Object invariants in dynamic contexts. In: Proceedings of ECOOP. pp. 491–516. Lecture Notes in Computer Science, Springer (2004)

16. Leino, K.R.M., Schulte, W.: Using history invariants to verify observers. In: Proceedings of ESOP. pp. 80–94. Lecture Notes in Computer Science, Springer (2007)

17. Liskov, B.H., Wing, J.M.: A behavioral notion of subtyping. ACM Trans. Program. Lang. Syst. **16**(6), 1811–1841 (1994). https://doi.org/10.1145/197320.197383, `https://doi.org/ 10.1145/197320.197383`

18. Maddox, J., Long, Y., Rajan, H.: Large-scale study of substitutability in the presence of effects. In: Leavens, G.T., Garcia, A., Pasareanu, C.S. (eds.) Proceedings of the 2018 ACM Joint Meeting on European Software Engineering Conference and Symposium on the Foundations of Software Engineering, ESEC/SIGSOFT FSE 2018, Lake Buena Vista, FL, USA, November 04-09, 2018. pp. 528–538. ACM (2018). https://doi.org/10.1145/3236024.3236075, `https://doi.org/10.1145/3236024.3236075`

19. Marcilio, D., Furia, C.A.: Lightweight precise automatic extraction of exception preconditions in Java methods. Empirical Software Engineering **29**(1), 30 (2024)

20. Meyer, B.: Object-oriented software construction. Prentice Hall, 2nd edn. (1997)

21. Owe, O.: Reasoning about inheritance and unrestricted reuse in object-oriented concurrent systems. In: Ábrahám, E., Huisman, M. (eds.) Integrated Formal Methods - 12th International Conference, IFM 2016, Reykjavik, Iceland, June 1-5, 2016, Proceedings. Lecture Notes in Computer Science, vol. 9681, pp. 210–225. Springer (2016). https://doi.org/10.1007/978-3-319-33693-0_14, `https://doi.org/10.1007/978-3-319-33693-0_14`

22. Paganoni, M., Furia, C.A.: Reasoning about exceptional behavior at the level of Java bytecode. In: Herber, P., Wijs, A., Bonsangue, M.M. (eds.) Proceedings of the 18th International Conference on integrated Formal Methods (iFM). Lecture Notes in Computer Science, vol. 14300, pp. 113–133. Springer (November 2023)

23. Paganoni, M., Furia, C.A.: Verifying functional correctness properties at the level of Java bytecode. In: Chechik, M., Katoen, J.P., Leucker, M. (eds.) Proceedings of the 25th International Symposium on Formal Methods (FM). Lecture Notes in Computer Science, vol. 14000, pp. 343–363. Springer (March 2023)

24. Paganoni, M., Furia, C.A.: ByteBack FASE 2025 replication package (Jan 2025). https://doi.org/10.6084/m9.figshare.28166951.v4, `https://doi.org/10.6084/m9.figsh are.28166951.v4`

25. Papi, M.M., Ali, M., Jr., T.L.C., Perkins, J.H., Ernst, M.D.: Practical pluggable types for Java. In: Ryder, B.G., Zeller, A. (eds.) Proceedings of the ACM/SIGSOFT International Symposium on Software Testing and Analysis, ISSTA 2008, Seattle, WA, USA, July 20-24, 2008. pp. 201–212. ACM (2008). https://doi.org/10.1145/1390630.1390656, https://doi.org/10.1145/1390630.1390656

26. Polikarpova, N., Tschannen, J., Furia, C.A., Meyer, B.: Flexible invariants through semantic collaboration. In: Proceedings of FM. Lecture Notes in Computer Science, vol. 8442, pp. 514–530. Springer (2014)

27. Pradel, M., Gross, T.R.: Automatic testing of sequential and concurrent substitutability. In: Notkin, D., Cheng, B.H.C., Pohl, K. (eds.) 35th International Conference on Software Engineering, ICSE '13, San Francisco, CA, USA, May 18-26, 2013. pp. 282–291. IEEE Computer Society (2013). https://doi.org/10.1109/ICSE.2013.6606574, https://doi.org/10.1109/ICSE.2013.6606574

28. Summers, A.J., Drossopoulou, S., Müller, P.: The need for flexible object invariants. In: Proceedings of IWACO. pp. 1–9. ACM (2009)

29. Tempero, E.D., Yang, H.Y., Noble, J.: What programmers do with inheritance in Java. In: Castagna, G. (ed.) ECOOP 2013 - Object-Oriented Programming - 27th European Conference, Montpellier, France, July 1-5, 2013. Proceedings. Lecture Notes in Computer Science, vol. 7920, pp. 577–601. Springer (2013). https://doi.org/10.1007/978-3-642-39038-8_24, https://doi.org/10.1007/978-3-642-39038-8_24

URL References

a. https://docs.oracle.com/en/java/javase/21/docs/api/java.base/java/util/List.html
b. https://github.com/openjdk/jdk/blob/master/src/java.base/share/classes/java/util/ImmutableCollections.java
c. https://guava.dev/
d. https://checkerframework.org/
e. https://checkerframework.org/manual/#annotating-libraries
f. https://fbinfer.com/docs/all-issue-types/#modifies_immutable
g. https://www.openjml.org/tutorial/SpecificationFiles

Advances in Automatic Software Testing: Test-Comp 2025

Dirk Beyer[(✉)] [iD]

LMU Munich, Munich, Germany
dirk.beyer@sosy.ifi.lmu.de
https://www.sosy-lab.org/people/beyer/

Abstract. The 7th edition of the Competition on Software Testing (Test-Comp 2025) provides an overview and comparative evaluation of automatic test-suite generators for C programs. The experimental evaluation was performed on a benchmark set of 11 226 test-generation tasks for C programs. Each test-generation task consisted of a program and a test specification. The test specifications included error coverage (generate a test suite that exhibits a bug) and branch coverage (generate a test suite that executes as many program branches as possible). Test-Comp 2025 evaluated 20 software systems for test generation that are all freely available. This included 13 test-suite generators that participated with active support from teams led by 12 different representatives from 8 countries (actively maintained software systems, participation in competition jury). Test-Comp 2025 had 1 new participant (Sikraken[new]) and 2 re-entries (ESBMC-incr, ESBMC-kind). The evaluation included also 7 test-generation tools from previous years.

Keywords: Software Testing · Test-Case Generation · Competition · Program Analysis · Software Validation · Software Bugs · Test Validation · Test-Comp · Benchmarking · Test Coverage · Bug Finding · Test Suites · SV-Benchmarks · BenchExec · TestCov · CoVeriTeam

1 Introduction

In its 7th edition, the International Competition on Software Testing (Test-Comp, https://test-comp.sosy-lab.org, [10, 11, 12, 13, 14, 16, 17]) again compares automatic test-suite generators for C programs, in order to showcase the state of the art in the area of automatic software testing. This competition report is an update of the previous reports, referring to the rules and definitions, presents the competition results, and give some interesting data about the execution of the competition experiments. We use BenchExec [31] to execute the benchmark runs, BenchCloud [24] to distribute the execution to a large and elastic set of computers, FM-Weck [33] to

---

This report extends previous reports on Test-Comp [10, 11, 12, 13, 14, 16, 17] by providing new results, while the procedures and setup of the competition stay mainly unchanged. Reproduction packages are available on Zenodo (see Table 3).

© The Author(s) 2025
A. Boronat and G. Fraser (Eds.): FASE 2025, LNCS 15693, pp. 257–274, 2025.
https://doi.org/10.1007/978-3-031-90900-9_13

execute tools from previous years using the container with all their requirements fulfilled, and the FM-TOOLS [18] collection to look up all the information we need about the tools for test-case generation, including their versions, parameters, and jury representatives. The results are presented in tables and graphs, also on the competition web site (https://test-comp.sosy-lab.org/2025/results), and are available in the accompanying archives (see Table 3).

Competition Goals. In summary, the goals of Test-Comp are the following [11]:

- Establish *standards* for software test generation. This means, most prominently, to develop a standard for marking input values in programs, define an exchange format for test suites, agree on a specification language for test-coverage criteria, and define how to validate the resulting test suites.
- Establish a set of *benchmarks* for software testing in the community. This means to create and maintain a set of programs together with coverage criteria, and to make those publicly available for researchers to be used in performance comparisons when evaluating a new technique.
- Provide an overview of *available tools* for test-case generation and a snapshot of the state-of-the-art in software testing to the community. This means to compare, independently from particular paper projects and specific techniques, different test generators in terms of effectiveness and performance.
- Increase the visibility and credits that *tool developers* receive. This means to provide a forum for presentation of tools and discussion of the latest technologies, and to give the participants the opportunity to publish about the development work that they have done.
- Educate PhD students and other participants on how to set up performance experiments, package tools in a way that supports reproduction, and how to perform *robust and accurate research experiments*.
- Provide *resources* to development teams that do not have sufficient computing resources and give them the opportunity to obtain results from experiments on large benchmark sets.

Related Competitions. In the field of formal methods, competitions are respected as an important evaluation method and there are many competitions [8, 26]. We refer to the report from Test-Comp 2020 [11] for a more detailed discussion and give here only the references to the most related competitions: Competition on Software Verification (SV-COMP) [19], Competition on Search-Based Software Testing (SBST) [54], and the DARPA Cyber Grand Challenge [56]. For the techniques used for automatic software testing, we refer to the literature [5, 41].

2   Definitions, Formats, and Rules

Organizational aspects such as the classification (automatic, off-site, reproducible, jury, training) and the competition schedule is given in the initial competition definition [10]. In the following, we repeat some important definitions that are necessary to understand the results.

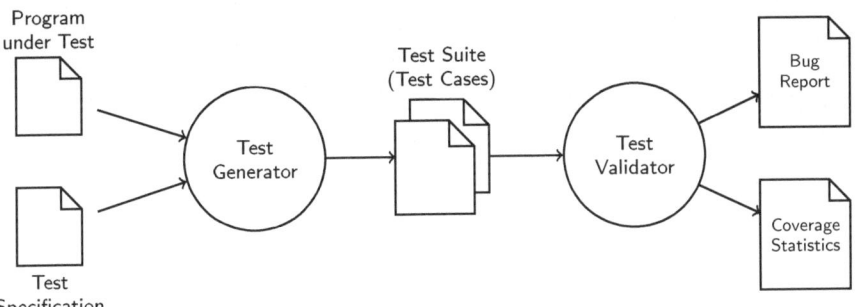

Fig. 1: Flow of the Test-Comp execution for one test generator (taken from [11])

Test-Generation Task. A *test-generation task* is a pair of an input program (program under test) and a test specification. A *test-generation run* is a non-interactive execution of a test generator on a single test-generation task, in order to generate a test suite according to the test specification. A *test suite* is a sequence of test cases, given as a directory of files according to the format for exchangeable test-suites.[1]

Execution of a Test Generator. Figure 1 illustrates the process of executing one test-suite generator on the benchmark suite. One test run for a test-suite generator gets as input (i) a program from the benchmark suite and (ii) a test specification (cover bug, or cover branches), and returns as output a test suite (i.e., a set of test cases). The test generator is contributed by a competition participant as a software archive in ZIP format on Zenodo, via a DOI entry of a version in the FM-Tools record of the test generator. All test runs are executed centrally by the competition organizer.

Execution of the Test Validator. The test-suite validator takes as input the test suite from the test generator and validates it by executing the program on all test cases: for bug finding it checks if the bug is exposed and for coverage it reports the coverage. We use the tool TESTCOV [30] [2] as test-suite validator.

In Test-Comp 2025, we used TESTCOV in four configurations: (a) We use separate validations based on the compiler, with GCC and with Clang. The motivation for this is that the two different compilers use different choices for unspecified behavior, where the C standard leaves certain choices up to the compiler (for example, the unspecified order of evaluation of function arguments). (b) We use separate validations based on the formatting after instrumentation, with and without formatting. The motivation for this is that due to incompatibilities of the tools for formatting and coverage measurement, we would like to make sure to obtain the best possible coverage measurement by using those variants. For each test-validation run, the best of the four results is used to determine the score.

---

[1] https://gitlab.com/sosy-lab/test-comp/test-format
[2] https://gitlab.com/sosy-lab/software/test-suite-validator

Table 1: Coverage specifications used in Test-Comp 2025 (similar to 2019–2024)

Formula	Interpretation
COVER EDGES(@CALL(reach_error))	The test suite contains at least one test that executes function reach_error.
COVER EDGES(@DECISIONEDGE)	The test suite contains tests such that all branches of the program are executed.

Test Specification. The specification for testing a program is given to the test generator as input file (either properties/coverage-error-call.prp or properties/coverage-branches.prp for Test-Comp 2025).

The definition init(main()) is used to define the initial states of the program under test by a call of function main (with no parameters). The definition FQL(f) specifies that coverage definition f should be achieved. The FQL (FSHELL query language [45]) coverage definition COVER EDGES(@DECISIONEDGE) means that all branches should be covered (typically used to obtain a standard test suite for quality assurance) and COVER EDGES(@CALL(foo)) means that a call (at least one) to function foo should be covered (typically used for bug finding). A complete specification looks like: COVER(init(main()), FQL(COVER EDGES(@DECISIONEDGE))).

Table 1 lists the two FQL formulas that are used in test specifications of Test-Comp 2025; there was no change from 2020 (except that special function __VERIFIER_error does not exist anymore).

Task-Definition Format 2.0. Test-Comp 2025 used again the task-definition format in version 2.0.

License and Qualification. The license of each participating test generator must allow its free use for reproduction of the competition results. The license for each tool is available in the FM-TOOLS entry for the tool, as well as in Table 4. Details on qualification criteria can be found in the competition report of Test-Comp 2019 [12].

3   Categories and Scoring Schema

Benchmark Programs. The input programs were taken from the largest and most diverse open-source repository of software-verification and test-generation tasks[3], which is also used by SV-COMP [19]. As in 2020 and 2021, we selected all programs for which the following properties were satisfied (see issue on GitLab[4] and report [12]):

---

[3] https://gitlab.com/sosy-lab/benchmarking/sv-benchmarks

[4] https://gitlab.com/sosy-lab/benchmarking/sv-benchmarks/-/merge_requests/774

1. compiles with **gcc**, if a harness for the special methods [5] is provided,
2. should contain at least one call to a nondeterministic function,
3. does not rely on nondeterministic pointers,
4. does not have expected result 'false' for property 'termination', and
5. has expected result 'false' for property 'unreach-call' (only for category *Cover-Error*).

This selection yielded a total of 11 226 test-generation tasks, namely 1 215 tasks for category *Cover-Error* and 10 011 tasks for category *Cover-Branches*. The test-generation tasks are partitioned into categories, which are listed in Tables 6 and 7 and described in detail on the competition web site.[6] Figure 2 illustrates the category composition.

Category Cover-Error. The first category is to show the abilities to discover bugs. The benchmark set consists of programs that contain a bug. We produce for every tool and every test-generation task one of the following scores: 1 point, if the validator succeeds in executing the program under test on a generated test case that explores the bug (i.e., the specified function was called), and 0 points, otherwise.

Category Cover-Branches. The second category is to cover as many branches of the program as possible. The coverage criterion was chosen because many test generators support this standard criterion by default. Other coverage criteria can be reduced to branch coverage by transformation [44]. We produce for every tool and every test-generation task the coverage of branches of the program (as reported by TESTCOV [30]; a value between 0 and 1) that are executed for the generated test cases. The score is the returned coverage.

Max Over All Validators. As mentioned before, TESTCOV is executed four times on each test suite, using four different configurations. The score of a test suite is the maximum of the four computed scores.

Ranking. The ranking was decided based on the sum of points (normalized for meta categories). In case of a tie, the ranking was decided based on the run time, which is the total CPU time over all test-generation tasks. Opt-out from categories was possible and scores for categories were normalized based on the number of tasks per category (see competition report of SV-COMP 2013 [9], page 597).

4   Reproducibility

We followed the same competition workflow that was described in detail in the previous competition report (see Sect. 4, [13]). All major components that were used for the competition were made available in public version-control repositories. An overview of the components that contribute to the reproducible setup of Test-Comp is provided in Fig. 3, and the details are given in Table 2. We refer to the report of Test-Comp 2019 [12] for a thorough description of all

---

[5] https://test-comp.sosy-lab.org/2025/rules.php
[6] https://test-comp.sosy-lab.org/2025/benchmarks.php

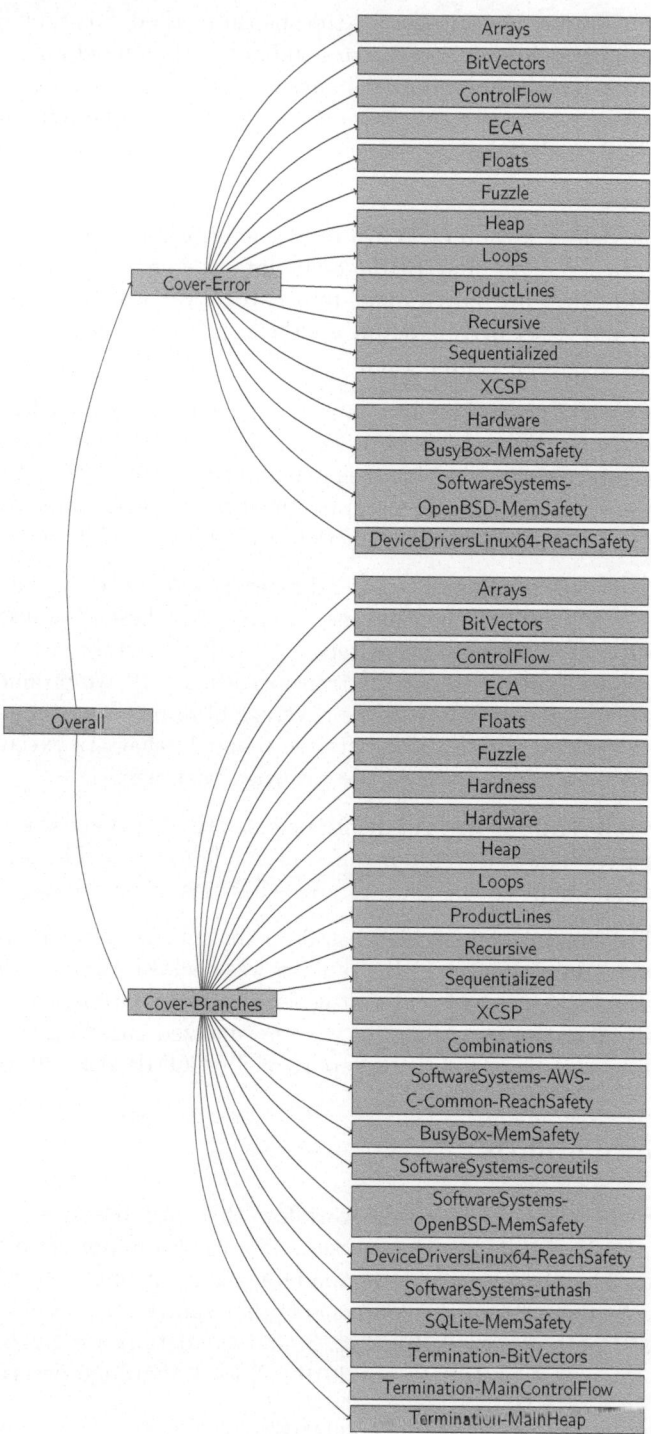

Fig. 2: Category structure for Test-Comp 2025

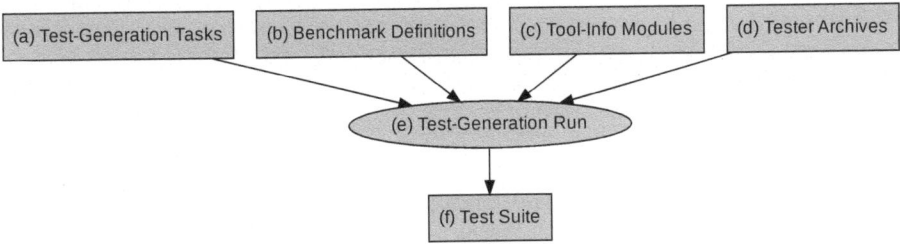

Fig. 3: Benchmarking components of Test-Comp and competition's execution flow (same as for Test-Comp 2020)

Table 2: Publicly available components for reproducing Test-Comp 2025

Component	Fig. 3	Repository at http://gitlab.com/sosy-lab/...	Version
Test-Generation Tasks	(a)	benchmarking/sv-benchmarks	testcomp25
Benchmark Definitions	(b)	test-comp/bench-defs	testcomp25
Tool-Info Modules	(c)	software/benchexec	3.29
Test-Generators	(d)	benchmarking/fm-tools	testcomp25
BENCHEXEC (Benchmarking)	(e)	software/benchexec	3.29
BENCHCLOUD (Distribution)	(e)	software/benchcloud	1.3.0
FM-WECK (Containers)	(e)	software/fm-weck	1.4.5
Test-Suite Format	(f)	test-comp/test-format	testcomp25
COVERITEAM for CI		software/coveriteam	1.2.1
Processing Scripts		benchmarking/competition-scripts	testcomp25

Table 3: Artifacts published for Test-Comp 2025

Content	DOI	Reference
Test-Generation Tasks	10.5281/zenodo.15034421	[22]
Competition Results	10.5281/zenodo.15034433	[21]
Test-Suite Generators	10.5281/zenodo.15055359	[20]
Test Suites (Witnesses)	10.5281/zenodo.15034431	[23]
BENCHEXEC	10.5281/zenodo.15007216	[61]
COVERITEAM	10.5281/zenodo.11193690	[32]

components of the Test-Comp organization and how we ensure that all parts are publicly available for maximal reproducibility.

In order to guarantee long-term availability and immutability of the test-generation tasks, the produced competition results, and the produced test suites, we also packaged the material and published it at Zenodo (see Table 3).

The competition used COVERITEAM [28]⁷ again to provide participants access to execution machines that are similar to actual competition machines. The competition report of SV-COMP 2022 provides a description on reproducing

---

⁷ https://gitlab.com/sosy-lab/software/coveriteam

Table 4: Competition candidates with tool references and representing jury members; [new] indicates first-time participants, [∅] indicates inactive (hors concours) participation; licenses are abbreviated, see the hyperlink or tool page at FM-Tools for the specific version of the license; TESTCOV is the validator that computes the score for each test-suite

Tester	Ref.	License	Jury member	Affiliation
CETFUZZ[∅]		Apache	–	–
COVERITEST	[27, 47]	Apache	M.-C. Jakobs	LMU Munich, Germany
ESBMC-INCR	[60]	Apache	C. Wei	U. of Manchester, UK
ESBMC-KIND	[42, 60]	Apache	C. Wei	U. of Manchester, UK
FDSE	[62]	Apache	Z. Chen	National U. Defense Techn., China
FIZZER	[48, 49]	Zlib	M. Trtík	Masaryk U., Brno, Czechia
FUSEBMC	[3, 4]	MIT	K. Alshmrany	U. of Manchester, UK and Inst. Public Admin., Saudi Arabia
FUSEBMC-AI[∅]	[1, 2]	MIT	–	–
HYBRIDTIGER[∅]	[34, 55]	Apache	–	–
KLEEF	[53]	NCSA	A. Misonizhnik	Independent Researcher, Neutral
KLEE[∅]	[35, 36]	NCSA	–	–
OWI[∅]		AGPL	–	–
PRTEST	[29, 51]	Apache	T. Lemberger	LMU Munich, Germany
RIZZER[∅]		Zlib	–	–
SIKRAKEN[new]		LGPL	C. Meudec	South East Technological U., Ireland
SYMBIOTIC	[37, 38]	MIT	M. Jonáš	Masaryk U., Brno, Czechia
TRACERX	[40, 46]	Apache	J. Jaffar	National U. of Singapore, Singapore
TRACERX-WP	[40, 46]	Apache	J. Jaffar	National U. of Singapore, Singapore
UTESTGEN	[6, 7]	LGPL	M. Barth	LMU Munich, Germany
WASP-C[∅]	[52]	Apache	–	–
TESTCOV	[30]	Apache	M. Kettl	LMU Munich, Germany

individual results and on trouble-shooting (see Sect. 3, [15]). A new component in Test-Comp 2025 was the use of the container solution FM-WECK [33], which makes it possible to include also older archives in the comparative evaluation, even if the tools were made for an older distribution of Ubuntu or use packages that are not available anymore. The tools can specify in their FM-TOOLS [18] entry a container in which they can run.

5   Results and Discussion

This section represents the results of the competition experiments. The report shall help to understand the state of the art and the advances in fully automatic test generation for whole C programs, in terms of effectiveness (test coverage, as accumulated in the score) and efficiency (resource consumption in terms of CPU time). All results mentioned in this article were inspected and approved by the participants.

Participating Test-Suite Generators. Table 4 provides an overview of the participating test generators and references to publications, as well as the team representatives of the jury of Test-Comp 2025. (The competition jury consists

Table 5: Technologies and features that the test generators used

Tester	Algorithm Selection	Bit-Precise Analysis	Bounded Model Checking	CEGAR	Concurrency Support	Evolutionary Algorithms	Explicit-Value Analysis	Floating-Point Arithmetics	Guidance by Coverage Measures	Portfolio	Predicate Abstraction	Random Execution	Symbolic Execution	Targeted Input Generation
CETFUZZ[∅]	✓					✓								
CoVeriTest		✓		✓	✓	✓	✓	✓			✓	✓	✓	
ESBMC-incr		✓	✓		✓									
ESBMC-kind		✓	✓		✓		✓	✓						
FDSE								✓	✓			✓	✓	
Fizzer		✓												
FuSeBMC			✓					✓	✓	✓				✓
FuSeBMC-AI[∅]			✓					✓	✓	✓				✓
HybridTiger[∅]				✓			✓	✓			✓			
KLEEF		✓						✓	✓				✓	✓
KLEE[∅]								✓					✓	✓
Owi[∅]		✓						✓				✓	✓	✓
PRTest								✓				✓		
Rizzer[∅]		✓											✓	
Sikraken[new]													✓	
Symbiotic		✓			✓			✓	✓	✓			✓	✓
TracerX			✓					✓					✓	✓
TracerX-WP														
UTestGen				✓							✓			
WASP-C[∅]								✓					✓	✓

of the chair and one member of each participating team.) An online table with information about all participating systems is provided on the competition web site.[8] Table 5 lists the features and technologies that are used in the test generators.

There are test generators that did not actively participate (tester archives taken from last year) and that are not included in rankings. Those are called *inactive* participation and the tools are labeled with a symbol ($^\varnothing$). In the past, we named those inactive tools 'hors concours', but since there could be other

---

[8] https://test-comp.sosy-lab.org/2025/systems.php

reasons for hors-concours participation (for example meta tools that consist of other participating tools), we now use the more specific term 'inactive'.

Computing Resources. The computing environment and the resource limits were the same as for Test-Comp 2024 [17], except for the upgraded operating system: Each test run was limited to 4 processing units (cores), 15 GB of memory, and 15 min of CPU time. The test-suite validation was limited to 2 processing units, 7 GB of memory, and 5 min of CPU time. The machines for running the experiments are part of a compute cluster that consists of 168 machines. Each machine had one Intel Xeon E3-1230 v5 CPU, with 8 processing units each, a frequency of 3.4 GHz, 33 GB of RAM, and a GNU/Linux operating system (x86_64-linux, Ubuntu 24.04 with Linux kernel 6.8). We used BENCHEXEC [31] to measure and control computing resources (CPU time, memory, CPU energy), BENCHCLOUD [24] to distribute, install, run, and clean-up test-case generation runs, and to collect the results, and FM-WECK [33] to prepare the correct container according to the tools' FM-TOOLS [18] entry. The values for CPU time are accumulated over all cores of the CPU. Further technical parameters of the competition machines are available in the repository which also contains the benchmark definitions. [9]

One complete test-generation execution of the competition consisted of 235 746 single test-generation run executions. The total CPU time was 3.7 years for one complete competition run for test generation (without validation). Test-suite validation consisted of 987 888 single test-suite validation runs. The total consumed CPU time was 0.95 years. Each tool was executed several times, in order to make sure no installation issues occur during the execution. Including preruns, the infrastructure managed a total of 968 364 test-generation runs (consuming 4.9 years of CPU time). The prerun test-suite validation consisted of 4 212 084 single test-suite validation runs (consuming 3.8 years of CPU time).

Quantitative Results. The quantitative results are presented in the same way as last year: Table 6 presents the quantitative overview of all tools and all categories. The head row mentions the category and the number of test-generation tasks in that category. The tools are listed in alphabetical order; every table row lists the scores of one test generator. We indicate the top three candidates by formatting their scores in bold face and in larger font size. An empty table cell means that the test generator opted-out from the respective main category (perhaps participating in subcategories only, restricting the evaluation to a specific topic). More information (including interactive tables, quantile plots for every category, and also the raw data in XML format) is available on the competition web site [10] and in the results artifact (see Table 3). Table 7 reports the top three test generators for each category. The consumed run time (column 'CPU Time') is given in hours and the consumed energy (column 'Energy') is given in kWh.

Score-Based Quantile Functions for Quality Assessment. We use score-based quantile functions [31] because these visualizations make it easier to under-stand the results of the comparative evaluation. The web site [10] and the results

---

[9] https://gitlab.com/sosy-lab/test-comp/bench-defs/tree/testcomp25
[10] https://test-comp.sosy-lab.org/2025/results

Table 6: Quantitative overview over all results; empty cells mark opt-outs; [new] indicates first-time participants, [∅] indicates hors-concours participation

Participant	Cover-Error 1215 tasks	Cover-Branches 10011 tasks	Overall 11226 tasks
CETFUZZ[∅]	323	2524	2906
CoVeriTest	552	4959	5333
ESBMC-incr	679	4380	5591
ESBMC-kind	680	4323	5565
FDSE	729	**5468**	6435
Fizzer	736	5429	**6446**
FuSeBMC	**994**	5656	**7763**
FuSeBMC-AI[∅]	853	4077	6228
HybridTiger[∅]	438	3866	4193
KLEE[∅]	804	3065	5434
KLEEF	969	**5734**	7692
Owi[∅]	281	2462	2677
PRTest	211	3191	2764
Rizzer[∅]	608		
Sikraken[new]		2469	
Symbiotic	**743**	4207	5793
TracerX	390	3327	3667
TracerX-WP	349	3275	3447
UTestGen	439	4393	4492
WASP-C[∅]	554	2740	4094

artifact (Table 3) include such a plot for each category; as example, we show the plot for category *Overall* (all test-generation tasks) in Fig. 4. We had 18 test generators participating in category *Overall*, for which the quantile plot shows the overall performance over all categories (scores for meta categories are normalized [9]). A more detailed discussion of score-based quantile plots for testing is provided in the Test-Comp 2019 competition report [12].

Table 7: Overview of the top-three test generators for each category (measurement values for CPU time rounded to two significant digits, in hours)

Rank	Tester	Score	CPU Time
Cover-Error			
1	**FuSeBMC**	**994**	75
2	KLEEF	969	9.5
3	Symbiotic	743	5.5
Cover-Branches			
1	**KLEEF**	**5734**	1 500
2	FuSeBMC	5656	2 500
3	FDSE	5468	2 200
Overall			
1	**FuSeBMC**	**7763**	2 600
2	KLEEF	7692	1 500
3	Fizzer	6446	2 100

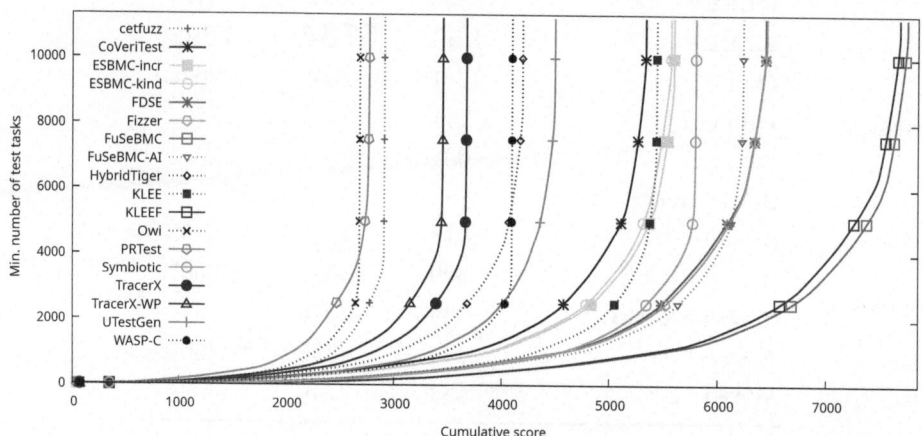

Fig. 4: Quantile functions for category *Overall*. Each quantile function illustrates the quantile (*x*-coordinate) of the scores obtained by test-generation runs below a certain number of test-generation tasks (*y*-coordinate). More details were given previously [12]. The graphs are decorated with symbols to make them better distinguishable without color.

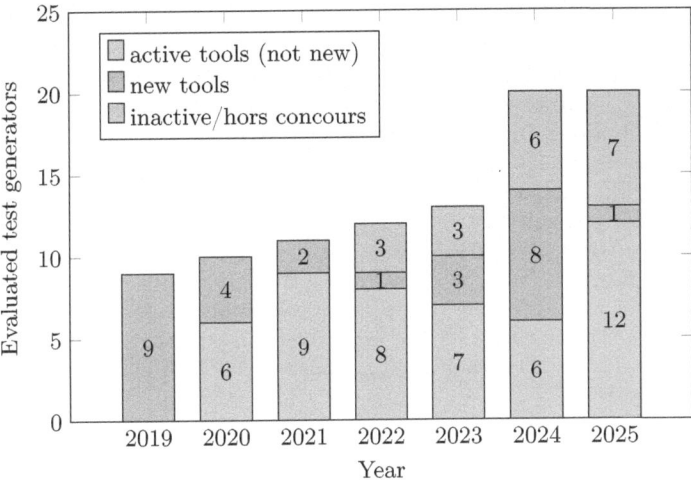

Fig. 5: Number of evaluated test generators for each year (blue/bottom: active participants from previous years, green/middle: number of first-time participants, gray/top: inactive participants from previous years)

6   Conclusion

The 7th Competition on Software Testing continues to provide an overview of fully-automatic test-generation tools for C programs. A total of 20 test-suite generators was compared (see Fig. 5 for the participation numbers and Table 4 for the details). This off-site competition uses a benchmark infrastructure that makes the execution of the experiments fully-automatic and reproducible. Transparency is ensured by making all components available in public repositories and have a jury (consisting of members from each team) that oversees the process. All test suites were validated by the test-suite validator TestCov [30] to measure the coverage. For the first time, the competition used several different validation runs for each test suite, in order to obtain the best possible coverage result, using different compiler backends and different formatting choices after instrumentation for coverage measurement. The results of the competition were presented at the 28th International Conference on Fundamental Approaches to Software Engineering (FASE) at ETAPS 2025 in Hamilton, Canada.

Data-Availability Statement. The test-generation tasks and results of the competition are published at Zenodo, as described in Table 3. All components and data that are necessary for reproducing the competition are available in public version repositories, as specified in Table 2. For easy access, the results are presented also online on the competition web site `https://test-comp.sosy-lab.org/2025/results`.

Funding Statement. This project was funded in part by the Deutsche Forschungsgemeinschaft (DFG) — 418257054 (Coop).

References

1. Aldughaim, M., Alshmrany, K.M., Gadelha, M.R., de Freitas, R., Cordeiro, L.C.: FuSeBMC_IA: Interval analysis and methods for test-case generation (competition contribution). In: Proc. FASE. pp. 324–329. LNCS 13991, Springer (2023). https://doi.org/10.1007/978-3-031-30826-0_18

2. Aldughaim, M., Alshmrany, K.M., Mustafa, M., Cordeiro, L.C., Stancu, A.: Bounded model checking of software using interval methods via contractors. arXiv/CoRR **2012**(11245) (December 2020). https://doi.org/10.48550/arXiv.2012.11245

3. Alshmrany, K., Aldughaim, M., Cordeiro, L., Bhayat, A.: FuSeBMC v.4: Smart seed generation for hybrid fuzzing (competition contribution). In: Proc. FASE. pp. 336–340. LNCS 13241, Springer (2022). https://doi.org/10.1007/978-3-030-99429-7_19

4. Alshmrany, K.M., Aldughaim, M., Bhayat, A., Cordeiro, L.C.: FuSeBMC: An energy-efficient test generator for finding security vulnerabilities in C programs. In: Proc. TAP. pp. 85–105. Springer (2021). https://doi.org/10.1007/978-3-030-79379-1_6

5. Anand, S., Burke, E.K., Chen, T.Y., Clark, J.A., Cohen, M.B., Grieskamp, W., Harman, M., Harrold, M.J., McMinn, P.: An orchestrated survey of methodologies for automated software test case generation. Journal of Systems and Software **86**(8), 1978–2001 (2013). https://doi.org/10.1016/j.jss.2013.02.061

6. Barth, M., Dietsch, D., Heizmann, M., Jakobs, M.C.: ULTIMATE TESTGEN: Test case generation with automata-based software model checking (competition contribution). In: Proc. FASE. pp. 326–330. LNCS 14573, Springer (2024). https://doi.org/10.1007/978-3-031-57259-3_20

7. Barth, M., Jakobs, M.C.: Test-case generation with automata-based software model checking. In: Proc. SPIN. Springer (2024). https://doi.org/10.1007/978-3-031-66149-5_14

8. Bartocci, E., Beyer, D., Black, P.E., Fedyukovich, G., Garavel, H., Hartmanns, A., Huisman, M., Kordon, F., Nagele, J., Sighireanu, M., Steffen, B., Suda, M., Sutcliffe, G., Weber, T., Yamada, A.: TOOLympics 2019: An overview of competitions in formal methods. In: Proc. TACAS (3). pp. 3–24. LNCS 11429, Springer (2019). https://doi.org/10.1007/978-3-030-17502-3_1

9. Beyer, D.: Second competition on software verification (Summary of SV-COMP 2013). In: Proc. TACAS. pp. 594–609. LNCS 7795, Springer (2013). https://doi.org/10.1007/978-3-642-36742-7_43

10. Beyer, D.: Competition on software testing (Test-Comp). In: Proc. TACAS (3). pp. 167–175. LNCS 11429, Springer (2019). https://doi.org/10.1007/978-3-030-17502-3_11

11. Beyer, D.: Second competition on software testing: Test-Comp 2020. In: Proc. FASE. pp. 505–519. LNCS 12076, Springer (2020). https://doi.org/10.1007/978-3-030-45234-6_25

12. Beyer, D.: First international competition on software testing (Test-Comp 2019). Int. J. Softw. Tools Technol. Transf. **23**(6), 833–846 (December 2021). https://doi.org/10.1007/s10009-021-00613-3

13. Beyer, D.: Status report on software testing: Test-Comp 2021. In: Proc. FASE. pp. 341–357. LNCS 12649, Springer (2021). https://doi.org/10.1007/978-3-030-71500-7_17

14. Beyer, D.: Advances in automatic software testing: Test-Comp 2022. In: Proc. FASE. pp. 321–335. LNCS 13241, Springer (2022). https://doi.org/10.1007/978-3-030-99429-7_18

15. Beyer, D.: Progress on software verification: SV-COMP 2022. In: Proc. TACAS (2). pp. 375–402. LNCS 13244, Springer (2022). https://doi.org/10.1007/978-3-030-99527-0_20

16. Beyer, D.: Software testing: 5th comparative evaluation: Test-Comp 2023. In: Proc. FASE. pp. 309–323. LNCS 13991, Springer (2023). https://doi.org/10.1007/978-3-031-30826-0_17

17. Beyer, D.: Automatic testing of C programs: Test-Comp 2024. Springer (2024)

18. Beyer, D.: Find, use, and conserve tools for formal methods. In: Proc. Festschrift Podelski 65th Birthday. Springer (2024), available online: https://www.sosy-lab.org/research/pub/2024-Podelski65.Find_Use_and_Conserve_-Tools_for_Formal_Methods.pdf

19. Beyer, D.: State of the art in software verification and witness validation: SV-COMP 2024. In: Proc. TACAS (3). pp. 299–329. LNCS 14572, Springer (2024). https://doi.org/10.1007/978-3-031-57256-2_15

20. Beyer, D.: FM-Tools Release 2.2: Data set of metadata about tools for formal methods (SV-COMP 2025, Test-Comp 2025). Zenodo (2025). https://doi.org/10.5281/zenodo.15055359

21. Beyer, D.: Results of the 7th Intl. Competition on Software Testing (Test-Comp 2025). Zenodo (2025). https://doi.org/10.5281/zenodo.15034433

22. Beyer, D.: SV-Benchmarks: Benchmark set for software testing (Test-Comp 2025). Zenodo (2025). https://doi.org/10.5281/zenodo.15034421

23. Beyer, D.: Test suites from test-generation tools (Test-Comp 2025). Zenodo (2025). https://doi.org/10.5281/zenodo.15034431

24. Beyer, D., Chien, P.C., Jankola, M.: BENCHCLOUD: A platform for scalable performance benchmarking. In: Proc. ASE. pp. 2386–2389. ACM (2024). https://doi.org/10.1145/3691620.3695358

25. Beyer, D., Chlipala, A.J., Henzinger, T.A., Jhala, R., Majumdar, R.: Generating tests from counterexamples. In: Proc. ICSE. pp. 326–335. IEEE (2004). https://doi.org/10.1109/ICSE.2004.1317455

26. Beyer, D., Hartmanns, A., Kordon, F.: TOOLympics Challenge 2023: Updates, Results, Successes of the Formal-Methods Competitions. LNCS 14550, Springer (2024). https://doi.org/10.1007/978-3-031-67695-6

27. Beyer, D., Jakobs, M.C.: COVERITEST: Cooperative verifier-based testing. In: Proc. FASE. pp. 389–408. LNCS 11424, Springer (2019). https://doi.org/10.1007/978-3-030-16722-6_23

28. Beyer, D., Kanav, S.: COVERITEAM: On-demand composition of cooperative verification systems. In: Proc. TACAS. pp. 561–579. LNCS 13243, Springer (2022). https://doi.org/10.1007/978-3-030-99524-9_31

29. Beyer, D., Lemberger, T.: Software verification: Testing vs. model checking. In: Proc. HVC. pp. 99–114. LNCS 10629, Springer (2017). https://doi.org/10.1007/978-3-319-70389-3_7

30. Beyer, D., Lemberger, T.: TESTCOV: Robust test-suite execution and coverage measurement. In: Proc. ASE. pp. 1074–1077. IEEE (2019). https://doi.org/10.1109/ASE.2019.00105

31. Beyer, D., Löwe, S., Wendler, P.: Reliable benchmarking: Requirements and solutions. Int. J. Softw. Tools Technol. Transfer **21**(1), 1–29 (2019). https://doi.org/10.1007/s10009-017-0469-y

32. Beyer, D., Wachowitz, H.: Coveriteam Release 1.2.1. Zenodo (2024). https://doi.org/10.5281/zenodo.11193690

33. Beyer, D., Wachowitz, H.: FM-WECK: Containerized execution of formal-methods tools. In: Proc. FM. pp. 39–47. LNCS 14934, Springer (2024). https://doi.org/10.1007/978-3-031-71177-0_3

34. Bürdek, J., Lochau, M., Bauregger, S., Holzer, A., von Rhein, A., Apel, S., Beyer, D.: Facilitating reuse in multi-goal test-suite generation for software product lines. In: Proc. FASE. pp. 84–99. LNCS 9033, Springer (2015). https://doi.org/10.1007/978-3-662-46675-9_6

35. Cadar, C., Dunbar, D., Engler, D.R.: KLEE: Unassisted and automatic generation of high-coverage tests for complex systems programs. In: Proc. OSDI. pp. 209–224. USENIX Association (2008)

36. Cadar, C., Nowack, M.: KLEE symbolic execution engine in 2019 (competition contribution). Int. J. Softw. Tools Technol. Transf. **23**(6), 867 – 870 (December 2021). https://doi.org/10.1007/s10009-020-00570-3

37. Chalupa, M., Novák, J., Strejček, J.: SYMBIOTIC 8: Parallel and targeted test generation (competition contribution). In: Proc. FASE. pp. 368–372. LNCS 12649, Springer (2021). https://doi.org/10.1007/978-3-030-71500-7_20

38. Chalupa, M., Strejček, J., Vitovská, M.: Joint forces for memory safety checking. In: Proc. SPIN. pp. 115–132. Springer (2018). https://doi.org/10.1007/978-3-319-94111-0_7

39. Cok, D.R., Déharbe, D., Weber, T.: The 2014 SMT competition. JSAT **9**, 207–242 (2016)

40. Dutta, A., Maghareh, R., Jaffar, J., Godboley, S., Yu, X.L.: TRACERX: Pruning dynamic symbolic execution with deletion and weakest precondition interpolation (competition contribution). In: Proc. FASE. pp. 320–325. LNCS 14573, Springer (2024). https://doi.org/10.1007/978-3-031-57259-3_19

41. Fraser, G., Wotawa, F., Ammann, P.: Testing with model checkers: A survey. STVR **19**(3), 215–261 (2009). https://doi.org/10.1002/stvr.402

42. Gadelha, M.Y., Ismail, H.I., Cordeiro, L.C.: Handling loops in bounded model checking of C programs via k-induction. Int. J. Softw. Tools Technol. Transf. **19**(1), 97–114 (February 2017). https://doi.org/10.1007/s10009-015-0407-9

43. Godefroid, P., Sen, K.: Combining model checking and testing. In: Handbook of Model Checking, pp. 613–649. Springer (2018). https://doi.org/10.1007/978-3-319-10575-8_19

44. Harman, M., Hu, L., Hierons, R.M., Wegener, J., Sthamer, H., Baresel, A., Roper, M.: Testability transformation. IEEE Trans. Softw. Eng. **30**(1), 3–16 (2004). https://doi.org/10.1109/TSE.2004.1265732

45. Holzer, A., Schallhart, C., Tautschnig, M., Veith, H.: How did you specify your test suite. In: Proc. ASE. pp. 407–416. ACM (2010). https://doi.org/10.1145/1858996.1859084

46. Jaffar, J., Murali, V., Navas, J.A., Santosa, A.E.: TRACER: A symbolic execution tool for verification. In: Proc. CAV. pp. 758–766. LNCS 7358, Springer (2012). https://doi.org/10.1007/978-3-642-31424-7_61

47. Jakobs, M.C., Richter, C.: COVERITEST with adaptive time scheduling (competition contribution). In: Proc. FASE. pp. 358–362. LNCS 12649, Springer (2021). https://doi.org/10.1007/978-3-030-71500-7_18

48. Jonáš, M., Strejček, J., Trtík, M.: FIZZER with local space fuzzing (competition contribution). In: Proc. FASE. LNCS , Springer (2025)

49. Jonáš, M., Strejček, J., Trtík, M., Urban, L.: FIZZER: New gray-box fuzzer (competition contribution). In: Proc. FASE. pp. 309–313. LNCS 14573, Springer (2024). https://doi.org/10.1007/978-3-031-57259-3_17

50. King, J.C.: Symbolic execution and program testing. Commun. ACM **19**(7), 385–394 (1976). https://doi.org/10.1145/360248.360252

51. Lemberger, T.: Plain random test generation with PRTEST (competition contribution). Int. J. Softw. Tools Technol. Transf. **23**(6), 871–873 (December 2021). https://doi.org/10.1007/s10009-020-00568-x

52. Marques, F., Santos, J.F., Santos, N., Adão, P.: Concolic execution for webassembly (artifact). Dagstuhl Artifacts Series **8**(2), 20:1–20:3 (2022). https://doi.org/10.4230/DARTS.8.2.20

53. Misonizhnik, A., Morozov, S., Kostyukov, Y., Kalugin, V., Babushkin, A., Mordvinov, D., Ivanov, D.: KLEEF: Symbolic execution engine (competition contribution). In: Proc. FASE. pp. 314–319. LNCS 14573, Springer (2024). https://doi.org/10.1007/978-3-031-57259-3_18

54. Panichella, S., Gambi, A., Zampetti, F., Riccio, V.: SBST tool competition 2021. In: Proc. SBST. pp. 20–27. IEEE (2021). https://doi.org/10.1109/SBST52555.2021.00011

55. Ruland, S., Lochau, M., Jakobs, M.C.: HYBRIDTIGER: Hybrid model checking and domination-based partitioning for efficient multi-goal test-suite generation (competition contribution). In: Proc. FASE. pp. 520–524. LNCS 12076, Springer (2020). https://doi.org/10.1007/978-3-030-45234-6_26

56. Song, J., Alves-Foss, J.: The DARPA cyber grand challenge: A competitor's perspective, part 2. IEEE Security and Privacy **14**(1), 76–81 (2016). https://doi.org/10.1109/MSP.2016.14

57. Stump, A., Sutcliffe, G., Tinelli, C.: STAREXEC: A cross-community infrastructure for logic solving. In: Proc. IJCAR, pp. 367–373. LNCS 8562, Springer (2014). https://doi.org/10.1007/978-3-319-08587-6_28

58. Sutcliffe, G.: The CADE ATP system competition: CASC. AI Magazine **37**(2), 99–101 (2016). https://doi.org/10.1609/aimag.v37i2.2620

59. Visser, W., Păsăreanu, C.S., Khurshid, S.: Test-input generation with Java PATHFINDER. In: Proc. ISSTA. pp. 97–107. ACM (2004). https://doi.org/10.1145/1007512.1007526

60. Wei, C., Wu, T., Menezes, R.S., Shmarov, F., Aljaafari, F., Godboley, S., Alshmrany, K., de Freitas, R., Cordeiro, L.: ESBMC v7.7: Automating branch-coverage analysis using CFG-based instrumentation and smt solving (competition contribution). In: Proc. FASE. LNCS , Springer (2025)

61. Wendler, P., Beyer, D.: sosy-lab/benchexec: Release 3.29. Zenodo (2025). https://doi.org/10.5281/zenodo.15007216

62. Zhang, G., Shuai, Z., Ma, K., Liu, K., Chen, Z., Wang, J.: FDSE: Enhance symbolic execution by fuzzing-based pre-analysis (competition contribution). In: Proc. FASE. pp. 304–308. LNCS 14573, Springer (2024). https://doi.org/10.1007/978-3-031-57259-3_16

FIZZER with Local Space Fuzzing*
(Competition Contribution)

Martin Jonáš⬤, Jan Strejček⬤, and Marek Trtík(✉)⬤

Masaryk University, Brno, Czech Republic
trtikm@mail.muni.cz

Abstract. FIZZER is a gray-box fuzzer introduced at Test-Comp 2024. This paper summarizes the lessons learned with the original version and describes the major changes including new analyses implemented in the current version of FIZZER. In particular, Fizzer now uses dynamic taint-flow analysis and local space fuzzing. We also provide experimental results showing the progress between the two versions.

Keywords: gray-box fuzzing · dynamic analysis · taint analysis

1 Test-Generation Approach

Fuzzers [8] are tools that generate test inputs for a given program with the use of dynamic analysis. Gray-box fuzzers first instrument the given program to get some information about each program execution (e.g., which basic blocks were visited during the run). The instrumented program is then executed on some input and the obtained information about the execution is used to prepare the input for the next execution with the aim to cover some previously uncovered code. This process is repeated until some goal or limit is reached. FIZZER focuses solely on achieving high branch coverage and applies the same process also in the *Cover-Error* category. Hence, only branch coverage is discussed in this paper.

While standard gray-box fuzzers prefer fast executions and thus gather only a little information, FIZZER collects more information and aims to create more targeted inputs. More precisely, FIZZER tracks the evaluation of *atomic Boolean expressions* (ABE) in the given program, which are the Boolean expressions built from expressions of other types, e.g., (x > 21) or (string[i] == 'B'). FIZZER instruments the program such that each time an ABE is evaluated, the program stores the current *calling context* (i.e., the sequence of function calls that are on the call stack), the value true or false of the ABE, and the *distance* to the opposite value. For example, if the ABE (x > 21) is evaluated to true, the distance to false is computed as x - 21. FIZZER aims to generate tests that evaluate each ABE in each reached calling context to both true and false.

Assume that some *input* leads to the evaluation of an ABE in some calling context to true. The original version of FIZZER [6] applies the following steps

---

* This work has been supported by the Czech Science Foundation grant GA23-06506S.
M. Trtík—Jury member.

A. Boronat and G. Fraser (Eds.): FASE 2025, LNCS 15693, pp.275–280, 2025.
https://doi.org/10.1007/978-3-031-90900-9_14

to evaluate it to `false`. First, it runs the *sensitivity analysis* to detect the *input* bytes that affect the distance (and thus probably also the value) of the considered ABE in the considered calling context. For each bit of *input*, sensitivity analysis executes the program on *input* with the bit flipped. If the distance changes, the whole byte containing the bit is marked as *sensitive*. As the second step, FIZZER runs the *byteshare analysis* if it has seen some *input'* that evaluates the same ABE to `false` in a different calling context. The analysis replaces sensitive bytes in *input* by the corresponding sensitive bytes of *input'* and executes the program. If this still does not evaluate the ABE in the considered calling context to `false`, FIZZER applies the last step. It performs a *gradient descent* on the sensitive bytes with the aim to minimize the absolute value of the distance and thus evaluate the ABE to `false`. We refer to the full paper [7] for more details.

The original version of FIZZER received the bronze medal in *Cover-Branches* category of Test-Comp 2024. Still, we have identified some drawbacks. One of them is that the sensitivity analysis is very slow on programs with a large input, because it may require a program execution for each bit of the input. Moreover, it does not detect bytes that affect the value of ABE if flipping more than one bit is needed to change the distance. In the new version of FIZZER, sensitive bytes are computed by a *dynamic taint-flow analysis*. The program is executed on *input* and bytes returned from each call to `__VERIFIER_nondet_*()` are tainted by a fresh taint. All the taints are propagated through instructions, from their input to output arguments. Input bytes whose taint reaches the expression of the ABE are marked as sensitive. While the original sensitivity analysis under-approximated the sensitive bytes, the new one over-approximates them.

The original approach also struggles with divergencies: a small modification of the input changes the execution path such that the desired ABE in the desired calling context is missed. On the positive side, these divergences can cover some program parts not covered so far. On the negative side, the divergencies disrupt the original sensitivity analysis and gradient descent. To prevent them, we developed the *local search analysis* that internally applies several strategies for input generation including gradient descent. An important feature of the local search analysis is that it runs all its strategies in a *local space* of the target ABE. We sketch this idea using an execution path with only two ABEs x = y and x = 1, where x, y are 32-bit signed integers. Assume that the path was explored using the input where $x = y = 0$ and that we want to evaluate the second ABE to `true`. The distance functions of the ABEs are $f(x, y) = x - y$ and $g(x) = x - 1$, respectively. Observe that the second distance depends only on x. Mutating x alone would produce an input for which the execution diverges from the original path on the first ABE. In order to prevent this, we build a stack of local spaces, one for each ABE along the path. Intuitively, the local space captures all values of sensitive bytes that keep the distance of the corresponding ABE unchanged. For example, the distance for the first ABE x = y given $x = y = 0$ is $f(0,0) = 0$ and thus the local space is given by equality $f(x, y) = f(0, 0)$, i.e., $x - y = 0$. Now assume that gradient descent applied on the distance of the second ABE wants to execute the program with $x = 1$. The original FIZZER would directly run the program on x = 1 and y = 0 and the execution would diverge on the first ABE. The local search analysis uses the local space of the first ABE to figure out that in order not to diverge from the path, y should be set to 1 and runs the program on x = y = 1 and the execution will not diverge. Due to space limitations we provide more details about the approach in [5].

2   Software Architecture

FIZZER is implemented in C++, significantly depends on the LLVM infrastructure, and is divided into two executable parts: INSTRUMENTER and SERVER. The task of INSTRUMENTER is to instrument a given program with the code tracking and reporting the information about program executions. SERVER schedules and runs the analyses described in the previous section, in particular for generating new inputs and starting executions of the instrumented program. The instrumented program runs in a separate process and communicates with the SERVER using shared memory, so if the program crashes, SERVER can still get the information about the run and continue with test generation.

The current version of FIZZER additionally compiles the given program to our new custom *Simple Assembly LAnguage* (SALA), which is basically a simplified version of LLVM, but SALA instructions do not contain type information, there are no LLVM registers nor intrinsics, and functions are not required to be in SSA form. SERVER contains a SALA interpreter that performs the taint-flow analysis described in the previous section.

3   Strengths and Weaknesses

The current FIZZER has mostly the same strengths and weaknesses as the original version [6]. FIZZER is still a relatively simple and very compact tool with minimal external dependencies. It can be applied to programs of arbitrary size and programs that use external functions available only in compiled form.

The main weaknesses of FIZZER stem from the fact that it is a fuzzer that significantly relies on gradient descent. First, being a fuzzer, it generates tests by executing the program. These executions must have some resource limits specified (e.g., number of evaluated ABEs, input size, size of calling context, time limit). FIZZER thus explores only *prefixes* of program paths and consequently tends to focus on parts of the program close to the entry point. This weakness is partially

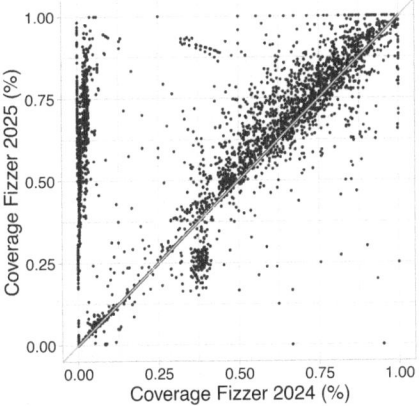

Fig. 1: Comparison of coverages achieved by the original [6] and new FIZZER on *Cover-Branches* benchmarks of Test-Comp 2024.

mitigated by running an *optimizer* after the fuzzing finishes. Optimizer extends the limits and re-runs the program executions that exceeded the standard limits. Second, being reliant on gradient descent, it tends to perform poorly if the branching conditions are non-linear as the standard gradient descent only computes information about linear approximations of the objective function.

Some of the weaknesses of the original FIZZER mentioned in Section 1, i.e., expensive sensitivity analysis and divergences caused by small modifications of inputs, are partially mitigated by the new taint-flow analysis and search in local spaces. This is supported by our experimental evaluation on all *Cover-Branches* benchmarks from Test-Comp 2024 [1] (our experiments use less resources than the Test-Comp 2024 setting, in particular the time limit was set to 300 s per benchmark). The results presented by the scatter plot in Figure 1 show that the new version of FIZZER generally achieves better branch coverage, sometimes even by an order of magnitude. On average, the new version of FIZZER achieved the coverage 66.5% while the original version achieved 59.8%. In Test-Comp 2025 [3], the new version of FIZZER finished in the 4th place in *Cover-Branches* category and won a bronze medal in *Overall* [2].

4   Tool Setup and Configuration

FIZZER can be downloaded either as a binary or as a source code (links are in Section 6). For the source code of the version used in the competition, check out the tag `TESTCOMP25`. The `README.md` file in the root of the repository contains instructions for building the tool. The tool is used via `sbt-fizzer.py` script:

```
sbt-fizzer.py [options] --input_file <c-program>
                        --output_dir <output-dir>
```

All results including the generated tests will be stored under the directory `<output-dir>`. The list of all available options can be obtained by the command `sbt-fizzer.py --help`. Options used in the competition are:

- `max_seconds 865`   The timeout for the entire fuzzing process.
- `optimizer_max_seconds 30`   The timeout for the optimizer.
- `max_exec_milliseconds 500`   The timeout for each program execution.
- `max_exec_megabytes 13312`   The memory limit for each program execution.
- `max_stdin_bytes 65536`   The upper bound for the number of input bytes.
- `stdin_model stdin_replay_bytes_then_repeat_zero`   An input model: given input bytes followed by bytes of the value 0.
- `test_type testcomp`   The format for the generated tests.

5   Software Project and Contributors

FIZZER has been developed at the Faculty of Informatics of Masaryk University by Marek Trtík and Lukáš Urban (contributed to the original version). Martin Jonáš and Jan Strejček participated in discussions and contributed to the project by some ideas. The tool is open-source and available under the ZLIB license.

6   Data-Availability statement

FIZZER is available in a binary form at Zenodo [4] and the source code is available at GitHub:

https://github.com/staticafi/fizzer

References

1. Test-Comp 2024 benchmarks repository (checkout testcomp24-final), https://gitlab.com/sosy-lab/benchmarking/sv-benchmarks/
2. Test-Comp 2025, table with results, https://test-comp.sosy-lab.org/2025/results/results-verified/
3. Beyer, D.: Advances in automatic software testing: Test-Comp 2025. In: Proc. FASE. Springer (2025)
4. Jonáš, M., Strejček, J., Trtík, M.: Fizzer: binary (Dec 2024). https://doi.org/10.5281/zenodo.14246517
5. Jonáš, M., Strejček, J., Trtík, M.: Gray-box fuzzing in local space (2025), https://arxiv.org/abs/2501.18046
6. Jonáš, M., Strejček, J., Trtík, M., Urban, L.: Fizzer: New gray-box fuzzer (competition contribution). In: Beyer, D., Cavalcanti, A. (eds.) Fundamental Approaches to Software Engineering - 27th International Conference, FASE 2024, Held as Part of the European Joint Conferences on Theory and Practice of Software, ETAPS 2024, Luxembourg City, Luxembourg, April 6-11, 2024, Proceedings. Lecture Notes in Computer Science, vol. 14573, pp. 309–313. Springer (2024), https://doi.org/10.1007/978-3-031-57259-3_17
7. Jonáš, M., Strejček, J., Trtík, M., Urban, L.: Gray-box fuzzing via gradient descent and Boolean expression coverage. In: Finkbeiner, B., Kovács, L. (eds.) Tools and Algorithms for the Construction and Analysis of Systems - 30th International Conference, TACAS 2024, Held as Part of the European Joint Conferences on Theory and Practice of Software, ETAPS 2024, Luxembourg City, Luxembourg, April 6-11, 2024, Proceedings, Part III. Lecture Notes in Computer Science, vol. 14572, pp. 90–109. Springer (2024), https://doi.org/10.1007/978-3-031-57256-2_5
8. Liang, H., Pei, X., Jia, X., Shen, W., Zhang, J.: Fuzzing: State of the art. IEEE Transactions on Reliability **67**(3), 1199–1218 (2018). https://doi.org/10.1109/TR.2018.2834476

ESBMC v7.7: Automating Branch Coverage Analysis Using CFG-Based Instrumentation and SMT Solving⋆
(Competition Contribution)

Chenfeng Wei[1], Tong Wu[1], Rafael Sa Menezes[1,6], Fedor Shmarov[2], Fatimah Aljaafari[3], Sangharatna Godboley[4], Kaled Alshmrany[1,5], Rosiane de Freitas[6], and Lucas C. Cordeiro[1,6 (✉)]

¹ The University of Manchester, Manchester, UK
lucas.cordeiro@manchester.ac.uk
² Newcastle University, Newcastle upon Tyne, UK
³ King Faisal University, Hofuf, Saudi Arabia
⁴ National Institute of Technology Warangal, Warangal, India
⁵ Institute of Public Administration, Jeddah, Saudi Arabia
⁶ Federal University of Amazonas, Manaus, Brazil

Abstract. ESBMC, a bounded model checking (BMC) verifier based on SMT solving, has demonstrated its effectiveness in bug detection in recent software verification competitions. We extend its capabilities to enable branch coverage analysis and test suite generation. Our contributions are twofold: (1) we define a branch coverage property and instrument the control flow graph (CFG) to compute branch coverage using SMT solving, and (2) we propose an incremental multi-property reasoning algorithm for efficient and sound test case generation. ESBMC is ranked 7th in the `Cover-Branches` category of Test-Comp 2025.

1 ESBMC's General Workflow

ESBMC [9] (Efficient SMT-Based Bounded Model Checker) verifies C programs for errors such as arithmetic overflow, array out-of-bounds, and user-defined assertions. Using a Clang-based [11] frontend, it converts the input program into a GOTO program [6], a simplified Control Flow Graph (CFG), to analyze the program's execution flow. The CFG is transformed into a state-space representation, specifically static single-assignment form (SSA) [7], for symbolic execution. This execution is performed symbolically [13] within defined bounds (e.g., through loop unrolling) and is eventually encoded as a verification condition (VC). This VC is an SMT formula incorporating constraints (execution conditions) and properties (expected behaviours). Backend solvers like Boolector [12] or Z3 [8] determine satisfiability, reporting failed properties with counterexamples. Additionally, ESBMC supports incremental and k-induction [4] reasoning for unbounded scenarios.

⋆ C. Wei—Jury member.

A. Boronat and G. Fraser (Eds.): FASE 2025, LNCS 15693, pp. 281–286, 2025.
https://doi.org/10.1007/978-3-031-90900-9_15

2   ESBMC's Test-Generation Approach

We extended ESBMC to include a *branch coverage* analysis capability, tracking the program execution across all decision branches and generating corresponding test suites. The process involves two main steps: branch coverage property instrumentation in the GOTO program and multi-property verification in the backend.

2.1   Coverage Property Instrumentation

Instrumentation. In symbolic execution of state systems, entering a branch requires satisfying a precondition, i.e., a branch constraint [1]. For instance, to execute a branch guarded by a non-constant condition like if(cond), there must exist an assignment that satisfies cond. This is equivalent to checking if a counterexample satisfies assert(!cond). Based on this insight, we introduce a method that models branch entry by transforming branch constraints into properties, represented as assertions, and instrumented into the program for verification. The instrumentation is applied to the GOTO program rather than the source code, as at this stage, control-flow constructs such as if-else statements, while loops, for loops, and switch-case statements are normalized into if-goto structures. This normalization simplifies subsequent operations and ensures the instrumentation is applied to all decision points, thereby maintaining soundness. Specifically, constraints from if statements (cond in statement if(cond)) are extracted and converted into two assertions: one representing the false condition (assert(!cond)) and the other representing its negation (assert(!(!cond))). These two assertions reflect the requirement for executing the if and else branches, respectively. Ultimately, they are inserted in sequential order before that if statement. Performing instrumentation before the if statement, rather than within its branches, enhances performance. Since the BMC engine unwinds loops, placing coverage properties inside loop bodies would result in duplicate assertion instances during unwinding, distorting coverage statistics, and hindering test generation. Additionally, this "instrument-before" strategy facilitates the elimination of redundant code, i.e., if-goto blocks, during the program slicing stage.

Isolation. Potential interferences are excluded to isolate the analysis of instrumented properties from others. First, all original program properties, e.g. user-defined assertions, are converted into tautologies (assert(True)), which are removed during the program slicing [5]. Second, internal safety checks within ESBMC are disabled to prevent unnecessary assertions from being introduced during analysis.

2.2   Multi-Property Verification

Multiple branch coverage properties are inserted during the CFG instrumentation. To reason and generate test suites for each property, we propose a method to verify multi-property in incremental, following these steps:

Symbolic execution & Slicing. The GOTO program is first symbolically executed with loops unwound up to a predefined threshold k, generating verification condition VC. Next, program slicing minimizes constraints by removing irrelevant parts based on the property under verification, reducing the state space.

Property Splitting. Given the sliced VC, the global property is decomposed into atomic properties, and the satisfiability of each assertion is verified within the bounded execution. Eq. (1) demonstrates the key process for this checking procedure, where C and P are used to denote the global constraints and properties of the state system (within bound k), respectively. The global property P is decomposed into a set of unit properties P_i. Thus, the verification condition VC is divided into a set of VC_i.

$$VC \Leftrightarrow C \wedge \neg P \Leftrightarrow \bigvee_i^n (C \wedge \neg P_i) \Leftrightarrow \bigvee_i^n VC_i \xrightarrow[\text{incr}]{\text{kind}} \bigvee_i^m VC'(m \leq n) \qquad (1)$$

Base Case. The base case evaluates whether each property P_i holds within k steps. For each VC_i, an SMT solver is set up, checking for satisfiability within a fixed bound k in isolation. Outcomes dictate subsequent actions: (1) Violation: A counterexample is identified and reported. Furthermore, the GOTO program is updated by converting the violated property P_i into a tautology (`assert(True)`). (2) Hold: Forward reasoning is performed to verify behaviour beyond k.

Forward Reasoning. This step evaluates program behavior for $k + 1$ steps and beyond, verifying that no violations occur beyond the k-bound (**Forward Condition**) and proving that if the property holds for k steps, it also holds for $k + 1$ steps (**Inductive Step**) [10]. Outcomes dictate subsequent actions: (1) Violation: A counterexample is reported, and the property P_i is converted into a tautology. (2) Hold: The property P_i is proven correct in an unbounded context and converted into a tautology. This indicates that the branch is unreachable. (3) Unknown: This indicates the bound k is insufficient to evaluate the property (e.g., k is too small to explore deep loop iterations), making forward reasoning undecidable. In such cases, the bound k is incremented for further re-verification.

Termination & Re-verification. The whole verification process terminates under the following conditions: (1) all remaining coverage properties are proven during forward reasoning, or (2) all properties are reduced to tautologies and removed through slicing, leaving no properties for further verification. Conversely, if any property remains unknown, a verification re-run is initiated. In this process, the bound k is incremented, and the updated GOTO program undergoes re-verification from symbolic execution until either a maximum k-threshold or a timeout is reached. Eq. 1 shows the reduction in VCs via slicing ($m \leq n$). The repeated program slicing removes the converted tautologies and their property-relevant code, mitigating state space explosion as the bound k increases. Additionally, to further accelerate k-increment verification, we implement a jump strategy starting k from a larger i and incrementing it by j, where $i, j > 1$.

Test Generation. Test generation occurs whenever a property P_i violation is reported during the **Base Case** or **Forward Reasoning** stage. Assignments with nondeterministic initial values are extracted from the counterexample traces and transformed into corresponding test suites.

3   Strengths and Weaknesses

ESBMC v7.7 uses forward reasoning for instrumentation-based branch coverage analysis, automatically exploring deeper execution paths and terminating when verification goals are met, ensuring full branch coverage. Furthermore, the repeated program slicing during incremental verification mitigates state-space explosion caused by the k-increment, limiting OUT-OF-MEMORY issues to 17 cases (esbmc-incr) and 12 cases (esbmc-kind) in Cover-Branches. The jump strategy offsets additional steps from forward reasoning, mitigating timeout issues as shown in Cover-Error. With a relatively high starting bound (5) and a jumping step (3), TIMEOUT cases decreased from 463 in 2024 Test-Comp [2] to 224 in 2025 [3] (a 48.38% reduction). However, disabling internal safety checks exposed incomplete pointer support within ESBMC. Previously, internal checks detected "null pointer" issues in the program and terminated verification; in their absence, ESBMC attempts to proceed with incorrect pointer encoding, leading to segmentation faults and resulting in 3 UNKNOWN cases in the Cover-Branches.

4   Tool Setup and Configuration

The tool is run via the wrapper: esbmc-wrapper.py [options] <PROGRAM>. Options used in the competition are: -p <PROPERTY> for the property path, -a 32 to set the architecture to 32-bit, -s kinduction to enable k-induction in esbmc-kind (incr for incremental BMC in esbmc-incr), and -o branch for coverage analysis in Cover-Branches. Based on these options, the following ESBMC flags are set during execution: --base-k-step 2 (3 for esbmc-incr) to set the initial bound, --k-step 3 to set the bound increment, --unlimited-k-steps to allow an unlimited upper bound, --generate-testcase to output test suites, and --no-standard-checks (for Cover-Branches) to disable internal safety checks. This configuration is applied globally across all benchmark categories.

5   Software Project and Contributors

ESBMC is open-source under the Apache License 2.0, primarily supported by the University of Manchester, with contributions from other universities and institutions. All people involved are listed as authors of this paper.

6   Data-Availability Statement

The version that participated in Test-Comp 2025 is available in binary form on Zenodo: https://doi.org/10.5281/zenodo.14340851. To set up and run ESBMC, follow the instructions in the README.md file. ESBMC's official website can be found at https://ssvlab.github.io/esbmc/. The ESBMC source code is written in C++ and publicly available for download on GitHub: https://github.com/esbmc/esbmc.

7   Funding Statement

The ESBMC development is funded by ARM, EPSRC EP/T026995/1, EPSRC EP/V000497/1, Ethereum Foundation, EU H2020 ELEGANT 957286, UKRI Soteria, Intel, and Motorola Mobility (through Agreement N° 4/2021).

References

1. Angeletti, D., Giunchiglia, E., Narizzano, M., Puddu, A., Sabina, S.: Automatic test generation for coverage analysis using cbmc. In: Computer Aided Systems Theory-EUROCAST 2009: 12th International Conference, Las Palmas de Gran Canaria, Spain, February 15-20, 2009, Revised Selected Papers 12. pp. 287–294. Springer (2009)
2. Beyer, D.: Automatic testing of C programs: Test-Comp 2024. In: TBA. Springer (2024)
3. Beyer, D.: Advances in automatic software testing: Test-Comp 2025. In: Proc. FASE. Springer (2025)
4. Beyer, D., Dangl, M., Wendler, P.: Boosting k-induction with continuously-refined invariants. In: International Conference on Computer Aided Verification. pp. 622–640. Springer (2015)
5. Cho, C.Y., D'Silva, V., Song, D.: Blitz: Compositional bounded model checking for real-world programs. In: 2013 28th IEEE/ACM International Conference on Automated Software Engineering (ASE). pp. 136–146 (2013). https://doi.org/10.1109/ASE.2013.6693074
6. Cordeiro, L., Fischer, B., Marques-Silva, J.: Smt-based bounded model checking for embedded ansi-c software. IEEE Transactions on Software Engineering **38** (07 2009). https://doi.org/10.1109/TSE.2011.59
7. Cordeiro, L., Fischer, B., Marques-Silva, J.: Smt-based bounded model checking for embedded ansi-c software. In: 2009 IEEE/ACM International Conference on Automated Software Engineering. pp. 137–148 (2009). https://doi.org/10.1109/ASE.2009.63
8. De Moura, L., Bjørner, N.: Z3: An efficient smt solver. In: International conference on Tools and Algorithms for the Construction and Analysis of Systems. pp. 337–340. Springer (2008)
9. Gadelha, M.R., Menezes, R.S., Cordeiro, L.C.: Esbmc 6.1: automated test case generation using bounded model checking. International Journal on Software Tools for Technology Transfer **23**, 857–861 (2021)

10. Gadelha, M.R., Monteiro, F.R., Morse, J., Cordeiro, L.C., Fischer, B., Nicole, D.A.: Esbmc 5.0: an industrial-strength c model checker. In: Proceedings of the 33rd ACM/IEEE International Conference on Automated Software Engineering. pp. 888–891 (2018)
11. Lattner, C., Adve, V.: LLVM: A compilation framework for lifelong program analysis and transformation. In: International symposium on code generation and optimization. pp. 75–88. San Jose, CA, USA (Mar 2004)
12. Niemetz, A., Preiner, M., Biere, A.: Boolector 2.0. Journal on Satisfiability, Boolean Modeling and Computation **9**(1), 53–58 (2014)
13. Ramalho Gadelha, M., et al.: Scalable and precise verification based on k-induction, symbolic execution and floating-point theory. Ph.D. thesis, University of Southampton (2019)

Author Index

A. Boronat and G. Fraser (Eds.): FASE 2025, LNCS 15693, pp. 287–288, 2025.
https://doi.org/10.1007/978-3-031-90900-9